QUEERING PUBLIC ADDRESS

Studies in Rhetoric/Communication
Thomas W. Benson, Series Editor

QUEERING PUBLIC ADDRESS

Sexualities in American Historical Discourse

EDITED BY CHARLES E. MORRIS III

The University of South Carolina Press

© 2007 University of South Carolina

Published by the University of South Carolina Press
Columbia, South Carolina 29208

www.sc.edu/uscpress

Manufactured in the United States of America

16   15   14   13   12   11   10   09   08   07   10   9   8   7   6   5   4   3   2   1

Library of Congress Cataloging-in-Publication Data

Queering public address : sexualities in American historical discourse / edited by
  Charles E. Morris III.
     p. cm. — (Studies in rhetoric/communication)
  Includes bibliographical references and index.
  ISBN-13: 978-1-57003-664-4 (cloth : alk. paper)
  ISBN-10: 1-57003-664-0 (cloth : alk. paper)
  1. Gay and lesbian studies—United States. 2. Homosexuality—United States—
History. I. Morris, Charles E., 1969–
  HQ75.16.U6Q445 2007
  306.76'60973—dc22

                                                                          2006038763

This book was printed on Glatfelter's Nature, a recycled paper with 50 percent
postconsumer waste content.

contents

series EDITOR's preface

In *Queering Public Address: Sexualities in American Historical Discourse*, Charles E. Morris III and his collaborators invoke, challenge, and invite a rewriting of public address studies in the discipline of rhetoric. Taken as a whole, their work, in its scrupulous logic and evident justice, is by no means unitary or merely programmatic. Rather, it works through processes of recovery and appropriation to normalize the nonnormative while at the same time it destabilizes and exposes the regime of the normal as itself arbitrarily and energetically exclusionary both in social practices and in the languages of disciplinary analysis. Morris writes that the recovery of queer historical texts is a way of constructing both history and identity, a worthy and necessary project of community-building that nonetheless risks accepting an essentialist vocabulary, thus reifying the untroubled assumptions of a dominant heteronormative regime. And so, at the same time that the work of recovery, assimilation, and shared historical identity proceeds, it is accompanied by a more radical aspiration to rearticulate the grounds of analysis, exposing and challenging the rhetorical constructions of the discipline itself. The eleven authors who have written this book are all leading figures in rhetorical studies, speaking with a deeply informed sense of the culture, the academy, and the discipline. Their work in this book will provoke conversations and reconsiderations that are long overdue.

THOMAS W. BENSON

ACKNOWLEDGMENTS

Queering Public Address, in many senses, has been long in the making; in another sense it is just beginning. At this moment I am smiling at the recognition that this project has at last come to fruition. Frustrations have been tempered along the way by my deep and abiding passion for the subjects of this volume and their promise, the manifold meanings of the labor, and the extraordinary collegiality and collaboration of my contributors (my heroes), who believed in my vision. It is wonderful indeed to be queer.

Queering Public Address commenced in 2000, when I joined the faculty of Vanderbilt University. During the five years I spent there, dear colleagues and friends supported this volume in diverse and memorable ways: John Sloop, who taught me much and made me laugh even more, the fellow traveler we all dream of having, as well as Lynn Clarke and Erika Johnson, Carolyn Dever, Tina Chen and Sean Goudie, Roger Moore, Mona Frederick, John English, Anne Demo, Brad Vivian, Kass Kovalcheck, Carole Kenner, M. L. Sandoz, Diane Banks, and the Gender and Sexuality Reading Group.

Queer life in Nashville with my tribe, especially Keith Blaydes and Bob Riedel (whom I cannot thank enough)—as well as John Jackson, Mark and Michael, Jim and Jack, Johnny Mac and Chris—generously offered the sweetest rewards for a hard day's work and a reminder that all we do to enrich our communities comes back to us tenfold. In addition to fabulous friends, I am exceedingly fortunate to have my family—Chuck and Ginny, Lew and Alana, Linda, Mary Kate, David, Jackie, Heather and Craig, Alyse and Carley, Augustine and Ophelia, Sharon and Brenda, Alex, and Elaine—always sustaining me with endless encouragement and great fun.

Colleagues and comrades throughout the discipline and beyond have also enriched the spirit and substance of this volume in ways large and small, for which I feel much gratitude: Alex Hivoltze, Rob Asen, and Dan Brouwer, Stephen Browne, Dick Gregg, Dana Cloud, Angela Ray, Barbara Biesecker, Josh Gunn, Bonnie Dow, Kathleen Domenig, Kyra Pearson, Jeff Sens, Lisbeth Lipari, Andrew Hansen, Dale Herbeck, Kent Ono, Carole Blair, Rosa Eberly, Davis Houck, Kendall Phillips, Lester Olson, Joan Faber McAlister, Cara Finnegan, John Murphy, Shawn and Trevor Parry-Giles, Mari Tonn, Mary Stuckey, Jim Jasinski, Karlyn Campbell, Barbara Warnick, David Henry, John Lucaites, Kevin Ayotte, Davin Grindstaff, John

Lynch, Erin Rand, Isaac West, James Darsey, Shea Doyle, Lance Baldwin, and my new colleagues at Boston College.

An early version of my chapter on Abraham Lincoln originally appeared as "My Old Kentucky Homo: Lincoln and the Politics of Queer Memory," *Framing Public Memory*, ed. Kendall R. Phillips (Tuscaloosa: University of Alabama Press, 2004), 89–114. Permission to use this material is courtesy of University of Alabama Press. I am also thankful to those who engaged this work with me in talks at Northwestern University, University of Maryland, Syracuse University, and University of Iowa.

This volume would not have been possible without the insight and endorsement of Barry Blose, acquisitions editor at the University of South Carolina Press, series editor Tom Benson, and the anonymous reviewers. Tom, in particular, has been a teacher and friend in so many ways since my first year in graduate school at Penn State. His belief in this project has meant a great deal to me.

Most of all, with great love and admiration I thank Virginia Blanck Moore and Scott Rose. By remarkable example, Aunt Ginny has taught me to celebrate difference and to strive to make a difference. Still writing poetry past age ninety, she is an inspiration. Her book *Seeing Eye Wife* first sparked my own desire to write, and her enthusiastic embrace has often given that desire flight.

With my heart's desire, queer work and life began in earnest a dozen years ago. After meeting my partner, Scott Rose, I could not imagine being or writing in any other way. To this day our life together gives rich purpose and texture to all that I do. Thank you, Gatto, for everything.

INTRODUCTION

Portrait of a Queer Rhetorical/
Historical Critic

Charles E. Morris III

To begin, a blushing confession: portraiture and America's queer past make me yearn. Each haunts me as a paradox, a refulgent eclipse, mute eloquence signifying so much and disclosing so little. Each possesses seductive mysteries—bodies, desires, agonies, knowledges, poses—produced by time, and worse: mysteries, like those embodied in Mona Lisa's smile, ineluctably inviting and maddeningly elusive, because, among other things, disciplined. Each is, from a unique vantage, vivaciously epideictic, bespeaking identifications and disidentifications we might voice or disavow, or perhaps bequeath to others, were we so inclined to enact a particular "persuasion." With this enactment in mind, and in the spirit of full disclosure, I admit that my yearning is expansive: I desire not just to be hailed by (or hail from) specific historical subjects, but indeed to hail them all. And yet, as a queer rhetorical/historical critic I understand, better than many, Simon Schama's wise monition, "We are doomed to be forever hailing someone who has just gone around the corner and out of earshot."[1]

As a means of introducing *Queering Public Address*, I offer an anonymous photographic portrait, which I have taken the liberty to entitle "Seneca Falls Boys."[2] I do so not to suggest a certain critical object or period of study in this volume, but rather to imagine the metonymic potential of our Seneca Falls Boys in figuring queer(ing) public address, a significant reconfiguration of historical-rhetorical studies. Like this project itself, the portrait is situated somewhere between distant history and cyberspace, a constitution of the past and, by its attributed virtues, the present and future; a text that speaks within its own context as eloquently as it did to me on eBay, when, fittingly, it eluded my grasp.

What our Seneca Falls Boys represent is, of course, subject to historically specific cultural performances, politics, and meanings. Within certain contemporary contexts, however, I believe that they could provocatively unsettle heteronormative business as usual: in excess of particular impositions, cultural as well as academic,

Seneca Falls Boys.
Collection of
Andrew K. Schultz

these boys desirously read as *waxing erotic*. To say as much is to posit critical potentialities for public address inquiry that commence with a reformulation of Quintil-
ian's familiar mandate of eloquence: *queer bonus dicendi peritus*. That is why I find
them such an appealing metonymy. For rhetorical critics committed to embracing
and explicating nonnormative sexualities in American historical discourse, our
Seneca Falls Boys exhibit well the many challenges and exhilarations of an endeavor
that finds us grappling at the intersection of rhetoric, history, and queerness; grappling with the historically situated cultural performances, politics, and meanings,
including our own, of the "good queer speaking well" and of queer sexuality as a
prism for the study of public address.

My impetus for this volume emerged not only from deep personal yearning for
a queer past, a peculiar sort of desire for historical desire, but from a professional
subject position perhaps best described as "vexed by disorientation." Situated during the past decade among those "doing rhetorical history,"[3] I have encountered,
on one hand, almost no effort to recover queer historical texts, and, on the other,
scant queer rhetorical-historical work that, beyond recovery, "[has] sought . . . to
probe the vast spectrum of conjunctions and interstices that exist between bodies,

genders, and desires, as well as how these formations relate to other discourses and institutions."[4] Strangely, I have felt, in a sense, rather like the "foundling" Christopher Nealon has so insightfully described, one struck with "an overwhelming desire to *feel historical*" and engaged in an "historiographical struggle . . . to find terms for historical narration that strike a balance between the unspeakability of desire, especially punishable desire, and group life."[5]

A few more words about this disciplinary disorientation will provide useful context for *Queering Public Address.* Traditionally conceived as the study of American eloquence, public address has taken as its critical object "the making and delivery of public speeches, the paradigmatic instance of which was the nineteenth century platform oration," and, more broadly, "oratory as a force in American history."[6] This neoclassical approach historically has centered on the "great" speaker and a single rhetorical "masterpiece," a canonical text of unique aesthetic, intellectual, or strategic merit performed in the face of often dramatic public exigencies and hence of historical significance. Under these conditions, it is easy to fathom the long absence of queer texts, especially the presumed void of discourse prior to the homophile movements of the 1950s and 1960s, prior to the "out" culture and politics that emerged from the Stonewall "revolution."[7]

However, the influences of poststructuralism, deconstruction, and cultural studies, although not eroding many of founding assumptions of public address, have produced meaningful transformations of this traditional model. For instance, scholarship now exhibits a heightened sensitivity to power, the multiplicity and fragmentation of textuality, the cultural conditions and discursive traditions that produce public discourse, as well as the various communities of reception, performance, and circulation that in another sense constitute public address. That said, unconventional encroachments more often than not get defined, reviewed, or edited out of the enclave.

Antiquated as it may generally seem to some readers, the art of public address as a mode of critical/historical inquiry—now having expanded its domain well beyond oratory, great speakers, and the single text—nevertheless continues to yield valuable insights into America's past. As Robert Hariman has argued, public address illuminates historical occasions and eras by providing a means of ingress into material culture, by disclosing the discursive structures that enable and constrain the dynamics of political culture, and by highlighting the texture of performative culture that strengthens historical interpretation of political praxis.[8]

A longstanding, accurate critique of public address scholarship (and its wider institutional regimes and academic regimens) is that its attentions, and thus legitimations, historically have been bestowed almost exclusively on the "great white straight male" historical subject or text. Since the 1980s strenuous efforts have undermined this sexist and racist hegemony, with promising results. Many traditionalist scholars now emphasize, if sometimes rather conspicuously, the "appearance" of women and African Americans in the history of public address; and race and gender increasingly shape field-specific discussions of rhetorical culture in American history.[9] If public address exhibits meaningful signs of being gendered and raced (and to an unfortunately lesser degree, classed), however, it has yet to be queered. Indeed sexuality stands among the last of the silent taboos, public address's shameful third persona.[10]

The absence of queer voice, visibility, and vision within public address—what we might call its "queer impoverishment"—highlights the forgotten or mangled assumption that, like historiography, public address is itself a rhetorical enterprise.[11] Rhetoricians are not always quick or willing to embrace this seemingly self-evident claim, with profound implications for the queer engagement of a rhetorical past. At a minimum, and without necessarily attributing nefarious motive, one can note with Dominick LaCapra that "any 'dialogue' with the past . . . takes place in a larger social, political, economic, and cultural context that places severe restrictions upon it."[12] The degree to which a particular historical account is inflected by those constraints depends on the critic, of course, but that those accounts are indeed inflected is difficult to gainsay. More pointedly, Carole Blair's insight that "rhetoricians, who have identified and explored rhetorics of various fields of inquiry, have neglected the rhetoricity of their own historical studies"[13] remains a valid critique not only of historians of rhetorical theory, but perhaps especially public address scholars. That history—its recovery and representation, theories and methods—is usable and used ideologically often escapes notice except by those for whom a relevant past has been "consigned to oblivion."[14]

At worst, a seemingly innocuous ideological dimension of critical invention shapes the academic norms by which, sometimes in pernicious fashion, marginalized voices and alternative perspectives are disciplined, if not silenced.[15] Thus we might consider carefully John Wrathall's astute observation that "scholars [of the history of sexuality] . . . have to contend with the problem of silences: silences created by the censorship of archival and educational institutions, silences created by historians' refusal to acknowledge the sexualities of individuals they study, and silences created by authors of the documents historians use to reconstruct the past."[16] In public address such silences echo throughout the archives, anthologies, syllabi, reviews, journals, bibliographies, and footnotes that fail to speak, or that distort and diminish, our names and the invisible processes by which they are achieved, normalized, and perpetuated. These silences need to be amplified in grating volume. Token voices, however heartening, need to be considered cautiously and critically. Opposition to queer impoverishment within public address, if it is to intervene meaningfully, needs to be revelatory of discipline and complicity, what has been said and not said, and how the history of American public address—the contexts, modes, and products of historical discourse, as well as the academic contexts, modes, and products of historical discourse—has or has not been spoken.

In *Queering Public Address*, therefore, we aim to disrupt the silence regarding nonnormative sexualities as it relates to American historical discourse, to undermine the governing heteronormativity[17] in its disciplinary conventions and articulations, and to queer (which, despite the nuances in definition offered throughout this collection, suggests the instantiation of sexuality as indispensable to the study of public address and a commitment to destabilizing sexual normalcy in its various contingent manifestations) the objects, methods, and theories within this field of inquiry.[18] It will become evident that this collection has broader implications for rhetorical studies: the essays are informed by contemporary social and political theories, often enact critical rhetoric, and merge quite well with many current rhetorical perspectives on public culture. Instead of abandoning public address for queer-hospitable academic locations within the discipline and beyond, however, we have decided to stay our home ground and render it pink, a rhetorical-historiographical version of what Lauren Berlant and Michael Warner have called "queer world making": "The queer project we imagine is not just to destigmatize those average intimacies, not just to give access to the sentimentality of the couple for persons of the same sex, and definitely not to certify as properly private the personal lives of gays and lesbians. Rather it is to support forms of affective, erotic, and personal living that are public in the sense of accessible, available to memory, and sustained through collective activity."[19]

As such, this volume specifically focuses on public address for at least two significant reasons. The first is that many of the contributors share my occupation with a queer rhetorical past, influenced as we have been by more than two decades of robust historical inquiry inspired by Foucault, pioneered by scholars such as Jonathan Ned Katz, Lillian Faderman, and John D'Emilio, and evolving into a rich diversity of approaches and insights, from historicist recuperation to deviant historiography, queer cultural studies of history, and queer historicism.[20] Recent scholarly proliferation in communication studies regarding contemporary queer culture, media, and politics, though invaluable, does not fully satisfy those of us for whom historical discourse, and the infrastructure that governs its study, matters greatly.

Second, to the extent that public address is understood as foundational to the tradition of rhetorical studies as a discipline,[21] queering it enacts the more radical vision of rearticulating that tradition from its very origins or roots: queering our disciplinary history, and thus our discipline, by queering rhetorical history. *Queering Public Address* therefore designates a domain of rhetorical inquiry and tropes an intervention into all domains of rhetorical inquiry. Our Seneca Falls Boys, for me, serve well as an emblem of this project's allure, as well as its inevitable troubles.

Those troubles must be candidly addressed, if not resolved. The eclectic nature of this collection of essays might signal to some a certain lack of cohesion, an uncertainty regarding what queer is meant to signify. There are, to be sure, a wide array of theoretical orientations and purposes, modes of investigation, and objects of study reflected in the pages of *Queering Public Address*. I read this richness of diversity as indicative of queerness itself, its purchase, for "the queer world is a space of entrances, exits, unsystematized lines of acquaintance, projected horizons, typifying examples, alternate routes, blockages, incommensurate geographies."[22] What is more, this volume exemplifies the tendencies and tensions among queer historical scholarship generally, which as Christopher Nealon points out, has simultaneously sought both "political" and "radical" ends in its inquiry.

The former represent recuperative projects—"the accumulated example of past attempts at survival"[23]—embodying one form of more traditional gay and lesbian cultural and political history that might be characterized by its ethnic or identitarian queer yearning. As David Deitcher has written of vintage same-sex photographs, "Being drawn in this way to enigmatic artifacts from the past provides evidence of longing: longing for the self-validation that results from having a history to refer to; longing for a comforting sense of connection to others—past as well as present—whose experience mirrors our own."[24] In this light, our Seneca Falls Boys bring to mind George Chauncey's reflections on the "folklore of the gay world" of the 1930s, equally applicable to the power of queer myth and memory that existed throughout the twentieth century and remains vital today: "Claiming historical figures was important to gay men not only because it validated their own homosexuality, but because it linked them to others. One of the ways groups of people constitute themselves as an ethnic, religious, or national community is by constructing a history that provides its members with a shared tradition and collective ancestors. . . . By constructing historical traditions of their own, gay men defined themselves as a distinct community. By imagining they had collective roots in the past, they asserted a collective identity in the present."[25]

This mode, signified best in my metonymy by the seemingly trivial marking designating the portrait's place of publication, Seneca Falls—especially for those familiar with Karlyn Kohrs Campbell's significant feminist recuperation of women's public address—is what Heather Love calls "affirmative history," "which seeks to confirm contemporary gay and lesbian identity by searching for moments of pride or past resistance."[26] Put somewhat differently, such "queer fictions of the past," to borrow Scott Bravmann's important concept, might be understood for their political utility as strategic essentialism. As Diana Fuss has observed, "Fictions of identity, importantly, are no less powerful for being fictions."[27]

No doubt with this perspective in mind, some of my contributors have noted that adopting our Seneca Falls Boys suggests that the project potentially smacks of (nonstrategic) essentialism, exhibiting what Lisa Duggan has described as "liberal assimilationist" gay politics: an emphasis on the primacy of sexual identity, an identity whose desire is fixed in a gendered direction, "residing clearly, intelligibly and unalterably in the body or psyche"[28] and, I might add, textually and critically instantiated as such by the (heroic) queer agent, all for the purposes of just inclusion, alongside other minority historical subjects, into that elusive "canon" of public address.[29] The risk here is that whatever rewards it might accrue, heteronormative structures and humanist assumptions remain uncontested, if not reified.

By contrast a more radical queer historical yearning seeks by means of cultural critique to explode the homo/hetero binary on which an ethnic perspective rests, to embrace and examine erotic identifications, past and present, instead of identity and sexual object-choice as an analytical category, to understand that "gay sexuality in its specific female and male cultural (or subcultural) forms acts as an agency of social process whose mode of functioning is both interactive and yet resistant, both participatory and yet distinct, claiming at once equality and difference, demanding political representation while insisting on its material and historical specificity."[30] In Michael Warner's influential postulation, such a project would primarily pose itself oppositionally and performatively against "regimes of the normal." As he explains, "[Queer theory] rejects a minoritizing logic of toleration or simple political interest-representation. . . . For both academics and activists, 'queer' gets a critical edge by defining itself against the normal rather than the heterosexual, and normal includes normal business in the academy."[31] A queer project so conceived would not be interested in our Seneca Falls Boys as gay rhetorical forebears, but rather in mapping their desire in relationship to culturally constructed, normative gender and sexual discursive conditions and performances of their historical moment, and the simultaneous mapping of our own desire for them, or its absence, in relation to contemporary discourses of academic and cultural "normalcy."[32]

From my perspective, *Queering Public Address* productively embodies the tendencies and tensions of queerness in both its political and radical meanings. As will become clear, some essays explore issues of identity and agency in a manner resembling more conventional gay and lesbian history and whose desire for assimilation into public address studies is palpable. Others, it is equally clear, eschew if not eradicate altogether such traditional assumptions and concerns, aiming instead for a rearticulation of the grounds of public address: by exposing the consequential privileges bequeathed under the guise of sexual normalcy (in relation, as well, to race, class, and gender), the historically situated intersecting discourses that constituted normalcy and queerness, and the symbolic and material conditions that shape contemporary reading practices, including public address as a regime of the normal. I find both of these perspectives necessary, not mutually exclusive but indeed already often confused and conflated in productive ways, and mutually beneficial, perhaps in part because of the inherent frictions between them.[33] Our Seneca Falls Boys therefore are fittingly paradoxical, representing at once the promises of gay, lesbian, bisexual, or transgender public address and the queer critiques that seek to deepen their fulfillment.

In moving from the already described disorientations to an orientation of *Queering Public Address*, I will briefly explain its organization and contents and then close by reflecting on some of the specificities bespoken paradoxically by our Seneca Falls Boys, and explored by my contributors. I have divided the volume into two sections, "Queer Interventions" and "Queer Figurations," groupings that serve broadly to emphasize shared dispositions—namely, goals, approaches, and thematics—among the essays.

Part 1 is labeled "Queer Interventions," by which I mean that these essays critically interrogate and disrupt from queer perspectives various principles, objects, methods, and theories that have directly or implicitly governed the practice and judgment of rhetorical-historical analysis; each in its own way constitutes a tipping of the sacred cows of public address. Dana Cloud insightfully examines the manifold recovery of Eleanor Roosevelt, asking that we take seriously, which is to say politically, the question: who from the past counts as queer? She also demands that we address the correlative but often overlooked questions of why, how, and for whom queer memory of historical subjects, and the process of reclamation, functions in relation to visibility—and what visibility does or should achieve—in the public sphere. Through Roosevelt, Cloud engages iconicity/canonicity, the disciplining of historical same-sex desire, and the critical obligations of queering the past that insist on activism as well as representation, the material as well as the symbolic.

Ralph Smith and Russel Windes offer in bold relief the central issue of identity, particularly collective identity, long assumed by scholars of historical rhetorics but, as they argue, insufficiently understood in its complexity, most often wrongly understood as natural and stable across time and historically negligent of marginal subjectivities, especially those of variant sexuality. In their critical genealogy of collective identity as manifested by variant sexuality movements, Smith and Windes unsettle the category of identity in critical praxis by demonstrating "the inevitability of a destabilizing rhetorical process" of "constitution, representation, deployment, and renegotiation of the marginal collective subject," from the homophile movement through civil rights and liberationist discourses to the contemporary identitarian/postidentitarian struggle.

In a tantalizing rendezvous, Karen Foss brings Lloyd Bitzer to bear on Harvey Milk, and vice versa, by queering Bitzer's germinal theory of the rhetorical situation. Employing Jennifer Terry's deviant historiography, Foss offers an "effective history" of Milk's political discourse, which she describes as "a rhetoric of contradiction that effectively created spaces and openings into which the gay/lesbian perspective could be acknowledged and discussed" and by which he "intervened into and disrupted the hegemony of San Francisco politics." In so doing, Foss performs her own deviant rethinking of exigence, discourse, audience, and constraints as constituent elements of historical-rhetorical action.

By means of Larry Kramer's explosive queer appropriation of Abraham Lincoln, Charles Morris "outs" the homophobic discourse of ostensibly apolitical, "objective" historians so as to reflect and disrupt a seemingly invisible disciplinary praxis.

Morris argues that, stricken by homophobic panic in the wake of Kramer's disclosure, Lincoln scholars dramatically enacted their custodianship of Lincoln's mutable memory by attempting what he calls "mnemonicide," or the assassination of memory. This disclosure of "academic" investments in the queer culture war, and the intermingling rhetorical labor of historiography and memory, is as significant here as the question of Lincoln's sexuality and its stake in American national identity.

I purposefully close the section with Julie Thompson's reading of Marlon Riggs's *Tongues Untied*, a manifesto in the best sense by virtue of its thoroughgoing confrontation of the key terms of this volume. In her "fundamental disruption of historical silences in rhetorical scholarship regarding human sexuality, race, gender, and class," Thompson "quares" (she rejects "queer" for the antiracist vocabulary adopted from E. Patrick Johnson's work) public address by engaging in "proselytical invention," or the quare recruitment of texts, to achieve a "homonormative" perspective on the history of American eloquence and its critical grammar. Through Riggs as an exemplar, she racializes and sexualizes the representational speaking subject as well as problematizes the representational speaking subject per se by placing it within its historically specific political economy.

Part 2 I have named "Queer Figurations," which signifies the focus each of these essays places on rhetorical productions of queerness in particular circumstances and locations in American history. Such rhetorical productions entail the figurations of specific historical subjects, voices, styles, and performances by means of various discourses that intersected in relation to ideologies, issues, and events, enabling and constraining, disseminating and retarding—in a word, constituting—queerness in multiple contexts over time. Through these essays we discover myriad mutations of queer experience and performance and heteronormative discourses, both pre- and post-Stonewall.

John Sloop explores the fascinating case of Lucy Lobdell, "The Female Hunter of Delaware and Sullivan County," who during the middle to late decades of the nineteenth century successfully and unsuccessfully passed as a man and lived with Mary Louise Perry. Reading extant discourses regarding Lobdell, Sloop offers an incisive view of the period's semiotics of gender and sexuality, as well as the moral, medical, and psychiatric discourses that sought jurisdiction over Lobdell's gender and sexual performance(s). Sloop also places Lobdell's "queer circumstances" within the contemporary politics of gender and sexuality to understand how such historical subjectivities and performances are retrieved, interpreted, appropriated, disciplined, and perhaps disrupted.

In his richly textured reading of Wallace Thurman's *Infants of the Spring*, Eric Watts takes us to the racial and sexual crucible known as Harlem during the height of its dramatic renaissance. Amid the struggle for a national African American ethos and "homeland," Thurman's "failure" exposes the centrality of sexuality as a constitutive force in shaping racial politics of identity and place for the New Negro.

Moreover Watts details how Thurman's novel and its surrounding discourses reveal the prospects and limitations of queer voice and a black gay utopia in the 1920s; the excessive queer sounds and sites interrupted African American sexual doxa, even if, tragically, they resulted in queer "voicelessness and homelessness."

Robert Brookey also meaningfully engages the issue of queer voice, in his case as the politically ambivalent productions emerging by means of psychoanalytic and psychological discourses across the twentieth century that have sought to define and regulate homosexuality. In keeping with Foucault, Brookey challenges us to deepen our perspective on power and discourse by demonstrating the ways in which disciplinary rhetorics produced queer sexuality, provided for queer voice through the rhetorical mode of "confession," and afforded various opportunities for queer resistance and advocacy. He examines "the ways queers have been allowed to speak, and in what ways they have been impelled to speak" by virtue (and vice) of institutional discourses, culminating in his genealogy with the removal of homosexuality from the American Psychiatric Association's catalog of mental disorders and the counterresistance waged by the homophobic reparative therapy movement.

Lisbeth Lipari provides yet another distinct approach to ethos and voice by countering the superficial reclamations of Lorraine Hansberry that have disfigured the complex textures of her multiple discourses—discourses that, when read within their queer historical contingencies of the 1950s and 1960s, reveal her as a less heroic and more formidable public intellectual than previously recognized. Lipari deftly "thickens" Hansberry's intertextual and contextual interpretation by reading the intersectionality of her discourse from within the "simultaneity of oppression" she experienced, situating her famous letters to the *Ladder* in relation to her plays, editorials, documentary narrative, and other political speech. As such, we come to understand Hansberry's political ethos and imagination—her rhetorical vision—as forged simultaneously by, and through speaking against, homophobia, racism, sexism, colonialism, and capitalism. This rhetorical vision is strikingly portrayed as both of its time and ahead of its time.

Finally Lester Olson examines discourse produced by material and symbolic violence, the traumas that far too frequently afflict gay, lesbian, bisexual, or transgender peoples and significantly shape their public voices. He considers such traumas in relation to style, a canon of public address more often assumed than explicated. In meticulously conceptualizing what he calls "traumatic styles," Olson engages as exemplary the liabilities and possibilities of Audre Lorde's rich rhetorical corpus to illustrate discursive constructions and implications of "unspeakable speech," "unlistenable speech," and "recovery, reintegration, and communal healing through political actions."

As I reflect on our Seneca Falls Boys and across these essays, I am struck by the figures themselves, desirable figures we might engage as reflections and refutations of ourselves and our communities, invited by their seductions (and our own), which suggests that they might indeed be suitable, available, for the taking. Similarly, we engage in this volume those queer voices (or those insufficiently queer) that might be made to signify, potentially forging meaningful political bonds and actions or creating significant dissonances: Abraham Lincoln, Lucy Lobdell, Wallace Thurman, Eleanor Roosevelt, Lorraine Hansberry, Harvey Milk, Audre Lorde, Marlon Riggs, Larry Kramer.[34] We need a vibrant imagination, and the fortitude to withstand even as we treat seriously the often insidious caution that we should avoid falling prey to wishful thinking. Wishful thinking, however, otherwise considered the art of the possible, or what Julie Thompson labels "proselytical invention," is at the rhetorical core of cultural and political transformation.

At the same time, we question what it is about those striking figures, and ourselves, that make them desirable, usable, avoidable. We recognize, as Dana Cloud and Charles Morris make clear in their analyses, Scott Bravmann's observation that "lesbian and gay historical self-representations—queer fictions of the past—help construct, maintain, and contest identities—queer fictions of the present. For this reason, we need to look at how the images of the gay and lesbian past circulating among us animate the present and to read lesbian and gay historical self-representations as sites of ongoing hermeneutic and political struggle in the formation of new social subjects and new cultural possibilities."[35]

We might imagine, too, that this sentimental portrait, not traditionally understood as a mode of public address (queer historical discourse is rarely, if ever, conventional, sanctioned), dares nonetheless to function rhetorically. Our Seneca Falls Boys perhaps perform the love that dare not speak its name: their dreamy gazes, their affectionate repose, solemnity that unapologetically—indeed proudly—reflects both occasion and betrothed hearts. As Lord Alfred Douglas and Oscar Wilde knew so well,[36] even the uttered denial of illicit same-sex love constitutes its own rather clever, even defiant, proclamation—a resistance. These boys speak through their closed lips; theirs is an iconic authorization of self and other.[37]

Such possibilities raise important questions regarding the means and ends of queering public discourse. On what disciplinary grounds, by what methods, might we interpret meaning in such ambiguous, if not surreptitious, expression? What, in historically specific circumstances, marks queer textuality? What, as Karen Foss asks, is distinctive stylistically and strategically in discourse manifested by queer rhetorical situations? What, Lisbeth Lipari, Eric Watts, and Dana Cloud query, constitutes a queer transformative vision, a queer political ethos? What warrants our queer hermeneutic claims on historical subjects who never fully substantiate them, whose very eloquence is vexed by silences and echoes with plausible deniability? By what means do we marshal adequate contexts to sustain such readings, overcoming the ever perilous politics of evidence, mindful, as is John Sloop, of the historical situatedness of gender and sexual articulations, then and now? How might we speak of such expressions, epistemologies, identities, articulated on their terms, without *merely* and dangerously (if, of course, always to some significant degree) reflecting ourselves?

Our Seneca Falls Boys must also be understood as a cultural production, manufactured in the Wale studio. Whatever their pose portrays, it does so through the mediating influences of broader social, cultural, and political meanings and matrices of power that animate the labor of that production. Their expression, however resistant, is simultaneously conventional.[38] Even as they speak, they are *spoken for* by means of various discourses, both in their time and our own, that inscribe, for instance, the gendered, raced, and classed virtues of masculinity and fraternity, and the (often unspoken) bogeys of erotic desire against which such homosociality is legible, legitimated, and limited.[39] In the interplay of these competing constitutive discourses, we discover the historical complexities of queer identity, identification, and invention.

Likewise many of the essays in this volume conceive of queering public address as rhetorically akin to "deviant historiography," offering, in Jennifer Terry's appropriation of Foucault, "*not* an alternative narrative with its own glorious tumescence peopled by previously elided but now recuperated Others. Effective history exposes not the events and actors elided by traditional history, but instead lay bare the *processes* and *operations* by which these elisions occurred. . . . [looking] not only for how subjects are produced and policed, but how they are resistant and excessive to the very discourse from which they emerge."[40] Both John Sloop and Robert Brookey explore the ways in which medical discourses create contexts of rhetorical performance and construct sexual identities. Eric Watts and Lisbeth Lipari examine the intersectionality of race and sexuality in the literary and political production of African American identity. Lester Olson considers violence as a condition of discourse, and Ralph Smith and Russel Windes analyze the mutability of identity as central to social movement strategy at any given historical locus. Historiography itself is understood as a regime of the normal in Charles Morris's reading of Kramer's Lincoln. In each instance the social relations and cultural constraints that shape the possibilities of rhetorical performance are central to a queer reading of public address.

Finally, however desirous we might be to identify with and reclaim—or, I think it important to acknowledge, at least in my case, to consume—our Seneca Falls Boys, we must do so keenly aware of the normalized and potentially problematic ideologies attending them (and, for that matter, us). They are men; they are white men; and, as their attire implies, they are economically privileged white men. As scholars across disciplines, especially those embracing queer theory, have emphasized, liberal assimilationist politics generally, and gay historiography specifically, has tended dangerously to naturalize the white, privileged gay male as representative of queer community and beneficiary of critical attention at the expense of a wide array of other subject positions, including lesbians, bisexuals, transgender people, people of color, the working class, and the disabled. We would ultimately fail in our antihomophobic efforts, therefore, if we replicate broader patterns of racism, sexism, and classism as we attempt to intervene in the contemporary critical practices of public address. Reminder of this is given its fullest articulation by Julie Thompson, and its application can be witnessed throughout the volume. Our Seneca Falls Boys therefore stand as a beacon for *Queering Public Address* in two senses, both lodestar and pharos.

Once more I return to the fortuitous coincidence that the portrait of our boys was created in Seneca Falls, New York. Where else (perhaps the Castro, Cherry Grove, Greenwich Village, or Harlem) to find an historical exemplar of the muscular recognition of difference, the resounding voice of queerness inspired by material and imagined sisterhood? That political spirit animates and pervades this volume. As so many of the contributors argue, the nature and scope of queer voice and advocacy, and how we interpret them, holds vitally significant cultural implications. In light of the vicissitudes and ambiguities of America's queer past, we question here the cultural and political prospects of queer public discourse, and queering public discourse. How those historical discourses have sought to forge queer resistance, counter-publics, individual and collective identities and identifications, and social transformation often, sometimes in contradictory ways, tell us much about our past and the challenges of our present and future. They remind us that we must listen not only for eloquent and disciplinary silences, but also for unconventional resistive articulations, muteness that articulated complicity in relations of power, and those powerful discourses that gave voice to the otherwise mute. And those multiple silences and voices puzzle for us the stakes involved in our own modes of inquiry.

Notes

1. Simon Schama, *Dead Certainties (Unwarranted Speculations)* (New York: Alfred A. Knopf, 1991), 320.

2. I am grateful to Mr. Schultz for his permission to use this photograph in the volume.

3. I take the phrase from Kathleen J. Turner, ed., *Doing Rhetorical History: Concepts and Cases* (Tuscaloosa: University of Alabama Press, 1998).

4. Anne G. Myles, "Queering the Study of Early American Sexuality," *William and Mary Quarterly* 60 (January 2003): 200.

5. Christopher Nealon, *Foundlings: Lesbian and Gay Historical Emotion before Stonewall* (Durham, N.C.: Duke University Press, 2001), 8, 13.

6. Martin J. Medhurst, "The Academic Study of Public Address: A Tradition in Transition," in *Landmark Essays on American Public Address*, ed. Martin J. Medhurst (Davis, Calif.: Hermagoras Press, 1993), xi; Stephen E. Lucas, "The Renaissance of American Public Address: Text and Context in Rhetorical Criticism," *Quarterly Journal of Speech* 74 (May 1988): 244.

7. Such discourse did, of course, exist, and as early as 1976 was made available thanks to Jonathan Ned Katz. Many of those texts, which included police reports and other disciplinary discourses, pseudonymous publications, and passing performances, however, would have required a more generous survey of the rhetorical landscape than the field was prepared to offer, even after the critical transformations of the 1970s and 1980s. See Katz, *Gay American History: Lesbians and Gay Men in the U.S.A.* (New York: Crowell, 1976).

8. Robert Hariman, "Afterword: Relocating the Art of Public Address," in *Rhetoric and Political Culture in Nineteenth-Century America*, ed. Thomas W. Benson (East Lansing: Michigan State University Press, 1997), 164–65.

9. In rightly touting the inclusion of numerous women in their survey among rhetorical scholars of the top hundred American speeches of the twentieth century, for instance, Stephen Lucas and Martin Medhurst observe, "While much work needs to be done, there can be little doubt that we have made great strides in the past two decades in recognizing the contributions of women speakers in all phases of American life and in recovering heretofore lost or neglected texts that manifest those contributions." Special note is also offered regarding the prominent appearance of African American discourse in the survey, a testament that "public speaking remains the single most important mode of expression for people seeking to broaden the lines of power and privilege in American society." Apparently, however, this is not the case for queers, who do not explicitly appear in either the list or the analysis. Lucas and Medhurst, "American Public Address: The Top 100 Speeches of the Twentieth-Century," unpublished essay, 7, 9. Although quantity is but one measure (and sometimes an unreliable and unsophisticated measure) of visibility and power, it is worth noting that between 2000 and 2005 in the *Quarterly Journal of Speech* and *Rhetoric & Public Affairs*, which in my opinion are the two flagship journals for public address studies within the discipline, scholarship related to race and/or gender has been consistently featured, constituting more than 20 percent of the published work. Similar commitment is evident in the titles published in the high-profile rhetoric series of Michigan State University, University of Alabama, and University of South Carolina presses.

10. Philip Wander, "The Third Persona: An Ideological Turn in Rhetorical Theory," *Central States Speech Journal* 35 (1984): 197–216. The exceptions that I believe in part prove the heteronormative rule within public address studies are manifest in the publication throughout the past five years of a limited number of queer public address studies, generously defined, in *Quarterly Journal of Speech*, *Rhetoric & Public Affairs*, and regional journals. See Lester C. Olson, "Liabilities of Language: Audre Lorde Reclaiming Difference," *Quarterly Journal of Speech* 84 (November 1998): 448–70; Charles E. Morris III, "'The Responsibilities of the Critic': F. O. Matthiessen's Homosexual Palimpsest," *Quarterly Journal of Journal of Speech* 84 (August 1998): 261–82; Robert A. Brookey, "Keeping a Good Wo/man Down: Normalizing Deborah Sampson Gannett," *Communication Studies* 49 (1998): 73–85; John M. Sloop, "Disciplining the Transgendered: Brandon Teena, Public Representation, and Normativity," *Western Journal of Communication* 64 (spring 2000): 165–89; Charles E. Morris III, "Pink Herring and the Fourth Persona: J. Edgar Hoover's Sex Crime Panic," *Quarterly Journal of Speech*, 88 (May 2002): 228–44; Brian L. Ott and Eric Aoki, "The Politics of Negotiating Public Tragedy: Media Framing of the Matthew Shepard Murder," *Rhetoric & Public Affairs* 5 (fall 2002): 483–505; Glenda Conway, "Inevitable Reconstructions: Voice and Ideology in Two Landmark

U.S. Supreme Court Decisions," *Rhetoric & Public Affairs* 6 (fall 2003): 487–507; Daniel C. Brouwer, "Privacy, Publicity, and Propriety in Congressional Eulogies for Representative Stewart P. McKinney (R-Conn.)," *Rhetoric and Public Affairs* 7 (summer 2004): 149–72; Lynn Clarke, "Contesting Definitional Authority in the Collective," *Quarterly Journal of Speech* 91 (February 2005): 1–36; John Lynch, "Institution and Imprimatur: Institutional Rhetoric and the Failure of the Catholic Church's Pastoral Letter on Homosexuality," *Rhetoric & Public Affairs* 8 (fall 2005): 383–404; Charles E. Morris III, "Passing by Proxy: Collusive and Convulsive Silence in the Trial of Leopold and Loeb," *Quarterly Journal of Speech* 91 (August 2005): 264–90. For a different sort of proof, I invite the reader to visit the touted website Americanrhetoric.com, perhaps now the most important archive in public address studies and pedagogy, where even the most casual survey will indicate the appalling paucity of queer texts (one entry, as of this writing), especially by contrast to the diverse array of discourse that is represented on the site. I do want to acknowledge here the early and contemporary efforts of gay, lesbian, bisexual, and transgender scholars who have explored broadly the relationship between sexuality and communication, whose vision for the discipline this volume charts with greater focus on rhetorical studies and public address. See James Chesebro, ed., *Gayspeak: Gay Male and Lesbian Communication* (New York: Pilgrim Press, 1981); R. Jeffrey Ringer, ed., *Queer Words, Queer Images: Communication and the Constructions of Homosexuality* (New York: NYU Press, 1994); and Gust A. Yep, Karen E. Lovaas, and John P. Elia, eds., *Queer Theory and Communication: From Disciplining Queers to Queering the Discipline(s)* (New York: Harrington Park Press, 2003).

11. See, for example, Michel Foucault, *The Archaeology of Knowledge: and the Discourse on Language*, trans. A. M. Sheridan Smith (New York: Pantheon, 1972); Hayden White, *Metahistory: The Historical Imagination in Nineteenth-Century Europe* (Baltimore: Johns Hopkins University Press, 1973), *The Tropics of Discourse: Essays in Cultural Criticism* (Baltimore: Johns Hopkins University Press, 1978), and *The Content of Form: Narrative Discourse and Historical Representation* (Baltimore: Johns Hopkins University Press, 1987); Dominick LaCapra, *Rethinking Intellectual History: Texts, Contexts, Language* (Ithaca, N.Y.: Cornell University Press, 1983); Allan Megill and Donald N. McCloskey, "The Rhetoric of History," in *The Rhetoric of the Human Sciences*, ed. John S. Nelson, Allan Megill, and Donald N. McCloskey (Madison: University of Wisconsin Press, 1987), 221–38; Michel de Certeau, *The Writing of History* (New York: Columbia University Press, 1988); Joan W. Scott, "The Evidence of Experience," in *Questions of Evidence: Proof, Practice, and Persuasion across the Disciplines*, ed. James Chandler, Arnold I. Davidson, and Harry Harootunian (Chicago: University of Chicago Press, 1994), 366; Alun Lunslow, *Deconstructing History* (London: Routledge, 1997); and E. Culpepper Clark and Raymie E. McKerrow, "The Rhetorical Construction of History," in *Doing Rhetorical History: Concepts and Cases*, ed. Kathleen J. Turner (Tuscaloosa: University of Alabama Press, 1998), 33–46.

12. Dominick LaCapra, "Rhetoric and History," in *History and Criticism* (Ithaca, N.Y.: Cornell University Press, 1985), 42–43.

13. Carole Blair, "Contested Histories of Rhetoric: The Politics of Preservation, Progress, and Change," *Quarterly Journal of Speech* 78 (November 1992): 403; see also Blair, "Octalog: The Politics of Historiography," *Rhetoric Review* 7 (fall 1988); and Blair and Mary L. Kahl, "Introduction: Revising the History of Rhetorical Theory," *Western Journal of Speech Communication*

54 (spring 1990): 148–59. Michael C. Leff, invoking the work of Steven Mailloux, has acknowledged the rhetoricity (if not ideological blindness) of close textual analysis: "A recognition of the contingency of interpretive work does not prevent us from taking a position; it only makes us more aware that interpretations of texts are like our other beliefs and commitments; they depend upon our historical situation, on our position in some particular time and place, and they are justified through argument to some particular audience." Leff, "Lincoln at Cooper Union: Neo-Classical Criticism Revisited," *Western Journal of Communication* 65 (summer 2001): 240. See also Mailloux, *Rhetorical Power* (Ithaca, N.Y.: Cornell University Press, 1989).

14. I borrow the phrase from John R. Gillis, ed., *Commemorations: The Politics of National Identity* (Princeton, N.J.: Princeton University Press, 1994), 9. Although his focus concerns literary studies, Eagleton's insights on ideology and academic writing are relevant here. Terry Eagleton, "Ideology and Scholarship," in *Historical Studies and Literary Criticism*, ed. Jerome J. McGann (Madison: University of Wisconsin Press, 1985), 114–25.

15. See Carole Blair, Julie R. Brown, and Leslie A. Baxter, "Disciplining the Feminine," *Quarterly Journal of Speech* 80 (November 1994): 383–409; Marouf Hasian, Jr., "Silences and Articulations in Modern Rhetorical Criticism," *Western Journal of Communication* 65 (summer 2001): 295–313.

16. John D. Wrathall, "Provenance as Text: Reading the Silences around Sexuality in Manuscript Collections," *Journal of American History* 79 (June 1992): 166. See also Blanche Wiesen Cook, "The Historical Denial of Lesbianism," *Radical History Review* 20 (spring–summer 1979): 60–65; Martin Bauml Duberman, "'Writhing Bedfellows': Two Young Men from Antebellum South Carolina's Ruling Elite Share 'Extravagant Delight,'" in *About Time: Exploring the Gay Past* (New York: Gay Presses of New York, 1986), 5–22; Blanche Wiesen Cook, "Outing History," *Out* (February/March 1994): 50–54; Estelle B. Freedman, "'The Burning of Letters Continues': Elusive Identities and the Historical Construction of Sexuality," in *Modern American Queer History*, ed. Allida M. Black (Philadelphia: Temple University Press, 2001), 51–68.

17. My understanding of heteronormativity is derived from Berlant and Warner: "By heteronormativity we mean the institutions, structures of understanding, and practical orientations that make heterosexuality seem not only coherent—that is, organized as a sexuality—but also privileged. Its coherence is always provisional, and its privilege can take several (sometimes contradictory) forms: unmarked, as the basic idiom of the personal and the social; or marked as a natural state; or projected as an ideal or moral accomplishment. It consists less of norms that could be summarized as a body of doctrine than of a sense of rightness produced in contradictory manifestations—often unconscious, immanent to practice or to institutions." Lauren Berlant and Michael Warner, "Sex in Public," *Critical Inquiry* 24 (winter 1998): 548.

18. For comparable efforts, see Jonathan Goldberg, ed., *Queering the Renaissance* (Durham, N.C.: Duke University Press, 1994); Steven Seidman, ed., *Queer Theory/Sociology* (Cambridge, Mass.: Blackwell, 1996); Gary David Comstock and Susan E. Henking, eds., *Que(e)rying Religion: A Critical Anthology* (New York: Continuum, 1997); William G. Tierney, *Academic Outlaws: Queer Theory and Cultural Studies in the Academy* (Thousand Oaks, Calif.: Sage, 1997); Allida M. Black, ed., *Modern American Queer History* (Philadelphia: Temple University Press, 2001); Ellen Lewin and William M. Leap, eds., *Out in Theory: The Emergence of*

Lesbian and Gay Anthropology (Urbana: University of Illinois Press, 2002); Yep, Lovaas, and Elia, eds., *Queer Theory and Communication*.

19. Berlant and Warner, "Sex in Public," 562. Although queering public address is not precisely the same as sex in public, the latter serves as an apt metaphor for this project (especially as it might be understood by traditionalists within the field), and I would argue that the telos is shared.

20. A full genealogy of queer American historical scholarship is too massive an undertaking for my purposes here. See, for example, Michel Foucault, *The History of Sexuality*, vol. 1: *An Introduction*, trans. Robert Hurley (New York: Vintage, 1978); Katz, *Gay American History*; John D'Emilio, *Sexual Politics, Sexual Communities: The Making of a Homosexual Minority in the United States, 1940–1970* (Chicago: University of Chicago Press, 1983); Martin Bauml Duberman, Martha Vicinus, and George Chauncey, Jr., eds., *Hidden from History: Reclaiming a Gay and Lesbian Past* (New York: New American Library, 1989); Allan Bérubé, *Coming Out under Fire: The History of Gay Men and Women in World War Two* (New York: Free Press, 1990); Lillian Faderman, *Odd Girls and Twilight Lovers: A History of Lesbian Life in Twentieth-Century America* (New York: Columbia University Press, 1991); Elizabeth Lapovsky Kennedy and Madeline D. Davis, *Boots of Leather, Slippers of Gold: The History of a Lesbian Community* (New York: Routledge, 1993); George Chauncey, *Gay New York: Gender, Urban Culture, and the Making of the Gay Male World* (New York: Basic Books, 1994); Thomas Waugh, *Hard to Imagine: Gay Male Eroticism in Photography and Film from Their Beginnings to Stonewall* (New York: Columbia University Press, 1996); Scott Bravmann, *Queer Fictions of the Past: History, Culture, and Difference* (New York: Cambridge University Press, 1997); Jennifer Terry, *An American Obsession: Science, Medicine, and Homosexuality in Modern Society* (Chicago: University of Chicago Press, 1999); John Howard, *Men Like That: A Southern Queer History* (Chicago: University of Chicago Press, 1999); Siobhan B. Somerville, *Queering the Color Line: Race and the Invention of Homosexuality in American Culture* (Durham, N.C.: Duke University Press, 2000); Lisa Duggan, *Sapphic Slashers: Sex, Violence, and American Modernity* (Durham, N.C.: Duke University Press, 2000); Nealon, *Foundlings*; Henry Abelove, *Deep Gossip* (Minneapolis: University of Minnesota Press, 2003); Kathryn R. Kent, *Making Girls into Women: American Women's Writing and the Rise of Lesbian Identity* (Durham, N.C.: Duke University Press, 2003); Graham Robb, *Strangers: Homosexual Love in the Nineteenth Century* (London: Picador, 2003); Gavin Butt, *Between You and Me: Queer Disclosures in the New York Art World, 1948–1963* (Durham, N.C.: Duke University Press, 2005).

21. See Thomas W. Benson, "History, Criticism, and Theory in the Study of American Rhetoric," in *American Rhetoric: Context and Criticism*, ed. Benson (Carbondale: Southern Illinois University Press, 1989), 1–17; Medhurst, "The Academic Study of Public Address," xi–xliii.

22. Berlant and Warner, "Sex in Public," 558.

23. Nealon, *Foundlings*, 17–18.

24. David Deitcher, *Dear Friends: American Photographs of Men Together, 1840–1918* (New York: Harry N. Abrams, 2001), 14.

25. Chauncey, *Gay New York*, 285–86. For a discussion of the persistence of this "ethnic" model of queer "cultural unity," see Rictor Norton, *The Myth of the Modern Homosexual: Queer History and the Search for Cultural Unity* (London: Cassell, 1997).

26. Seneca Falls was the site of the first women's rights convention in 1848, the birthplace of the movement. Karlyn Campbell's pathbreaking recovery and analysis of early feminist texts—what might be called the gender turn within rhetorical studies—is generally considered a landmark moment in the history of public address. Karlyn Kohrs Campbell, *Man Cannot Speak for Her*, 2 vols. (New York: Praeger, 1989); Heather K. Love, "'Spoiled Identity': Stephen Gordon's Loneliness and the Difficulties of Queer History," *GLQ: A Journal of Lesbian and Gay Studies* 7 (2001): 487–519.

27. Bravmann, *Queer Fictions of the Past*; Diana Fuss, *Essentially Speaking: Feminism, Nature, and Difference* (New York: Routledge, 1989), 104.

28. Lisa Duggan, "Making It Perfectly Queer," *Socialist Review* 22 (January–March 1992): 18.

29. For an instructive discussion of the perils and possibilities of a minority canon, see Eve Kosofsky Sedgwick, *Epistemology of the Closet* (Berkeley: University of California Press, 1990), 48–59. Christopher Lane has provided a provocative critique that identifies the pitfalls of seeking resemblance and similarity in queer engagements of the past. Lane, "Afterword: The Homosexual in the Text," in *The Burdens of Intimacy: Psychoanalysis and Victorian Masculinity* (Chicago: University of Chicago Press, 1999), 224–45. In terms of a "canon" within public address studies, I share James Aune's belief that "the salutary move toward greater coherence in graduate education about public address studies and the defense of close readings of rhetorical documents do not, it seems to me, entail an acceptance of 'canon' language in describing our field of study." I would argue, however, that "the salutary move" he describes suggests a disciplinary fiction that a canon does exist, with political implications for queer discourses of the past. James Arnt Aune, "'The Power of Hegemony' and Marxist Cultural Theory," in *Rhetoric and Community: Studies in Unity and Fragmentation*, ed. J. Michael Hogan (Columbia: University of South Carolina Press, 1998), 72.

30. Teresa de Lauretis, "Queer Theory: Lesbian and Gay Sexualities: An Introduction," *differences* 3 (summer 1991): iii. See also Jennifer Terry, "Theorizing Deviant Historiography," *differences: A Journal of Feminist Cultural Studies* 3 (1991): 55–74; Lisa Duggan, "The Discipline Problem," *GLQ: A Journal of Lesbian and Gay Studies* 2 (August 1995): 179–91; Donna Penn, "Queer: Theorizing Politics and History," *Radical History Review* 62 (1995): 24–42; Henry Abelove, "The Queering of Lesbian/Gay History," *Radical History Review* 62 (1995): 44–57; John Howard, "Where Are We to Begin," in *Modern American Queer History*, ed. Allida M. Black (Philadelphia: Temple University Press, 2001), 3–10.

31. Michael Warner, introduction to *Fear of a Queer Planet: Queer Politics and Social Theory*, ed. Warner (Minneapolis: University of Minnesota Press, 1993), xxvi.

32. Rhetorical scholars will recognize this as a queer version of "critical rhetoric." See Raymie E. McKerrow, "Critical Rhetoric: Theory and Praxis," *Communication Monographs* 56 (June 1989): 91–111.

33. For a useful parallel, see the meaningful exchange between Karlyn Kohrs Campbell and Barbara Biesecker regarding approaches to gender in public address studies. Barbara Biesecker, "Coming to Terms with Recent Attempts to Write Women into the History of Rhetoric," *Philosophy and Rhetoric* 25 (1992): 140–61; Karlyn Kohrs Campbell, "Biesecker Cannot Speak for Her Either," *Philosophy and Rhetoric* 26 (1993): 153–59; Biesecker, "Negotiating with Our Tradition: Reflecting Again (without Apologies) on the Feminization of Rhetoric," *Philosophy and Rhetoric* 26 (1993): 236–40.

34. As with our anonymous boys, we emphasize the rhetorical significance of a range of voices, not merely the culturally prominent but also the ordinary or obscure, such as Lucy Lobdell or members of the Mattachine Society or Daughters of Bilitis, an inhabitant of Harlem, or any gay, lesbian, bisexual, or transgender person who experiences trauma.

35. Bravmann, *Queer Fictions of the Past*, 4.

36. The phrase "the love that dare not speak its name" is derived from Lord Alfred Douglas's poem "The Two Loves" (1894), which was used as evidence in the infamous trials of Oscar Wilde in 1895. To his peril, Wilde's defense of the poem's depiction of same-sex love constitutes one of the most eloquent apologias in Western queer public discourse. See H. Montgomery Hyde, *The Trials of Oscar Wilde* (New York: Dover Publications, 1962), 200–201.

37. Although Walt Whitman's "Calamus photographs" are in a class unto themselves, the extent to which they functioned as "icons of male-male affection," circulating among devotees, and publicly, with tacit meanings both exhilarating and threatening in their erotic charge, their queer compulsion, is illuminating here. See Ed Folsom, "Whitman's Calamus Photographs," in *Breaking Bounds: Whitman and American Cultural Studies*, ed. Betsy Erkkila and Jay Grossman (New York: Oxford University Press, 1996), 193–219. See also John Ibson, *Picturing Men: A Century of Male Relationships in Everyday American Photography* (Washington, D.C.: Smithsonian Institution Press, 2002).

38. Deitcher notes that in nineteenth-century studio portraiture, the "adhesive" pose ("in which men are seen in tight close-ups with their heads inclined so that they touch above, and often a little behind, the ear") suggested in commercial form the "shared choreography of everyday bodily experience" derived from dominant cultural meanings of male affection and friendship (and phrenology), and much older traditions of iconic representation. Deitcher, *Dear Friends*, 138–39.

39. See Mark C. Carnes and Clyde Griffen, eds., *Meanings for Manhood: Constructions of Masculinity in Victorian America* (Chicago: University of Chicago Press, 1990); E. Anthony Rotundo, *American Manhood: Transformations in Masculinity from the Revolution to the Modern Era* (New York: Basic Books, 1993); Laura McCall and Donald Yacovone, eds., *A Shared Experience: Men, Women, and the History of Gender* (New York: NYU Press, 1998); Mary Chapman and Glenn Hendler, eds., *Sentimental Men: Masculinity and the Politics of Affect in American Culture* (Berkeley: University of California Press, 1999); Caleb Crain, *American Sympathy: Men Friendship, and Literature in the New Nation* (New Haven, Conn.: Yale University Press, 2001); Chris Packard, *Queer Cowboys and Other Erotic Male Friendships in Nineteenth-Century American Literature* (New York: Palgrave Macmillan, 2005).

40. Jennifer Terry, "Theorizing Deviant Historiography," 56–57. See also Michel Foucault, "Nietzsche, Genealogy, History," in *Language, Counter-Memory, Practice: Selected Essays and Interviews by Michel Foucault*, ed. Donald F. Bouchard (Ithaca, N.Y.: Cornell University Press, 1977), 139–64.

Part One

queer
interventions

THE FIRST LADY'S PRIVATES

Queering Eleanor Roosevelt for Public Address Studies

Dana L. Cloud

Dear one, & so you think they gossip about us. . . . I am always so much more optimistic than you are. I suppose because I care so little what "they" say!

Eleanor Roosevelt to Lorena Hickok, 1933,
in Roger Streitmatter, ed., *Empty without You*

About an hour and fifteen minutes into the two-hour Public Broadcasting Service (PBS) *American Experience* episode produced in 2000 about the life of Eleanor Roosevelt, the video introduces the openly lesbian figure of Lorena Hickok ("Hick"), described as Roosevelt's closest friend. A gray-haired, sharp-featured woman identified as Roosevelt family friend Trude Lash comments that Eleanor Roosevelt was extremely affectionate with Hick, but "she definitely was not a lesbian."[1] Roosevelt's granddaughter in the next sequence is more tolerant (perhaps to the point of oppression). "I have no idea if Lorena Hickok had a homosexual relationship with my grandmother. And my feeling about that is, kind of, who cares? They were very good friends. And if they could make each other happy in any way, then that's what's important."

Was Eleanor Roosevelt one of us? This, I will argue, is the wrong question. Yet it is difficult to let it remain a mystery. I enjoy announcing to my undergraduate students in my course "Communicating Gender in America" that Eleanor Roosevelt very likely had sex with another woman, much in the same way that I revel in telling them that Helen Keller was a member of Eugene Debs's Socialist Party.[2] This news is most often surprising, even shocking, to undergraduates and offers a significant set of pedagogical and political opportunities: namely, with such tidbits I can expose the partiality of mainstream historical narratives, attribute value to lesbian existence (to the extent that students admire Roosevelt), and encourage skepticism about received knowledge and public memory. A gay student might feel more confident and self-affirming on finding out that an admired historical figure was gay or lesbian. There is a powerful sense in which breaking historical silences makes a significant contribution to criticism, pedagogy, and politics. In Julie Thompson's phrasing, queering Eleanor Roosevelt makes it possible "to render non-normative standpoints regarding desire intelligible and authoritative in public."[3]

Even so, I will argue throughout this chapter that there are two reasons for caution in this project: first, we cannot claim Roosevelt as if her identity were a knowable, fixed essence; second, in spite of the common scholarly argument that any visibility is good for queer people,[4] I will argue that it matters how we approach the recovery of queer[5] memory and how visibility is shaped in the public sphere. Thus it is not my purpose to weigh in on whether Roosevelt was or was not a lesbian. Rather this chapter argues for getting beyond the logic of outing, choosing rather to queer public knowledge and memory of prominent public figures such as Eleanor Roosevelt.

To this end, the chapter examines popular video and print biographies of Eleanor Roosevelt and Lorena Hickok. The biographies reveal the twin perils of the logic of outing, either attempting to locate her among prominent gay public figures or rendering the private past as titillating scandal. The first strategy, assimilationist recovery of "great gays," lays claim to Roosevelt as representing queer people and oppression in some authentic way. The second strategy refuses to embrace Roosevelt, inviting voyeuristic distance from her scandalous historical secrets. Both approaches risk locating what it means to be queer in the practices of private life and away from public political intervention. For these reasons, I argue that, rather than claiming or outing people as queer, scholars and activists can queer the public's knowledge and memory of them. Rhetoricians can circulate new meanings of their private and public lives in order to shape how they are remembered and to encourage public reflection on the conditions of possibility for particular kinds of identities to be intelligible in public.

The chapter proceeds, first, by surveying the range of scholarly and political stances toward the critique of queer public address; second, by recounting the controversy over Eleanor Roosevelt's sexuality; third, by examining a number of popular film and written biographical narratives framing her sexuality; and finally, by arguing that the texts and the theoretical stances toward them are homologous in the bifurcation between assimilation and scandal. These observations warrant reflection on the goals of theory and criticism of queer public address.

Swinging Both Ways: Approaches to Queer Public Address

There are two dominant theoretical frames in which the project of recovery could be undertaken. Both are freighted with intellectual and political problems. The first is the liberal/assimilationist paradigm represented by gay and lesbian advocates such as Andrew Sullivan. Sullivan argues that gays and lesbians will only win their due rights if we can demonstrate to the public at large that we are just like everyone else: gays go to work, raise children, own property, engage in political life, consume goods, and so on.[6] For Sullivan and other liberals, claiming Eleanor Roosevelt would add evidence to the claim that "we are (and have been) everywhere"—including the White House. Further, Roosevelt's established greatness and public credibility could lend ethos to gays and lesbians among those who already respect her. Not only are "we" like other mainstream Americans—we are represented among the most revered of American heroes.

Scholars of every historically marginalized and oppressed group, including feminist scholars, have argued that the integration of new groups into scholarly canons and academic theory goes through several stages, beginning with the discovery and recovery from the past of "great" representatives of the oppressed category. Recovery movements then traverse the stages of distinguishing the voices of marginalized groups from dominant voices and criticizing the ways in which such distinctions are produced culturally and politically.[7] Work in contemporary queer theory demonstrates that this sequence is collapsed in our case: studies of famous gay people in history appear alongside work exploring the possibilities of agency in regimes of heteronormative distinctions.[8]

Although the simple recognition that there have been gays and lesbians among American political figures is still a useful and politically progressive impulse, the assimilationist framework privileges gays and lesbians who otherwise do not contest normative social, political, and economic boundaries. In much the same way that the making into cultural icons of Oprah Winfrey and Colin Powell and Bill Cosby tokenizes "American Dream"–friendly black Americans,[9] the liberal gay and lesbian rights advocates imply that the only "good gays" are those who do not challenge mainstream norms of intimate and familial behavior, the rules of capitalist society (to work and consume), and the assumption that one will work within a mainstream political framework. Those of us who might be more unruly—in our sexual, familial, political, and economic lives—are left out in the cold.

As Lauren Berlant and Michael Warner put it, "The national lesbian and gay organizations have decided to float with the current, arguing that lesbians and gays should be seen just as the people next door, well within a mainstream whose highest aspirations are marriage, military patriotism, and protected domesticity."[10] Further, if rhetorician Barbara Biesecker is correct in her argument regarding Karlyn Campbell's necessary and pioneering recovery of women's public address texts, the project of liberal recovery risks replicating an unhelpful ideological individualism that fails to recognize the structural contexts of and possibilities for queer subjects to emerge.[11]

Thus the most visible alternative to the liberal assimilationist framework comes to us from a poststructuralist-inflected queer theory. As represented by Berlant and Warner, queer theory challenges the humanism of the liberal approach, troubling the assumption of individual agency and free will and challenging the idea that people have sexual identity essences that are part of an individual self.[12] In the words of queer theorist Lisa Duggan, for example, "I want to take up the position of 'queer' largely in order to criticize the liberal and nationalist strategies in gay politics and to advocate the constructionist turn in lesbian and gay theories and practice."[13] For queer theory, privates are public and political; Berlant and Warner suggest that queer theory's program is "to mess up the desexualized spaces of the academy, exude some rut, re-imagine the publics from and for which academic intellectuals write, dress, and perform."[14]

As I have argued elsewhere, this perspective poses problems for a queer public address studies that wants to retain some investment in the idea of public human agency.[15] Avoiding essentialism, conservatism, and a politics of performance of the self, a historical materialist perspective can engage the intersections of class and queerness.[16] This perspective criticizes the spaces of self-cultivation celebrated in queer theory as inadequate to address the exclusion of the oppressed from spheres of deliberation and agency. Speaking in public on matters of importance has long been the prerogative of propertied white males; subaltern subjects have had to fight for access to the spaces of public, instrumental political agency. Thus it is tempting to valorize the private and cultural spaces of the oppressed and exploited as the spheres of hidden agency, as do some contemporary cultural studies scholars.[17] Eleanor Roosevelt demonstrated to an enormous degree a kind of traditional, public, instrumental agency in the political sphere, but her private life remains clouded in ambiguity, and its relevance to her public, political persona is likewise unclear.

Did She or Didn't She? Historiography, Eleanor, and Lorena

There is convincing evidence that First Lady Eleanor Roosevelt had a long-term, intimate, homosexual relationship with journalist Lorena Hickok. Blanche Wiesen Cook's definitive biography of Eleanor Roosevelt contains hundreds of mentions of the intimate relationship the two women shared.[18] Cook describes the relationship as marked by ardor, intensity, and jealousy, even though she remains discreet about the former First Lady's sexual behaviors. An out lesbian, Hickok is described as flirtatious and attractive to women, many of whom wined, dined, and shared weekend dalliances with her.[19] When, in 1978, the Franklin D. Roosevelt Library opened eighteen cartons containing Eleanor's correspondence with Hick, the public was shocked to discover numerous erotic passages exchanged between them.

Prominent scholars, including Arthur M. Schlesinger, Jr., denied the sexual element of the relationship or dismissed allegations of lesbianism in an argument that the women were merely passionate friends.[20] Joseph P. Lash[21] had, even before the opening of the letters, denied that there was a sexual dimension to the relationship and insisted on a passionate romance between Eleanor and Franklin.[22] In a book about Eleanor Roosevelt's personal life, Lash attributes the affection expressed between Hick and Roosevelt as an instance of the nineteenth-century custom of "smashing" (romantic crushes between girls or women), a usually nonsexual form of homoemotional behavior that, according to Lash, does not indicate lesbianism.[23]

On the other side of the debate, the gay historian Neil Miller notes that Roosevelt kept company with lesbians, and she considered the lesbian couples Marion Dickerman and Nancy Cook and Esther Lappe and Elizabeth Read as a second family. Quoting Cook, Miller argues that the relationship cannot be dismissed as a chaste friendship: "The fact is that E.R. and Hick were not involved in a schoolgirl 'smash.' They were neither saints nor adolescents. Nor were they virgins or mermaids. . . . They knew the score. They wrote to each other exactly what they meant to write."[24]

Likewise Roger Streitmatter, who edited a published volume of the letters, notes that, although Roosevelt also had intense correspondence with men, "None of those letters . . . approaches the emotional intensity found in Eleanor and Hick's correspondence; only these two women spoke of lying down together and kissing each other on the mouth."[25] He also writes that Eleanor's intense friendships with women and her correspondence with Hick "show that love between women was definitely not an alien concept for Eleanor. She was a professed believer in sexual freedom—including people acting on homosexual desires. In 1925, she wrote in her personal journal: 'No form of love is to be despised.'"[26] In one memorable 1934 letter to Hick, Eleanor wrote,

> If I just could take you in my arms. Dear, I often feel rebellious too & yet I know we get more joy when we are to-gether than we would have if we had lived apart in the same city & could only meet for short periods now & then. Someday perhaps fate will be kind & let us arrange a life more to our liking but for the time being we are lucky to have what we have. Dearest, we are happy to-gether & strong relationships have to grow deep roots. . . . I shall feel you are terribly far away & that makes me lonely but you are happy I can bear that & be happy too. Love is a queer thing, it hurts but it gives one so much more in return![27]

The letter concludes, "I do put my arms around you in my dreams dear one."

On the publication of Streitmatter's book, conservative columnists revisited the controversy. Noemie Emery, writing in the *Weekly Standard*, commented that Streitmatter ignores evidence to the contrary of his assumption that Roosevelt and Hick had a lesbian affair, noting that we ought not trust this evidence because "the Roosevelt mystery is being fought, not on the grounds of probability, but on the bloody terrain of the culture wars. . . . Historians from both these camps follow their own interests and give their readers what they want to believe."[28] In a strategic attempt to defuse the newly available evidence of the possibility of the affair, Emery argues that all biography should be rejected as specious because all biographical writing is political. Emery discredits those who would emphasize the affair's likelihood as victims of political correctness fighting a misguided culture war, neglecting her own political investments in that war.

Along with Streitmattter's book (which excerpts only the romantic passages of a few hundred of the letters), Cook's first two volumes of the Eleanor Roosevelt biography indicate a lesbian relationship. Evan Thomas in *Newsweek* commented, "Historians harrumphed that Cook could not prove a physical relationship, but the letters she excerpts in her second of presumably several volumes are suggestive."[29] And if the mainstream historical establishment went to great pains to turn ambiguity in the service of heteronormativity, gay and lesbian reviewers gave the news another, more celebratory, spin.

For example, in *Lambda Book Report*, Sandra de Helen notes that in Cook's biography readers "learn more about ER's love affair with Lorena Hickok, and follow along with ER in her real life, based on extensive research and written with the intimate knowledge of one who has known lesbian love."[30] Likewise, Barbara Grier, also writing in the *Lambda Book Report*, asserts, "that Eleanor Roosevelt and Lorena Hickok, a reporter, friend, and advisor for the First Lady, were lovers, has long been known and discussed and rehashed since the public release of their letters in 1978."[31] Grier marvels "that they managed to do all this under the noses of the world without being noticed."

In the *Advocate*, Streitmatter praises books that "tell the whole truth about people we admire."[32] He comments, "Although Eleanor did not, during her lifetime, publicly define herself either as a lesbian or a bisexual woman, the more than 300 letters that I have transcribed and annotated in *Empty without You* leave no question that Eleanor had a loving relationship with Lorena that was intense, passionate, and physical." Michelangelo Signorile, in an essay about historical events of the twentieth century for which he would have liked to be present, includes Roosevelt's 1934 vacation with Hick.[33] He describes Hick as "the Associated Press reporter with whom she shared a longtime passionate relationship. . . . I'd learn what historians can never be certain of: the true nature of the relationship that led Eleanor to send 'Hick' many tender and romantic notes and letters."

Echoing Signorile's hopeful uncertainty, Allida Black, in the *Lesbian Review of Books*, calls Cook's volume two of the Eleanor biography "the one we've been waiting for"[34] and notes that although Cook does not "categorize ER's devotions" she does suggest repeatedly that the women had a sexual liaison. "With a skillful use of letters, interviews, and ER's public writings, she moves what in less skilled hands could easily become the ER-FDR-Lorena Hickok ('Hick') triangle into a continuum in which all struggled to balance the need for devotion with a desire to create a politics responsive to the needs of America."[35] For her part, Cook says that although Streitmatter's book is faithful to the arc of Roosevelt and Hick's relationship he overpersonalizes the relationship and omits its political content. For similar reasons, Cook is also critical of the only serious biography we have of Lorena Hickok, by Doris Faber. Faber's *The Life of Lorena Hickok: E.R.'s Friend* represents Hick as a desperate, insecure, and troubled woman whose connection to the White House was her only claim to respect and credibility.

In contrast, Eleanor Roosevelt has been a tremendous political figure in the American political imagination, authoring newspaper articles, radio reports, editorials, legislation, and public addresses. She wrote "four autobiographies, seven monographs, seven children's books, and more than 550 articles. In February 1933, she began a monthly column, which existed in a variety of forms until her death in November 1962. On December 30, 1935, she began 'My Day,' a 500–word column published five days a week, which ran continuously until September 27, 1962. And she wrote more than 100,000 letters."[36] She was incredibly independent from both her husband and the Democratic Party in her views, which ranged from support for labor rights to opposition to racism; from support for increases in welfare provisions to anticommunism; from opposition to war to defense of women's rights to independent careers and political voice. But was she queer?

Outing and the Problem of Representation: Who Counts as Queer?

Any claims to a universal or permanent gay essence are put to the lie by "down low" sexuality (in which persons engaged in same-sex sex do not identify as gay), transgendering, and transsexualism. Clearly we need other, nonessentialist criteria for queerness. Establishing whether someone is queer is a social question; one can be queer only to the extent that one is intelligible to others as such. More important, to articulate queerness as a challenge to heteronormative social relations entails some degree of public visibility and advocacy. Eleanor Roosevelt, in all of her political writings,[37] addressed issues of war, labor, human rights, the cold war, freedom of speech, housing, education, and the status of women—but never the rights of the homosexual. Reading between the lines of an essay on freedom and human rights, today's queer scholar might think she or he spotted something like advocacy: "You are going to live in a dangerous world for quite a while I guess, but it's going to be an interesting and adventurous one. I wish you the courage to face it. I wish you the courage to face yourselves and when you know what you really want to be and when you know what you really want to fight for, not in a way, but in order to gain a peace, then I wish you imagination and understanding."[38]

Likewise, in remarks at the United Nations in 1953, Roosevelt said, "Where, after all, do universal human rights begin? In small places close to home—so close and so small that they cannot be seen on any map of the world. . . . The neighborhood, the school, the factory, farm, or office. . . . Such are the places where every man, woman, and child seeks equal justice, equal opportunity, equal dignity without discrimination."[39] These are noble sentiments that may speak to us because they recognize the "small places close to home" as political. Just as present-day cultural-studies scholars often prioritize the local, the personal, and the cultural, Roosevelt seems to warrant a closer look at the spaces of freedom oppressed persons make for themselves in the margins.

One key component of queerness is *the development of subaltern identity out of shared experience of oppression.* This criterion emerges from historians' observation that gay identity as such did not exist prior to the systematic attempts in capitalist society to name and prohibit homosexual acts.[40] Oppression is not merely a perceptual or subjective state; otherwise any rich, white, heterosexual man could claim to be oppressed. Extending Iris Marion Young's argument about gender, belongingness to any group depends on having a shared "structural relation to material objects as they have been produced and organized by a prior history."[41] Belonging to an oppressed group entails sharing a structural relationship of austerity and to the "objects"—including discourses and institutions—of heteronormativity.

Thus I do not mean to dismiss entirely the kinds of private survival strategies and localized cultural resistance hailed by Robin Kelley and James Scott, who have noted that oppressed groups engage in "infrapolitics," or a series of nuanced intersubjective and mutually intelligible practices of survival and identity maintenance.[42] The closet may be one such space. George Chauncey describes the appearance of gay men in public in New York in the 1920s and 1930s, but it was a particularly privatized kind of publicness: "Given the risks involved in asserting a visible presence in the streets, most gay people chose not the challenge the conventions of heterosexual society so directly. But they resisted and undermined them nonetheless by developing tactics that kept them hidden from the dominant culture, but not from one another."[43] Being out and politically outspoken about queer existence may be treacherous for those vulnerable to stigmatization and repression by the state, employer, or community. Outing vulnerable gays and lesbians is not a progressive act. Eleanor Roosevelt, however, bore greater responsibility on this criterion than would someone with less access to public platforms and less class-based and institutional protection.

On this argument, Roosevelt was not queer in any practical sense of the word. I cannot say that she absolutely escaped (or wanted to escape) the oppression of heteronormativity and homophobia. Yet, as a member of the American ruling class, she was buffered by wealth and privilege from the experience of oppression. Of course, even in her position of First Lady, Roosevelt would not have been entirely immune from risk. It is important to remember, however, that journalists in the 1930s kept the private lives of public figures out of print, in general, even to the extent that they worked with the Roosevelt administration to keep Franklin Roosevelt's polio-related disabilities hidden.[44] Furthermore, the position of First Lady is an office without accountability to the electorate and with a role between public and private life. In this context, Eleanor had a huge opportunity to speak, at least obliquely, about the cause of gay rights. She took many other controversial stands on questions of labor and civil rights, which in the time period might have been equally risky. Especially after Franklin's death, she had the freedom and the support from the circle at Val-Kill to be more open, if she had so chosen.

Janice Raymond and Lillian Faderman have argued that Roosevelt's love for Lorena Hickok was a "bisexual compromise" that could not be publicly acknowledged.[45] As historian Neil Miller and a number of other scholars point out, however, in the 1920s and 1930s sexual mores loosened for both men and women, and lesbianism entered the public vocabulary of the American and European mainstream.[46] With the publication in 1928 (and its banning by the English courts until 1949) of Radclyffe Hall's *Well of Loneliness*, "for the first time, lesbianism truly entered public consciousness both in England and the United States. . . . As a result, large numbers of lesbians were able to recognize themselves and their sexuality."[47]

In an era of increasing public acknowledgment of homosexuality and the growing prestige of psychoanalytic understandings of sexuality, "World War II marked the first time the U.S. military asked recruits the question, 'Are you homosexual?'"[48] Miller adds, "Suddenly those who were attracted to members of the same sex had an identity, at least in the eyes of the military."[49] As Michel Foucault noted in his *History of Sexuality*, subaltern identities often take shape, ironically, in response to institutional definition and repression.[50] Thus the emergence of an even stronger sense of homosexual identity came into being at the moment of military sanction. It is clear not only in the U.S. and British contexts, but also in the context of Stalinist and Nazi repression of gays and lesbians beginning, respectively, in the 1920s and 1930s that homosexuality in general and lesbian desire in particular were linguistically available subjects and sites for identification.

In refusing such public identification, Eleanor Roosevelt did not exert agentive control over how her sexual identity and life would be remembered in generations to come. Even if she had done so, the project of queer public address should look beyond the "was she or wasn't she" question to understand how public memory about ER shapes and sustains shared definitions of what it means to be queer. The texts of Eleanor Roosevelt embrace a logic of outing that renders queerness as a matter of either truth or secrecy, a paradigm that can trap a public in denial and/or voyeurism rather than enabling critical reflection and public political intervention on behalf of gay, lesbian, bisexual, or transgendered persons. To make the discussion about whether someone simply is, or is not, queer is overly simple; further, it fails to ask what someone's being queer means and does in the public sphere. In theory and public culture alike, making the question personal rather than political is an ideological strategy of containment.

Small Places Close to Home: The Public, the Private, and Biography

Popular biographical narration, at least in American culture, negotiates the public and private lives of celebrities and the powerful in a peculiar way, weaving them together in a story in which private foibles and personal history determine and explain public actions and achievement. Thus political life is personalized, historical greatness, both good and evil, is psychoanalyzed, and efforts for social change are explained in terms of intimate motivations of individual champions. Rather than politicizing the personal—in other words, revealing the structural, socioeconomic, political, social, and cultural bases for features of life that people tend to regard as merely personal—such texts are relentless in their attempts to personalize everything, private or public.[51] Biography can produce a persona of the heroic individual, but individuals are generally allowed to occupy those personae only under certain conditions. As I have argued elsewhere, for example, Oprah Winfrey is iconized as living proof of the American Dream only so long as she refuses identification with the civil rights movement or any critique of systemic racism and capitalism.[52] Noting the general conservative function of this kind of discourse amplifies my earlier point that one cannot simply "recover" "great gays in history" for critical scholarly purposes.

Although there are some exceptions to this ideological pattern in popular biography,[53] the popular film and video biographies of Eleanor Roosevelt are not among them. One other written text deserves mention before I move to an examination of the videos. In *The Life of Lorena Hickok, E.R.'s Friend*, Faber enacts all four of the strategies I have identified to contain the import of the correspondence between Roosevelt and Hick. The biography describes Hickok's lesbianism in pathological terms: sexual and physical abuse at the hands of her father led her to hate and distrust men.[54] Hickok appears here to be lumpish and antisocial, secretly craving influence and affection. Faber acknowledges the love Hick had for Roosevelt but diminishes its importance in the book's introduction, where she worries that the story of the affair will "eclipse" her important role as reporter for the New Deal.[55]

Most prominent among this text's strategies is ambiguity. Faber writes, "Still there were personal matters that neither Lorena Hickok nor Eleanor Roosevelt would ever write about, except obliquely. Nobody else had been with them on many occasions since the election; nobody ever can say what had occurred privately before the Cornell visit, or what occurred during it. But it is likely that the friendship between these two women changed in the course of their sojourn there."

Probably Eleanor Roosevelt confided to Hick then about her affair with Lucy Mercer, which, fifteen years later, still tortured her. Furthermore it appears that as Franklin reached ever closer to *his* goal of the presidency, his wife was increasingly distraught by the prospect of having to bear new constraints on *her* hard-won independence; she even seems to have contemplated leaving her husband. Thus Hick's sympathy, personally and patriotically, would have been overwhelming.

But despite many uncertainties that can never be resolved, one fact must now be recorded. Just a few weeks after returning from Ithaca, on March 4, 1933, when the forty-eight-year-old Eleanor Roosevelt did become the First Lady, she was wearing the same sapphire ring with which an opera singer had rewarded an enthusiastic young reporter many years earlier. And from the White House three days afterward, on Lorena Hickok's fortieth birthday, Eleanor wrote to her: "Hick, darling, All day I've thought of you and another birthday I *will* be with you. . . . Oh! I want to put my arms around you, I ache to hold you close. Your ring is a great comfort. I look at it & think she does love me or I wouldn't be wearing it!"[56]

So far, Faber is highlighting the possibility of a romantic, sexual attachment between the two women. Yet, she also goes on at some length to describe their correspondence as incomplete and cryptic: "Of course, in the best of all possible worlds the private behavior of any adults would be only their own concern. Even in this far from perfect world, until quite recently it would have been all but unthinkable to raise such a question involving a woman of Eleanor Roosevelt's stature. Indeed that word—*unthinkable!*—was the reaction of the senior archivists at Hyde Park when they first scanned The Papers of Lorena Hickok. To them, the effusively affectionate passages in numerous letters were the expression of just an intense, if unusually belated, schoolgirl crush. At least with regard to Roosevelt herself, this verdict is, I believe, essentially justified. The preponderance of the evidence, and the total context of her life, does support it. Nevertheless there undoubtedly were nuances of less naïveté in her relationship with Hick; their correspondence contains dozens of passages that offer some grounds for such an assumption. But there are also, it must be added, ample grounds for rejecting the immediate implication of the letter that ended the last chapter. The fact is that no way exists to banish uncertainty because Hick did deposit a mass of ambiguous material where it was bound to be perused."[57]

Faber's assertion in the passage quoted above that in an ideal world, the women's sex lives would be only their own business echoes contemporary liberal tolerance in a way that diminishes the political, social, and historical importance of lesbian existence. Further, this extended argument with herself clearly concludes on a note of denial, in legal language: the verdict of heterosexuality is justified. Faber was so frightened, apparently, by the possible scandal of Eleanor Roosevelt's lesbianism that she wanted the FDR archives to keep the letters under wraps for another two decades.[58]

Not all of the video biographies of Eleanor Roosevelt are so determined to deny the possibility of the lesbian affair as Faber's print version of Hick's life, yet all of them exhibit containment strategies, frames of interpretation that minimize or trivialize the possibility of lesbian love on the part of a First Lady. Here I am considering three such texts: Richard Kaplan's 1965 *Eleanor Roosevelt Story;* Henry Rasky's "Eleanor Roosevelt: A Restless Spirit," broadcast in 1994 as part of the Arts and Entertainment (A & E) network's *Biography* series; and the PBS documentary about Roosevelt made for the *American Experience* series.[59] In all three, the audience is told again and again about Eleanor's unhappy though wealthy childhood, about the deaths of her mother and father in the 1890s and her subsequent years with her stern grandmother. Viewers learn about her marriage to Franklin Roosevelt in 1903, his mother's domineering role in their married life, their five surviving children, his subsequent political career and philandering with Lucy Mercer and Missy LeHand, and Eleanor's unwillingness to settle for the role of obedient political wife. By all accounts, Eleanor was an ugly duckling in a family of beautiful society women transformed by the end of her life into "the first lady of the world."[60] All of the documentaries describe Eleanor and Franklin as moving in separate orbits and holding separate courts. All three mention her close friendships with women, her establishment of the women's school and furniture factory at Val-Kill, New York, during the Depression, and her ardent independence in political matters. All three end with footage and narration regarding her role in the U.S. delegation to the United Nations after World War II and her lead role in the production and adoption of the Universal Declaration of Human Rights. The films are also very different from one another, ranging a spectrum from staid silence on one end to spectacular exposure on the other.

Silence and Image in *The Eleanor Roosevelt Story*

Of the three, the 1965 documentary *The Eleanor Roosevelt Story*, which won an Oscar for best documentary feature that year, is focused most heavily on the public Eleanor Roosevelt. Reflecting the conventions of reporting that prevailed until after the 1960s in the United States, the video emphasizes Eleanor's public work beginning in World War I in the Red Cross. Although this documentary does tell the story of her awkward childhood, it spends proportionally little time on this subject, moving quickly into documenting her political life. It explains her devotion to social causes in terms of the sense of "noblesse oblige" instilled in her from childhood. The theme throughout the film builds on Roosevelt's own words, "What one has to do usually can be done."

The Eleanor Roosevelt Story is rich in archival footage of election campaigns, inaugural speeches, social movement protests, and war. Here Eleanor is revealed to be an inexhaustible traveler, political activist, researcher, writer, and spokesperson for the poor, unemployed, sick, and aged. "The issue everywhere was human rights and human freedom," intones Eric Severeid, narrator of much of the film. According to this text, Eleanor was "an American myth of inexhaustible energy." Eliding questions such as her silence regarding the Holocaust before the U.S. entry into World War II (the film even praises her for understanding the perils of fascism before most other people), the film constructs her as an American hero championing freedom and human dignity against the repression represented by both communism and fascism abroad. Except for the childhood story, the film also elides all questions of a personal nature, including FDR's extramarital affairs and Eleanor's own private life. There is no verbal mention of Hick anywhere in this text.

It is interesting, however, that the images tell a more unruly story. As Charles Morris has argued, queer texts can often be found embedded within dominant texts; these subtexts may be recognizable to those in the know as queer while remaining oblique to other audiences.[61] In much of the footage in *The Eleanor Roosevelt Story* of Eleanor's travels and work, there is a woman, the same woman, beside her—entering airplanes, riding horses, visiting soldiers, riding in a gondola over the Tennessee Valley, entering the White House. She is, of course, Lorena Hickok. In this staunchly public and propagandistic narrative, the fleeting glimpses of Lorena might be read as representing the private side of Eleanor, which here is rendered unimportant, if not unspeakable. In a scene in which Roosevelt and Hick are riding horses together on a trail among some trees, Eleanor is heard commenting in voice-over, "Everything passes if you just live it through. If there is criticism and there is a foundation of right in it, then it's fair criticism and you have to take it. If there is no foundation in it, sooner or later people are going to notice."

These remarks refer to the increasing controversy surrounding the First Lady and her independent activities—including sponsoring a concert by the black contralto Marion Anderson at the Lincoln Memorial when the Daughters of the American Revolution refused Anderson a venue—during FDR's presidency. Alongside the accompanying visuals (who is that unidentified woman who keeps appearing next to Eleanor?), however, the words invite another reading. Eleanor seems to be standing up to potential criticism of her relationship with Hick, remonstrating that criticism of her choices may be unfair and without foundation. "Sooner or later people are going to notice." Indeed later, rather than sooner, people did notice the possibility of lesbian love in Roosevelt's life. As Marguerite Moritz has argued, feminist film scholarship "attempts to uncover the ways in which cinema specifically creates meaning through its visual as well as its spoken story. . . . Feminist film theory asks how women are *not* represented in a script; it also asks how women are represented visually, what fixed images of women are appealed to, and how those images operate interactively in the story line and in the visual structuring."[62]

On the one hand, I am grateful to have had access to feminist and queer interpretive communities and literatures so that I know to look for the ways in which images of Lorena Hickok might cut against a conservative narrative that negates her presence in Eleanor Roosevelt's life. On the other hand, one might consider such a reading an amusing stretch for most viewers of this documentary watching it outside an academic, critical context. One can presume that viewers of the film in 1965, even more so than viewers among today's audience, would not have had the resources with which to conduct such a reading. And on the whole, *The Eleanor Roosevelt Story* can be characterized as silent when it comes to allowing the whole Eleanor Roosevelt, both public and private, to be remembered in the American imaginary.

Transferred Heterosexual Longing on PBS

Predictably, the documentaries made later in the century are inflected with the urge to titillate audiences and to expose the private person under the public veneer. Thus the PBS documentary made in 2000 openly, if ambivalently, acknowledges the extramarital relationships of both Franklin and Eleanor. "Eleanor Roosevelt" describes its subject as happiest in public life and unhappy in private. Uniquely in this text, listeners hear that Eleanor was dispassionate toward her children, who later resented her absence and lack of concern for their well-being. In the narrative about her own unhappy childhood, the emphasis here is on her longing for her father and her father's approval, which, it is implied, explains her passion for public life.

The video describes Roosevelt's time in boarding school in Europe at some length. At Madame Marie Souvestre's London girls' school in 1899, she learned about the importance of activism for social justice. The school was a place where intellect and strength among women were highly valued. This section of the documentary serves another purpose, too: to set up its eventual argument that affection among girls and women of social standing was common and unremarkable at the turn of the century and that such passionate friendships did not necessarily mean that the girls and women involved were lesbians. This narrative thus deals with the potential scandal of Eleanor's lesbianism with partial acknowledgment: girls had crushes on other girls, to whom they brought flowers. Homesick girls often came to the levelheaded Eleanor for comfort.

This partial acknowledgment is followed by overt denial of lesbian existence. The narrative of her romance with Franklin is marked by its insistence on their devotion to one another and passion for each other. Viewers also learn that Eleanor craved intimacy, which was the one thing that Franklin could not give her. Implicitly, any forays outside marriage for intimacy on Eleanor's part would stem from this initial rejection and explicitly heterosexual craving. Likewise the documentary explores the subject of Franklin's affairs at some length, describing how traumatic knowledge of them was for Eleanor. Again extramarital dalliances, heterosexual or homosexual, can thus be explained as a product of original heterosexual rejection and hurt.

Here Eleanor Roosevelt is described as relishing the company of strong, independent women. She had a circle of close friends that included the open lesbian couple Nancy Cook and Marian Dickerman. It seems that Val-Kill may even have been the site of an open lesbian coterie. Yet scenes of her independent women's circle at Val-Kill are interspersed with speculation that she had a romantic involvement with her male bodyguard, former state trooper Earl Miller, again affirming Roosevelt's heterosexual desire. The film represents Hick as the agent of the romance with Roosevelt, stating that Hick fell in love with her and implying that the romantic feelings were not mutual. Further, the film portrays the relationship as pathological, rooted in both women's need for affection, "two needy people" who could fulfill each other's needs. Following this minimization of their attachment, the audience witnesses Trude Lash's denial of Eleanor's lesbian identity. It is diffi-cult to accept her flat statement in light of the images that accompany it: scenes of the women's 1934 Caribbean vacation, including tickling and giggling on the air-plane. The narrator comments, "Eleanor had never looked happier." Obliquely, this segment invites continued questioning on the part of astute viewers.

During the Second World War, the relationship between Roosevelt and Hick became more distant and diminished in intensity. The documentary notes a poten-tial later romantic liaison between Roosevelt and a young communist named Joseph Lash (later to become a biographer-historian and Trude's husband) based on evidence from Roosevelt's three-thousand-page FBI file. Apparently J. Edgar Hoover had felt that Roosevelt's commitment to civil rights for black Americans was a perpetual threat to American society and had her watched almost constantly. The film notes yet another heterosexual possibility in Eleanor's involvement during the 1950s with her doctor and companion, David Gurewitsch. The pattern of acknowledgment then denial of lesbian desire and affirmation of active heterosex-ual desire is complete in this episode. Coming as it did twenty-two years after the revelation of the letters exchanged between Hick and Roosevelt, the PBS documen-tary "Eleanor Roosevelt" could not be silent about the possibility of the First Lady's affection for women. Instead this text's strategy is to recognize but disavow the pos-sibility of lesbianism.

The Scandal of Eleanor's Restless Spirit on A & E

This disavowal does not characterize the third text under consideration here. Although the A & E network's biography of Eleanor Roosevelt was produced six years before the PBS version of the story, it is by far the most open about her per-sonal life. "Eleanor Roosevelt: A Restless Spirit" promises to go beyond the familiar images of Eleanor's political persona at the beginning: host Jack Perkins invites the audience to stay tuned for another side, the personal side, of the story. Then the video runs through the generic story of Roosevelt's troubled childhood, moving rather quickly through the romance with FDR and on to the pair's political promi-nence. As does the 2000 documentary, this one features historian Blanche Wiesen Cook, foregrounding her as the authoritative expert on Eleanor Roosevelt. Cook describes Eleanor as establishing close relationships with a number of lesbian and feminist friends in a "world of political activism, art, and poetry." In the video, Cook is pitted against another historian, Steven Gillon, who insists, with somewhat less authority, on redeeming the conventional heterosexual narrative.

Discussing the correspondence between Roosevelt and Hick, Cook notes, "I think over time Eleanor Roosevelt's friendships, which involved passion and com-mitment and intensity, probably did also involve physical intimacy. I think her great friendship with Earl Miller was an intimate and passionate friendship. I think her great friendship with Lorena Hickok was an intimate and *physical* and passionate friendship."[63] Gillon responds to the effect that Victorian friendships were often intense and not necessarily indicative of lesbian identity or activity. Then the video allows Cook to respond. She reads from the correspondence between the women: "'I cannot wait for your return so I can lie down beside you and take you in my arms.' [Cook speaking as herself now] I don't think that's a rhetorical Victorian flourish, I think that's real." Nowhere else has Cook made such a definitive statement, made even more conclusive in its placement against Gillon's point of view. After Cook's statement, which implies that the correspondence should be taken as patent evidence of a physical relationship, Gillon is given another chance. He says, "If ER was a bisexual, she certainly went to great lengths to see that we would never find out. My own feeling is that we don't know what the extent of many of these relationships were, whether they were consummated. Whether they went beyond just an emotional attachment or not. And I believe it is very unlikely that given the evidence that exists that we'll ever know."

This attempt at restoring ambiguity falls short. Ultimately Cook's testimony has more weight. It is clear, from the ordering of the story and the text's titillating emphasis on Eleanor's multiple affairs, that the producers of this documentary are encouraging viewers to accept a view of her as actively bisexual. From this point, the documentary rushes through Roosevelt's later political career and the end of her life, continuing to focus on personal tidbits, such as the fact that Lucy Mercer, not Eleanor, was at FDR's side when he died.

On the one hand, this text's openness about the possibility of a lesbian love affair between Roosevelt and Hick is refreshingly unconventional. To use Michael Warner's words, "it exudes some rut"; it offers viewers a "carnivalesque display" of nonnormative sexuality.[64] Perhaps it should be lauded as a progay (or queer-friendly) text. On the other hand, however, it exploits the juicy tidbits of Eleanor's life that are most likely to garner better ratings and audience interest. Unlike PBS, the A & E network seeks a younger, less socially conservative audience to whom advertising could appeal, relying on the sensational and the shocking to attract viewers to its programming.[65] Although in this documentary, Roosevelt's relationship with Hick is situated briefly in the context of women's community and activity, the video foregrounds this and other relationships in terms of scandal and shock value. The host explicitly promises viewers that they will get something different, new, and shocking to chew on, something that might tarnish the reverence held by many Americans for Eleanor Roosevelt.

Shallow irreverence and sexual scandal may attract viewers and in this case, may actually inform audiences of little-known dimensions of even the most publicly conventional lives; however, acknowledging lesbian existence in a scandal frame still serves to discredit it. Rather than transferring reverence from a respected Eleanor Roosevelt to lesbians in general, it encourages audiences to come away from the viewing with less respect for the former First Lady. The documentary shows its audiences the possibility of a lesbian First Lady but invites the audience to react with shock and distance as well.

It matters how a truth is admitted, and a public sphere based on the sharing of scandalous trivia about famous people from celebrities to politicians might be an impoverished public indeed. In an article on "freak" talk shows on television, Joshua Gamson wonders whether shows that feature a spectacularized representation of those designated as "freaks"—including gays and lesbians—perform a ritual of debasement that ultimately reassures audiences of the superiority of a heteronormative social order.[66] Likewise, it is possible that the A & E appropriation of Roosevelt's relationships trades on voyeurism and encourages audiences to frame the information as scandalous rather than as acceptable in a normative frame. This narrative participates in a problematic logic of outing.

Michaelangelo Signorile has argued that there are gay and lesbian people in high places who do not act responsibly toward their secret constituency.[67] Therefore he has taken it on himself to expose the sexual lives of the rich and famous, including, most notably, Malcolm Forbes.[68] Signorile's argument that homosexuality would become less stigmatized if powerful gays and lesbians were to leave the closet behind is a powerful one. Likewise Larry Gross has argued that any visibility is good visibility and that outing is therefore a productive strategy for queer people.[69]

The essentialist logic of outing, in expecting individuals to be one thing (gay) consistently across contexts, however, is theoretically simplistic. If sexual identity is not a biological essence, but rather a set of culturally constituted and collectively and individually performed semiotics and behaviors, queer scholars cannot say with any certainty that anyone, including Eleanor Roosevelt, was "one of us" (whoever "we" are). Rather than claiming Roosevelt, we can *queer* her by pointing out how her private life, if brought by rhetorical criticism into public memory—which has sublimated, if not erased, this relationship—can trouble the assumptions of heteronormativity. We may out the *texts* of Eleanor Roosevelt, but we may not out *Eleanor*. In the A & E documentary, the logic of outing also participates in the scandal frame that sensationalizes queer lives as freakish and titillating rather than as a serious challenge to social norms and discipline. It could be, however, that, as Gamson concludes, the "freaks" on talk TV "talk back" and that, although their voices are officially discounted, "they wind up messing with sexual categories in a way that goes beyond a simple expansion of them. . . . Talk show producers often make entertainment by mining the in-between: finding guests who are interesting exactly because they don't fit existing notions of 'gay' and 'straight' and 'man' and 'woman,' raising the provocative suggestion that the categories are not quite working."[70]

Conclusion: Against the Pubic Public

In this chapter I have argued that neither Eleanor Roosevelt nor the texts that constitute public memory of her sexuality enable us to get beyond what is, essentially, the wrong question. If it is enough that Eleanor Roosevelt existed, perhaps as a lesbian, then maybe it is enough that individuals in the present simply live private lives and feel no obligation to take part in a public, instrumental project on behalf of gay, lesbian, bisexual, and transgender persons who may be less buffered from the effects of oppression. We—gays, lesbians, bisexuals, and the transgendered; feminists, socialists, and antiracist activists and theorists; fighters for freedom on all fronts—thirst for representation.[71] Yet a sexual politics of intimacy, and the attendant valorization of publicly eloquent but only privately homosexual persons, risks settling for the freedoms of intimacy and desire while ignoring the political and material exclusion of most gays, lesbians, bisexuals, and the transgendered from the prerogatives of full citizenship. In this context, it matters less what someone is than what they and the texts that represent them do; queering public address must do more than affirm queer existence.

Eric Clarke has argued that intimacy and erotic experience are political and ought not belong only to the intimate sphere.[72] Yet Clarke also describes how late capitalist society channels discussion of homoeroticism in two equally limiting directions: in the assimilationist affirmation that gays and lesbians are "just like everyone else," or in the production of commodified enclaves that offer identification and spectacle instead of actual social transformation.[73] The biographical texts analyzed here replicate this logic, emphasizing the ways in which Roosevelt was conventional or attempting to tease out, in the context of sensational televisual narrative, her secrets.

I write in the moment of political ferment instigated by the new civil rights movement for queer liberation.[74] In acts of civil disobedience, queer people in cities across the United States are lining up to demand marriage licenses and are receiving them in San Francisco and in Portland, Oregon. One license seeker commented to a National Public Radio reporter, "In our country people have gone into places to demand civil rights that they never had before. We are doing the same thing." This is the kind of instrumental project to which our work should be connected. We ought not settle for scandalous visibility when there are major instrumental projects—including equal rights and protection in the workplace and in private life and a real fight against AIDS—that need real advocates, not mysterious figures from the past.

Notes

I would like to thank Charles Morris, John Sloop, Lisbeth Lipari, Julie Thompson, and Katie Feyh for their thoughtful and very helpful suggestions and support regarding this work.

1. PBS Home Video, *American Experience: Eleanor Roosevelt*, PBS Paramount, 2000.

2. Helen Keller and Philip Foner, *Helen Keller: Her Socialist Years, Writings and Speeches* (New York: International, 1967).

3. Julie Thompson, "On the Development of Counter-Racist Quare Public Address Studies," present volume.

4. See Larry Gross, *The Contested Closet* (Minneapolis: University of Minnesota Press, 1993).

5. Here I will admit to a certain discomfort with using the word "queer," because it has so many pejorative connotations and uses historically and today; however, I cannot think of a more inclusive shorthand for the identities and experiences of gay, bisexual, lesbian, transgendered, gender-ambiguous, and transsexual persons, so I use it advisedly.

6. Andrew Sullivan, *Virtually Normal: An Argument about Homosexuality* (New York: Knopf, 1995). For a critique of Sullivan's position, see Michael Warner, *The Trouble with Normal: Sex, Politics, and the Ethics of Queer Life* (Cambridge, Mass.: Harvard University Press, 1999).

7. Carole Spitzak and Kathryn Carter, "Women in Communication Studies: A Typology for Revision," *Quarterly Journal of Speech* 73 (1987): 404–5. For other works "recovering" figures from the past for a new canon, see Karlyn Kohrs Campbell, *Man Cannot Speak for Her*, 2 vols. (Greenwood, N.J.: Praeger, 1989); and Angela Davis, *Women, Race, and Class* (New York: Random House, 1983). Campbell's pioneering work introduced early feminist orators to the field of American public address. Davis brings into the early feminist canon neglected working-class radicals and black women such as Ida B. Wells and Maria Miller Stewart.

8. See, for example, Lauren Berlant and Michael Warner, "Sex in Public," *Critical Inquiry* 24 (1998): 547–60; Judith Butler, *Gender Trouble* (New York: Routledge, 1993); Charles E. Morris III, "My Old Kentucky Homo: Abraham Lincoln, Larry Kramer, and the Politics of Queer Memory," present volume; John Sloop, "Disciplining the Transgendered: Brandon Teena, Public Representation, and Normativity," *Western Journal of Communication* 64 (2000): 165–90; Eve Kosofsky Sedgwick, *Epistemology of the Closet* (Berkeley: University of California Press, 1990); Mas'ud Zavarzadeh, Teresa Ebert, and Donald Morton, eds., *Marxism, Queer Theory, Gender*, special issue of *Transformation: Marxist Boundary Work in Theory, Economics, Politics and Culture* 2 (2001).

9. Dana L. Cloud, "Hegemony or Concordance? The Rhetoric of Tokenism in Oprah Winfrey's Rags-to-Riches Biography," *Critical Studies in Mass Communication* 13 (1996): 115–37.

10. Lauren Berlant and Michael Warner, "What Does Queer Theory Teach Us about *X*?" *PMLA* 110 (May1995): 345.

11. Barbara Biesecker, "Coming to Terms with Recent Attempts to Write Women into the History of Rhetoric," *Philosophy and Rhetoric* 25 (1992): 155–66.

12. Michael Warner, *Fear of a Queer Planet* (Minneapolis: University of Minnesota Press, 1993), xxvi.

13. Lisa Duggan, "Making It Perfectly Queer," *Socialist Review* 22 (January–March 1992): 11.

14. Warner, *Fear of a Queer Planet*, xxvi.

15. Dana L. Cloud, "Queer Theory and Family Values," *Transformation* (Syracuse, N.Y.) 2 (2000): 71–114.

16. Cloud, "Queer Theory"; Teresa Ebert, *Ludic Feminism and After* (Ann Arbor: University of Michigan Press, 1995); Donald Morton, "The Politics of Queer Theory in the (Post)Modern Moment," *Genders* 17 (fall 1993): 121–50; Carol Stabile, "Feminism and the Ends of Postmodernism," in *Materialist Feminism: A Reader in Class, Difference, and Women's Lives,* ed. Rosemary Hennessy and Chrys Ingraham (New York: Routledge, 1997), 395–408.

17. Robin D. G. Kelley, *Race Rebels* (New York: Free Press, 1994); James C. Scott, *Domination and the Arts of Resistance: Hidden Transcripts* (New Haven, Conn.: Yale University Press, 1990).

18. Blanche Wiesen Cook, *Eleanor Roosevelt*, vol. 2, *1933–1938* (New York: Viking, 1999).

19. Cook, *Eleanor Roosevelt*, 199–200.

20. Arthur M. Schlesinger, Jr., Review of *Lorena Hickok: ER's Friend. New York Times*, February 17, 1980, sect. 7, p. 3.

21. The biographer was the husband of Trude Lash, family friend of the Roosevelts, quoted above.

22. Joseph P. Lash, *Love, Eleanor: Eleanor Roosevelt and Her Friends* (New York: McGraw-Hill, 1985); and *Eleanor and Franklin* (New York: Signet, 1981). See *Eleanor and Franklin*, 192–217, for discussion of their courtship and honeymoon. Interestingly, however, Lash notes, "Sex was an ordeal to be borne, she would later confide to her daughter Anna" (211).

23. Lash, *Love, Eleanor*, 146–47. The book highlights the possibility of a heterosexual liaison between Roosevelt and her male friend Earl Miller in a much more open way.

24. Neil Miller, *Out of the Past: Gay and Lesbian History from 1869 to the Present* (New York: Vintage, 1995), 170–71.

25. Roger Streitmatter, ed., *Empty without You: The Intimate letters of Eleanor Roosevelt and Lorena Hickok* (New York: Da Capo Press, 1998), xvii.

26. Ibid., xix.

27. Ibid., 78–79.

28. Noemie Emery, "Looking for Lesbians under Every Bed," *Weekly Standard* (October 2, 1998): 34.

29. Evan Thomas, "The Private Eleanor," *Newsweek* 134, no. 2 (July 12, 1999): 62.

30. Sandra deHelen, "Reviews: The Rest of the Story," *Lambda Book Report* 7, no. 12 (July/August 1999): 1.

31. Barbara Grier, "First Lady Love," *Lambda Book Report* 7, no. 7 (February 1999): 30.

32. Roger Streitmatter, "Out after Death," *Advocate* 770 (October 13, 1998): 60–61.

33. Michangelo Signorile, "A Journey through Our Gay Century," *Advocate* 802 (January 18, 2000): 26.

34. Allida Black, "The One We've Been Waiting For," *Lesbian Review of Books* 7, no. 2 (winter 2000–2001): 3.

35. Ibid.

36. Allida Black, ed., *Courage in a Dangerous World: The Political Writings of Eleanor Roosevelt,* (New York: Columbia University Press, 1999), 2.

37. Collected in Black, ed., *Courage.*

38. Black, ed., *Courage,* frontispiece.

39. Ibid., 190.

40. John D'Emilio, *Making Trouble: Essays on Gay History, Politics, and the University* (New York: Routledge, 1992), 3–16.

41. Iris Marion Young, "Gender as Seriality," *Signs: Journal of Women in Culture and Society* 19 (1994): 720.

42. Kelley, *Race Rebels*; Scott, *Domination and the Arts of Resistance*.

43. Chauncey, *Gay New York*, (New York: BasicBooks, 1994); 187.

44. See Vermont Royster's history, *FDR* (New York: Simon and Schuster, 1985).

45. Lilian Faderman, *Odd Girls and Twilight Lovers* (New York: Penguin, 1991), 99. See also Janice Raymond, *A Passion for Friends* (Boston: Beacon, 1986). Doris Faber also makes this claim in *The Life of Lorena Hickok: E.R.'s Friend* (New York: Morrow, 1980), 33.

46. Miller, *Out of the Past*. See also Allan Bérubé, *Coming Out under Fire* (New York: Plume, 1990); Chauncey, *Gay New York*; John D'Emilio, *Sexual Politics, Sexual Communities: The Making of a Homosexual Minority in the United States, 1940–1970* (Chicago: University of Chicago Press, 1983); Paula Fass, *The Damned and the Beautiful* (Oxford: Oxford University Press, 1977); Kevin White, *The First Sexual Revolution* (New York: NYU Press, 1993).

47. Miller, *Out of the Past*, 199. Radclyffe Hall, *The Well of Loneliness* (1928; New York: Anchor, 1990). From the literature one gets the impression that the speakability of homosexuality was much greater for men than for women. For example, White argues that in spite of Victorian morality's dominance, homosexual men took part in an "underground primitivism" (8), to which women had little access. It could be that consciousness of oneself as homosexual and the articulation of a situation in common with other homosexuals was more prominent among men at this time, and still operating mainly undercover in social life. Likewise, Chauncey emphasizes the emergence of gay men in public in the 1920s and 1930s (179–206) but says nothing about women. Further, the culture he describes is not public, but a set of coded performances that allowed gay men to recognize each other without being recognized or policed by others (187). D'Emilio argues that lesbianism did not fully enter into visibility until the 1950s; similarly Bérubé notes that lesbianism was a category of identity among the armed forces during World War II. Thus, it is fair to say that it may not have been so easy for Roosevelt and Hick in the early 1930s to find language for their desires.

48. Miller, *Out of the Past*, 231. See also Bérubé, *Coming Out under Fire*.

49. Miller, *Out of the Past*, 232.

50. Michel Foucault, *History of Sexuality*, vol. 1, *An Introduction*, trans. Robert Hurley (New York: Random House, 1980).

51. For this argument, see Cloud, "Hegemony"; and Jeffrey Decker, *Made in America* (Minneapolis: University of Minnesota Press, 1997).

52. Cloud, "Hegemony."

53. One thinks of Alex Haley, *Autobiography of Malcolm X* (New York: Ballantine, 1965).

54. Doris Faber, *The Life of Lorena Hickok: E.R.'s Friend* (New York: Morrow, 1980), 33.

55. Ibid., 6.

56. Ibid., 110.

57. Ibid., 112.

58. Ibid., 332.

59. Richard Kaplan (dir.), *The Eleanor Roosevelt Story* [motion picture] (Roosevelt Story Company / Kino Video, 1965); PBS Home Video, *American Experience: Eleanor Roosevelt* [motion picture] (2000); Harry Rasky (dir.), *Eleanor Roosevelt: A Restless Spirit* [motion picture] (A&E Television, 1994).

60. "Eleanor: First Lady of the World" is the title of a 1982 Columbia Pictures video about Roosevelt, directed by John Erman. This video focuses exclusively on the years after 1945, when she served as a delegate to the United Nations.

61. Charles E. Morris III, "'The Responsibilities of the Critic': F. O. Matthiessen's Homosexual Palimpsest," *Quarterly Journal of Speech* 84 (August 1998): 261–82.

62. Marguerite J. Moritz, "Old Strategies for New Texts: How American Television Is Creating and Treating Lesbian Characters," in *The Columbia Reader on Lesbians and Gay Men in Media, Society, and Politics*, ed. Larry Gross and James Woods (New York: Columbia University Press, 1999), 324.

63. Emphasis added; the relationship with Miller is not described as physical.

64. Warner, *Fear of a Queer Planet*, xxvi.

65. I have been unable to get information about demographics of A & E's viewership for the Biography program; however, the A & E website provides demographic data for website visitors, which presumably represents some of the most engaged and serious viewers of the network's offerings. According to the site, website viewers have the following characteristics: age range: 25 percent, 25–34 years; 27 percent, 35–44 years; 27 percent, 45–54 years; male : female ratio, 41 : 59.

66. Joshua Gamson, "Do Ask, Do Tell: Freak Talk on TV," in *Columbia Reader*, ed. Gross and Woods, 333.

67. Michelangelo Signorile, *Queer in America: Sex, the Media, and the Closets of Power* (New York: Random House, 1993).

68. Michelangelo Signorile, "How I Brought Out Malcolm Forbes and the Media Flinched," in *Columbia Reader*, ed. Gross and Woods, 429–30. Signorile also outed former Pentagon spokesperson Pete Williams in 1993.

69. Gross, *The Contested Closet*.

70. Gamson, "Do Ask, Do Tell," 334.

71. And now are offered an abundance of it in texts such as *The L Word, Queer as Folk, Will and Grace*, and *Queer Eye for the Straight Guy*. These texts offer images of gays and lesbians that affirm the poles of problematic representation I have identified here: assimiliationist paradigms in which lesbians and gay men (on behalf of straight men) shop, get married, and have babies, on the one hand, and a theatrical paradigm in which sexual carnival and slapstick offer the only alternative to being like everyone else, on the other. *Queer Eye* puts gays in the service of straight men, whose objectives seem to be advancing their careers in capitalism and getting married. The show affirms both capitalism and heteronormativity disguised as democratic representation.

72. Eric O. Clarke, *Virtuous Vice: Homoeroticism and the Public Sphere* (Durham, N.C.: Duke University Press, 2000).

73. Ibid., 50.

74. March 5, 2004.

CIVIL RIGHTS MOVEMENTS AND QUEER IDENTITIES

Complexities of the Collective Subject

Ralph R. Smith and Russel R. Windes

The constructing attitude is skeptical. It is also humanist. It says that the demands of morality do not come from the idealized and not-human Father or even the idealized posthuman Son. They come from the demands on rationality that free agents place on themselves.

Ian Hacking, *The Social Context of What?*

Historians of public address and other rhetorical critics should recognize that the term "collective identity" has supplied in recent years an important conceptual perspective on social movement action, supplementing and enriching, if not displacing, older explanatory constructs such as collective behavior/mass society, Marxism, and resource mobilization theory.[1] From this perspective, the production of collective identity is both a significant influence on, and a result of, movement strategy and action embedded in discourses. Ways in which movement members define their characteristics, boundaries, and relationships with other groups deeply influence how they articulate grievances, represent potential recruits and enemies, project organizational forms and models of leadership, and, important for rhetorical critics, select forms and content of persuasive messages. Equally important, grieving, recruiting, eliminating, and persuading create the personae of movement subjects who are simultaneously rhetors and auditors.

Although the concept of collective identity has long been recognized, increasing emphasis is now being placed on identity as an outcome of shared group experiences arising out of common struggle.[2] Verta Taylor and Nancy Whittier stress that "to understand any politicized identity community, it is necessary to analyze the social and political struggle that created the identity."[3] Identity-forming struggle, as Joshua Gamson demonstrates, occurs both within the movement and between the movement and exogenous groups and structures of power and belief.[4]

Identity production in movements is now recognized as neither a single generative act nor a stable final outcome, but as a continuous process in which a multitude of a movement's identities are created, often in internal opposition to one
another. As Hank Johnston, Enrique Larana, and Joseph Gusfield conclude, "[T]he
collective identity of social movements is a 'moving target' with different definitions predominating at different points in a movement career."[5] Collective identities, then, are the result of exchanges, negotiations, conflicts, and strategic choices.
Bearers of a movement's collective identities operate in a "field containing a system
of vectors in tension. These vectors constantly seek to establish an equilibrium
between the various axes of collective action and between identification declared
by the actor and the identification given by the rest of the society."[6]

Study of complex processes of collective identity formation is interdisciplinary.
Identity is a topic of investigation in sociology, anthropology, political science, history, and philosophy.[7] Central to several paradisciplinary fields is recognition that
identity formation is a continuing and complex process to which discursive practices are central.[8]

Interest in movement identities goes beyond academic theorizing. Movement
action itself, for at least the past several decades, has increasingly invoked identity
accounts and narratives. Valentine Moghadam observes that, "during the 1980s, discourses and movements centered on issues of identity erupted around the world
with considerable force. . . . Cultural revivalism, national liberation, religious 'fundamentalism' and sexual affirmation all constituted some of the most vocal and visible political movements of recent history."[9]

For rhetorical critics, a broad avenue is provided into the complexity of movement identity production by the truism that movement subjects are created
through communication. Ian Hacking summarizes this premise by postulating that
(1) people are inherently interactive kinds—that is, self-aware through social interaction of being a member of a classification; (2) all identity behavior is the result of
"looping effects" through which individual behavior comes to conform to socially
ascribed identity. He writes that knowledge about "'the homosexual' becomes
known to the people classified, changes the way these individuals behave, and loops
back to mandate changes in the classification and knowledge about them."[10]

The multiple interactive effects that are central to this chapter concern self- and
other-definitions, a segment of the wider subject of the rhetorical creation of definitional contests, a field until recently little explored by students of argument.[11] In
his exploration of the rhetoric of definition, Edward Schiappa suggests important
directions for examining classification contests that are, with respect to persons, disagreements over identity. He writes that "definitional disputes should be treated
less as philosophical or scientific questions of 'is' and more as sociopolitical and
pragmatic questions of 'ought.'"[12] Recently Lynn Clarke's lucid study of definitional

controversy and the power to define provides important insight into identity formation and dispersal, especially with respect to minority sexuality. She correctly
argues that definitional struggle has material consequences and that "definitional
controversies may give way to communicative interaction."[13]

For students of public address, Maurice Charland's earlier analysis of "constitutive identity" provides an excellent beginning point for describing processes of collective identity formation through discursive definitional strategies.[14] He implies
that an account of identity-forming discourses is crucial to understanding social
movement, maintaining that political identity is inevitably an ideological fiction,
though one that is historically material. Narrative ideological effects are created
through the process of interpellation, of being hailed through discourse as a certain
kind of person. Individuals who recognize and acknowledge being addressed become a subject of discourse since "acknowledgment of an address entails an acceptance of an imputed self-understanding which can form the basis of an appeal."[15]
Recognition of the operation of constitutive rhetoric leads to the conclusion that
rhetorical critics should investigate the "very nature of the subjects that rhetoric
both addresses and leads to come to be." Such an understanding of constitutive
rhetoric allows for the possibility that rhetorical subjects evolve, their nature shifting with modification in ideology.[16]

Despite such a useful beginning toward developing a rhetorical approach to
understanding discursive creation of collective subjects, rhetorical theory and criticism of movement public address has not built on developments in other fields in
two important respects: (1) recognition of the complexity of identity formation and
(2) concern for marginal identity. In other fields, Hetherington believes, the "interest in questions of identity and identity politics is one that has principally focused
over the past few years . . . on issues associated with . . . topological complexity: dispersal, fragmentation, uncertainty, difference, contingency, hybridity, ambivalence
and multiplicity."[17] Accompanying complexity in recent study of collective identity
is a concern with the construction of marginal groups. Identity scholarship has
evolved within a social and historical context of intense movement activity centered on gender, race, and sexuality. These "movements—and the scholarship they
spawned—feminist, black, postcolonial, lesbian and gay, queer—pushed from the
margins to demand attention to the identities of those who were outside the normative framework."[18]

This chapter will illuminate the difficult conceptual terrain of contested discursive marginal collective identity formation in order to encourage efforts to understand processes and effects of collective identity constitution, representation,
deployment, and renegotiation of the marginal movement subject. The phalanx of
movements to be examined here generally revolves around variant sexuality. The
politics of sexuality has frequently been examined by using the vocabularies of

movement analysis.[19] These collective efforts have generally been considered partially responsible for achieving significant change in social norms and values with respect to sexuality.[20]

Our project focuses on three terms: "constitution," "conflict," and "conciliation." We will (1) describe a series of collective subjectivities that have been constituted by movements centered on variant sexuality; (2) outline grounds of conflict that occur among bearers of these subjectivities; and (3) sketch some of the proposals for accommodation to such conflicts. The theme throughout this chapter is that one aspect of "queering public address" is to recognize and become reconciled with, even to embrace, the inevitability of a destabilizing rhetorical process as a concept that is well on its way to replacing fixed, naturalized identities that have, in the past, interested rhetorical critics. This approach provides rhetorical critics with a productive entry into public policy disputes such as the current contest over gender-neutral marriage.

Constituting of Marginalized Sexual Identities

In the course of organized political and cultural action to change our society's public regime of sexuality, many identities have been advanced for sexually variant actors, ranging from thickly described gay men and lesbians to thinly described straight queers. A place to begin analysis of these sexually centered identities is by asking how a variety of change-demanding discourses changed the cast of movement actors.

Early development of homophile movement organizations in the 1940s and 1950s demonstrated both the necessity for creating a collective identity and the paradoxical divisive effect of identity construction. John D'Emilio, a leading historian of the inception phase of the gay movement, argues that "activists had not only to mobilize a constituency; first they had to create one."[21] The identities thus created were responses to longstanding negative descriptions (sin, crime, mental illness) of homosexuality. In response to their stigmatized identities, organizers of the Mattachine Society, the nation's first homophile organization, developed an understanding of gay people as an oppressed minority. This understanding produced a clear line of collective action—raising the consciousness of a class "in itself" to a class "for itself."[22] Among those few homosexuals who affiliated with the Mattachine Society, disagreement soon arose over this minority class analysis. Control of the organization soon passed to a majority that espoused an assimilationist interpretation of homosexual identity. In this interpretation, gay and lesbian people do not form a distinct social group, because homosexuality is a minor and personal difference that should not, if the larger society were properly informed, prevent integration of gay men and lesbians into the social mainstream.[23] Under the Mattachine Society's new leadership, "accommodation to social norms replaced the affirmation of a distinctive gay identity, collective effort gave way to individual action."[24]

The early ideological contests within homophile organizations introduced issues that continue to be important: "whether homosexuality was an unimportant characteristic or an aspect of a person's life so significant that it bound gay men and women together as a minority group; whether homosexuals and lesbians should accommodate themselves to the mores of society or assert their difference; whether they were victims of prejudiced opinion or of a system of oppression inherent in the structure of Americans society; and whether patient educational work or militant political action was the key to social change."[25] The ideological position of gay advocates continues to be steered by either a preference for a collective identity that blurs or one that makes salient differences between heterosexuals and homosexuals.[26]

Sexual variance as the basis for distinct minority status became a dominant movement theme in the 1960s as civil rights emerged as the master action frame to express gay and lesbian political interests.[27] The rise of the New Left also had a powerful catalyzing influence on gay and lesbian collective action.[28] By the late 1960s, despite continuing internal dissension, a wide range of gay organizations articulated a variety of civil rights goals, including repeal of sodomy laws, prohibition of entrapment, elimination of employment and housing discrimination, and the right to serve openly in the military.[29] Equally important, discourses through which gay men and lesbians described themselves changed. The previously dominant "stigmatized discourse of homosexuality" was displaced by a gay-positive representation of self that affirmed an "accrediting political identity to be openly enacted in public as well as private arenas."[30]

In the late 1960s and early 1970s, gay liberationist leaders, radicalized by experiences in black and student organizations, seriously challenged gaining civil rights as the goal of gay collective action. They were motivated by hatred of a corrupt establishment that led them to conclude that "civil rights had become passé: why petition to be let into a social system so deeply riven by racism, sexism, militarism, and heterosexism."[31] An important effect of the rise of gay liberation was division of gay advocates into (1) rights activists who wanted to reinforce the homosexual/heterosexual distinction to achieve minority status and (2) liberationists who sought to erase this distinction through a global revolutionary crusade and as part of a general sexual revolution that would celebrate many forms of erotic behavior and relationships.

Central to gay liberation theory was the premise that human nature is polymorphous and androgynous. "Liberation politics aimed at freeing individuals from the constraints of a sex/gender system that locked them into mutually exclusive homo/hetero and feminine/masculine roles."[32] Rather than espousing specific civil rights projects, gay liberationists opposed social conventions that confined sexuality to monogamous heterosexual families.[33] They took the position that struggle for freedom entailed a "much broader challenge to the commonly held notions regarding sexuality that now prevail."[34] They did not seek civil rights per se, but the "pleasures and joy in all their multiform ways of the whole body."[35]

Gay liberation expressed through movement organizations was short-lived during the 1970s. Liberationist organizations ceased to exist soon after their founding, riven by internal discord and demoralized by consistent failure to mobilize supporters. In contrast, gay and lesbian civil rights leaders were encouraged by the growth of gay enclaves, increasing visibility, the doctrine of gay pride, and a modicum of media support and legislative success.[36] Movement organizations that promote lesbian and gay civil rights, however, did not entirely dominate collective action. Recently the most significant internal challenge to the gay and lesbian civil rights movement has come from those working under the sign "queer" to challenge the ethnic identity model on which civil rights movements are built. "Queer," in its current political usage, signifies a protest by individuals who are marginal to the mainstream gay movement dominated by a white, middle-class, and, often, male cadre. Steven Seidman characterizes this protest as a "revolt of the social periphery against the center, only this time the center was not mainstream America but a dominant gay culture."[37]

Queer activism emphasized change in the culture, not the state. Culture must be changed, Warner concludes, "because the logic of the sexual order is so deeply embedded by now in an indescribably wide range of social institutions. . . . Queer struggles aim not just at toleration or equal status but at challenging those institutions and accounts."[38] Queer thought was deeply influenced by academic postmodern fashions.[39] Queer political action followed the earlier liberationist modes of engaging in a "politics of carnival, transgression, and parody which leads to deconstruction, decentering, revisionist readings." The goal of queer action therefore is to revolutionize the culture by challenging a civil rights politics based on a well-defined identity. Such an identity serves primarily to normalize the lesbian/gay subject and thereby rationalize and consolidate "heterosexuality and homosexuality as master categories of sexual and social identity."[40]

Strategic and tactical constraints exercised considerable power over selection of identity accounts by movement activists. Mainstream gay and lesbian movements sought to consolidate their constituency into a unified movement, and queer advocates aggressively divided themselves from white, middle-class, mainstream gays. Lesbian and gay movements emphasize the importance of identity-confirming action, whereas queer spokespersons have been concerned with homophobia and the enemies of difference. Heather Love observes that "queer critics have tended to be less invested than gay and lesbian critics in consolidating a positive tradition of gay and lesbian identity; instead, they have turned their attention to the effects of homophobia in a range of historical contexts."[41] In contrast to mainstream lesbian, gay, bisexual, and transgendered leaders, queer activists attacked homophobia as a restraint on freedom rather than stigmatization of class membership, a limit on individual experiential potential rather than on public group recognition.

Gay and lesbian identity accounts closely fit attempts to recruit broadly, seeking to include even nongay people, efforts to attack enemies who are depicted as reactionary bigots, an interest group politics with strong organizational structure and formal leadership, and persuasive strategies that feature insider politics and simplistic public messages. Queer identity accounts, by contrast, fit comfortably with recruiting the marginal inhabiting the periphery of the gay community, demonizing mainstream gay leaders, organizing loose and anarchic discussion groups and spontaneous action to achieve publicity, and mounting persuasive efforts featuring close nominalistic analysis expressed in an arcane vocabulary.

The creativity and perseverance of movements concerning sexual variance, elaborated during the current flowering of academic discussion of sexuality and gender, have thus produced fiercely contesting discourses accounting for identities and narrating them into existence.[42]

Antagonistic Discourses of Identity

This brief and partial historical narrative focused on minority group and constructionist identity accounts explains ongoing contention among advocates invoking incompatible identities. Beneath this divergence are distinctly different ways of understanding what identity is and how identities are produced. Rather than attempting to assess the strength and weakness of appeals for one or another understanding of identity and its uses, we simply contend that movements positive toward variant sexuality are deeply divided in response to questions of identity. We first describe justifications for essentialized identity and then, synoptically and without extended argumentative evaluation, examine refutation and rebuttal on these claims.

Gay and lesbian political action in support of civil rights is dominated by an essentialized subject whose sexual orientation is a "culture-independent, objective and intrinsic property."[43] Such a subject is a biologically determined product of nature.[44] This account locates "sexuality within the individual as a fixed essence, leading to a . . . variety of psychological determinisms, and, often enough, to a full-blown biological determinism as well."[45] In the essentialist conception, differences that define lesbians and gay men are beyond social influence and therapeutic intervention.

The naturalized gay or lesbian subject dominates the civil rights politics of sexual orientation. Steven Epstein correctly asserts that this naturalized "'ethnic' self-characterization by gays and lesbians has obvious political utility, permitting a form of group organizing that is particularly suited to the American experience, with its history of civil rights struggles and ethnic-based, interest-group competition."[46]

Legal scholars Davida Cooper and Didi Herman observe that "identity politics have played a powerful part in political struggles, in the past focusing on ethnicity, religion, and class, and in contemporary times on race, gender, sexual orientation, and disability."[47] The dominant paradigm of liberal pluralism emphasizes differences between groups in the effort to supply "legal protection for identities through anti-discrimination statutes, sexual harassment policies, constitutional rights, hate crime statutes and affirmative action policies."[48] Thus gay men and lesbians are following well-trod paths to political influence by locating identity in nature.[49] The result, Larry Gross points out, is that the "preponderance of lesbian and gay political rhetoric, both within the community and externally, reflects an essentialist position, insisting that one doesn't 'choose' to be gay, but 'recognizes and accepts' that one is so."[50]

The dominant gay and lesbian political discourse of civil rights hinging on a naturalized gay subject working for a place within an uninterrogated gender and civic order is articulated in popular books on gay strategy and in progay legal discourse.[51] Marshall Kirk and Hunter Madsen's *After the Ball* (1989), Bruce Bawer's *Place at the Table* (1993), Michael Nava and Robert Dawidoff's *Created Equal* (1994), and Andrew Sullivan's *Virtually Normal* (1995) share a commitment to a natural and unitary gay identity. A distinct class of immutable gay subjects is assumed in legal arguments for privacy and for consideration of homosexuals as a protected category under the equal protection clause.[52] Diane Helene Miller observes that the gay and lesbian civil rights argument "implicitly draws on, at the same time it creates, an essentialized understanding of gays and lesbians as constituting a distinct and identifiable class of people. It then deploys this understanding as a means of seeking 'suspect class' status and of gaining legal protections for gays and lesbians based on equal protection laws."[53]

Several scholars have perceptively described the dominance of an essentialist gay and lesbian subject in legislative debate. Herman examined Canadian civil rights struggles involving variant sexuality with special reference to Ontario's 1986 Bill 7 to add the words "sexual orientation" to that province's Human Rights Code. She observes that progay political advocacy assumes a liberal equality paradigm that "has contributed to the public presentation and perception of lesbians and gay men as a discrete minority community, whose innate 'difference' should not result in prejudice and discrimination."[54] Smith analyzed the debate surrounding Section 28 of Britain's Local Government Act of 1987–1988, which forbade local authorities to "promote homosexuality" or teach the "acceptability of homosexuality as a pretended family relationship."[55] In reaction to homophobic (and racist) Thatcherite discourses, a "response that sexual difference is genetic became hegemonic among the gay and lesbian community leaders and politicians." From this perspective, sexuality and gender became fixed positions, and disruption of sexual categories was depicted as "nonsensical and even illegitimate."[56]

The extensive deployment of an essentialized lesbian and gay subject in public debate on legislative measures is confirmed by analysis of the 1996 U.S. congressional debates on the Defense of Marriage Act (DOMA) and the Employment Non-Discrimination Act (ENDA). Progay advocates in each debate represented gay men and lesbians as persons biologically determined as members of a distinct class to be protected under civil rights law against public discrimination and loss of public benefits. At no time in these debates did either openly gay or gay-friendly legislators question an essentialist view of gay identity or the appropriateness of classifying gay men and lesbians as a group with common characteristics.[57]

Many factors explain the power of an essentialist identity for gay and lesbian politics. Creation of the naturalized gay subject is consistent with gay self-perception and the dominant political culture. With respect to individuals, Sullivan asserts that, for most gays, the "condition of homosexuality is as involuntary as heterosexuality is for heterosexuals. Such an orientation is evident from the very beginning of the formation of a person's emotional identity."[58] From another perspective, Richard Mohr suggests that, because an effect of the political culture is that "society treats gays *as though* they constitute an ethnic minority," an appropriate response is to demonstrate the immorality of the treatment without disturbing the fundamental identity.[59]

An essentialist identity is also crucial to a variety of powerful arguments against opponents of full citizenship for gay men and lesbians. The antigay contention that visible homosexuality must be suppressed because intolerant societies have fewer homosexuals than tolerant societies is deflated by the response that the "formation of homosexual preference, at least in males, appears to be deeply rooted in genetic, hormonal, and (or) developmental factors unlikely to be offset by purely social influences."[60] The essentialist premise also provides a refutation of the antigay argument that homosexuality is a sinful chosen behavior, providing the counterpoint that homosexuality is natural for some persons.[61] More generally, progay self-representation is pushed by antigay depiction toward essentialized identity. Because antigay denunciation causes progay defenders to adopt an essentialist position, there is widespread acceptance that gay men and lesbians need a immutable identity if they are to represent themselves in the public sphere.[62] Simon LeVay supports this strategy, pointing out that survey results consistently demonstrate that individuals who believe that same-sex sexual orientation is genetically caused are consistently more gay positive than those who believe that homosexual identity is a chosen behavior.[63]

Beyond tactical advantage, the essentialization of the gay and lesbian identity can also be understood as grounded on the unexamined assumption that identity formation precedes rhetorical action. For example, Craig Calhoun observes that Jurgen Habermas "presumes that the private sphere provides [the public sphere] with fully formed subjects, settled identities and capacities."[64] Many rhetorical critics, unmindful of the concept of constitutive rhetoric discussed earlier, are Habermasian in that they take for granted that collective actors speak automatically from a transparent identity, and therefore the only rhetorical decisions are those that concern how a given identity is to be presented to a particular audience. Such essentializing theory is wedded to the conception that transcendental subjects exist before communication begins.[65]

Essentialist gay and lesbian civil rights discourse has been attacked on the grounds that it (1) is not effective; (2) ignores the truth of constructionist thought; (3) suppresses "difference" among sex-variant individuals; (4) makes invisible individuals who hold multiple identities; (5) maintains the current regime of sexual normalization; and (6) prevents creation of a broad progressive coalition.

Essentialist discourse has been denounced frequently as an inadequate defense against oppression. For example, essentialist identity grounded in biology fails to prevent oppression because, "from the Holocaust to the history of racial prejudice in America, one can see that being born a certain way does not cushion anyone against persecution."[66] Biological essentialism even welcomes prenatal intervention to prevent the birth of sex-variant individuals.[67] More fundamentally, however, David Halperin links the reason for essentialism's weakness as a political stance to the fact that no identity account "is so positive as to be proof against hostile appropriation and transformation."[68] Alan Sinfield confirms this view, arguing that if homosexuality were genetically determined, "it might seem futile to harass people who are only manifesting a natural condition; on the other hand, our enemies might regard us as an inferior species."[69]

The essentialist representation of a natural gay subject is opposed on intellectual grounds by constructionists who believe that such self-presentation is fundamentally false. In their view, all forms of identity politics perpetuate disabling myths of the social agent as transparent, natural, and homogenous. Drawing primarily on the works of Foucault, and secondarily on Judith Butler, anti-identity theorists "slide into viewing identity itself as the fulcrum of domination."[70] Most basically, they argue, identities are simply false, based on "our 'misrecognition' of their origins; despite, that is, their roots in myths and lies."[71] Such a view traces back to the concept that "symbolic representation always distorts the subject."[72] With respect to sexuality, an essentialized identity denies the continual transformation of the boundaries among socially constructed types of sexual and social actors.[73] Further, essentialization abrogates the individual's right to have a fluid sexual identity contingent on circumstances or phases of life.[74]

Essentialism has the additional effect of making differences among gay and lesbian people less visible. The gay "community" consists of many different demographic groups and of individuals who are in deep disagreement with one another about political philosophy and objectives. In the positing of a single essentialized gay identity, some groups of gay people are disadvantaged in relation to others.[75]

Eric Rofes correctly observes that the "formidable challenge facing any gay organizing has been to take men whose values and original identities were formed in vastly different cultures and corral them into some semblance of a cohesive movement."[76] Men and women involved in the gay community consistently demonstrate that they have divergent political perspectives and goals.[77]

Divisions also exist along ideological lines. Gerre Goodman and her collaborators note that, throughout the history of gay and lesbian politics, participants have brought many different perspectives to the collective effort: "countercultural, personal growth, bourgeois reformist, Marxist, anarchist, pacifist, socialist, feminist, radical feminist, effeminist, and lesbian separatist."[78] In general, Miller argues, various essentialist political projects do not "challenge the misleading notion of a single, homogeneous gay and lesbian 'lifestyle.' They preclude exploration of the wide range of differences between and among gays and lesbians, prohibiting the formulation of broader definitions and better understanding of the gay and lesbian movement."[79] Duggan asserts that essentialist gay politics "ultimately represents the view from the subject position 'twentieth century, Western white gay male.'"[80] As a consequence, other groups are rendered invisible, illustrating the need to recognize the principle that "past campaigns for political or social unity endangered the autonomy and at times the very existence of individuals identified with one or another minority group."[81]

Suppression of difference and willful ignorance of the many grounds of difference are also alleged to be characteristic of essentialism. The first allegation is that a civil rights strategy based on essentialism tends to impose "a unitary identity upon gay men, lesbians, and bisexuals [that] is alienating to those who do not fit into the mold constructed by the leaders of the movement."[82] A second charge is that an essentialist politics fails to allow individuals to realize the multiplicity of identities that they must perform.[83]

Essentialism is also seen as reinforcing the existing heterosexual order, in which homosexuals necessarily remain unprivileged. Adoption of an essentialized gay and lesbian identity, Diana Fuss asserts, may simply operate "as an indispensable interior exclusion . . . a transgression of the border which is necessary to constitute the border as such."[84] Thus the possibility exists that "basing legal protections for gay men and lesbians on the fundamental difference of their sexual orientation reinforces the very repression sought to be removed."[85] Seidman provides a typical statement of this position: "Gay identity constructions reinforce the dominant hetero/homo sexual code with its heteronormativity. If homosexuality and heterosexuality are a coupling in which each presupposes the other . . . and in which this coupling assumes hierarchical forms, the epistemic and political project of identifying a gay subject reinforces and reproduces this hierarchical figure."[86]

Critique of lesbian and gay identity, along with criticism of feminist essentialism, has been roughly grouped under the term "queer theory," a generalized approach that has come to dominate academic study of variant sexuality. Through disruption of foundational constructs, queer theory "rejects a minoritizing logic of toleration or simple political interest-representation in favor of a more thorough resistance to regimes of the normal."[87] Queer theorists have attempted to move beyond dispute over collective identity, shifting from "an anti-identity politics to a politics against identity *per se*. Implicit in this subversion of identity is a celebration of liminality, of the spaces between or outside structure, a kind of anarchistic championing of 'pure' freedom from all constraints and limits."[88] In its attack on gay and lesbian identity, queer theory "describes those gestures or analytical models which dramatize incoherencies in the allegedly stable relations between chromosomal sex, gender and sexual desire . . . demonstrating the impossibility of any 'natural' sexuality."[89] Despite its indeterminacy, the generalization is possible that queer theory's derivation from postmodernism and poststructuralism leads to the rejection of all categorizations as controlling limitations imposed by dominant power structures.[90]

Essentialists respond to postidentitarian criticism in a number of ways. Constructionism has been criticized because it erases the gay subject, disorganizes gay political action, undercuts moral claims to equality, is intellectually vacuous, and offers a reductionist, even essentializing, version of identity processes and outcomes.

Constructionism threatens to destroy identity consciousness necessary for political and cultural action. Leo Bersani, for example, argues that constructionism, deconstruction, and postidentitarian politics in general threaten erasure of gay people. He maintains that "we have erased ourselves in the process of denaturalizing the epistemic and political regimes that have constructed us."[91] The consequences of this erasure are unilateral disarmament, desexualization, and assimilation. In rejecting essentializing identities, advocates must mount a "resistance to homophobia in which the agent of resistance has been erased." Further, the current political expression of deconstructionism "puts all resisters in the same queer bag—a universalizing move I appreciate but that fails to specify the sexual distinctiveness of the resistance." Moreover, having "degayed" themselves, "gays [will] melt into the culture they like to think of themselves as undermining."[92]

The argument is also made that, without a well-defined collective subject, political action is impossible. Sullivan asserts that constructionist appeals impede gay and lesbian mobilization because "its politics was inevitably a confused and seamless flux of competing constructions; a recipe for political paralysis and chaos [that] stemmed from the core meaning of what such a movement should be about; and it made it impossible for the movement to move anywhere coherently or together."[93]

The constructionist frame is further alleged to deny warrant to claims of gay and lesbian oppression. Mohr complains of the "dissipating indeterminacy from the contemporary intellectual forces of deconstructionism, historicism, and relativism. If all norms are socially relative, as most gay academics now hold, there can be no concept of oppression, only more or less pervasive regimes of knowledge, discourse and power."[94]

The postidentitarian position is also attacked because it lacks ideological substance. Constructionism emphasizes the operation of language at the expense of analysis of the material world. Rosemary Hennessy suggests that "because it is the social order—the distribution of wealth, of resources, and power—that is at stake in the struggle over meanings, a politics that contests the prevailing constructions of sexual identity and that aims to disrupt the regimes they support will need to address more than discourse."[95]

Finally, constructionism limits freedom. Wayne Dynes offers the proposition that "while [constructionism's] malleability offers a promise of openness, it does so at the cost of a reductive portrayal of the individual as a mere puppet jerked about by collective forces."[96] In support of Dynes's concept, Calhoun contends that "social constructionist approaches could be just as determinist as naturalizing approaches, for example, when they denied or minimized personal or political agency by stressing seemingly omnipresent but diffuse social pressures as the alternative to biological causation."[97] In this view, constructionism fails to fulfill its promises to gain freedom from identity's constraints or to dissolve the boundaries of social categories. For some critics, the narratives of constructionism are not, as a practical matter, much different from essentialist narratives since each leads to a fixed identity. Seidman points out that "both essentialist and social constructionist versions of lesbian/gay theory in the 1970s and 1980s have related stories of the coming of age of a collective gay subject."[98] In Calhoun's words, "emphases on early socialization and on the power of social structure also lead many social constructionists to treat identities in terms nearly as 'essentialist' as those of biological determinists"[99]

Queer theory, and the blurring of identity implicated in it, has been criticized in ways parallel to identitarian critique of constructionism, mainly by highlighting its failures to provide a starting point for collective action, promote public engagement, and build modes of social action. The effect of acceptance of queer theory is to suppress creation and maintenance of identities necessary to projects of resistance.[100] Most important, queer theory, as an expression of consumerist individualism, reinforces the structure of power within late capitalism. Max Kirsch observes, "Queer theory's highlighting of the impossibility of identity and the relativity of experience closely follows the development of current capitalist relations of production, where the self-contained individual is central to the economic goal of creating profit through production and its by-product, consuming. . . . The tenets of Queer theory closely pattern the characteristics of social relations that it claims to reject. Rather than building resistance to the capitalist production of inequality, it has, paradoxically, mirrored it."[101] In similar fashion, Sue-Ellen Case asserts that the "rise of 'queer performativity,' then, accompanies the victory of global capitalism in the new Europe as well as the complete commodification of the sexual movement."[102]

This summary of conflicting assertions about identity does not serve here as a springboard to weighing truth claims and assessing consequences of different positions. Instead the significance of these disagreements lies in leading rhetorical critics to recognize how challenges to the fundamental belief of others about the self further fracture the already fractious constituencies for variant sexuality movements. Elaboration of impulses to blur or harden identities, and to multiply or reduce their number, frustrates the process of reaching a critical mass of advocates for any form of sexual citizenship or liberation.

Conciliations in Identity Contests

Three types of proposals have been advanced to ameliorate problems in the creation and presentation of gay and lesbian public identities appropriate to movement mobilization and maintenance. They are (1) changing how the politics of civil rights is strategized; (2) modifying how the nature of identity is understood; and (3) restrategizing specific identity representations. The first concerns the public justification for having an identity, the second, naturalization of struggles over the self, and the third, forms of rhetorical action.

With respect to identity and citizenship, suggestions have been made that underlying conceptions of civil rights protections should be modified to de-emphasize essentialized identity. Some legal scholars argue that civil rights cases have been misconceived as hinging on an essentialized identity. Thus effective advocacy of legal protection depends on changing popular conceptions of the nature of civil rights.

Jane Schacter provides an insightful analysis of what she calls the "discourse of equivalence," which hinges on "whether sexual orientation is sufficiently 'like' race, gender, disability, religion or national origin to merit the legal protection of civil rights laws."[103] She points toward a conception of civil rights law consistent with more or less unstable and diffuse identity characteristics. The notion that the meaning of civil rights law is constant and stable, Schacter believes, should be displaced by a "conception of civil rights laws as fluid social constructs that may legitimately be directed at very different kinds of social subordination and stigmatization."[104] Consequently, she argues, simply "recognizing the open texture of civil rights laws suggests the advocates for gay rights must make their case by communicating the distinctive circumstances of antigay subordination and stigmatization."[105] In Schacter's view, statutory protection can be given on the basis of sexual orientation while maintaining an "open-ended, fluid" definition of who is protected.[106]

Denial that immutable identity is a primary qualification for civil rights protection is central to Schacter's argument. Janet Halley confirms that civil rights claims do not require fixed categories of persons, but rather recognition of processes bringing social actors into and out of existence. Therefore she rejects the position taken by "gay rights activists [who] have fairly consistently argued that homosexual orientation is so unitary, fundamental, irresistible, and inalterable that homosexuals meet a supposed requirement of suspect classification, that of immutability."[107] Instead, Halley asserts, there is ample precedent for belief that the equal protection clause "vigilantly protects not monolithic groups but rather the dialogue that generates group identity and suggests that gay rights advocates and courts attend not to . . . the class but to the *classification* of homosexuals."[108]

David Richards proposes a more generalized approach to movements against antidiscrimination, suggesting that the key appeal is based not on a fixed identity, but on the social prejudices that underlie discrimination. He argues that advocacy of gay rights "is not to reflect an identity which is somehow naturally given, but quite the opposite, to protest the cultural stereotype of naturally given difference that, in a vicious circle, rationalize injustice."[109] In this way, the exigence of gay movement becomes abstract structural injustice, "namely, abridgment of basic human rights of conscience, speech, intimate life, and work, unjustly rationalized in terms of dehumanizing stereotypes."[110] The object of collective action is not reinforcement of a gay identity, but demolition of misrepresentation of homosexuals.

Richards's analysis neatly fits another approach to gay and lesbian identity politics premised on equivalence between gay and lesbian identities and racial and ethnic identities as constructed, contingent, and unstable. Certainly the "naturalness" of ethnic and racial identity has recently been severely questioned. With respect to ethnic group membership, Joanne Nagel demonstrates that "while ethnicity is commonly viewed as biological in the United States . . . research has shown people's conception of themselves along ethnic lines, especially their ethnic identity, to be situational and changeable."[111] She concludes that the production of ethnic identity, like gay and lesbian identity, is "strongly limited and influenced by external forces that shape the options, feasibility, and attractiveness of various ethnicities."[112] Racial identity has also been described as a socially constructed category. Henry Louis Gates asserts that race as a scientific concept is a fiction.[113] Davis confirms this view, claiming that the "black population of the United States is a socially constructed category backed by law, not a grouping established by physical anthropologists and biologists."[114] Many scholars have concluded that, in the words of Janet Jakobsen and Ann Pellegrini, "identity categories that seem so self-evident and so natural to us today are and have been contingent, changeable, and confused."[115]

Loosening the categories of civil rights protection and denaturalizing ethnic and racial identity is, however, a difficult, if not insurmountable, task. Racial groups, no less than gay men and lesbians, engage in rancorous struggle over the expediency of particular identity representations. Gamson describes the conflict between a politics of "identity-building and identity blurring [that] has erupted in recent debates in African American movements over multiracialism."[116] Opponents of multiracialism have vehemently resisted deconstruction of naturalized racial identity because access to both a set of rich identity narratives and civil rights protection are understood to be based on existing essentialist racial categories. In addition, these approaches do not reconcile essentialism and constructionism within the public sphere but merely proclaim the triumph of constructionism within it.

Linda Alcoff provides possible remedies to the difficulty of deconstructing categories that individuals deeply value and to the loss of politically useful essentialist categories. In analyzing constructionism and gender, she recommends to feminists a "politics of positionality" within which "'woman' is defined not by a particular set of attributes but by a particular position, the internal characteristics of the person thus identified are not denoted so much as the external context within which that person is situated."[117] Identity, Alcoff argues, is most usefully defined for feminists as a series of relationships—exploitation, dominance, exclusion—through which individuals in a culture understand their nature and obligations. She retains the identity "woman" as a point of departure for feminist action while, at the same time, neither invoking the falsity and fixity of an essentialist category nor risking the relativism and nihilism of deconstructionism. In parallel fashion, a politics of positionality for sex-variant actors might identify relationships within civic life that disadvantage them, while retaining a sense of both shifting contexts that modify positions and a spirit of relationship leading to common action on the part of those who share disadvantaged sexualities. Susan Bickford extends this position, observing that at the heart of successful identity politics will be recognition that "prevailing relations of power allow institutions and individuals to define less powerful groups—through cultural images, bureaucratic practices, economic arrangements—in order to control, constrain, condemn or isolate them."[118]

Apart from changing concepts of civil rights, some legal scholars have suggested that equal protection could be justified through an assimilated and ill-defined gay identity. Peter Cicchino, Bruce Deming, and Katherine Nicholson traced the seventeen-year-long struggle for passage of the Massachusetts Gay Civil Rights Bill. A key feature of the approach used in this protracted but ultimately successful struggle was the choice of a "rhetoric [that] emphasized similarities over differences. Rather than depicting the gay and lesbian community as a distinctive subgroup within society, advocates for the bill . . . tended to emphasize that gay people were, apart from their sexual orientation, not much different from the general population."[119] In such a discourse featuring similarity, the analogy of gays and lesbians to racial and ethnic groups was replaced by argument involving harm avoidance. The central premise of this argument was that "regardless of whether being gay or lesbian is natural or unnatural . . . it is not so great a harm as to justify discrimination."[120] Such a strategy, however, carried high costs, including neglect of political mobilization of the gay community, shirking responsibility to alter public perception through education about gay and lesbian issues, and, most important, "excluding those gay and lesbian people who do not conform to the carefully cultivated images that the strategy projects."[121]

A second way of arriving at accommodation in struggles over identity is to recognize that contests between essentialists and constructionists, or between gay civil rights and queer activists, should be recognized as a natural and altogether unavoidable element in movements. Through this approach, identity itself is denaturalized while contention over identity is naturalized. Attempts to understand the inevitable presence of identity-constructing and identity-deconstructing forces in movements have been made on the levels of language, philosophy, and social theory.

Harrison White draws a distinction between "language that coordinates action-in-the world and language that is world disclosing."[122] Strategic claims to fixed identity have been used opportunistically in civil rights discourses to coordinate the action necessary to address social justice issues. At the same time, deconstruction of the language of identity has been employed in the project of disclosing oppressive institutional identity models and social norms.

An ironic stance can also help put gay and lesbian identity disagreements into a naturalizing perspective. Richard Rorty argues that all "final vocabularies," including the vocabularies of essential identity and deconstruction, should be used with a sense of irony. He defines a final vocabulary as the justificatory words "in which we tell, sometimes prospectively, sometimes retrospectively, the story of our lives."[123] Such an ironic approach suggests that any final vocabulary of collective self-description is more or less politically efficacious depending on the rhetorical effects that seem appropriate to a given situation. No single mix of political strategy, mode of representation, or identity politics captures the realities of variant sexuality or automatically results in full citizenship for gay men and lesbians. Lives as lived are irreducibly diverse, and life strategies are both complex and banal.

Some social theorists have recently come to naturalize struggle over identity through the conception that the effective production and communication of identity is controlled by rhetorical goal and situation. With respect to goals, the presentation of identity may be influenced by whether reform effort is directed at modifying the political system or at changing the culture. Gamson suggests that both a fixed essentialist identity and the deconstruction of identity are useful strategies in light of the "simultaneity of cultural sources of oppression (which make loosening categories a smart strategy) and institutional sources of oppression (which make tightening categories a smart strategy)."[124] The location of advocates may have an important effect. Adoption of an essentialist identity is reinforced by proximity to confrontation. Constructionism is the reigning position within queer studies programs, and in the academy in general, which is to say it is prevalent in those places where opposition to homosexuality is least likely to be articulated. Essentialism, in contrast, is the dominant assumption among progay activists and organizations, and for gay and lesbian people who seek to legitimate themselves in both public and private spheres.[125]

Finally the degree to which gay and lesbian people are understood to be a discrete minority depends on a host of specific factors. Mary Bernstein, for instance, argues that the celebration or suppression of differences within political campaigns depends on the structures of movement organizations, access to the polity, and type of opposition.[126] Thus lack of an organizational infrastructure produces emphasis difference through a strong identity conception. Conversely movements with access to the political structure feature sameness through a discourse of assimilation. The strategy for deploying identity, of course, depends on a complex interaction of a variety of situational factors.

A third approach to managing conflict over identity combines ironic and realist views to produce gay representation as strategic essentialism. Central to such an approach is strategic use of multiple identities in which one chooses to emphasize one identity over another as the rhetorical situation demands, enacting what Gayatri Spivak labels "operational essentialism." She asserts that the "strategic use of essentialism [is] something one cannot not use."[127] Other writers have recognized that even constructionists for whom identity is anathema "acknowledge the mobilizing power implicit in the use of terms like 'lesbian,' 'gay,' 'bisexual,' 'transsexual,' and so on."[128] Kath Weston takes this position to mean that progressive advocates should "operate as though you are one thing through and through, a model of consistency and conviction . . . as though each identity you claim is natural and inescapable and quite simply 'who you are.'"[129] William Connolly asserts that such a position "accepts the indispensability of identity while refusing (while struggling to refuse) to live its own identity as intrinsic truth."[130]

There is little doubt that in many situations, essentialism will remain the dominant interpretation of variant sexuality. For example, in her recent study of initiative politics in Oregon, Arlene Stein found that "essentialist understandings of homosexuality were strategically useful as a means of presenting homosexuality to a community with limited knowledge," even at the expense of understanding homosexuals as a "tightly bound minority group that posed little challenge to the heterosexual norm." In situations that seem to demand the normalizing of homosexuality and in which most individuals lack an elaborated vocabulary of sexuality, however, researchers have also heard an emergent "folk" constructionism that "grappled with individual differences, understood that homosexuality challenges the way that people 'do' gender, and acknowledged that even many straight people find heteronormativity to be restrictive."[131]

Tolerance of difference must extend beyond recognition of individual variance in self-definition to include the constant wrangling and compromise that accompanies movement renegotiation of the collective subject. Manuel Castells believes that students of movement representation should encourage an understanding that "no identity has, *per se*, progressive or regressive value outside its historical context.

A different, and very important matter, is the benefits of each identity for the people who belong."[132]

Rhetorical Criticism of Movement Identities

The chapters in this volume demonstrate that a primary concern of rhetorical critics interested in discourses of variant sexuality should be contests over the definition of identities, the historical forces that shape these contests, and the agonistic genealogies of specific identities. Byrne Fone observes that all aspects of variant sexuality, including persecution of sexual "others," are constructions "responding to historical and social forces."[133] Scholarship in the last century demonstrates decisively that, in Louis Crompton's words, the "history of civilization reveals above all how differently homosexuality has been perceived and judged at different times and in different cultures."[134] Gay identity developed its many faces from identity-forming communication expressing these perceptions and judgments. As the substance of the essays collected here show, the moment has now fortunately arrived when no single history or body of criticism of discourses concerning homosexuality is possible.[135]

Rhetorical critics, in our view, ought to enter more fully into the complexities of identity accounts and narrations by attending to the discursive creation and representation of sexual identities. Gender-neutral marriage is now the most visible contest in which progay and antigay movements are engaged. A new and unanticipated identity has been conjured out of this contest. Our discussion of identity formation is well illustrated by the emergence of this identity of the gay or lesbian couple that has emerged out of the complex interplay of many situational factors and strategies. Rather than doing criticism of the discursive contest over identity in the "gay marriage" controversy, we are simply outlining a project that, if executed adequately, could only be written at greater length.

Gay identity as a collective subject has historically been limited to the singular —the gay individual transformed from abject to rights bearer. Whereas plural collective subjects—for example, "community" or "family"—have been figuratively invoked, the gay movement has featured the individual struggling for freedom, rights, and responsibilities, a representation reinforced by the antigay movement's depiction of the solitary gay. Understood this way, gender-neutral marriage concerns the right of individuals to marry persons of their choice; however, because gender-neutral marriage provides a significant political opportunity for both progay and antigay movements that can only be exploited within the constraints of the present political system, the organized gay movement has now tentatively acted to explore the discursive uses of a new sentimentalized plural subject, thereby causing division within the gay movement.

Achieving gender-neutral marriage is a project that has made significant judicial progress since 1993, when Hawaii's court system began to move toward what seemed inevitable recognition of same-sex marriage.[136] Electorates, even in Hawaii, however, have repeatedly and usually overwhelmingly endorse restricting marriage to male-female couples and have even enacted prohibitions against same-sex domestic partnerships and civil unions.[137] Since the Massachusetts Supreme Judiciary Court's ruling that marriage licenses must be granted to same-sex couples in the Bay State, fourteen other states have approved by popular vote amendments to their state constitutions to prohibit same-sex marriage and, in some states, marriage-like legal arrangements between same-sex individuals.[138] These amendments were approved by significant margins, ranging from 56.8 percent in favor of such prohibition in Oregon to 85.6 percent in favor in Mississippi.[139]

Expansion of the same-sex marriage debate from elite venues such as courts to include elected representatives and the voting public changes a fundamental rhetorical dynamic. As many scholars pointed out, when cultural issues such as gay marriage become ballot measures, electoral contests turn into moralistic symbolic crusades in which voices pleading for civil rights are drowned out.[140]

Striving to defeat anti–gay-marriage initiatives, advocates for gender-neutral marriage struggle with the problem of making their rights appeals heard. In a gay marriage discourse where marriage figures as a "bundle of rights," the counter-rhetoric that celebrates "traditional" marriage easily wins. Different-sex marriage as sentimentalized cultural icon trumps gay marriage as a civil right.[141]

An important countermeasure recently used by gay advocates is to sentimentalize the gay male or lesbian couple. Although same-sex couples have long existed and were sometimes publicly acknowledged, they have become only in the past several years the subject of an effort within the gay movement to emotionalize appeals for same-sex marriage, representing the gay couple as both object of discrimination and rights bearer.

The move toward creation of the couple as a plural movement subject is visible in books advocating same-sex marriage. The exclusive emphasis on civil rights in "gay marriage" appeals is well illustrated in two of the most important works in the mid-1990s phase of the marriage debate, Andrew Sullivan's *Virtually Normal* (1995) and William Eskridge's *Case for Same-Sex Marriage* (1996). Although such works continue to be written, newer books in the civil rights tradition now stress that gay couples are the chief actors in the marriage drama. Evan Wolfson, a prominent litigator on behalf of gay couples, finds room for what he terms the "civil rights poetry" of actual gay couples. He asserts that "through the example of same-sex couples who already are getting married . . . society is coming to learn that gay people are no different when it comes to their desire to marry the person of their choice."[142] Perhaps the most complete rendering of the marrying gay couple is to be found in Amy Rennert's celebration of gay and lesbian marriage, *We Do*, which reproduces pictures of gay couples during their wedding ceremonies in February 2004 in San Francisco City Hall. This work captures expressions of enduring relationships between couples in all their idiosyncratic, exuberant, and moving ways.[143] The conscious choice to make individuated gay and lesbian couples the center of the gay marriage struggle has recently become obvious in the strategic choices of pro–gay-marriage advocates to make public their stable and loving relationships. In the successful Massachusetts litigation over same-sex marriage, gay and lesbian couples of a publicly acceptable type were very much the center of the case. Following success in the Massachusetts case, proponents of gay marriage looked forward to being able to "humanize an abstraction, putting real faces on what polls show most Americans think is a scary idea."[144]

While many news articles increasingly highlight gay and lesbian couples as the subject of cultural struggle over marriage, editorials and other opinion pieces have made the gay couple the center of this discussion.[145] By their very nature, same-sex-marriage and celebration announcements in newspapers prominently feature specific gay couples.[146]

Many gay organizations also contribute to increasing the prominence of the gay and lesbian couple. To use only one example, Freedom to Marry has established a "Story Center" in cooperation with the American Civil Liberties Union. This effort consists of requesting submissions from gay couples in which they answer basic questions—thereby providing a statistical database—and submit the story of their relationships. The Story Center proclaims that "when Americans began to see real, committed, loving couples—patiently and joyously—standing in the rain and waiting for the historic opportunity to get married, many saw reality for the first time. And witnessing these couples' and their families' love changed many opinions from opposition to support of our cause."[147]

Another way of observing the possibility of shift toward a plural gay and lesbian couple identity and away from the singular gay subject is to note the concern—indeed, anger—of many gay and queer advocates toward the same-sex marriage crusade. Opposition to focusing on same-sex marriage has been significant within the gay community, with many commentators seeing marriage as a normalizing strategy that leaves noncoupled gay people even more stigmatized than they were in earlier eras. As Warner asserts, promotion of same-sex marriage is a mainstreaming strategy for "allowing married gay couples to be relieved of the stigma in order to make its coercive effects felt all the more by the unmarried."[148] Miller insists that such demands for marriage may well "foreclose any interrogation of heterosexuality, refusing to challenge its compulsory nature or privilege." [149]

Gender-neutral marriage can illustrate some aspects of the interplay of many forces in the constitution of identities, as well as the play of identities in conflict, the gestures of conciliation made by advocates, and the divisiveness of deploying one identity rather than another. Further progress away from simply assuming the self-definition of actors in movement communication will be made when a more general recognition is achieved that gender and race are also good beginning points for understanding the process of identity construction. Success of a queer under-standing of rhetorical action will be achieved when so-called normal movement subjectivities, for example, worker, survivalist, environmentalist, are not simply taken for granted but have their turn at careful analysis.

Notes

1. Marcy Darnovsky, Barbara Epstein, and Richard Flacks, *Cultural Politics and Social Movements* (Philadelphia: Temple University Press, 1995), vii–xiii. See also Sue-Ellen Case, "Toward a Butch-Feminist Retro-Future," in *Queer Frontiers: Millennial Geographies, Genders, and Generations*, ed. Joseph A. Boone, Martin Dupuis, Martin Mecker, Karin Quimby, Cindy Sarver, Debra Silverman, and Rosemary Weatherston (Madison: University of Wisconsin Press, 2000), 32; Andre Krouwel and Jan Willem, "The Private and the Public: Gay and Lesbian Issues in Political Science," in *Lesbian and Gay Studies: An Introductory, Interdisciplinary Approach*, ed. Theo Sandfort, Judith Schuyf, Jan Willem Duyvendak, and Jeffrey Weeks (London: Sage, 2000), 113.

2. Charles J. Stewart, Craig Allen Smith, and Robert E. Denton, Jr., *Persuasion and Social Movements*, 4th ed. (Prospect Heights, Ill.: Waveland Press, 2001), 42–43.

3. Verta Taylor and Nancy E. Whittier, "Collective Identity in Social Movement Communities: Lesbian Feminist Mobilization," in *Frontiers in Social Movement Theory*, ed. Aldon D. Morris and Carol McClurg Mueller (New Haven, Conn.: Yale University Press, 1992), 109.

4. Joshua Gamson, "Messages of Exclusion: Gender, Movements, and Symbolic Boundaries," *Gender & Society* 11 (1997): 178–99.

5. Hank Johnston, Enrique Larana, and Joseph R. Gusfield, "Identities, Grievances, and New Social Movements," in *New Social Movements: From Ideology to Identity*, ed. Larana, Johnston, and Gusfield (Philadelphia: Temple University Press, 1994), 15.

6. Alberto Melucci, *Challenging Codes: Collective Action in the Information Age* (New York: Cambridge University Press, 1996), 76.

7. Richard Jenkins, *Social Identity* (London: Routledge, 1996), 7.

8. Dorothy Holland, Debra Skinner, and Carole Cain, *Identity and Agency in Cultural Worlds* (Cambridge, Mass.: Harvard University Press, 1998), 4. See also Madan Sarup, *Identity, Culture and the Postmodern World* (Athens: University of Georgia Press, 1996).

9. Valentine M. Moghadam, "Introduction: Women and Identity Politics in Theoretical and Comparative Perspective," in *Identity Politics & Women: Cultural Reassertions and Feminisms in International Perspective*, ed. Moghadam (Boulder, Colo.: Westview, 1994), 3.

10. Ian Hacking, *The Social Construction of What?* (Cambridge, Mass.: Harvard University Press, 1999), 104, 34.

11. Brian R. McGee, "The Argument from Definition Revisited: Race and Definition in the Progressive Era," *Argumentation and Advocacy* 35 (1999): 141.

12. Edward Schiappa, *Defining Reality: Definitions and the Politics of Meaning* (Carbondale: Southern Illinois University Press, 2003), 3.

13. Lynn Clarke, "Contesting Definitional Authority in the Collective," *Quarterly Journal of Speech* 91 (2005): 27–28.

14. Maurice Charland, "Constitutive Rhetoric: The Case of the *Peuple Quebecois*," *Quarterly Journal of Speech* 73 (1987): 133–50.

15. Ibid., 138.

16. Ibid., 148.

17. Kevin Hetherington, *Expressions of Identity: Space, Performance, Politics* (London: Sage, 1998), 25. See also Cathy J. Cohen, "Contested Membership: Black Gay Identities and the Politics of AIDS," in *Creating Change: Sexuality, Public Policy, and Civil Rights*, ed. John D'Emilio, William B. Turner, and Urvashi Vaid (New York: St. Martin's Press, 2000), 382–406.

18. Sasha Roseneil and Julie Seymour, "Practising Identities: Power and Resistance," in *Practising Identities: Power and Resistance*, ed. Sasha Roseneil and Julie Seymour (New York: St. Martin's Press, 1999).

19. See, for example, Barry D. Adam, *The Rise of a Gay and Lesbian Movement* (Boston: Twayne, 1987); Margaret Cruikshank, *The Gay and Lesbian Liberation Movement* (New York: Routledge, 1992); John Loughery, *The Other Side of Silence: Men's Lives and Gay Identities: A Twentieth Century History* (New York: Henry Holt, 1998).

20. Jeni Loftus, "America's Liberalization in Attitudes toward Homosexuality, 1973 to 1998," *American Sociological Review* 93 (2001): 762–82; David Rayside, "The Structuring of Sexual Minority Activist Opportunities in the Mainstream: Britain, Canada, and the United States," in *Sexual Identities, Queer Politics*, ed. Mark Blasius (Princeton, N.J.: Princeton University Press, 2001), 23–55.

21. John D'Emilio, *Sexual Politics, Sexual Communities: The Making of a Homosexual Minority in the United States, 1940–1970* (Chicago: University Press of Chicago, 1983), 4.

22. Ibid., 63–75.

23. Ibid., 79.

24. Ibid., 81.

25. Ibid., 89–90.

26. For an excellent analysis of conflicting ideologies in the gay "movement," see Paul Robinson, *Queer Wars: The New Gay Right and Its Critics* (Chicago: University of Chicago Press, 2005).

27. Douglas McAdam, "Culture and Social Movements," in *New Social Movements: From Ideology to Identity*, ed. Larana, Johnston, and Gusfield, 41–42.

28. Barry D. Adam, Jan Willem Duyvendak, and Andre Krouwel, eds., *The Global Emergence of Gay and Lesbian Politics: National Imprints of a Worldwide Movement* (Philadelphia: Temple University Press, 1999), 1.

29. Loughery, *The Other Side of Silence*, 306.

30. Dana Rosenfeld, *The Changing of the Guard: Lesbian and Gay Elders, Identity, and Social Change* (Philadelphia: Temple University Press, 2003), 3. Rosenfeld further claims that this shift from a discredited to an accredited identity was produced in the course of political action (3, 9). Because of political involvement, "passing" became a less frequently used term, "coming out" ceased to mean revealing one's homoerotic desires to similar persons and became a public declaration, and "queer" shifted to a positive rather than a pejorative term.

31. Adam, *The Rise of a Gay and Lesbian Movement*, 76.

32. Eric Rofes, *Reviving the Tribe: Regenerating Gay Men's Sexuality and Culture in the Ongoing Epidemic* (New York: Harrington Park Press, 1996), 110.

33. Adam, *The Rise of a Gay and Lesbian Movement*, 78.

34. Kenneth Birch, "The Politics of Autonomy," in *Homosexuality: Power and Politics*, ed. Gay Left Collective (London: Allison & Busby, 1980), 86.

35. Jeffrey Weeks, "Capitalism and the Organization of Sex," in *Homosexuality*, ed. Gay Left Collective, 20.

36. Adam, *The Rise of a Gay and Lesbian Movement*, 97–99; Randy Shilts, *Conduct Unbecoming: Gays & Lesbians in the U.S. Military* (New York: St. Martin's Press, 1993), 213, and *The Mayor of Castro Street: The Life and Times of Harvey Milk* (New York: St. Martin's Press, 1982).

37. Steven Seidman, "Identity and Politics in a 'Postmodern' Gay Culture: Some Historical and Conceptual Notes," in *Fear of a Queer Planet: Queer Politics and Social Theory*, ed. Michael Warner (Minneapolis: University of Minnesota Press, 1993), 118.

38. Warner, introduction to *Fear of a Queer Planet*, ed. Warner, xiii.

39. David Bell and Jon Binnie, *The Sexual Citizen: Queer Politics and Beyond* (Cambridge, Mass.: Polity, 2000), 17. For a good, brief summary of queer theory, see William G. Tierney, *Academic Outlaws: Queer Theory and Cultural Studies in the Academy* (Thousand Oaks, Calif.: Sage, 1997), 35.

40. Steven Seidman, introduction to *Queer Theory/Sociology*, ed. Seidman (Cambridge, Mass.: Blackwell, 1996), 12.

41. Heather K. Love, "'Spoiled Identity': Stephen Gordon's Loneliness and the Difficulties of Queer History," *GLQ: A Journal of Lesbian and Gay Studies* 7 (2001): 492.

42. Jeffrey Escoffier, *American Homo: Community and Perversity* (Berkeley: University of California Press, 1998), 64.

43. Edward Stein, "Conclusion: The Essentials of Constructionism and the Construction of Essentialism," in *Forms of Desire: Sexual Orientation and the Social Constructionist Controversy*, ed. Stein (New York: Garland, 1990), 325.

44. John Lyne, "Bio-Rhetorics: Moralizing the Life Sciences," in *The Rhetorical Turn: Invention and Persuasion in the Conduct of Inquiry*, ed. Herbert W. Simons (Chicago: University of Chicago Press, 1990), 35–57.

45. Robert A. Padgug, "Sexual Matters: On Conceptualizing Sexuality in History," in *Forms of Desire*, ed. Stein, 50.

46. Steven Epstein, "Gay Politics, Ethnic Identity: The Limits of Social Constructionism," in *Forms of Desire*, ed. Stein, 255.

47. Davina Cooper and Didi Herman, "Getting the 'Family Right': Legislating Heterosexuality in Britain, 1986–1991," in *Legal Inversions: Lesbians, Gay Men, and the Politics of Law*, ed. Didi Herman and Carl Stychin (Philadelphia: Temple University Press, 1995), 211.

48. Dan Danielson and Karen Engle, introduction to *After Identity: A Reader in Law and Culture*, ed. Danielson and Engle (New York: Routledge, 1995), xiv.

49. Adam, *The Rise of a Gay and Lesbian Movement*, 121.

50. Larry Gross, *Contested Closets: The Politics and Ethics of Outing* (Minneapolis: University of Minnesota Press, 1993), 113.

51. See John D'Emilio, *Making Trouble: Essays on Gay History, Politics, and the University* (New York: Routledge, 1992), 181; Adam, *The Rise of a Gay and Lesbian Movement*, 121.

52. Janet E. Halley, "The Politics of the Closet: Towards Equal Protection for Gay, Lesbian, and Bisexual Identity," *University of California at Los Angeles Law Review* 36 (1989): 359.

53. Diane Helene Miller, *Freedom to Differ: The Shaping of the Gay and Lesbian Struggle for Civil Rights* (New York: NYU Press, 1998), 41.

54. Didi Herman, *Rights of Passage: The Shaping of the Gay and Lesbian Struggle for Civil Rights* (Toronto: University of Toronto Press, 1994), 5.

55. Anna Marie Smith, *Representing the Enemies Within: British New Right Discourse on Race and Sexuality* (Cambridge: Cambridge University Press, 1994), 183.

56. Ibid., 236.

57. Ralph R. Smith, "Legislative Discourse on Justice, Morality, and Power: The Defense of Marriage Act," National Communication Association Convention, 1997.

58. Andrew Sullivan, *Virtually Normal: An Argument about Homosexuality* (New York: Knopf, 1995), 17.

59. Richard D. Mohr, *Gay Ideas: Outing and Other Controversies* (Boston: Beacon Press, 1992), 251, 256.

60. Richard A. Posner, *Sex and Reason* (Cambridge, Mass.: Harvard University Press, 1992), 163.

61. Didi Herman, *The Antigay Agenda: Orthodox Vision and the Christian Right* (Chicago: University of Chicago Press, 1997), 71–75.

62. Ralph R. Smith and Russel R. Windes, *Progay/Antigay: The Rhetorical War over Sexuality* (Thousand Oaks, Calif.: Sage, 2000), 96–104.

63. Simon LeVay, *Queer Science: The Use and Abuse of Research into Homosexuality* (Cambridge, Mass.: MIT Press, 1996).

64. Craig Calhoun, "Social Theory and the Politics of Identity," in *Social Theory and the Politics of Identity*, ed. Calhoun (Oxford: Blackwell, 1994), 23.

65. Lawrence Grossberg, "Marxist Dialectics and Rhetorical Criticism," *Quarterly Journal of Speech* 65 (1979): 249.

66. Urvashi Vaid, *Virtual Equality: The Mainstreaming of Gay and Lesbian Liberation* (New York: Anchor, 1995), 136.

67. Donald J. West and Richard Green, "Conclusion," in *Sociolegal Control of Homosexuality*, ed. West and Green (New York: Plenum Press, 1997), 334.

68. David M. Halperin, *One Hundred Years of Homosexuality: And Other Essays on Greek Love* (New York: Routledge, 1990), 52.

69. Alan Sinfield, *Cultural Politics—Queer Reading* (Philadelphia: University of Pennsylvania Press, 1994), 70.

70. Seidman, "Identity and Politics," 132.

71. Kwame A. Appiah, "African Identities," in *Social Postmodernism*, ed. Linda Nicholson and Steven Seidman (New York: Cambridge University Press, 1995), 110.

72. Slavoj Žižek, *The Sublime Object of Ideology* (London: Verso, 1989), 175.

73. George Chauncey, *Gay New York: Gender, Urban Culture, and the Making of the Gay Male World, 1890–1940* (New York: Basic Books, 1994), 12–13.

74. Shane Phelan, introduction to *Playing with Fire: Queer Politics, Queer Theories*, ed. Phelan (New York: Routledge, 1997), 4; John P. DeCecco and John P. Elia, "A Critique and Synthesis of Biological Essentialism and Social Constructionist Views of Sexuality and Gender," *Journal of Homosexuality* 24 (1993): 16–17.

75. John D'Emilio, *The World Turned: Essays on Gay History, Politics, and Culture* (Durham, N.C.: Duke University Press, 2002), 143.

76. Rofes, *Reviving the Tribe*, 30.

77. Dudley Clendinen and Adam Nagourney, *Out for Good: The Struggle to Build a Gay Rights Movement in America* (New York: Simon and Schuster, 1999), 85–105, 261–66.

78. Gerre Goodman, George Lakey, Judy Lashof, and Erika Thorne, *No Turning Back: Lesbian and Gay Liberation for the '80s* (Philadelphia: New Society, 1983), 30.

79. Miller, *Freedom to Differ,* 77.

80. Lisa Duggan, "Making It Perfectly Queer," in *Sex Wars: Sexual Dissent and Political Culture,* ed. Duggan and Nan S. Hunter (New York: Routledge, 1995), 162.

81. Martha Minow, "Rights and Cultural Differences," 348.

82. Anthony Slagle, "In Defense of Queer Nation: From *Identity Politics* to a *Politics of Difference,*" *Western Journal of Communication* 59 (1995): 86.

83. Phelan, introduction, 90–91.

84. Diana Fuss, *Inside/Out: Lesbian Theories, Gay Theories* (New York: Routledge, 1991), 3.

85. Editors of the *Harvard Law Review, Sexual Orientation and the Law* (Cambridge, Mass.: Harvard University Press, 1990), 17.

86. Seidman, "Identity and Politics," 130.

87. Warner, introduction, xxv.

88. Seidman, "Identity and Politics," 105.

89. Annamarie Jagose, *Queer Theory: An Introduction* (New York: NYU Press, 1996), 3.

90. Max H. Kirsch, *Queer Theory and Social Change* (London: Routledge, 2000), 33.

91. Leo Bersani, *Homos* (Cambridge, Mass.: Harvard University Press, 1995), 4.

92. Ibid., 56, 71, 4.

93. Sullivan, *Virtually Normal,* 89.

94. Mohr, *Gay Ideas,* 4.

95. Rosemary Hennessy, "Queer Visibility in Commodity Culture," in *Social Postmodernism,* ed. Linda Nicholson and Steven Seidman (New York: Cambridge University Press, 1995), 152.

96. Wayne Dynes, "Wrestling with the Social Boa Constructor," in *Forms of Desire,* ed. Stein, 233.

97. Craig Calhoun, "Social Theory and the Politics of Identity," in *Social Theory and the Politics of Identity,* ed. Calhoun (Oxford: Blackwell, 1994), 16.

98. Steven Seidman, "Deconstructing Queer Theory or the Under-Theorization of the Social and the Ethical," in *Social Postmodernism,* ed. Nicholson and Seidman, 125.

99. Calhoun, "Social Theory," 16.

100. Kirsch, *Queer Theory,* 8, 9,17,31,81.

101. Ibid., 17.

102. Case, "Retro-Future," 32.

103. Jane S. Schacter, "The Gay Civil Rights Debate in the States: Decoding the Discourse of Equivalents," *Harvard Civil Rights and Civil Liberties Review* 29 (1994): 286.

104. Ibid., 312.

105. Ibid., 313.

106. Jane S. Schacter, "Skepticism, Culture, and the Gay Civil Rights Debate in a Post-Civil-Rights Era," *Harvard Law Review* 110 (1997): 720.

107. Janet E. Halley, "The Politics of the Closet: Towards Equal Protection for Gay, Lesbian, and Bisexual Identity," *University of California at Los Angeles Law Review* 36 (1989): 920.

108. Ibid., 924. Halley maintains, relying on, among other precedents, analyses in *Shaare Tefila Congregation v. Cobb*, *St. Francis College v. AlKhazraji*, and *San Antonio Independent School District v. Rodriguez*, that process analysis of identity construction has largely replaced immutability as the standard for recognition of a suspect class. As she concludes, "Where immutability does figure in the Court's analysis it is merely a factor in the Court's review of two different sorts of process failure: mere irrationality and a pervasive prejudice" (927). Rhetorical critics should thus consider that communication that creates, changes, and distorts concepts of identity is shielded by equal protection, rather than a stable and immutable identity characteristic such as skin color or sexual object choice.

109. David A. J. Richards, *Identity and the Case for Gay Rights: Race, Gender, Religion as Stereotypes* (Chicago: University of Chicago Press, 1999), 72.

110. Ibid., 90.

111. Joanne Nagel, "Constructing Ethnicity: Creating and Recreating Ethnic Identity and Culture," *Social Problems* 41 (1994): 154.

112. Ibid., 161.

113. Henry L. Gates, Jr., "The Black Man's Burden," in *Fear of a Queer Planet*, ed. Warner, 230–38.

114. F. James Davis, *Who Is Black: One Nation's Definition* (University Park: Pennsylvania State University Press, 1991), 3.

115. Janet R. Jakobsen and Ann Pellegrini, *Love the Sin: Sexual Regulation and the Limits of Religious Tolerance* (New York: NYU Press, 2003).

116. Joshua Gamson, "Must Identity Movements Self-Destruct? A Queer Dilemma," *Social Problems* 42 (1995): 401.

117. Linda Alcoff, "Cultural Feminism Versus Poststructuralism: The Identity Crisis in Feminist Theory," *Signs: Journal of Women in Culture and Society* 13 (1988): 433.

118. Susan Bickford, "Anti-Anti-Identity Politics: Feminism, Democracy, and the Complexities of Citizenship," *Hypatia* 12, no. 4 (1997): 119.

119. Peter M. Cicchino, Bruce R. Deming, and Katherine M. Nicholson, "Sex, Lies, and Civil Rights: A Critical History of the Massachusetts Gay Civil Rights Bill," in *Legal Inversions*, ed. Herman and Stychin, 144.

120. Ibid., 145.

121. Ibid., 153.

122. Harrison C. White, *Identity and Control: A Structural Theory of Social Action* (Princeton, N.J.: Princeton University Press, 1992), 25.

123. Richard Rorty, *Contingency, Irony, and Solidarity* (New York: Cambridge University Press, 1989), 73.

124. Gamson, "Must Identity Movements Self-Destruct," 403.

125. Ralph R. Smith and Russel R. Windes, "The Progay and Antigay Issue Culture: Interpretation, Influence and Dissent," *Quarterly Journal of Speech* 83 (1997): 32–33.

126. Mary Bernstein, "Celebration and Suppression: The Strategic Uses of Identity by the Lesbian and Gay Movement," *American Journal of Sociology* 103 (1997): 532.

127. Gayatri C. Spivak, *Outside the Teaching Machine* (New York: Routledge, 1993), 5.

128. Sarah Chinn and Kris Franklin, "'I Am What I Am' (Or Am I?): The Making and Unmaking of Lesbian and Gay Identity in *High Tech Gays*," *Discourse* 15 (1992): 15.

129. Kath Weston, *Render Me, Gender Me: Lesbians Talk Sex, Class, Color, Nation, Stud-muffins* (New York: Columbia University Press, 1996), 43.

130. William E. Connolly, *Identity/Difference: Democratic Negotiations of Political Paradox* (Ithaca, N.Y.: Cornell University Press, 1991), 46.

131. Arlene Stein, *The Stranger Next Door: The Story of a Small Community's Battle over Sex, Faith, and Civil Rights* (Boston: Beacon Press, 2001).

132. Manuel Castells, *The Power of Identity* (Malden, Mass.: Blackwell, 1997), 8.

133. Byrne Fone, *Homophobia: A History* (2000; New York: Picador, 2004), 13.

134. Louis Crompton, *Homosexuality & History* (Cambridge, Mass.: Belknap Press, 2003), p. xiii.

135. David Halperin, *How To Do a History of Homosexuality* (Chicago: University of Chicago Press, 2002), 109.

136. Barbara J. Cox, "Same-Sex Marriage and Choice-of-Law: If We Marry in Hawaii, Are We Still Married When We Return Home," *Wisconsin Law Reporter* (1994), 1033–18; Joseph W. Hovermill, "A Conflict of Laws and Morals: The Choice of Law Implications of Hawaii's Recognition of Same-Sex Marriage," *Maryland Law Review* 53 (1994): 450–93; Larry Kramer, "Same-Sex Marriage, Conflict of Laws, and the Unconstitutional Public Policy Exception," *Yale Law Journal* (1907): 1965–2007; Ken I. Kersch, "Full Faith and Credit for Same-Sex Marriages?" *Political Science Quarterly* 112 (1997): 117–36.

137. The Defense of Marriage Act passed in the House of Representatives by a margin of 342 in favor, 67 opposed; in the Senate, the bill received 85 yes votes and 14 no votes. In late 1998, voters in both Alaska and Hawaii approved by better than a two-to-one margin through the initiative process constitutional amendments unfavorable to same-sex marriage. See Elaine Herscher, "Same-Sex Marriage Suffers Setback: Alaska, Hawaii Voters Say 'No,'" *San Francisco Chronicle*, November 5, 1998, A2.

138. Kava Peterson, "50–State Rundown on Gay Marriage Laws," http://www.stateline.org (August 18, 2005).

139. James Dao, "Same-Sex Marriage Issue Key to Some GOP Races," *New York Times*, November 4, 2004, P4.; Katharine Q. Seelye, "Moral Values Cited as a Defining Issue of the Election," *New York Times*, November 4, 2004, P4.

140. Donald P. Haider-Markel and Kenneth. J. Meier, "The Politics of Gay and Lesbian Rights: Expanding the Scope of Conflict," *Journal of Politics* 58 (1996): 332–49; Todd Donovan and Shaun Bowler, "Direct Democracy and Minority Rights: Opinions on Anti-Gay and Lesbian Ballot Measures," in *Anti-Gay Rights*, ed. Stephanie L. Witt and Suzanne McCorkle (Westport, Conn.: Praeger, 1997), 107–26.

141. On the comparative power of civil rights appeals versus sentimentalization of different-sex marriage, see Mary Adamski, "Same-Sex Issue Debated on TV," *Honolulu Star-Bulletin*, October 17, 1998, http://www.starbulletin.com (July 23, 2001); Mike Yuen, "'Yes' Won with Focus, Clear Message," *Honolulu Star-Bulletin*, November 5, 1998, http://www.starbulletin.com (July 23, 2001).

142. Evan Wolfson, *Why Marriage Matters: America, Equality, and Gay People's Right to Marry* (New York: Simon and Schuster, 2004), 186.

143. Amy Rennert, ed., *We Do: A Celebration of Gay and Lesbian Marriage* (San Francisco: Chronicle Books, 2004).

144. Carolyn Lochhead, "Pivotal Day for Gay Marriage in U.S. Nears: Massachusetts Move to Legalize Weddings May Intensify Backlash in Other States," *San Francisco Chronicle*, May 2, 2004, http://www.sfgate.com (July 26, 2004).

145. For examples of such news stories and features, see Clifford Krauss, "A Few Gay Americans Tie the Knot in Canada," *New York Times*, June 2, 2003, A2; Kate Zernike, "As Debate Rages, Gays Meld with Straights," *New York Times*, August 24, 2003, A12. For an example of an editorial featuring the gay couple, see "For Gay Marriage," *Boston Globe*, July 8, 2003, http://www.ftmmass.org/GlobeGayMarriageEditorial.htm (July 26, 2004).

146. Matthew A. Hennie, "Wedded Bliss: Daily Newspapers Differ on Treatment of Gay Marriage Announcements," *Southern Voice*, March 19, 2004, http://www.sovo.com (July 26, 2004).

147. Story Center, Freedom to Marry, http://www.freedomtomarry.org (September 19, 2004).

148. Michael Warner, *The Trouble with Normal: Sex, Politics, and the Ethics of Queer Life* (New York: Free Press, 1999), 114.

149. Miller, *Freedom to Differ*, 77.

Harvey Milk and the Queer Rhetorical Situation

A Rhetoric of Contradiction

Karen A. Foss

And the young gay people in the Altoona, Pennsylvanias and the Richmond, Minnesotas who are coming out. . . . The only thing they have to look forward to is hope. And you have to give them hope. . . . Without hope, not only gays, but the blacks, the seniors, the handicapped . . . will give up. And if you help elect more gay people, that gives a green light to all who feel disenfranchised, a green light to move forward. It means hope to a nation that has given up because if a gay person makes it, the doors are open to everyone.

Harvey Milk, quoted in Randy Shilts,
The Mayor of Castro Street

In 1977, Harvey Milk was elected the first openly gay supervisor in San Francisco. On virtually every front, his campaign discourse deserves consideration as a case study of queer[1] public address in action. That he was elected when gay politicians were closeted would make his case interesting enough. That he ran three unsuccessful campaigns before winning adds the possibility of an evolutionary perspective. And these campaigns spanned significant shifts in gay culture—from a time when gays and lesbians thought the best they could do was to support sympathetic liberal candidates to a full-fledged gay/lesbian liberation movement with considerable political clout.[2] Finally, the outcome demands a straightforward, pragmatic assessment from the vantage of hindsight: Milk, along with San Francisco mayor George Moscone, was assassinated by fellow supervisor Dan White.[3] What can be learned about the possibilities and limitations of scripts and strategies for marginalized rhetors seeking the mainstream?

In this chapter, I explore the rhetoric of Harvey Milk within the frame of public address and specifically within the frame of Lloyd Bitzer's rhetorical situation. Though implicit in treatises on rhetoric since at least the time of Aristotle, the notion of the rhetorical situation was articulated specifically by Bitzer in his 1968 essay of the same name. Bitzer argued that any rhetorical situation comes into being "because of some specific condition or situation which invites utterance"[4] an *exigence* or imperfection. A rhetorical situation also contains a *rhetor* whom is invited by the situation to create and present *discourse,* an *audience* capable of modifying thought or action so as to affect the exigence, and *constraints* that influence the rhetor and the audience.[5] The rhetorical situation, in sum, is "a complex of persons, events, objects, and relations presenting an actual or potential exigence which can be completely or partially removed if discourse, introduced into the situation, can so constrain human decision or action as to bring about the significant modification of the exigence."[6] Milk's campaigns offer an opportunity to view the interplay of exigence, audience, rhetor, discourse, and constraints from a queer standpoint to explore the nature of the queer rhetorical situation. I suggest that, in the case of Harvey Milk, Bitzer's theory usefully can be extended beyond mainstream contexts.[7]

The Rhetor

Harvey Milk was born and raised in New York and moved to San Francisco permanently in 1973, the year of his first campaign for supervisor. His early years gave little indication of the path his life would take. He joined the navy, taught high school, and became a financial analyst on Wall Street. He worked on a friend's Broadway productions in his free time, which gave him exposure to the counterculture of the 1960s. When his partner took a job as stage manager for the San Francisco production of *Hair,* Milk moved with him to San Francisco. Although he found work as a financial analyst, his values were becoming increasingly countercultural, and he was fired for burning his BankAmericard during a demonstration against the Vietnam War. Milk returned to New York briefly to work in theater but soon moved back to San Francisco with his new partner, Scott Smith, where the two of them opened a camera store in the Castro.[8]

Milk's decision to run for the board of supervisors came from frustration over government's unresponsiveness to people's needs. Already disgusted by government's lack of honesty in the Watergate scandal, Milk was upset about a special tax charged him as a small business owner. The last straw for Milk was when a teacher came into the camera store to borrow a projector because her district could not afford to buy one.[9] Deciding he could "make a difference,"[10] Milk ran as a representative for all underrepresented groups in the city, playing up his own outsider status as Jewish, gay, hippie, newcomer to the city, and newcomer to politics. In that election, he finished tenth in a field of thirty candidates—a solid showing for an unknown.[11] Milk ran again for the board of supervisors in 1975, this time coming in seventh after the six incumbents running for reelection. Because of Milk's strong showing, the new mayor, George Moscone, appointed him to a seat on the board of permit appeals.[12]

Milk gave up his seat on the board in 1976, only a few months into his term, to run for the Democratic nomination for a seat in the California state assembly.[13] He decided to run after learning that Art Agnos had been selected by the Democratic leadership far in advance of the primary election to be the Democratic candidate. Milk believed representatives should be selected by the people and thus challenged the process of political deal making by running himself. He lost the election to Agnos by a narrow margin.

Milk ran again for the board of supervisors of San Francisco in 1977, and this time he succeeded.[14] He was responsible for two pieces of legislation during his eleven-month tenure—a gay rights bill and a pooper-scooper law that required pet owners to clean up after their animals on city streets. His term was cut short when he was assassinated on November 27, 1978, along with Mayor George Moscone, by fellow supervisor Dan White.[15] White had resigned his supervisorial seat and then asked for it back; on the day of the killings, Moscone was to have announced that he had decided not to reappoint White to the seat. White's trial generated the "Twinkie defense"—that junk food exacerbated White's depression and caused him to react abnormally. White was sentenced to seven years and eight months— the maximum possible for his dual convictions for involuntary manslaughter—but served fewer than five years. On October 21, 1985, within a year of his release, he committed suicide.[16]

The Rhetorical Frame

In the case of Harvey Milk the rhetorical situation seems simple on the surface: a gay man elected to the San Francisco Board of Supervisors in 1977. Milk's exigence was a desire to achieve public office in order to deal with inequities he perceived in city politics. Milk's audience was the voters of San Francisco, and a major constraint operating in the situation was that Milk was gay—and open about it. Milk as rhetor managed the situation by becoming increasingly astute over the course of his campaigns about the interests and needs of his audience until he finally was elected to office.

But are there other, different·stories, embedded in this rather generic version of the rhetorical situation Milk encountered? Multiple stories exist for the same set of facts, each with different consequences for rhetorical action and analysis. W. Barnett Pearce suggests that "the stories told are *underdetermined* by the facts of life; whatever set of stories has been told, an additional story can be constructed that meets the 'facts' sufficiently well to make them coherent."[17] The story I offered about Milk above is that of an aspiring politician who adapted to his audiences until he finally was successful. The focus of this story is the concessions or accommodations Milk made in each campaign. In the first campaign, we would learn, for instance, that he refused to give up his jeans or to cut his long hair—his only concession was to pull his hair back into a ponytail.[18] For the second campaign, his accommodations grew:

he cut his hair, began wearing suits purchased second-hand from a dry cleaners, and gave up smoking marijuana and going to bath houses.[19] In his third campaign, to broaden his base of support, Milk presented himself as a conservative business-person.[20] And in the fourth campaign, Milk offered a different image yet—that of a true incumbent because of his knowledge of the city—even though he never had held office.[21] This scenario privileges the rhetor as politician and the deliberate choices he made to try to win election. That Milk was gay is secondary here to the focus on political adaptation.

If Milk's identity as a gay man is made the focus of the rhetorical situation, the story shifts in yet another way. The story told is that of a politician who achieved a "first" by becoming the first openly gay supervisor in San Francisco. He is "special" and "noteworthy" because of this "first," but that is as far as the story goes.[22] His gay identity is not seen as connected to his politics. In essence, he is a politician who, by the way, happens to be gay.

Yet another approach to this rhetorical situation might center on the audience and the ways voters ignored, were repulsed by, or celebrated Milk's honesty and openness about being gay. In this story, Milk as rhetor is given limited agency, and his audiences are given more; their perceptions control the situation because their reactions and votes determine Milk's political future. In this scenario, Milk becomes the object to the audience's agency: he is presented as having little choice but to respond to and deal with the homophobic hegemony of the times.

These various stories not only suggest different ways the rhetorical situation might be viewed, but they point to larger issues involved in the study of queer pub-lic address. They suggest that the rhetorical situation is complicated by the gay rhetor and that the approach of rhetorical scholars must be similarly complicated as well. To truly make public address theory queer—and not simply construct a theory about queers—requires attention to the complications that accompany the ways a queer rhetor manages a rhetorical situation. It is not enough, then, to treat Milk as a traditional politician, as the first scenario does, but telling the story with only a focus on the "firsts" he achieved as a gay politician is similarly distorting and tokenizing. The scenario featuring audience is also only a partial picture; it puts cul-tural stereotypes about homosexuality in charge of the rhetorical situation, reduc-ing the rhetor's agency to little or nothing.

Instead, the gay rhetor must be understood within a multitude of complex dimensions and even contradictions. The queer rhetor asks society to confront sex-uality and the place of identity issues in politics, which create a distinctive stand-point that needs to be part of how the rhetoric is understood and analyzed. A queer theory about Milk, then, will have Milk's gay identity as central rather than periph-eral to it. His gay sexuality will be considered a cultural and personal standpoint in its own right and not simply a "marginal" one juxtaposed to a "dominant, stable" heterosexuality.[23] That he did not hide his sexuality and even flaunted it also will need to be part of the story. And his exigence was not merely to get elected to office; it was to get elected to office as a gay man at a time when that was not considered a possibility.

Jennifer Terry, referring to her own role as an historian of homosexual subjectivity, uses the phrase "our presence under the present circumstances of widespread homophobia,"[24] which aptly describes the rhetorical situation Milk faced. Milk talked a lot about the city of San Francisco and how it could be made better at the same time that he talked about how to end oppression against gays and lesbians. Every nuance of audience reaction thus was constantly filtered through—but not confined to—Milk's gay identity. This was always a complication on the exigence that Milk would not allow his audience to ignore.

Queerness, then, permeates Milk's rhetorical situation, and his story demands to be told in a way that makes that queerness central. I argue that when the rhetorical situation is framed in this way, Milk's discourse emerges as a "deviant subjectivity" that "looks not only for how subjects are produced and policed, but how they are resistant and excessive in the very discourses from which they emerge."[25] I will argue that his approach constitutes a rhetoric of contradiction that effectively created spaces and openings into which the gay/lesbian perspective could be acknowledged and discussed—not just by Milk, but by all of the communities that comprise San Francisco. His campaign discourse intervened into and disrupted the hegemony of San Francisco politics, creating what Terry calls an "effective history."[26] Taking this label from Foucault, Terry defines *effective history* as attention not to some "ideal continuity" of events but to *effects* that are manifestations of ruptures and discontinuities in history.[27] An effective history traces the conditions under and means by which marginalized rhetors find moments for self-expression and self-representation.

As such, an effective history is not so much an alternative narrative as a place that notes the possibilities and limitations that arise in the jarring juxtaposition where margins push against the dominant culture. Milk's campaigns intervene in just such a way, offering traces or effects of the conditions, structures, and possibilities of queer in the study of public address. These effects contain powerful contradictions that exist side by side: effective political maneuvering that gained Milk election within the political mainstream juxtaposed with disruptions of such magnitude that his death was the result. Ultimately, then, I argue that Milk's rhetoric creates a space in which new opportunities emerge within the disruptions that create such space.

Managing the Rhetorical Situation

Milk's campaign discourse reveals two pairs of strategies that both created and managed a place of contradiction: (1) antithesis and synthesis and (2) enactment and violation. As contradictory strategies, these reveal the manner in which Milk played on and with his deviance to challenge the political status quo in San Francisco. In combination, these strategies allowed Milk not simply to negotiate his gay identity in relation to politics—what would be a traditionally political accommodation—but also to create a queer subjectivity that used contradiction to forge a new rhetorical space that both resisted and transcended traditional political expectations.

Antithesis and Synthesis

Milk's first pair of strategies was antithesis and synthesis. He consistently paired opposing or contrasting ideas in such a way to ensure that the contradictions themselves remained paramount. In his first campaign, he presented himself as an outsider, marginalized in every possible way because he was gay, Jewish, and a newcomer to San Francisco and to politics. Despite his outsider status, however, he also presented himself as capable of representing or standing for all of the outsider positions: "I stand for all those who feel that the government no longer understands the individual and no longer respects individual rights."[28] He concentrated on being the outsider while simultaneously turning himself into the universal insider able to compete in the mainstream world. His campaign slogan, "Milk Has Something for Everybody," articulated his universal appeal—an appeal constructed on his outsider status.

Milk also incorporated antithesis in his use of human billboards, a tactic in his first campaign that became a favorite throughout all four. Rows of gay men lined the streets of San Francisco holding signs bearing the legend "Milk for Supervisor."[29] In this way, Milk took one of the city's most invisible groups in terms of city politics and made it highly visible. Long before "We are Everywhere" became a gay/lesbian mantra, Milk demonstrated its truth indirectly as a group ignored as a political force came out in force to become "placeholders" for Milk's campaign signs.

In his second campaign for supervisor, Milk continued his oxymoronic pairing, this time with gays and labor unions. The Teamsters' Union had been attempting, with limited success, to effect a boycott of Coors beer because of Coors's refusal to sign a labor contract.[30] Milk convinced the gay bars in San Francisco to boycott Coors beer—an action crucial to the boycott's success—and one that earned Milk the endorsement of several labor unions. One labor leader's comment is typical and shows how unusual and oppositional this pairing was: "*Whaddaya mean you're thinkin' of endorsin' this Harvey Milk guy? For Chrissakes, I'm supposed to go back to work and tell the guys we endorsed some goddamn fruit for a supervisor.*"[31] Milk showed his ability to identify with blue-collar workers—often viewed as the antithesis of the gay man—during his campaigns. A labor leader supporter summarized his appeal: "A lot of our guys think gays are little leprechauns tip-toeing to florist shops, but Harvey can sit on a steel beam and talk to some ironworker who is a mean sonuvabitch and probably beats his wife when he has a few too many beers, but who would sit there and talk to Harvey like they knew each other for years."[32]

Also in this campaign, Milk was given—or perhaps gave himself—the title of the "unofficial mayor of Castro Street."[33] The terms *unofficial* and *mayor* are strikingly antithetical and further Milk's ability to present himself as someone who is capable of bringing together characteristically oppositional attributes. In this case, he preserved his outsider status—his unofficial status—while also suggesting his prominent role in the life of the city: he had started the highly successful Castro Street fair, revived a neighborhood business association, wrote a column for the *Bay Area Reporter*, and registered two thousand new voters in the city.

Milk juxtaposed two additional antithetical categories—insider/outsider and human/machine—in his third campaign, the run for the Democratic nomination for state assembly. The focus of his campaign was on the insider/outsider, with Milk reversing the meanings of the two in his campaign rhetoric. He consistently described himself as the true insider to politics while making his opponent, Art Agnos, the outsider: "He's been an observer, not a participant, and has never really experienced the daily fight for survival that most of us have to face. I'm not being accusatory here—in some respects, I may be envious. I'm a small business man and I'm well aware of the uncertainties of the economy, exactly what the 'inflationary spiral' means when I'm forced to raise prices to my customers, and how taxes can eat into your earnings."[34]

Milk similarly paired the antithetical terms of *human* and *machine* in this third campaign, which he made the core of his campaign slogan, "Milk versus the Machine." Milk argued that the political machine—and not the people of the state of California—was making the decisions about who would run for office: "The overriding issue is simply: do the people . . . that make up the Sixteenth Assembly District have the right of political self-determination—or, can the machine take that right away? Machines operate on oil and grease; they're dirty, dehumanizing, and too often unresponsive to any needs by those of the operators."[35] By pitting himself against the machine and focusing on his human agency, Milk also implicitly managed the unspoken belief that gays and lesbians are deviant and thus somehow "less than" human.

In Milk's final and successful run for supervisor, he took the term *incumbent* for himself, in spite of never having held office—another instance of antithesis. Milk saw himself as the incumbent in terms of the things that mattered—knowledge of the city, city involvement, and experience with its daily challenges—even though technically he did not qualify as an incumbent.[36]

For Milk, antithesis was a consistent campaign strategy and cornerstone of his rhetoric. Whether linking large concepts such as insider and outsider or creating specific oxymorons—such as the "unofficial mayor of Castro Street"—his campaigns were grounded in the juxtaposition of unlikely and contradictory ideas. By allowing contradictions to exist side by side, Milk's rhetoric opened a space for different discursive possibilities than those that previously had existed in San Francisco politics. These possibilities did not reject or embrace either the straight political hegemony or a resistant gay discourse. Instead Milk's rhetoric intervened between these oppositions, allowing for new combinations to emerge.

With the incorporation of synthesis as a rhetorical strategy, Milk continued to work with the binary categorizations that he often brought together in antithesis—whether gay/straight, insider/outsider, visible/invisible, insider/outsider, unofficial/official. With synthesis, however, he transcended the tension between oppositions. In his first campaign, his creation of a coalition of "outsiders" is one form this synthesis assumed. Milk did not simply assert his outsider role, but offered himself as the candidate who would represent all marginalized groups. Also in the first campaign, the opportunity for synthesis presented itself when an ideologically conservative Arab Republican businessman took one of Milk's flyers, crossed out Milk's name, and inserted his own. Rather than get angry, Milk called a press conference and used it as an opportunity to point out that he must be doing a good job of bridging ideologies if someone whose politics were so different from his could use his campaign flyer without revision.[37] As a final example, Milk developed a flyer that listed his position on thirteen city issues on the left-hand side and the present board's stance on each on the right-hand side of the page. In the middle, complete with blank lines, was a column titled, "Write in Your Position."[38] Milk encouraged his audience to engage in synthesis themselves after examining his position and the often antithetical one of the current board of supervisors. Milk took the opportunities offered to move beyond dichotomies and to focus on what could be fashioned from their juxtaposition.

Milk's ability to manage and bridge dichotomies did not occur with simply the content of his campaigns. He also positioned himself as rhetor between the dichotomies of agent and victim, often striking a pose that contained both at once. This tactic was evident in his first campaign, when he presented himself as the outsider, the victim, the one left out of city politics. His announcement of his candidacy offers one example of this stance: "Having a small business and being one of thousands of people whom no one in government will listen to, I have decided to run for supervisor as a person."[39] That he was running anyway, despite his outsider position, immediately removed him from the victim position; that he saw himself as the representative of the underrepresented suggested a strong sense of agency: "Give me your support and I'll fight for you. . . . I'll fight for you because I am you."[40]

In the assembly campaign, Milk moved between his outsider stance and his own sense of agency. He presented himself as victim when talking about the political machine that ran the state; he presented himself with considerable agency when he self-represented as a business leader who was a true insider in terms of what was important to the people of the state. In his final campaign, he even created situations of victimage in terms of his past to highlight his maverick status and its resulting agency even more. For example, in one campaign flyer, he said he had been fired for failing to play by the rules: "Harvey was appointed to the Board of Permit Appeals, the first gay person appointed to a city commission. Later he was fired for his political independence."[41] In fact, Mayor Moscone had told him he could not keep his seat if he chose to run for the assembly. Similarly, in describing his navy background, Milk implied that he had been dishonorably discharged from the service because he was gay, when in actuality he completed his term of enlistment without incident: "Harvey Milk was a decorated deep-sea rescue diver during the Korean War. Then the Navy found out he was gay."[42]

In each of these cases, Milk placed himself in a position of victimage while simultaneously bestowing on himself agency. He preserved his outsider persona, which allowed a considerable degree of political independence, while also overcoming victimage in a strong assertion of self. Thus he acknowledged and in a sense maintained both the roles of victim and agent, preserving the history of oppression as a critical starting point for gay men and lesbians but not a place to stay.

The strategies of antithesis and synthesis set the tone for the ways in which Milk constructed a queer rhetoric. He used antithesis to both exceed and resist the limits of the rhetorical situation he faced; he used synthesis to bring together elements in new juxtapositions. Together they demonstrate how Milk shook up the existing worldview by unsettling categories and putting them together in unexpected ways. His disruptions of the norm and creation of a queer sensibility are evident in his second pair of strategies as well—enactment and violation.

Enactment and Violation

Enactment, defined by bell hooks as "the lived practice of interaction,"[43] was evident in that Milk consistently enacted or served as an example of his politics. He did what he believed in, and he did what he said he was going to do. For the most part, this assumed the form of attending to and meeting basic human needs—those often ignored by the political mainstream. In his first campaign, he set the stage for the form his enactment would take when he described his vision for San Francisco: "San Francisco can start right now to become number one. . . . We can start overnight. We don't have to wait for budgets to be passed, surveys to be made, political wheelings and dealings . . . for it takes no money . . . it takes no compromising to give people their rights . . . it takes no money to respect the individual. It takes no political deal to give people freedom. It takes no survey to remove repression."[44]

Milk also made clear that, for him, the key to the city was its neighborhoods: "The American Dream starts with the neighborhoods. If we wish to rebuild our cities, we must first rebuild our neighborhoods. And to do that, we must understand that the quality of life is more important than the standard of living."[45]

The specific proposals Milk offered to enact his vision for the city were simple and direct, and in each case, they appreciably would improve the quality of life for its citizens. Milk proposed, for example, that cars be banned in the "downtown core area"; the current board of supervisors, in contrast, supported a plan for more garages.[46] Milk suggested that city officials be required to ride Muni (San Francisco's rapid transit system) to work every day. According to Milk, "It's the only way that the people of San Francisco will ever get better Muni service."[47]

By the time of his second campaign, Milk personally had worked to enact the vision he had for the city, starting with his own neighborhood, the Castro. As a local business owner in the Castro, he threw himself into efforts to make it a place where people talked to their neighbors and talked through issues and problems. He organized the Castro Street fair and resurrected the Castro Village Association, both of which fit his image of what a neighborhood' should be.

Milk's decision to run for the California assembly—his third campaign—also conveyed his commitment to enactment. When he learned that the Democratic candidate has been selected far in advance of the election, he ran to enact his vision of an open political system and provide a true alternative to the machine. And when he did win election to the board of supervisors, he did not abandon his concern with the basic rights and issues that make a city livable. He gave top priority to fixing potholes and was responsible for the installation of more than fifty new stop signs in his district. The two bills he managed to get passed before his death were a pooper-scooper ordinance and a gay-rights bill: "Harvey's political philosophy was never more complicated than the issue of dogshit; government should solve people's basic problems."[48]

Perhaps Milk's most important form of enactment, however, was being out as gay. Milk did not hide his sexuality in any way; in fact, it was crucial to his cultivation of contradiction. By making his gay identity the subject of attention, discussion, and humor, he articulated the notion of queer rhetor for his audiences. Beginning with his first campaign, Milk listed *gay* as among the outsider characteristics he proudly brought to the political table in San Francisco, and he used gay supporters in very public ways in his campaigns—with his human billboards a striking example. His marshalling of the gay bars to support the Coors boycott in his second campaign also meant that he was very public and vocal about the existence of and concerns of the gay community. In the assembly campaign, Milk developed his "hope" speech, in which he made the disenfranchisement of gays and lesbians the epitome of what it means to be disenfranchised: "And the young gay people in the Altoona, Pennsylvanias and the Richmond, Minnesotas who are coming out. . . . The only thing they have to look forward to is hope. And you have to give them

hope. . . . Without hope, not only gays, but the blacks, the seniors, the handicapped
. . . will give up. And if you help elect . . . more gay people, that gives a green light
to all who feel disenfranchised, a green light to move forward. It means hope to a
nation that has given up because if a gay person makes it, the doors are open to
everyone."[49] No matter what other issues he was addressing, Milk ended with this
reference to gays and lesbians. He did not let the subject lie, even when speaking
on issues that had nothing to do with being gay, and he refused to separate his gay
identity from other issues.

When Milk became a city supervisor, he continued to be extremely vocal about
the gay community. Perhaps the fact that he now held political office made him
even more adamant about this form of enactment: "I'm tired of the silence, so I'm
going to talk about it. And I want you to talk about it."[50] He suggested that if "every
Gay person were to come out only to his/her own family, friends, neighbors and fellow workers, within days the entire state would discover that we are not the stereotypes generally assumed."[51]

The introduction of Proposition 6 upped the ante even more in terms of Milk's
stance on coming out, giving it the status of a moral imperative for him. This ballot initiative, introduced about the time Milk took office, would allow school boards
to fire teachers who practiced, advocated, or indicated an acceptance of homosexuality.[52] For Milk, coming out became the ultimate enactment of an authentic personal and political response to this repressive measure: "Gay brothers and sisters,
what are *you* going to do about it? You must *come out.* Come out . . . to your parents. . . . I know that it is hard and will hurt them but think about how they will
hurt you in the voting booth! *Come out to your friends* . . . if they indeed they [*sic*]
are your friends. *Come out* to your neighbors . . . to your fellow workers . . . to the
people *who work* where you eat and shop. . . . *Come out* only to the people you
know, *and who know you.* Not to anyone else. But once and for all, break down the
myths, destroy the lies and distortions."[53]

Milk's advocacy of coming out, then, enacted the vision he had for society in
which the closet no longer was acceptable for any reason: "So break out of yours
today—tear the damn thing down once and for all!"[54] Through enactment, he transformed the constraints of the closet into resources, both personal and political, that
he believed could transform the social landscape.

At the same time that Milk consistently enacted his worldview and especially his
gay identity, he also made sure to do the unexpected—to disrupt, deviate, and violate. Just as with the antithesis/synthesis pairing, he rhetorically chose to assert and
resist, to show he could play the game but chose not to. In the first campaign, his
use of violation as a strategy manifested both nonverbally and verbally. He refused
to dress the part of a politician—he did not dress up or cut his long hair—and
instead wore blue jeans and pulled his hair back into a ponytail. He repeatedly
made remarks that would be the kiss of death for most politicians simply because

of how outrageous they were. Michael Wong, who ultimately became a Milk supporter, described their first meeting and how such statements affected his image of
Milk: "I had heard from the so-called gay leaders—Jim Foster and the Alice B. Tok-
las Gay Democratic Club—that this guy was a nut. I was very wary of even talking
to him. But in the course of the conversation, I was really impressed with the issues
he brought up. . . . But halfway through this conversation, . . . Harvey told us that
he thought . . . that some father who learned that he's homosexual will come out
and shoot at him and he'll survive the shooting but that'll give him so much sympathetic publicity that he'll win on that. . . . And then I thought, Jim Foster was
right—this guy is a nut."[55]

As another example, in his second campaign, he successfully brought gays
together with labor unions to boycott Coors beer—a pairing that violated traditional political alliances. Milk's irreverence about and willingness to violate traditional political decorum earned him considerable negative publicity. Milk knew,
however, that even this kind of press kept his name before the public. "Sticks and
stones may break my bones, but just spell my name right"[56] was his response; he
preferred to be noticeable and thus remembered on Election Day rather than appropriate and forgotten.

Violation, then, features the disruptions of the rhetorical situation just as enactment fully offered who Milk was to that situation. Both strategies were necessary
for Milk to create a queer rhetorical space that simultaneously expressed an exuberant deviance but also managed it, that pushed at and resisted the boundaries
of traditional politics while allowing him to enter that system. The contradictory
forces he fostered wrested a space of contradiction out of the exigence to create the
possibility of a new and queer rhetorical space for San Francisco.

A Rhetoric of Contradiction

Harvey Milk's rhetorical strategies—antithesis versus synthesis and enactment versus violation—provide important clues to a queer rhetorical situation. These strategies embody the approach Milk used not simply to respond to a rhetorical situation,
but also to transform it—and in the process invite transformation on the part of his
audiences as well. This analysis also expands the theory of the rhetorical situation
to make it suitable for understanding the rhetorical dimensions of marginalized
situations and rhetors.

It is significant that Milk's rhetorical strategies simultaneously embodied and
challenged the oppositions that constructed the rhetorical situation in place when
Milk entered the scene. The situation of San Francisco politics was framed in
dichotomous terms: gay/straight, public/private, appropriate/inappropriate, open/
closed. From his first campaign, however, Milk refused to accept these boundaries.
He consistently acknowledged the boundaries of the dominant worldview and
stirred them up; he recognized the limits and at the same time crossed them. These

strategies allowed him to negotiate an opening—a rhetorical space for "both-and" rather than "either-or"—in which a different world could emerge. And it is in this particular combination of contradictory strategies that a queer rhetorical space emerges. It is as if the juxtaposition of contrasting strategies literally pushed open the boundaries of the straight political world so that Milk could pose different possibilities for it. According to Mary Alice Speke Ferdig, staying in contradiction—learning to "hold the paradox" and "stay in the heat" of the conversational tension that results—is the ideal climate for generating new points of view.[57] Milk's pairs of contrasting strategies created and managed a space in which the queer could become part of the San Francisco political landscape. Milk's use of contradictory strategies also accomplished a "normalizing" of gay identity. By *normalize*, I do not mean assimilate; Milk did not whitewash, deny, or distort his identity in any way, but he made his gay identity critical and at the same time just another part of who he was. He was different from some people because he was gay, but he was similar to many people in spite of being gay. In other words, Milk presented shifting and multiple framings of his identity at any one time and invited others to similarly consider the various ways they also negotiate and present their own identities to others. He refused static definitions in favor of shifting one to heighten the variety of perspectives available.

I argue that Milk's discursive space, with its expanding and shifting sense of space and identity and its embrace of contradictions, is at the core of a queer rhetoric that has at its core the potential to envision and act into situations in new ways. I propose that this rhetoric anticipates three possibilities in particular—a spirit of freedom, a spirit of identification, and a spirit of inclusion. I refer to these dimensions as *possibilities* to signal their ideal nature.[58] Each demands the collaboration and resistance that Milk accomplished with his contradictory strategies.

A Spirit of Freedom

First, a spirit of freedom emerged in the contradictions that defined Milk's queer rhetoric and the juxtapositions and disruptions that emerged. In the moments of contradiction, Milk offered participants the opportunity to attend to all of the ways their own identities and meanings could be shaken up; they were free to invent themselves in new ways, just as Milk himself was doing, usually to excess. At the same time, the sense of community similarly was released from homophobic constraint, and the collective exploration of new identities and meanings became possible. Milk valued the possibility of an engaging, distinctive, productive dialogue in which all freely participated in order to freely imagine, design, and construct a new vision of self and community.

Experimentation and exploration are important to the spirit of freedom as it played out in Milk's queer rhetoric. In a space that privileges contradiction, change, and uncertainty, openness to the expression and exploration of ideas is necessarily a value. All ideas, no matter how new or uncertain, can be proposed and made available in the community for consideration and reflection. This does not mean, of course, that all participants agreed with one another about the issues that emerged in the spaces Milk's rhetoric created. What is important is not agreement so much as the freeing up and fluidity of possibilities—new ways of thinking and behaving—that were not available before. This meant that some now would have the courage to speak a personal truth—to come out of the closet. For others, it meant letting others lead the lives of their own choosing, no matter how uncomfortable that might be. It also meant being free to be undecided—to remain in the contested queer space—unsure about how to interpret things and perhaps still uncomfortable with the very space itself. Although the process of exploration is not tidy, the process of growth has value, no matter how messy, tentative, and hesitant.

A Spirit of Identification

In addition to creating a sense of freedom, Milk's strategies created the possibility of identification with the queer experience. Milk's strategies were effective because they decentered the norms and boundaries of his audiences, and in the resulting imbalance his audience members were able more easily to hear and see new possibilities. Being at odds with the expected was normal for and valued in Milk's queer world, and he brought the experience to his campaign audiences. In this manner, Milk allowed his gay/lesbian audiences to find themselves acknowledged rhetorically because he presented their disequilibrium in his discourse. At the same time, his straight audiences were given the opportunity to experience rhetorically the tensions of the gay world—to occupy queer spectator positions. This position was one no longer at the "edge of culture" but rather one that participates in and resists that culture at the same time.[59] Milk's notion of identification, then, was a complex one, founded on disruption and disequilibrium rather than accommodation. He centered the queer experience and used it as the basis for identification with all of his audience members.

A Spirit of Inclusion

When there is freedom to discuss, acknowledge, understand, and identify with different points of view, a spirit of inclusion is a third possible outcome. There are no topics that cannot be spoken about, no desire to hide deviant dimensions, no effort at camouflage. Not all participants will agree with all positions, but their right to be in the conversation is accepted and valued. Milk's strategies ultimately encompassed gay and straight and valued all perspectives as necessary to a successful San Francisco. He folded the ends into a middle in a queer construct that was unexpected and full of possibility for resistance and transformation at the same time.

Milk's rhetorical strategies ultimately negotiated a different rhetorical situation, a queer rhetorical space, for his audience than the one in place when he first ran for office. His strategies deliberately challenged essentialist, hegemonic categories and replaced them with a complex world in which contradictions coexist and categories dissolve. Through his rhetoric, he constructed a queer world in which the possibilities of freedom, identification, and inclusion were privileged and could be used to co-construct a different meaning of community for San Francisco.

This does not mean, however, that everyone welcomed or appreciated the queer possibilities that Milk's discursive tactics created in the city. Ideally Milk's rhetoric of contradiction would bring the different constituencies of the city together in appreciation of the different ways to do life. But there always will be those for whom a different world is not an option because dialogue is threatening rather than liberating. In Milk's case, with four campaigns in the space of five years, there was some time—though not much—for the public to get used to his rhetorical approach. And no matter the benefits of a queer rhetoric in the abstract, it is a rhetoric built on the deliberate disruption of established ways of doing and being.

Not surprising, then, is that in actuality, there were many in Milk's audience who chose to focus on the disruptions his rhetoric caused rather than the possibilities it contained, who were afraid of rather than willing to embrace the contradiction and change inherent to his queering of the rhetorical situation. Dan White, of course, is the obvious example of this kind of response to Milk's rhetoric, and his assassination of Milk suggests the extreme outcomes possible with such rhetorical disruptions. Milk himself moved between seeing the possibilities and potential that disruption and deviance can create and understanding the risks. At times, he was convinced that discussion and debate could win anyone over, including White, yet throughout his life he had forebodings of an early violent death because of his frankness about his sexuality.[60] He told friends, for example, that he would not make it to fifty, and in fact he did not. When asked, in his first campaign, if he really thought he could win, he said he could because he would probably be shot by someone who hated gays, giving him sympathy votes in addition to gay and liberal votes. Most telling, Milk recorded three audiotapes a week after his election to supervisor to serve as his political will. One of these contains the passage: "If a bullet should enter my brain, let that bullet destroy every closet door."[61] Disruptions have considerable potential, but their very essence means they cannot be completely controlled.

Despite these limitations, Milk's approach to his rhetorical situation offers a model for queer public address that perhaps can be used as a template by other marginalized groups. He used the contradictory features of his own experience as a starting point to create a queer discursive space that contained, played with, and used deviance to create new possibilities. It is a space that simultaneously resisted but also managed and opened up possibilities of collaboration within a traditional political system. Milk's discursive practices suggest that traditional models of rhetoric can be expanded to encompass the rhetorical margins as well as the rhetorical mainstream. In the case of Bitzer's theory, I suggest that it is flexible enough to reveal the undercurrents and nuances of a rhetorical situation that are not evident in an initial or mainstream reading.

Whereas Bitzer envisioned a separation between rhetor and exigence—the rhetor addressed an exigence outside of self—his theory has proved useful in the situation of a gay rhetor whose identity complicates and becomes an additional exigence to the external constraints of achieving political office against a backdrop of homophobia. Just as Milk collapsed binaries into a new space, the theory of the rhetorical situation similarly can negotiate a queer rhetorical situation that collapses boundaries across exigence, audience, and rhetor. The queer space expects and achieves an integration of rhetor and audience by not simply addressing the exigence, but transforming it. Together rhetor and audience disrupt the traditional rhetorical situation and create another that is fluid, appreciative, and even audacious in its acceptance of a range of subject positions, strategies available to address issues, and outcomes allowed and envisioned. The result is a more nuanced, complete, and engaging picture of the marginalized rhetor in relation to the exigence and audience. Milk's story, then, shows how he first queered and then transformed the rhetorical situation he faced in San Francisco, the audiences he addressed, and ultimately the theory of rhetorical situation itself.

Notes

1. The ways I will use the words *queer* and *gay* in this chapter need to be addressed directly. Recognizing the many meanings attached to the term *queer*, I use it in the sense that De Lauretis does—"to mark a certain critical distance from . . . 'lesbian and gay' or 'gay and lesbian.'" Teresa Le Lauretis, "Queer Theory: Lesbian and Gay Sexualities. *An Introduction*," *Differences: A Journal of Feminist Cultural Studies* 3 (summer 1991): iv. I follow William Tierney's lead in seeing queer theory as disruptive, seeking to uncover and decode ideological norms and practices in terms of sexual identity and politics. William G. Tierney, *Academic Outlaws: Queer Theory and Cultural Studies in the Academy* (Thousand Oaks, Calif.: Sage, 1997), 35. For me, queer theory is a theoretical and academic stance that serves as a lens by which to problematize, deconstruct, transgress, and transcend gay, lesbian, bisexual, and transgendered identities. It is separate from the "life-styles, sexualities, sexual practices, communities, issues, publications, and discourses" (De Lauretis, v) that designate particular individuals—some of whom would identify with the queer label and others who would not. From this vantage point, I use the term *gay* when referring specifically to Harvey Milk and the phrase *gay/lesbian* to refer to the social movement for gay rights that became increasingly vocal and visible during his campaigns because these were the preferred labels of that era. I am well aware of the considerable differences in the experiences of lesbians and gay men and the difficulties of theorizing them collectively. In this study of Milk—a gay man—however, the gay male experience is predominant, and I prefer to use the terminology of his time to map the rhetorical situation as he conceptualized it. I will use *queer*, however, when I am imposing my critical frame of a queer rhetorical situation—when my focus is on the conceptual and critical deconstruction of Milk's discourse and situation.

2. For a summary of the different stages in the gay rights/gay liberation struggle, see Dudley Clendinen and Adam Nagourney, *Out for Good: The Struggle to Build a Gay Rights Movement in America* (New York: Simon and Schuster, 1999); for actual documents from gay liberation, see Mark Blasius and Shane Phelan, eds., *We Are Everywhere: A Historical Sourcebook of Gay and Lesbian Politics* (New York: Routledge, 1997); and Barry D. Adam, *The Rise of a Gay and Lesbian Movement* (Boston: Twayne, 1987). Randy Shilts, *The Mayor of Castro Street: The Life and Times of Harvey Milk* (New York: St. Martin's Press, 1982), also details the emergence and different manifestations of gay liberation as they intersected with Milk's career.

3. Despite the distinctive features of Milk's case, he is largely unknown today, even among gay men, for whom he could be expected to be a model and source of inspiration. My own work on Milk is all I could locate in terms of scholarship about him. See Karen A. Foss, "Harvey Milk: 'You Have to Give Them Hope,'" *Journal of the West* 27 (April 1988): 75–81, and "The Logic of Folly in the Political Campaigns of Harvey Milk," in *Queer Words, Queer Images: Communication and the Construction of Homosexuality,* ed. R. Jeffrey Ringer (New York: NYU Press, 1994), 7–29. Popular articles available about Milk today include his listing as one of a hundred heroes by *Time* magazine (http://www.time.com/time/time100/heroes/profil/milk01.html); and an article published on the twentieth anniversary of his death. See "Why Milk Is Still Fresh," *Advocate,* November 10, 1998, available at http://www.findarticles.com/m1589/1998_Nov_10/54879326/p1/article.jhtml. Milk is also the subject of a play; see Dan Pruitt and Patrick Hutchison, "The Harvey Milk Show," in *Staging Gay Lives: An Anthology of Contemporary Gay Theater,* ed. John M. Clum (Boulder, Colo.: Westview, 1996), 5–62.

4. Lloyd Bitzer, "The Rhetorical Situation," *Philosophy and Rhetoric* 1 (winter 1968): 4.

5. Ibid., 8.

6. Ibid., 6.

7. This effort is certainly not the first to reconfigure, extend, or elaborate notions of Bitzer's rhetorical situation. See, for example, Richard L. Larson, "Lloyd Bitzer's 'Rhetorical Situation' and the Classification of Discourse: Problems and Implications," *Philosophy and Rhetoric* 3 (summer 1970): 165–68; Richard E. Vatz, "The Myth of the Rhetorical Situation," *Philosophy and Rhetoric* 6 (summer 1973): 154–61; Scott Consigny, "Rhetoric and Its Situations," *Philosophy and Rhetoric* 7 (summer 1974): 175–86; and John H. Patton, "Causation and Creativity in Rhetorical Situations: Distinctions and Implications," *Quarterly Journal of Speech* 65 (February 1979): 36–55.

8. For background material on Milk see Shilts, *The Mayor of Castro Street;* and Foss, "Harvey Milk."

9. Shilts, *The Mayor of Castro Street,* 71.

10. Ibid., 90.

11. Ibid., 79.

12. Ibid., 128.

13. "Milk Will Run: Loses Permit Board Seat," *San Francisco Chronicle,* March 10, 1976, 6.

14. "The Complete Election Results," *San Francisco Chronicle,* November 10, 1977, 4.

15. For information about the killings, see "Another Day of Death," *Time* (December 11, 1978): 24–26; "Mayor Was Hit 4 Times," *San Francisco Chronicle,* November 28, 1978, 1, 12;

and Mike Weiss, *Double Play: The San Francisco City Hall Killings* (Reading, Mass.: Addison-Wesley, 1984).

16. For information about White's trial, see Michael Weiss, "Trial and Error," *Rolling Stone*, (July 12, 1979): 47–49; and Katy Butler and Randy Shilts, "Big S. F. Protests against Dan White," *San Francisco Chronicle*, January 7, 1984, 2. The film *The Times of Harvey Milk*, produced by Richard Schmeichen and directed and coproduced by Robert Epstein (Cinecom International Films, 1986), also gives considerable coverage to the killings, White's trial, and the response of the gay/lesbian community to his sentence. For more on White's suicide, see "S. F. Mayor's Killer Dies in His Garage," *San Francisco Chronicle*, October 22, 1985, 1.

17. W. Barnett Pearce, *Communication and the Human Condition* (Carbondale: Southern Illinois University Press, 1989), 21.

18. Shilts, *The Mayor of Castro Street*, 76.

19. Ibid., 80.

20. Ibid., 143–44.

21. Harvey Milk, "The Campaign: General Notes," 1977, 1, Harvey Milk Archives.

22. The problem of "first woman" news stories is discussed by Barbara F. Luebke, "'First Woman' Stories: A Sign of Progress or More Special Treatment?" *Women's Studies in Communication* 9 (spring 1986): 30–37. Luebke found that, because of such stories, "women continue to be thought of as a special class of people, still needing special treatment." She suggests that such stories are equally damaging for "blacks in the Sixties, women in the Seventies, and Hispanics in the Eighties" (30). Gay men and lesbians easily could have been added to the list.

23. De Lauretis, "Queer Theory," iii.

24. Jennifer Terry, "Theorizing Deviant Historiography," *Differences: A Journal of Feminist Cultural Studies* 3 (summer 1991): 55.

25. Ibid., 55, 57.

26. Ibid., 56.

27. Ibid., 56.

28. "Shopowner Runs for Supervisor," *San Francisco Examiner*, 27 July 1973, 3.

29. Shilts, *The Mayor of Castro Street*, 101.

30. Ibid., 83.

31. Ibid., 95.

32. Ibid., 97–98.

33. Ibid., 87.

34. Harvey Milk, "Milk Forum: My Concept of a Legislator," *Bay Area Reporter*, 27 May 1976.

35. Harvey Milk, "Statement of Harvey Milk: Candidate for the 16th Assembly District," 9 March 1976, Harvey Milk Archives, San Francisco, California.

36. Milk, "The Campaign: General Notes."

37. Shilts, *The Mayor of Castro Street*, 78.

38. "S.F.'s Strange Alliance," *San Francisco Chronicle*, September 22, 1973; and Harvey Milk, "An Open Letter to the Mayor of San Francisco," September 22, 1973, Harvey Milk Archives.

39. "Shopowner Runs for Supervisor," 3.

40. "Harvey Milk: Harvey Comes Down On: The Waste of Taxpayers' Money," 1975, Harvey Milk Archives.

41. Harvey Milk, "The Day after Election Day Is Too Late to Find Out Where Your Candidate Stands on the Issues," 1977, Harvey Milk Archives.

42. Milk, "The Day after Election Day Is Too Late."

43. bell hooks, *Teaching to Transgress: Education as the Practice of Freedom* (New York: Routledge, 1994), 48.

44. Harvey Milk, "Address to the Joint International Longshoremen and Warehousemen's Union of San Francisco and to the Lafayette Club," September 10, 1973, 2, Harvey Milk Archives.

45. Shilts, *The Mayor of Castro Street*, 353.

46. Harvey Milk, "Harvey Milk for Supervisor: 'Positions' Paper," 1973, Harvey Milk Archives.

47. "New Ploy: Make VIPs Ride Muni," *San Francisco Examiner*, September 28, 1973, 4.

48. Shilts, *The Mayor of Castro Street*, 203.

49. Harvey Milk, "The Hope Speech," in Shilts, *The Mayor of Castro Street*, 363.

50. Harvey Milk, "That's What America Is," in Shilts, *The Mayor of Castro Street*, 366.

51. Harvey Milk, *Coast to Coast Times*, June 13, 1978, Harvey Milk Archives.

52. For information about Milk's campaign against Proposition 6, see Harvey Milk, "Milk Forum: Gay Freedom Day Speech," *Bay Area Reporter*, July 6, 1978, 11; Stephen Hall, "Fiery Clash over Prop. 6," *San Francisco Chronicle*, September 16, 1978, 7; and Eugene Robinson, "A Wild Debate: Briggs vs. Milk," *San Francisco Chronicle*, October 12, 1978, 6.

53. Milk, "That's What America Is," 368.

54. Ibid.

55. Michael Wong, interviewed by David Lamble in *Harvey Milk Remembered*, an audio documentary compiled and produced by David Lamble, San Francisco, Calif., 1979.

56. Shilts, *The Mayor of Castro Street*, 78. Ironically, when Milk finally did win election to the board of supervisors, the *San Francisco Chronicle* spelled his name *Nilk* rather than *Milk*. See Jerry Burns, "New S. F. District Supervisors: Six Incumbents Are Elected," *San Francisco Chronicle*, November 9, 1977, 1.

57. Mary Alice Speke Ferdig, "Exploring the Social Construction of Complex Self-Organizing Change: A Study of Emerging Change in the Regulation of Nuclear Power," Ph.D. dissertation, Benedictine University, 2000.

58. I am indebted to Ferdig for the terminology of "spirit" by which to label these qualities.

59. De Lauretis, "Queer Theory," iii.

60. Milk's attitude about White was optimistic: "'As the years pass, the guy can be educated. . . . Everyone can be reached. Everyone can be educated and helped.'" See Shilts, *The Mayor of Castro Street*, 185.

61. Milk's forebodings of death are described in Shilts, *The Mayor of Castro Street*, 33–34; his line about getting sympathy votes after being shot by a homophobic voter are described by Shilts in *The Mayor of Castro Street*, 70. Milk's political will can also be found as an appendix in Shilts, *The Mayor of Castro Street*, 372–75.

MY OLD KENTUCKY HOMO

Abraham Lincoln, Larry Kramer, and the Politics of Queer Memory

Charles E. Morris III

O Memory! Thou midway world / 'Twixt earth and paradise, / Where things decayed and loved ones lost / In dreamy shadows rise, // And, freed from all that's earthly vile, / Seem hallowed, pure, and bright, / Like scenes in some enchanted isle, / All bathed in liquid light.

> Abraham Lincoln, "My Childhood-Home I See Again,"
> in *Collected Works of Abraham Lincoln*, ed. Roy P. Basler

The sacred thing is *par excellence* that which the profane should not touch, and cannot touch with impunity.

> Emile Durkheim,
> *The Elementary Forms of Religious Life*

Nearly vanquished by the ravages of AIDS, National Book Award–winner Paul Monette somehow mustered the requisite fortitude for his last sojourn to the nation's capital, so that he might join his brethren in April 1993 for their March on Washington. Too debilitated to participate fully, he garnered energy enough to fulfill those obligations he deemed most significant to the symbolic advancement of the cause. And so he stood at the feet of Lincoln. His reflections on this occasion bear mentioning in full:

> There is nothing to match the Lincoln, in America anyway, for noble proportion and spiritual lift. On the wall to the left is the Gettysburg Address; on the right the Second Inaugural. *With malice toward none, with charity for all.* I suddenly needed to stand in the spot where Marian Anderson sang her Easter concert, barred from Independence Hall by the D.A.R. . . . . All under the eyes of Lincoln, eighty years after the Emancipation Proclamation. Another quarter century later, and the tempered gaze of Lincoln—warrior and wise man—bore witness to the passion of Dr. King. I didn't think the

Lincoln of my understanding would have any trouble equating the Civil Rights struggle of people of color with the latter-day dreams of the gay and lesbian movement. There's too much compelling evidence in his own life—the bed he shared for four years with Joshua Speed above the general store in Springfield; the breakdown he suffered when family duties sent them apart—of the "dear love of comrades." In any case, I was choked with tears and in awe to be there. . . . And oh, how we needed a Lincoln to stand for equal justice and bind us all together again.[1]

In Monette's memoir we find an articulation of public memory itself: a purposeful engagement of the past, forged symbolically, profoundly constitutive of identity, community, and moral vision, inherently consequential in its ideological implications, and very often the fodder of political conflagration. That Monette would find both universal and particular value in this American icon—Lincoln's eloquence, monument—is not surprising. As his recuperation of Anderson and King suggests, our history is, in one sense, a chronicle of those, perhaps especially oppressed Americans, who have found solace and inspiration in Lincoln's rather malleable legacy.

Noteworthy is the revolutionary mettle potentially derived from such mnemonic encounters. As David Blight has written of Frederick Douglass's appropriation of Lincoln and the Civil War, "Historical memory . . . was the prize in a struggle between rival versions of the past, a question of will, of power, of persuasion. The historical memory of any transforming or controversial event emerges from cultural and political competition, from the choice to confront the past and to debate and manipulate its meaning."[2] Monette understood well what African Americans before him conceived of as memory's political grounds for cultural transformation. Scott Sandage has observed, "Black protestors refined a politics of memory at the Lincoln Memorial. Within the sacred, national space of the memorial, activists perfected a complex ritual of mass politics, one that exploited the ambiguities of cherished American values to circumvent opposition, unify coalitions, and legitimate black voices in national politics."[3] The political struggle between rival versions of Lincoln's queer memory is the subject of this chapter.

A dying Monette could only articulate a fleeting if hopeful vision of Lincoln's memory as an animating force that might bind gays to each other and to national identity. His comrade Larry Kramer—whom Monette once described as "more than a witness, more than a leader, in his own way like the Elie Wiesel who stood on the heath tearing his hair"[4]—soon did more. In February 1999, Kramer—author, playwright, father of AIDS activism, and notorious polemicist—would transform Monette's queer vision into the struggle Blight and Sandage describe. Those familiar with Kramer's penchant for political theater might have expected his "outing" of Lincoln in a speech at the University of Wisconsin to be quickly dismissed as merely the latest expression of his creative propagandistic imagination. For residents of Springfield, Illinois, and Lincoln scholars, however, Kramer's gay public memory of the Great Emancipator constituted a salvo that incited homosexual panic, exposing a cultural fault line implicating rhetoric, historiography, public memory, and queer politics.

As I will explain in this chapter, the "revolution" of memory attempted by Kramer illustrates the complex dynamics initiated when public memory and sexuality collide, allowing us to examine these explosive components as they are marshaled in a symbolic contest for the communal and national meanings of historical, and therefore contemporary, identity, community, and politics. That contest reveals much about historiography as a "regime of the normal," the wages of official memory, and the prospects of a queer past.[5]

Queer Memory and Its Discontents

I use the word "revolution" carefully and deliberately for what it suggests about memory and gay (male) identity in American culture, and its potential for a queer present and future.[6] In a rudimentary sense, what is described here is a deliberate *turn toward* memory in a subculture for which public memory itself is defined more by absence and negation than presence and affirmation. Often fractured by sexual practice, generation, race, class, and organization, haunted still by stigma, disease, and the legacy of the closet, and hindered by institutional and cultural amnesia, gay men often find memory remote, debilitated, irrelevant. For many, a preliberation past seems too obscure or ambiguous, too closeted, insufficiently political or insufficiently queer to be usable.[7] Martin Duberman argues, "The decades preceding Stonewall . . . continue to be regarded by most gays and lesbians as some vast Neolithic wasteland—and this, despite the efforts of pioneering historians . . . to fill the landscape of those years with vivid, politically astute personalities."[8]

If we consider the last two decades of the twentieth century, AIDS has contributed profoundly to the material and political depletion of public memory. For example, the AIDS Quilt, perhaps the most powerfully symbolic gay memorial, poignantly and vibrantly remembers lost lives and community, yet at the same time represents a memory void: a lost generation of memory agents who serve as markers of a gay male past but speak as eloquently of their incapacity to convey and preserve that past.[9] Those lost to AIDS create a memory void in another sense by undermining the will to remember in an ongoing context of the disease. As Kramer argues, "How do I know our AIDS dead are forgotten? Because so many gay men and lesbians and the gay movement have forgotten AIDS, do not want to remember it is still here."[10]

Moreover, during the 1990s, Christopher Castiglia explains, AIDS resulted in "the increased normalization of sexual representation and the concomitant refashioning of intimate memory brought about by years of right-wing politics and AIDS phobia, which are orchestrated to obliterate memory by re-creating the values of the 'sexual revolution' as deadly and infantile, irresponsible and narcissistic, anything but revolutionary."[11] This "counternostalgia," as Castiglia calls it, practiced especially by neoconservative gay journalists, enacted a "form of enforced amnesia" that severed gay men from the "hedonistic trauma of the gay past," consequently "cutting off gay men from sexual memories that provide alternative models of public intimacy and political union."[12]

Kramer offers his own explanation of the diminution of gay memory: "'To write a history composed mostly of events like this [oppression of gays] is a depressing undertaking. I suspect there is much less joy than sorrow buried in our graves.'"[13] But in those graves Kramer saw the very bonds of gay identity and community, a vital past that, although often ignored, must be remembered if that community is to prosper in the future.[14] Thus Lincoln's embodiment in gay public memory emerged viscerally in Kramer's lecture, "Our Gay President," at the University of Wisconsin's Midwest GLBT College Conference in February 1999. For the edification and inspiration of a relatively small crowd, Kramer boldly claimed to have new documentary evidence that clarified the nuances of a longstanding and fragmentary narrative regarding the nearly four years Abraham Lincoln and Kentucky merchant Joshua Speed spent as young bedfellows in Springfield, Illinois.

Abe and Joshua

To appreciate Kramer's fulgurous contribution to this tale, its general contours and controversial elements must briefly be recounted.[15] An aspiring lawyer and politician, twenty-eight-year-old Abraham Lincoln nevertheless arrived penniless in Springfield in April 1837. Already deeply in debt, Lincoln seemed crestfallen over the cost of seventeen-dollar bedding in twenty-two-year-old Joshua Speed's general store, which touched the proprietor: "The tone of his voice was so melancholy that I felt for him. I looked up at him, and I thought then as I think now, that I never saw so gloomy a face. I said to him: 'The contraction of so small a debt, seems to affect you so deeply, I think I can suggest a plan by which you will be able to attain your end, without incurring any debt. I have a very large room, and a very large double bed in it; which you are perfectly welcome to share if you choose.'" Lincoln's decision was swift. After immediately climbing the stairs to the bedroom, he returned, "a face beaming with pleasure and smiles," exclaiming, "Well Speed I'm moved."[16]

The two bachelors slept in the same bed through the spring of 1841. Such an arrangement was quite common at the time, as historians are quick to observe, but it is not too fanciful to suggest that that bed might be read as a metonymy for their intense emotional bond, which could not be equaled during their years together.[17] They were, even by conservative estimate, "something like soul mates."[18] Lincoln's friend and future bodyguard Ward Lamon called Speed "the most intimate friend

Mr. Lincoln ever had."[19] William Herndon, roommate, friend, and Lincoln biographer, balked jealously at Nicolay and Hay's claim that Speed was Lincoln's *only intimate friend*, but nevertheless conceded that "Lincoln loved this man more than any one dead or living."[20] On the eve of Speed's marriage, an event that marked the final emotional juncture in their friendship, Lincoln wrote, "You know my desire to befriend you is everlasting—that I will never cease, while I know how to do any thing."[21]

Their friendship derived from not only material generosity, but also a shared interest in law, politics, poetry, and a variety of other subjects, some of which they discussed (along with bawdy tales) at great length on many evenings with male friends at Speed's store.[22] Perhaps especially they shared their mutual anxieties regarding women. Both men, despite their numerous attractions and courtships, seemed to struggle intensely with the idea of physical intimacy with women.[23] Lincoln apparently fell in love twice (if not three times) during the late 1830s, only to thwart engagement plans with Mary Owens and Mary Todd. Charles Strozier argues that in the face of such romantic tension, these friends found in each other succor if not a resolution to their troubles: "It would appear, therefore, that Lincoln and Speed's close relationship centered on their similar and reinforcing conflicts. . . . It is probable that such close male contact during the years of Lincoln's greatest heterosexual tension heightened the difficulty he found in securing intimacy with a woman. . . . Speed provided an alternative relationship that neither threatened nor provoked Lincoln. Each of the two men found solace in discussing their intimate maleness that substituted for the tantalizing but frightening closeness of women."[24] Most prominent Lincoln scholars share Strozier's account of Lincoln's angst regarding the opposite sex, though they minimize or ignore its centrality to his friendship with Speed, and particularly its emotional implications for both men.

Lincoln's feelings for Speed are evident most explicitly, and mysteriously, in the closing year of their intimate friendship. In December 1840 Speed disclosed to Lincoln that he intended to sell the store, which fell short of his financial aspirations, and to return to his Kentucky home in the wake of his father's death. Dashed hopes for love with Matilda Edwards, whom Lincoln too may have been courting, also likely influenced Speed's decision. "There is nothing here," he wrote his sister, "but some of the cleverest fellows that God ever made—the truest friends and warmest hearts—that is worth living in this country for."[25] Lincoln's reaction remains a contested issue, one that emanates from conflicting interpretations of what he called "that fatal first of Jany. '41."[26] On that day the sales notice for Speed's store appeared in the local paper, and Lincoln broke off his engagement to Mary Todd. Whether he lost his nerve, as some thought, loved Matilda Edwards too much, as others surmised, or rather was despondent over Speed's imminent departure, which too few are willing to entertain, is uncertain. That Lincoln fell into a terrible depression during the early weeks of January 1841 is certain, documented by those who thought him "crazy as a loon" and suicidal.[27] In his own estimation, "I am the most miserable man living. If what I feel were equally distributed to the whole human family, there would not be a cheerful face on earth."[28]

Lincoln recovered quickly, if not fully, perhaps in part because Speed did not actually leave Springfield until May 1841. In August of that year Lincoln paid an extended visit to Speed's family home outside of Louisville, during which his friend experienced a budding romance with Fanny Henning. They almost immediately became engaged. Between September and the end of 1841 the men were again in Springfield together, likely discussing Speed's intense, escalating doubts about his relationship with Henning. As many have observed, Lincoln served well in the role of trusted and patient confidant and counselor, returning the cherished favor he had enjoyed during his own failed engagements.[29] His flurry of passionate correspondence to Speed in January and February of 1842 bespeaks the depth of their friendship, even as it raises questions about its nature.

Lincoln's version of a pep talk is, to say the least, peculiar, though lack of interpersonal context makes reading the only extant (one-sided version of) exchange between the men rather difficult. Articulating his "deepest solicitude for the success of the enterprize [sic] you are engaged in," Lincoln claims in his first letter to "adopt this as the last method I can invent to aid you, in case (which God forbid) you shall need any aid." Evidently Lincoln expected ("hoped" perhaps more accurately describes his feeling) that the case would, in fact, present itself, for he meticulously outlined "*three special causes*" and "*one general one*" to explain his "reasonable" belief that Speed "would feel verry [sic] badly some time between this and the final consummation of your purpose." This latter point in time, they both knew, represented the stressful consummation of heterosexual commitment, sexual intercourse as much as marriage, as it seemed to be constituted in their anxious imaginations. In addition, generally, to his "*naturally . . . nervous temperament*," Lincoln explained, Speed would be vulnerable to bad weather, a lack of conversation with friends, and "*the rapid and near approach of that crisis on which all your thoughts and feelings concentrate.*" In response to that crisis, which Lincoln defined as the "apprehension that you do not love her as you should," he reassured Speed that it was not because she expected it or because she was wealthy. No, he had not "*reasoned* [himself] *into* it," for he did not then know her to be "moral, amiable, sensible, or even of good character." Reassurances, indeed! In truth, Lincoln argued, Speed had found himself "unable to *reason* himself *out* of it" because her "*personal appearance and deportment*" had impressed "the *heart* and not the head." It was those "heavenly black eyes."

As a final measure of comfort, Lincoln urged that Speed not worry about Fanny "scouting and despising you, and giving herself up to another," because he had had no such apprehension in the first place and therefore could not "bring it home to your feelings."[30] Consensus has not been achieved regarding Lincoln's use of

praeteritio in this letter, but it is clear that, as before, the trials of love were weath-
ered, and romance endured, because of their friendship.

A month later, and just weeks before the wedding, Fanny Henning nearly died,
or so Speed feared. Again Lincoln wrote with conspicuous words of solace. "I hope
and believe, that your present anxiety and distress about *her* health and *her* life,
must and will forever banish those horrid doubts, which I know you sometimes felt,
as to the truth of your affection for her." Those doubts, Lincoln observed, could not
be matched in "their immeasurable measure of misery," even by the prospect of
Fanny's death. "The death scenes of those we love, are surely painful enough; but
these we are prepared to, and expect to see. They happen to all, and all know they
must happen." If, perhaps, Speed could not fully appreciate Lincoln's resignation to
Fanny's mortality, further consolation followed. "Should she, as you fear, be destined
to an early grave," Lincoln reminded Speed, she has prepared well through the religion "he once disliked so much." He expressed his hope that Speed's "melancholly
[*sic*] bodings" were unfounded and optimistically concluded that, whatever happened, his worry provided "indubitable evidence of your undying affection [and
love] for her."[31] Without any sense of irony, David Donald's interpretation of these
letters, like Lincoln's advice, is both clinical and presumably salubrious: "In effect,
Lincoln and Speed were acting out a game of doctor and patient; in the winter
of 1840–1841 Lincoln had been the sufferer and Speed had offered encouraging
advice; now it was Speed who was at risk and Lincoln was trying to save his health
and sanity."[32]

Fanny lived. More consequentially, with Lincoln's able assistance, embodied in a
final prenuptial pledge that his "desire to befriend" Speed was "everlasting" and the
sensible advice that Speed only need go through the ceremony "calmly, or even
with sufficient composition not to excite alarm," his friend married.[33] In what
might be rightly called Lincoln's swan song,[34] he wrote days after the marriage that
his anticipation on Speed's behalf (news of the February 15 consummation did not
arrive until the twenty-fourth) was such that "I opened the letter, with intense anxiety and trepidation—so much, that although it turned out better than I expected,
I have hardly yet, at the distance of ten hours, become calm." Relieved that their
"*forebodings*" were, in the end, "all the worst sort of nonsense," Lincoln offered one
last bit of advice to settle Speed, who seemed plagued still by doubts. Speed had
written that "something indescribably horrible and alarming still haunts [me]" and
confessed his fear that the "Elysium" of which he had "dreamed so much, is never
to be realized." Lincoln responded,

> Well, if it shall not, I dare swear, it will not be the fault of her who is now
> your wife. I now have no doubt that it is the peculiar misfortune of both you
> and me, to dream dreams of Elysium far exceeding all that any thing earthly
> can realize. Far short of your dreams as you may be, no woman could do

more to realize them, than that same black eyed Fanny. . . . My old Father used to have a saying that "If you made a bad bargain, *hug* it the tighter"; and it occurs to me, that if the bargain you have just closed can possibly be called a bad one, it is certainly the most pleasant one for applying the maxim to, which my fancy can, by any effort, picture.

If their dreams of Elysium also included an intense bond with each other, that too must be tempered with the bromide of homely maxims and practical relations. Lincoln married Mary Todd, with whom he resumed a courtship after Speed's marriage, in November 1842.

It is worth closing this tale, however, with the provocative query Lincoln himself posed to Speed just a month before his nuptials: "The immense sufferings you endured from the first days of September till the middle of February you never tried to conceal from me, and I well understood. You have now been the husband of a lovely woman nearly eight months. That you are happier now than the day you married her I well know, for without, you could not be living. . . . But I want to ask a closer question—'Are you in *feeling* as well as *judgement*, glad you are married as you are?' From any body but me, this would be an impudent question not to be tolerated; but I know you will pardon it in me. Please answer it quickly as I feel impatient to know."[35]

What would Lincoln have done if his friend had answered in the negative? Was he envisioning a reunion? We cannot know; however, years later, after Lincoln's death, Speed wrote to William Herndon, "One thing is plainly discernible; if I had not been married and happy—far more happy than I expected to be—he would not have married."[36] Whatever one's interpretation, it is difficult to mistake the echoes of Lincoln's pining heart. His friendship with Speed persisted throughout their lives, though it would never again, in word or deed, match the emotional intensity palpable in those remarkable letters of devotion and love.

Kramer's Lincoln

Considering Larry Kramer's vitriolic rhetorical career, his sentimental reclamation of Lincoln seems a rather queer episode. It is, however, part of a longstanding polemical assault on America's erasure of gay men, past and present. Kramer is best known for sounding the first alarm of the AIDS epidemic and founding Gay Men's Health Crisis (GMHC) in 1981 and AIDS Coalition to Unleash Power (ACT UP) in 1987—two of the most influential AIDS organizations in the plague's history.[37] Already controversial, if not an outright pariah, for his 1978 novel *Faggots*, a moralistic satire of the sexual profligacy of gay male urban culture, Kramer found powerful political ethos in the jeremiadic mode he hoped would save the lives of his gay brothers. He is generally considered a firebrand, public nuisance, prophet, and, given his tragic prescience, the Cassandra of the epidemic.[38]

Kramer's signature voice—what one observer defines as *the* "rhetoric of AIDS,"[39] at least in the formative years of the epidemic—has been widely and variously described as acerbic criticism, vilification, shrill rant, righteous anger, and histrionics. As Michael Specter observes, "In fact, Kramer uses anger the way Jackson Pollock worked with paint; he'll fling it, drip it, or pour it onto any canvas he can find—and the bigger the canvas the more satisfied he is with the result. Subtlety repulses him. His novels, plays, and essays are filled with lists of enemies, hyperbolic cries of despair, and enough outrage to fill the Grand Canyon."[40] His famous opening lines of "1,112 and Counting" summarize well his rhetorical strategy: "If this article doesn't scare the shit out of you, we're in real trouble. If this article doesn't rouse you to anger, fury, rage, and action, gay men have no future on this earth. Our continued existence depends on just how angry you get."[41] Whatever one thinks of his approach, there is no gainsaying the fact that his diverse forms of virulent discourse ("1,112 and Counting," *The Normal Heart, Reports from the Holocaust, The Destiny of Me,* "Sex and Sensibility") created anew direct action politics, spread that politics to a mass audience, rendered the "AIDS Establishment" (embodied memorably in scapegoats ranging from the *New York Times* and Ed Koch to the National Institutes of Health, among an inexhaustible list) accountable and to varying degrees responsive, and even revolutionized the patient's role in medical treatment.

His lecture "Our Gay President" is part of a larger, in fact enormous, project —now at least 1,500 pages—begun in 1978, entitled *The American People.* Kramer describes it as an epic history of America in novel form, "as reflected through disease, through illness," or what he calls "the perversion of sexual instincts"—namely, homophobia.[42] It originally focused only on AIDS, but eventually spanned the whole of the American past: "What existed in the '80s was there for a reason, and the reason did not start in 1981. It started . . . in 1935, which was the year I was born. But then I realized it didn't start in 1935 either. You've got to go back even further; and before I knew it, I was back to the Indians—I mean the Indians before George Washington!"[43] His personal and political impetus for *The American People* is reclamation in the face of homophobic erasure: "Most of the books I have been reading are history books. The main thing I'm learning from reading them is that we aren't in them. It's hard to believe so many books can be so filled with lies. Because we are not in these histories, in the eyes of most people, especially academics, we therefore don't exist."[44]

The genesis of the Lincoln chapter is traceable to Kramer's early 1980s interview of Gore Vidal in which Vidal shared intuitions forged in the writing of his historical novel *Lincoln.*[45] Kramer claims that he did not intend to disclose the Lincoln material; his presentation of it at the Midwest GLBT conference on February 22, 1999, was a "spur-of-the-moment stopgap measure" to save him the trouble of preparing another speech for a second appearance at the gathering.[46] But having committed himself, Kramer ventured, in typical bullish fashion, and with Wisconsinites in tow, where all others had feared to tread.[47]

In terms of subtlety and indirection, Kramer's rendering of the Lincoln-Speed affair paled in comparison to Lincoln's gymnastic letters and historians' sterile interpretations of them. "Between 1839 and 1842 Abraham Lincoln and Joshua Speed loved each other." Far from being the crucible of economic hardship, Speed's bed fostered a blossoming (and not merely fraternal) love that began at first sight and was only sundered by (tortured) political choices that required, among other sacrifices, wives. "For years they shared a bed and their most private thoughts. They fell in love with each other and slept next to each other for four years." Like Lincoln scholars, Kramer substantiated his interpretation in part by reference to extant correspondence. "One only has to read the letters between these two to know the depth of their love." Unlike Lincoln scholars, however, Kramer without qualification concluded that Lincoln and Speed were gay.[48]

More provocatively, Kramer's strikingly romantic narrative was purportedly legitimated, and certainly amplified, by letters and diary entries allegedly found buried beneath the floorboards of Speed's old store and housed currently in a private, unnamed collection in Davenport, Iowa. Lush with witness to their love, those diary entries resolved any ambiguity about the nature of their friendship: "He ["Linc," as Speed affectionately called him] often kisses me when I tease him, often to shut me up. . . . He would grab me by his long arms and hug and hug." Anticipating the incredulity of posterity, Speed apparently writes, "Yes, our Abe is like a school girl."

Kramer's disclosure, of course, sought to titillate the historical imagination and provoke collective memory. I want to clarify, however, how it might be understood as a performance distinguishable from typical nonacademic discourses that grope for queer historical subjects. Kramer's lecture was not simply a manifestation of familiar gossip meant to intrigue by raising the specter of homosexuality; nor was it, in keeping with Kramer's long career of diatribe, a demolition of the historical closet designed to expose and condemn the hypocrisy of heteronormative power. To the contrary, his protectiveness of the lecture (which to date he has refused to share and has not published), his uncharacteristically temperate persona, and the care with which he constituted Lincoln's ethos reveal a political but not necessarily polemical motive.[49]

Kramer offered what Roger Simon calls "insurgent commemoration": "attempts to construct and engage representations that rub taken-for-granted history against the grain so as to revitalize and rearticulate what one sees as desirable and necessary for an open, just and life-sustaining future."[50] Insurgency, in this sense, should not be construed as strategic *impiety*, to borrow Kenneth Burke's term. He did not, in other words, defile Lincoln's sacred memory for the sake of political confrontation. Rather, in filling a void perpetuated by the caretakers of official memory,

Kramer exhibited a will to piety, which Burke characterizes as a "loyalty to the sources of our being. . . . [creating] the deep connection [with] . . . the 'remembrance of things past.'"[51] As Kramer argued, "To know that Abraham Lincoln and Joshua Speed were in love with each other for all of their adult lives and that no history book will record this essential truth that could so radically alter how gay people are accepted in this country that worships Lincoln is very painful."[52] "History is about possession," Kramer concluded. "History is about claiming what is ours."[53]

Proprietary claims are not novel in public memory. Indeed their dynamic social construction and currency, and competition among them, provide the vital sustenance for memory's endurance. The agon of Lincoln's memory, as Barry Schwartz and Merrill Peterson's studies richly demonstrate, has long contributed fundamentally to his becoming an "inexhaustible resource," an exemplar so deeply forged, so iconic, so permanent, that he is unquestionably "part of the soul of American society."[54] It is noteworthy, however, that Kramer's insurgent commemoration, admittedly a radical reconfiguration of the American soul, provoked responses attempting what I call *mnemonicide*—the assassination of memory—to assuage the anxieties attending their homosexual panic.[55] Mindful of Schwartz's thoughtful reservations regarding the praxis of John Bodnar's "official memory,"[56] I aim nonetheless to account for this rhetoric of control seeking to preserve Lincoln's, and thus our own, hegemonic heterosexuality.

Lincoln's Queer Mnemonicide

This account of Lincoln's queer mnemonicide begins with a simple question: why would anyone care if a known gay extremist delivered a fantastic rendering of an American icon's homosexuality at a gathering of Midwestern collegiate queers? In response, I turn to the notion of homosexual panic, the homophobic terror of guilt by homosexual association that subtly governs our social bonds and warrants visceral and vicious responses to any potential encroachment by the queer contagion.[57] In view of the magnitude of Lincoln's memory in forging our collective, national identity, with obvious implications for individual identity, conviction of his homosexuality would necessarily implicate us all, by means of this inescapable heritage, as practitioners and progenitors of same-sex love. The threat elicits not only fear of homosexual complicity, but also, perhaps more consequentially, that of normalizing and centralizing queerness as a national value. That said, my query reminds us that this panic, while potentially dispersed throughout a culture, most keenly strikes locally those in particular proximity to the stakes. In this case, I highlight two of these panic-stricken communities to demonstrate mnemonicide at work.

You do not need to be a queer theorist to fathom the reaction of Springfield residents as they opened their Sunday *State Journal-Register* on May 16, 1999, to find, just beneath Lincoln's picture on the masthead, a headline that read "Writer asserts proof Lincoln was gay."[58] Staff writer Jefferson Robbins's judicious account[59] of Kramer's speech, its key arguments and the merits of its evidence as interpreted by historians, evoked a tirade by local residents sparked by an immediate and intense flash of homosexual panic. They answered this betrayal of their civic pride and collective memory with cancellations and a flurry of e-mails, phone calls, and editorials chastising the *State-Journal-Register* for its sensationalism (what one reader described as "dredg[ing] up all the trash lying on the bottom of the ocean for the world to ponder"), its advancement of the gay "agenda," its endangerment of Springfield's prosperous tourism industry, and its "smearing of President Lincoln's reputation."[60] Even editor Barry Locher's immediate (if qualified) apology could not quell a feeling that most shared with a resident who wrote, "Honest Abe must be spinning in his Oak Ridge grave wondering what he did to Springfield to make them shame him in this manner."[61] What these local stewards of Lincoln did not articulate fully was the motive that animated so many of their explicitly pragmatic and patriotic appeals: to constitute Lincoln's memory is to be constituted by Lincoln's memory.[62] As one outraged subscriber astutely, if unfortunately, observed, "Families need good values, not gay values."[63]

The rather predictable volley of ad hominem and threat exhibits the limited rhetorical options available to those locals threatened by an "out-law" memory, a flexing of vernacular muscle so as to insulate and protect the multiple (economic, social, familial) investments in a sanctioned and cherished official memory.[64] Interested in neither the historical merits of Kramer's claims nor their newsworthiness, Springfield residents did not seek to refute a competing memory out of existence; instead they formed a posse comitatus and performed the rhetorical equivalent of running the "out-law" memory out of town on a rail.

Such tar-and-feather mnemonicide is not nearly as complex or interesting as that attempted by those Lincoln scholars who readily answered Kramer's folly. Any claim that professional historians suffered equally the moral, cognitive, and emotional constrictions of homosexual panic or, more precisely, that consequently they would deploy themselves, consciously or unconsciously, in the service of public memory's political battle over Lincoln is tantamount to fighting words. Many historians would deny that, in the words of one London reporter, "scholars . . . consider it their business to safeguard the memory of the Father of the Nation."[65] Thomas Fleming, in distinguishing between the objectivity of history and the ideological labor of public memory, stated the case in unequivocal terms: "My painfully acquired belief [is] that the historian's chief task is to separate history from memory. . . . memory is not history. It is too clotted with sentiment, with the kind of retrospective distortion that we constantly inflict on the past. History gives us, not the past seen through the eyes of the present, but the past in the eyes, the hearts and minds of the men and women who lived through a particular time, and experienced it."[66] Merrill Peterson maintains this distinction regarding the nation's memory of

Lincoln, arguing that "the public remembrance of the past, as differentiated from the historical scholars', is concerned less with establishing its truth than with appropriating it for the present. . . . While heightening consciousness of the nation's heritage, it restages it and manipulates it for ongoing public purposes."[67]

Such, no doubt, is the expected professional response that readily dismisses Kramer's gay memory of Lincoln, that all-too-familiar speculative imagining that has circulated at least since Carl Sandburg's capricious characterization, seventy-five years ago, of Lincoln and Speed as having "a streak of lavender, and spots soft as May violets."[68] The seasoned and serious historian, with instant discernment, should rightly conclude with Douglas Wilson: "It sounds like this might be a case of taking a 19th century event and giving it a 20th century context."[69]

How, then, does one explain the passionate engagement of this controversy by Lincoln historians? Ideological investments, despite strenuous claims to the contrary, do indeed manifest themselves. As Barry Schwartz has argued, "That Americans constantly reinvent their past to fit the present is a tedious proposition, but no one can deny it—nor can one deny that some historians take as many liberties with the past as laymen, perhaps more because of the depth of their ideological commitments. Events of ambiguous meaning and consequence, however, are more susceptible to ideological interpretations than others. The blurring of the line between thinking *about* history and thinking *with* history, between describing or explaining reality and modifying the past to fit reality, is a major problem of contemporary scholarship."[70] I would further argue that some historians' passionate differentiation between history and collective memory might be read as symptomatic of a fear that their ideological investments, however minimal, will be exposed in the comparison.[71]

In short, in certain cases historians doth protest too much. Queer history and memory is certainly one of them. The story of gay, lesbian, bisexual, or transgender historiography cannot be told but as one of struggle against discipline, a term that designates not only an academic field but the rhetorical efforts, often cloaked as "objective" praxis and judgment, which preserve hegemonic constructions of sanctioned domains of inquiry into the past.[72] Despite a contemporary climate of relative legitimacy, queer history continues to struggle, particularly in subfields such as Lincoln studies. Philip Nobile has argued, "Ever since talk about Lincoln's possible bisexuality crept into the mainstream circa 1995 . . . Lincoln scholars have been unanimously skeptical and sometimes even hostile to the idea. Perhaps the best word to describe their reaction is homophobic, that is, fear of a lavender Lincoln."[73]

Homophobic fear when intensified becomes homosexual panic, as I believe occurred in the wake of Kramer's speech. Threatened by memory-making that claimed historical authenticity of Lincoln's homosexuality by virtue of documentary evidence, Lincoln scholars blurred Peterson's distinction between establishing history's truth and appropriating, restaging, and manipulating the nation's heritage for ongoing ideological purposes. I would argue that Joshua Speed's diary entries, on which Kramer's public memory rests, and which, to date, historians have not seen, marks that collision of history and memory that is born of the most dangerous forms of "insurgent commemoration." Speed's diary portends a radical disruption and transformation—a revolution, we might say—of national collective identity as constituted by Lincoln's memory. In view of the stakes—what one author astutely labeled the "second Civil War"[74]—scholars, many of whom as American citizens share the values embedded in the dominant memory of Lincoln, have reacted to their own homosexual panic by forming the last battalion capable of preserving Lincoln's heterosexual ethos.

Because, as David Thelen has observed,[75] historians professionally are most concerned with the accuracy of memory, their ethos when defending a particular version of the past derives from the same source, namely, the legitimacy of a detached voice authorizing the verified remembrance of the historical subject. In the face of what could amount to exculpatory evidence—namely, Speed's alleged diary—we find a consistent gesture toward the *plausibility* of Kramer's narrative, remote as historians may will it to be, that preserves this ethos of objectivity. Michael Burlingame, for instance, comments, "'If this is an authentic diary and it does contain homoerotic passages, I'm willing to believe it if the evidence is there.'"[76] Others, including Illinois state historian Thomas Schwartz, establish similar ethos by clarifying the burden of proof: "'You can't prove a negative. There's always a possibility that anything exists, until you can absolutely demonstrate it not being true. On the other hand, if the thing does exist, it's really incumbent upon Kramer to prove his assertion rather than for others to disprove it.'"[77] Beyond good method, however, these expressed deferrals of judgment, which *do not conclude* historians' response (they express deferrals that are belied by extended commentary), serve to cloak the ideological work that will get done in the explicit judgments that follow. This rhetoric of objectivity and deferral strategically grounds enthusiastic arguments that aim precisely to prove the negative in Lincoln's case.

In varying degrees of development and sophistication, Lincoln historians have challenged Kramer's memory *without waiting* for Kramer's disclosure of Speed's diary. Lincoln was "very, very unlikely" a gay man, they argue, for the following circumstantial reasons: because many nineteenth-century frontiersmen shared beds for the same reason Lincoln did—economic necessity; because Lincoln courted women, several prior to Mary Todd, and then fathered four children with her; because of the "very personal and very rough politics of the time," which certainly would have produced evidence of blackmail had there been a romance between Lincoln and Speed.[78] Each of these arguments provides useful contextual frames through which inferences regarding the Lincoln-Speed relationship, and their texts (extant correspondence), might be derived. As Thomas Schwartz rightly observes, "History is always interpreted. Facts don't speak for themselves. Evidence has to be cemented together with imagination and interpretation."[79]

What marks these accounts ideologically, however, is their rather indiscriminate if not desperate application, their insistent tone. Although none of the contextual frames are mutually exclusive in their relation to a queer reading of Lincoln and Speed, nor comprehensive, they are presented *as if* that were the case, meant to raise doubt sufficiently to eliminate homosexuality as a credible inference. The issue of romance is particularly illuminating. In newspaper interviews, Michael Burlingame forcefully dismisses the possibility of Lincoln's homosexuality by asserting that, "there is too much evidence that Lincoln was strongly attracted to women."[80] In his book *The Inner World of Abraham Lincoln*, however, Burlingame unambiguously charts the tortured history of Lincoln's relationship with women, aptly summarized in the opening sentence of the chapter-long discussion: "Abraham Lincoln did not like women." He quotes one love interest from the 1830s who observed that Lincoln seemed to be "a very queer fellow" and another whom Lincoln courted in Springfield during his residency in Speed's bed: "'While he was never at ease with women, with men he was a favorite companion.'" Complexities Burlingame methodically elucidates for a narrower academic audience are absent in summary judgments that appear, in mass-mediated sources, to seek foreclosure of same-sex desire as a dynamic force in Lincoln's heterosexual congress.[81]

Perhaps more telling, Burlingame offers as evidence of Lincoln's heterosexuality his famous love affair with Ann Rutledge, whom Lincoln apparently engaged on her deathbed. Historians have long contested the existence and nature of this affair on evidentiary grounds. In his book, Burlingame endorses those Lincoln scholars who rebut James G. Randall's early skepticism regarding the veracity of the affair. Among his favored revisionists is Douglas Wilson, who argued that Randall "insists on an extremely high standard of proof" that befits legal judgment but not historical inquiry. Wilson, arguing that the Rutledge story is a "positive gain for all who seek to understand the man and the circumstances that brought him forth," dismissed Randall's standard of proof because "observing the evidentiary safeguards of a criminal trial would, after all, bring a substantial portion of historical inquiry to a halt, for much of what we want to know about the past simply cannot be established on these terms. Abraham Lincoln's early life is a perfect example." By stark contrast, both Burlingame and Wilson seemingly impose Randall's impossibly rigorous standards in interpreting the evidence—of comparable, if not sounder, documentary merit, from the same time period—of Lincoln's relationship with Speed. Their heteronormative, if not homophobic, bias is unmistakable here and tells us much about the largely invisible ideological assumptions at work in their historical method.[82]

Others have employed definitional argument to limit interpretive ground for assessing such evidence. Thomas Schwartz, for example, is more forthright than Burlingame in dealing with the complexities of Lincoln's love affairs, only to dismiss them as a definitional warrant for a queer reading. "I don't think anyone would deny that you find [in Lincoln] an ambivalence and awkwardness toward women. Whether you could make the case that he experienced not only homosexual attraction but also had homosexual partners is something else." Lest that case be made, Michael Rogin deepens the definitional burden: "There may be evidence of male-male desire, but that's not gay. If 'gay' is going to mean anything it's got to mean orgasms with other men. There's got to be some sense of transgression and forbiddenness."[83] The ambiguity of establishing "something else," or the impossibility of discovering in some archive the fluid proof of "transgression and forbiddenness," insulates Lincoln, and his custodians, from interpretation that defies heternormative memory.

Beyond the convulsions that have passed during this homosexual panic as coolly objective responses to Kramer's assertions, this discourse exhibits further assurances that control is both means and end in this struggle. Absent silencing Kramer by way of an authoritative historical interpretation of Lincoln's love of Speed, contingency plans lurk everywhere among circumstantial and evidentiary claims. First, ad hominem and well-poisoning abound, as one historian proclaimed on the *History News Network:* "every gay historian, or gay activist who claims to be an historian, wants to 'out' all of our great historical figures."[84] Second, is an admonishment against certain revisionist history, which Gabor Boritt articulates in *The Lincoln Enigma:* "Lincoln strongly bonded with men but what may suggest homosexuality in our time most likely did not so much occur to most people in his time. . . . In history, context is all-important and the first duty of the historian is to understand the past in terms understood by those who lived in the past."[85] Finally, queer distinctions are distinctions without meaningful difference. As Harold Evans argues, "If it was an isolated, earlier event that occurred decades before a person rose to prominence, the public should use their own good judgment and common sense and not take it very seriously."[86]

Fearing their incapacity to discipline memory, some historians have sought the diminution of any queer interpretive grounds that would sustain the meaning for collective memory potentially derived from counter-evidentiary authority. Ironically, Lincoln scholars have embodied their own critique of Kramer. As Norman Hellmers, superintendent of the Lincoln Home National Historic Site, put it so well, "People find it useful to exploit Mr. Lincoln for their own purposes. They'll do whatever it takes to make the connection."[87] In this case, we witness not a disciplining or domestication of memory's imaginative excess, but the assassination of memory, or mnemonicide, for the sake of perpetuating a hegemonic connection to our ostensibly straight past.

Conclusion

By way of conclusion, let me offer a few relevant clarifications and implications. I am not claiming that historians are necessarily elites whose standard practice, whose guiding impulse—as Bodnar might argue—functions as the ballast of hegemonic memory. Indeed I have in principle much sympathy for Timothy Garton Ash's characterization of Holocaust historians: "Thank God for historians . . . [their] fairness, representation, completeness . . . the historians are our protectors. They protect us against forgetting—that is a truism. But they also protect us against memory."[88] Gay and lesbian historians have, in this spirit, labored to discover a past that both founds queer memory and dismantles the myths that have trivialized and scapegoated homosexuals into obscurity. I join Martin Duberman in pressing for the "right of a people to a knowledge of its own history (its *memory*), an indispensable prerequisite for establishing collective identity and for enjoying the solace of knowing that we too have 'come through,' are the bearers of a diverse, rich, unique heritage."[89] I also draw, however, from this study of Lincoln's memory the inherent danger in historians' ability to "protect us against memory." Induced (occasionally, but not always, unknowingly) by circumstance into the political fray, bolstered by a professional ethos that positions them as arbiters and advocates of memory's struggle, historians threaten to become the midwives of the forgotten.

Take, for striking example, the 2003 publication of *"We Are Lincoln Men": Abraham Lincoln and His Friends* by David Herbert Donald, Pulitzer Prize–winning author of *Lincoln* and arguably the dean of Lincoln studies in America. In his exploration of Lincoln's "special friends," Donald graciously engages queer scholars and activists—even Larry Kramer, who, as he notes, called him "a dried old heterosexual prune at Harvard"—on the question of Lincoln's sexuality.[90] "The subject," he observes with reference to the Lincoln-Speed relationship, "deserves careful and cautious discussion."[91]

Yet Donald's discussion of Lincoln and Speed, conspicuously free of queer theory, queer sociology, and, for the most part, queer history, seems to reach a rather familiar and definitive heteronormative judgment: homoeroticism means sex, for which there is no evidence; bed sharing by members of the same sex was normative, therefore not romantic or erotic; sodomy was illegal, rarely prosecuted, and therefore rarely occurred; only younger men were romantically, but rarely sexually, involved; Lincoln's letters to Speed "are totally lacking in expressions of warm affection"; Lincoln, while president, "publicly" referred to having slept with Speed, which establishes its innocence; both were "eagerly trying to get married"; they eventually married Mary Todd and Fanny Henning.[92]

More dangerous than the conclusiveness of many of Donald's fragile warrants and evidence denying the homoeroticism of Lincoln and Speed's relationship is the fact that *David Herbert Donald* has apparently foreclosed the debate. Is the venerable historian simply "protecting us from memory"? In response, and in light of the conspicuous timing of his publication, I dare ask, do we witness here an apologia?[93] To what lengths will disciplined scholars reach to insure that, with firm conviction, straight Americans can proclaim, "We Are Lincoln Men"?

110 CHARLES E. MORRIS III

For Kramer, recuperating Lincoln was necessary not foremost as a form of gay protest, but instead as a mandate that gays and lesbians, to survive, must learn to remember: "A lot of our brothers and sisters, the generations that came before us, our blood kin, died, and we must never for one second forget the fact that each and every one of us is related by blood to every single other gay man and lesbian who not only died from AIDS but who has ever lived."[94] His astuteness regarding the moral and rhetorical imperatives inherent to such a mandate of memory is revealed in his repeated appropriation of the Gettysburg Address: "By their dying, it has been, over and over again, our own brothers and sisters who have shown us also this path to freedom, that our gay nation might live. . . . They died for us, and we must recall some mighty words inspired by Lincoln himself. It is for us, the living, from these honored dead, to take increased devotion, to be dedicated to the great task remaining before us that we shall not perish from the earth."[95] Kramer's radical appropriation of Lincoln would extend beyond this rather typical if meaningful invocation of sacred words; indeed, like Lincoln himself, he would *innovate* in deploying the usable symbolic resources of the past as an organizing principle in the present and moral vision for a sustainable queer future.[96]

Notes

Earlier versions of this essay were presented at the Framing Public Memory Conference at Syracuse University, September 2001; the University of Maryland Communication Collo-quium Series, May 2002; and the Summer Institute of the Center for Global Culture and Communication at Northwestern University, 2004. The essay was first published as "'My Old Kentucky Homo': Lincoln and the Politics of Queer Public Memory," in *Framing Public Memory*, ed. Kendall R. Phillips (Tuscaloosa: University of Alabama Press, 2004). I am grateful to many colleagues for their valuable insights and suggestions, especially John Sloop, Barry Schwartz, Carolyn Dever, Tina Chen, and the Vanderbilt Gender & Sexuality Reading Group.

1. Paul Monette, "Mustering," in *Last Watch of the Night* (New York: Harcourt Brace, 1994), 147–49.

2. David W. Blight, "'For Something beyond the Battlefield': Frederick Douglass and the Struggle for the Memory of the Civil War," *Journal of American History* 75 (March 1989): 1159. See also Frederick Douglass, "Oration in Memory of Abraham Lincoln," in *The Life and Writings of Frederick Douglass*, ed. Philip S. Foner (New York: International Publishers, 1955), 4: 309–19; David W. Blight, *Frederick Douglass and Abraham Lincoln: A Relationship in Language, Politics, and Memory* (Milwaukee: Marquette University Press, 2001).

3. Scott A. Sandage, "A Marble House Divided: The Lincoln Memorial, the Civil Rights Movement, and the Politics of Memory, 1939–1963," *Journal of American History* 80 (June 1993): 135.

4. Monette, "Mustering," 149.

5. Michael Warner draws on Hannah Arendt's notion of society in characterizing "regimes of the normal": "She identifies society in this sense with 'conformism, the assumption that men had become social beings and unanimously followed certain patterns of behavior, so that those who did not keep with the rules could be considered asocial or abnormal.' The social

realm, in short, is a cultural form, interwoven with the political form of the administrative state and with the normalizing methodologies of modern social knowledge." Queer theory functions oppositionally and performatively to disrupt regimes of the normal. Michael Warner, introduction to *Fear of Queer Planet: Queer Politics and Social Theory*, ed. Warner (Minneapolis: University of Minnesota Press, 1993), xxvii. Here I would also clarify my use of the terms "gay" and "queer." I use the term "gay" in characterizing Larry Kramer's memory of Lincoln because his political focus is largely gay male, essentialist, and assimilationist. Although these assumptions are antithetical to queer theory, I also use the term "queer" in this essay as it accurately describes my own critical exposure of the politics of historiography, and my thinking about the possibilities of Lincoln's counter-memory instigated by Kramer. In this sense I am responding to Scott Bravmann's compelling call for a "queer cultural studies of history" that aims in part to disrupt historiography as a regime of the normal by exploring queer historical imaginations. Bravmann, *Queer Fictions of the Past: History, Culture and Difference* (New York: Cambridge University Press, 1997).

6. My description of Kramer's memory of Lincoln is most accurately characteristic of gay male culture and thus I resist generalizing these observations in regard to lesbians. Indeed, any generalizations here should be understood as qualified, recognizing as I do the multifariousness within gay male culture. I am not suggesting that the queering of Lincoln's memory is irrelevant or insignificant for lesbians. I am, however, concerned that such functions be carefully situated within a specific discussion of lesbians and public memory, which, for better or worse, is beyond the scope of this essay.

7. Michael Warner argues similarly, "One reason we have not learned more from this history is that queers do not have the institutions for common memory and generational transmission around which straight culture is built. Every new wave of queer youth picks up something from its predecessors but also invents itself from scratch. Many are convinced they have nothing to learn from old dykes and clones and trolls, and no institutions—neither households nor schools nor churches nor political groups—ensure that this will happen. And since the most painfully instructed generation has been decimated by death, the queer culture of the present faces more than the usual shortfall in memory." Warner, *The Trouble with Normal: Sex, Politics, and the Ethics of Queer Life* (Cambridge, Mass.: Harvard University Press, 1999), 51–52.

8. Martin Duberman, *Stonewall* (New York: Plume, 1994), xvii. Moreover, significant post-Stonewall figures are, even in conspicuous sites of memory, forgotten. In writing of Harvey Milk, for instance, historian John D'Emilio observes, "The memory in this community doesn't last more than a few years." John Cloud, "Why Milk Is Still Fresh," *Advocate* (November 10, 1998): 33.

9. As Cleve Jones observed, "The Quilt was not the forum to pass on gay and lesbian history, but I, like many others, felt it was important that the history of the struggle for gay rights be rescued even as so many of its leaders were being lost to AIDS. At this time there was a terrible toll in the activist community; some of the most brilliant leaders were dying before they'd achieved their goals or had time to pass on their skills and their contacts and accumulated wisdom. Given the dramatic changes and equally startling continuities in gay experience over the past forty years, there was a sense that history must be preserved lest it be forgotten, and so repeated." Jones, *Stitching a Revolution: The Making of an Activist* (San

Francisco: HarperSanFrancisco, 2000), 207. See also Christopher Capozzola, "A Very American Epidemic: Memory Politics and Identity Politics in the AIDS Memorial Quilt, 1985–1993," *Radical History Review* 82 (2002): 91–109; Marita Sturken, *Tangled Memories: The Vietnam War, the AIDS Epidemic, and the Politics of Remembering* (Berkeley: University of California Press, 1997); Peter S. Hawkins, "Naming Names: The Art of Memory and the NAMES Project AIDS Quilt," *Critical Inquiry* 19 (summer 1993): 752–79.

10. Larry Kramer, "Yesterday, Today, and Tomorrow," *Advocate*, March 30, 1999, 67.

11. Christopher Castiglia, "Sex Panics, Sex Publics, Sex Memories," *boundary 2*, no. 27 (2000): 156–57.

12. Castiglia, "Sex Panics, Sex Publics, Sex Memories," 158–59.

13. John Nichols, "History Out in the Open; AIDS Activist Says the Missing Chapters on Gays Must Be Written," *Capital Times* (Madison, Wisconsin), February 26, 1999, 11A; Kramer, "Yesterday, Today, and Tomorrow," 67.

14. It is worth noting that Kramer is a prominent example of those neoconservative gay men whom Castiglia describes as the perpetrators of "counternostalgia." Note, for instance, Robert Chesley's frequently quoted assessment of Kramer, which is as apt a characterization of Kramer today as it was when published by the *New York Native* in 1981: "I think the concealed meaning in Kramer's emotionalism is the triumph of guilt: that gay men deserve to die for their promiscuity. . . . Read anything by Kramer closely. I think you'll find that the subtext is always: the wages of gay sin are death." Quoted in Larry Kramer, *Reports from the Holocaust: The Making of an AIDS Activist* (New York: St. Martin's Press, 1989), 16. It is likely not coincidental, therefore, that Kramer reclaims not the Stonewall generation, which for him might well represent the "hedonistic trauma of the gay past," but instead the romantic, homosocial, and sexually ambiguous nineteenth-century "homosexual" icon.

15. See Charles B. Strozier, *Lincoln's Quest for Union: A Psychological Portrait*, 2nd ed. (Philadelphia: Paul Dry Books, 2000), 53–65; Jonathan Ned Katz, "No Two Men Were Ever More Intimate," in *Love Stories: Sex between Men before Homosexuality* (Chicago: University of Chicago Press, 2001), 3–25; Douglas L. Wilson, *Honor's Voice: The Transformation of Abraham Lincoln* (New York: Alfred A. Knopf, 1998), 245–59; Charley Shively, "Big Buck and Big Lick: Lincoln and Whitman," in *Drum Beats: Walt Whitman's Civil War Boy Lovers* (San Francisco: Gay Sunshine Press, 1989), 71–88; Robert L. Kinkaid, *Joshua Fry Speed: Lincoln's Most Intimate Friend* (Harrogate, Tenn.: Department of Lincolniana, Lincoln Memorial University, 1943).

16. Douglas L. Wilson and Rodney O. Davis, eds., *Herndon's Informants: Letters, Interviews, and Statements about Abraham Lincoln* (Urbana: University of Illinois Press, 1998), 588–91; Joshua F. Speed, *Reminiscences of Abraham Lincoln and Notes of a Visit to California: Two Lectures* (Louisville: John P. Morton, 1884), 21–22.

17. In addressing the bed question, Charles Strozier is the most sensible of Lincoln scholars, most of whom refuse to consider its emotional dimensions: "Social custom and individual experience, however, are not always congruent. Just because many men slept together casually in inns and elsewhere during this period by no means proves that it was unimportant that Lincoln lay down in a crowded bed night after night for well over three years with his best male friend, whom he trusted above all with his deepest feelings. The question is, what does it mean?" Strozier, *Lincoln's Quest for Union*, 57. On male bed sharing generally in

the nineteenth century, see Anthony Rotundo, *American Manhood: Transformations in Masculinity from the Revolution to the Modern Era* (New York: Basic Books, 1993), 85; and Donald Yacovone, "'Surpassing the Love of Women': Victorian Manhood and the Language of Fraternal Love," in *A Shared Experience: Men, Women, and the History of Gender,* ed. Laura McCall and Donald Yacovone (New York: NYU Press, 1998), 195–221.

18. Wilson, *Honor's Voice,* 245.

19. Ward H. Lamon, *The Life of Abraham Lincoln: From His Birth to His Inauguration as President* (1872; Lincoln, University of Nebraska Press, 1999), 231.

20. Herndon here exhibits irritation about the implications of the term "intimacy." Although this must be read in its cultural context, it might be understood as the first in a long line of chronicles that resist depictions of same-sex affection or desire. For the purposes of my argument, it is all the more interesting for its injunction against the excesses of memory: "Who authorizes H. and N. to assert what they do assert? How do H. and N. know that Lincoln and Speed poured out their souls to one another? If to tell a friend some facts in *one line* or direction constitutes *intimate* friendship, then Lincoln always, before and after Speed left Illinois, had *intimate* friends, and if Lincoln's refusal to tell all the secrets of his soul to any man shows a want of intimate friendship, then Lincoln never had an intimate friend. Poetry is no fit place for severe history. I think the truth is just here, namely, that under peculiar conditions and under *lines of love* and in that direction they were *intimate* friends. No man pours his whole soul to any man" (William H. Herndon to Jesse W. Weik, January 22, 1887, in *The Hidden Lincoln: From the Letters and Papers of William H. Herndon,* ed. Emanuel Hertz [New York: Blue Ribbon Books, 1940], 159.)

21. Abraham Lincoln to Joshua Speed, February 13, 1842, in Basler, *Collected Works of Abraham Lincoln,* 1: 269. Lincoln's son, Robert Todd Lincoln, confirmed the depth of his father's affection in a letter to Speed's nephew, Gilbert Speed Adams: "I have no doubt that your uncle, Joshua F. Speed, was the most intimate friend that my father ever had." Abraham Lincoln to Gilbert Speed Adams, June 15, 1915, Filson Club [Louisville, Ky.], quoted in Gary Lee Williams, "James and Joshua Speed: Lincoln's Kentucky Friends," Ph.D. dissertation, Duke University, 1971.

22. Speed, *Reminiscences of Abraham Lincoln,* 23. At one time two of those friends shared the upstairs sleeping quarters with Lincoln and Speed. See William H. Herndon and Jesse W. Weik, *Abraham Lincoln: The True Story of a Great Life* (New York: D. Appleton, 1896), 1: 179.

23. Wilson, *Honor's Voice,* 195–264; Strozier, *Lincoln's Quest for Union,* 41–65. Others suggest that Lincoln's struggles with women spanned his lifetime and stemmed not merely from anxiety about sex. See Katz, *Love Stories,* 14; Burlingame, *The Inner World of Abraham Lincoln,* 123–46.

24. Strozier, *Lincoln's Quest for Union,* 56.

25. Quoted in Wilson, *Honor's Voice,* 247.

26. See Douglas L. Wilson, "Abraham Lincoln and 'That Fatal First of January,'" in *Lincoln before Washington: New Perspectives on the Illinois Years* (Urbana: University of Illinois Press, 1997), 99–132; Wilson, *Honor's Voice,* 233–38; Strozier, *Lincoln's Quest for Union,* 58–59; David Herbert Donald, *Lincoln* (New York: Simon and Schuster, 1995), 86–88; Katz, *Love Stories,* 18.

27. William H. Herndon to Isaac N. Arnold, November 20, 1866, in Hertz, *The Hidden Lincoln*, 37.

28. Abraham Lincoln to John T. Stuart, January 23, 1841, in Basler, *Collected Works of Abraham Lincoln*, 1: 229.

29. Wilson, *Honor's Voice*, 251–59; Donald, *Lincoln*, 89–90; Strozier, *Lincoln's Quest for Union*, 60–65; Katz, *Love Stories*, 18–24.

30. All quotations from Abraham Lincoln to Joshua F. Speed, January 3[?], 1842, in Basler, *Collected Works of Abraham Lincoln*, 1: 265.

31. All quotations from Abraham Lincoln to Joshua F. Speed, February 3, 1842, in Basler, *Collected Works of Abraham Lincoln*, 1: 267–68.

32. Donald, *Lincoln*, 89.

33. Abraham Lincoln to Joshua F. Speed, February 13, 1842, in Basler, *Collected Works of Abraham Lincoln*, 1: 269–70.

34. All quotations from Abraham Lincoln to Joshua F. Speed, October 5, 1842, in Basler, *Collected Works of Abraham Lincoln*, 1: 303.

35. Abraham Lincoln to Joshua F. Speed, February 13, 1842, in Basler, *Collected Works of Abraham Lincoln*, 1: 269–70.

36. Herndon and Weik, *Abraham Lincoln*, 204.

37. For Kramer's career, see Kramer, *Reports from the Holocaust*; Michael Shnayerson, "Kramer vs. Kramer," *Vanity Fair* (October 1992): 228–31, 293–97; Lawrence D. Mass, ed., *We Must Love One Another or Die: The Life and Legacies of Larry Kramer* (New York: St. Martin's Press, 1997); Dudley Clendinen and Adam Nagourney, *Out for Good: The Struggle to Build a Gay Rights Movement in America* (New York: Simon and Schuster, 1999); Michael Specter, "Public Nuisance," *New Yorker* (May 13, 2002): 56–65; John D'Emilio, "A Meaning for All Those Words: Sex, Politics, History and Larry Kramer," in *The World Turned: Essays on Gay History, Politics, and Culture* (Durham, N.C.: Duke University Press, 2002), 64–77.

38. Michael Denneny writes, "And here the figure of the Old Testament prophet gives way to the image of Cassandra—'I wanted to be Moses but I could only be Cassandra,' says Ned Weeks in *The Destiny of Me*—Cassandra who saw so clearly the terrible vision of the destruction of her beloved city, who tried to warn her fellow citizens of their impending doom, but whose prophesies failed to avert the destruction of Troy." Denneny, "A Mouthful of Air," in *We Must Love One Another or Die*, ed. Mass.,180. John D'Emilio, in describing the aptness of the Cassandra analogy, observed, "And I was shocked to realize that, in this encounter with them [Kramer's collected discourse in *Reports from the Holocaust*] as historical documents, I found myself thinking: 'Virtually everything that Larry said has turned out to be true; the worst case scenarios have become fact.'" D'Emilio, "A Meaning for All Those Words," 73–74.

39. David Bergman, "Larry Kramer and the Rhetoric of AIDS," in *AIDS: The Literary Response*, ed. Emmanuel S. Nelson (New York: Twayne, 1992), 175–86.

40. Specter, "Public Nuisance," 59.

41. Kramer, *Reports from the Holocaust*, 33. For a good analysis of Kramer's rhetorical strategy, see Bonnie J. Dow, "AIDS, Perspective by Incongruity, and Gay Identity in Larry Kramer's '1,112 and Counting,'" *Communication Studies* 45 (fall–winter 1994): 225–40.

42. Lawrence D. Mass, "Interview with a Writer," in *We Must Love One Another or Die*, 324, 334.

43. Mass, "Interview," 333.

44. Kramer, "Yesterday, Today, and Tomorrow," 67.

45. Donald Weise, ed., *Gore Vidal: Sexually Speaking, Collected Sex Writings* (San Francisco: Cleis, 1999), 265–66.

46. Carol Lloyd, "Was Lincoln Gay?" *Salon.com* (May 3, 1999), http://www.salon.com/books/it/1999/04/30/lincoln/index.html (November 22, 2000).

47. Kramer has refused to provide a transcript of this speech or the chapter on Lincoln in his unpublished work-in-progress, *The American People*. Excerpts and description of the speech are found in Samara Kalk, "Lincoln Was Gay, Activist Contends," *Capital Times* (Madison, Wisconsin), February 23, 1999, 2A; Kate Kail, "Lecturer Suggests Lincoln Was Gay," *Cardinal News* (Madison, Wisconsin), February 23, 1999; Nichols, "History Out in the Open," 11A; Lloyd, "Was Lincoln Gay?"

48. Although determining the nature of the Lincoln-Speed relationship, even if it were possible, is not the point of this essay, I would argue that Kramer's interpretation of the men as "gay" does not account sufficiently for nineteenth-century American gender and sexuality and is also problematically essentialist. I do think, however, that Kramer is right to fathom eros as part of male homosociality before the "invention" of homosexuality. Many queer historians are unwilling to go so far. D'Emilio, for instance, is willing to acknowledge the homosocial bond between Lincoln and Speed, but not necessarily an erotic affiliation: "Of course, in prosperous 21st.-century America everyone has his or her own bed. But that was not the case in the early part of the nineteenth century, where it was very common for men of Lincoln's class to share a bed with another man. I don't doubt that Lincoln and Speed had an intimate relationship—lots of men did then. It was totally typical, viewed as completely normative." Richard A. Kaye, "Outing Abe," *Village Voice*, June 25–July 1, 2003, http://www.villagevoice.com/issues/0326/kaye.php (July 2, 2003).

49. Note, for instance, that in response to Carol Lloyd's question regarding his refusal to share his evidence, "he confesses that he fears the vitriol, or worse, that may rain down upon him from outraged defenders of Lincoln's sullied honor. 'Don't tell them where I live,' he adds at the end of the conversation, with no hint of irony." Quoted in Lloyd, "Was Lincoln Gay?" Kramer's response seems uncharacteristic, given that his career is marked by an unflinching candor and willingness, if not passion, to enter the fray. It is impossible to know his motives more fully (he has not said more on the subject), but one could argue that his hesitancy, his protectiveness has something to do with his understanding of the preciousness and precariousness of a gay past.

50. Roger I. Simon, "Forms of Insurgency in the Production of Popular Memories: The Columbus Quincentenary and the Pedagogy of Counter-Commemoration," *Cultural Studies* 7 (January 1993): 76. Kramer's essentialism in reclaiming Lincoln is at odds with what might otherwise be reconfigured as the work of "countermemory," in Foucault's terms. Both share a sense of the significance of remembering previous struggles of the homosexual and the homophobia that shaped those struggles. Their positions on how those memories might be used perhaps differ, but I think Kramer would agree with Foucault that "if one controls people's memory, one controls their dynamism. And one also controls their experience, their knowledge of previous struggles." Michel Foucault, "Film and Popular Memory," in *Foucault Live: Interviews, 1966–84*, ed. Sylvère Lotringer (New York: Semiotext[e], 1989), 92. See also

Foucault, "Nietzsche, Genealogy, History," in *Language, Counter-Memory, Practice: Selected Essays and Interviews by Michel Foucault*, ed. Donald F. Bouchard (Ithaca, N.Y.: Cornell University Press, 1977), 139–64.

51. Kenneth Burke, *Permanence and Change: An Anatomy of Purpose* (Los Altos, Calif.: Hermes, 1954), 71, 74.

52. Kramer, "Yesterday, Today, and Tomorrow," 67.

53. Nichols, "History Out in the Open," 11A.

54. Merrill D. Peterson, *Lincoln in American Memory* (New York: Oxford University Press, 1994); Barry Schwartz, *Abraham Lincoln and the Forge of National Memory* (Chicago: University of Chicago Press, 2000). See also John Hope Franklin, "The Use and Misuse of the Lincoln Legacy," *Papers of the Abraham Lincoln Association* 7 (1985): 30–42.

55. In using the term *mnemonicide*, I mean to imply the rhetorical nature of collective forgetting or repression of memory, and thus want to retain and emphasize a sense of agency in thinking about the social construction, transmission, and erasure of memory as it occurs at a specific historical moment. I recognize that the rhetorical acts I explore are part of the broader social/cultural dynamics of collective "amnesia" that can occur over much longer periods of time. See Michael Schudson, *Watergate in American Memory: How We Remember, Forget and Reconstruct the Past* (New York: Basic Books, 1992); Barry Schwartz, "Deconstructing and Reconstructing the Past," *Qualitative Sociology* 18 (1995): 263–70.

56. Schwartz qualifies Bodnar and other theorists of the politics of memory who emphasize the retention of state hegemony in social constructions of an "official past": "Collective memory is in truth an effective weapon in contemporary power struggles, but the battlefield image of society, taken alone, distorts understanding of collective memory's sources and functions, leaving out, as it does, the cultural realm within which the politics of memory is situated." Schwartz, *Abraham Lincoln and the Forge of National Memory*, 15–17. See John Bodnar, *Remaking America: Public Memory, Commemoration, and Patriotism in the Twentieth Century* (Princeton, N.J.: Princeton University Press, 1992).

57. Homosexual panic functions by means of an ideologically driven fear that one might be homosexual, harbor homosexual longings, or, most important, be perceived as homosexual by others. It thus bolsters and perpetuates heternormativity through its terrorizing discourse or by force of gay bashing. See Edward J. Kempf, *Psychopathology* (St. Louis: Mosby, 1920), 477–515; Eve Kosofsky Sedgwick, *Between Men: English Literature and Male Homosocial Desire* (New York: Columbia University Press, 1985), 83–96; Charles E. Morris III, "Pink Herring and the Fourth Persona: J. Edgar Hoover's Sex Crime Panic," *Quarterly Journal of Speech* 88 (May 2002): 228–44. See also Sedgwick, *Epistemology of the Closet* (Berkeley: University of California Press, 1990), 182–212.

58. Jefferson Robbins, "Writer Asserts Proof Lincoln Was Gay/Gay Activist Claims Mystery Diary Shows Recollections of Affair," *State Journal-Register* (Springfield, Ill.), May 16, 1999, 1.

59. Robbins detailed the relationship and the controversy in three articles published in the same edition. Robbins, "Writer Asserts Proof Lincoln Was Gay"; Jefferson Robbins, "Joshua Speed was longtime friend, prototypical frontier settler," *State Journal-Register* (Springfield, Ill.), May 16, 1999, 1; Jefferson Robbins, "Joshua Speed suffered a case of cold feet before his 1842 marriage to Fanny Henning," *State Journal-Register* (Springfield, Ill.), May 16, 1999, 6.

60. For editorial responses see the *State Journal-Register* (Springfield, Ill.), May 20, 1999, 6; Stephanie Simon, "Lincoln Country Aghast as Local Paper Prints Gay Allegation; Activist

Claims He's Seen the Diary of the 16th President's Homosexual Lover. Historians Deride the Idea as Springfield Fumes," *Los Angeles Times*, June 22, 1999, A5.

61. Barry Locher, "Claims about Lincoln Deserved Investigation," *State Journal-Register* (Springfield, Ill.), May 20, 1999, 7.

62. On the relationship between identity and memory, see Maurice Halbwachs, *On Collective Memory*, ed. Lewis A. Coser (Chicago: University of Chicago Press, 1992); John R. Gillis, "Memory and Identity: The History of a Relationship," in *Commemorations: The Politics of National Identity*, ed. Gillis (Princeton, N.J.: Princeton University Press, 1994), 3–24.

63. Quoted in Locher, "Claims about Lincoln," 7.

64. Bodnar's discussion of vernacular memory is useful here; however, in this instance we witness a struggle between two vernacular memories, one of which (in Springfield) mirrors and supports, rather than disrupts, the "official" memory. Bodnar, *Remaking America*. My rendering of Kramer's counter-memory of Lincoln as an "out-law" memory is in keeping with Sloop and Ono's broader conception of "out-law discourse." John M. Sloop and Kent A. Ono, "Out-law Discourse: The Critical Politics of Material Judgment," *Philosophy and Rhetoric* 30 (1997): 50–69.

65. Andrew Gumbel, "Abe Lincoln's Home Town Outraged at His 'Outing,'" *Independent* (London), June 27, 1999, 21.

66. Thomas Fleming, "History and Memory: They're Different," *History News Network* (July 24, 2001), http://www.historynewsnetwork.org/articles/article.html?id=159 (September 3, 2001).

67. Peterson, *Lincoln in American Memory*, 35.

68. Sandburg wrote, suggestively, "A streak of lavender ran through him [Speed]; he had spots soft as May violets. . . . Lincoln too had . . . a streak of lavender, and spots soft as May violets. . . . Their births, the loins and tissues of their fathers and mothers, accident, fate, providence, had given these two men streaks of lavender, spots soft as May violets." Carl Sandburg, *Abraham Lincoln: The Prairie Years* (New York: Blue Ribbon Books, 1926), 1: 166–67. For an analysis of the homoerotic subtext here, see Katz, *Love Stories*, 354.

69. Quoted in Lloyd, "Was Lincoln Gay?"

70. Barry Schwartz, "The New Gettysburg Address: A Study in Illusion," in *The Lincoln Forum: Rediscovering Abraham Lincoln*, ed. John Y. Simon and Harold Holzer (New York: Fordham University Press, 2002), 160.

71. See Peter Novick, *That Noble Dream: The "Objectivity Question" and the American Historical Profession* (New York: Cambridge University Press, 1988). On rhetoric and historiography, see Stephen E. Lucas, "The Schism in Rhetorical Scholarship," *Quarterly Journal of Speech* 67 (February 1981): 1–20; "Octalog: The Politics of Historiography," *Rhetoric Review* 7 (fall 1988): 5–49; Marouf Hasian, Jr., and Robert E. Frank, "Rhetoric, History, and Collective Memory: Decoding the Goldhagen Debates," *Western Journal of Communication* 63 (winter 1999): 95–114.

72. See Blanche Wiesen Cook, "The Historical Denial of Lesbianism," *Radical History Review* 20 (spring/summer 1979): 60–65; Lisa Duggan, "History's Gay Ghetto: The Contradictions of Growth in Lesbian and Gay History," in *Presenting the Past: Essays on History and the Public*, ed. Susan Porter Benson, Steven Brier, and Roy Rosenzweig (Philadelphia: Temple University Press, 1986), 281–92; George Chauncey, Jr., Martin Bauml Duberman, and Martha Vicinus, introduction to *Hidden from History: Reclaiming the Gay and Lesbian Past*, ed. Duberman,

Vicinus, and Chauncey (New York: NAL Books, 1989); John D'Emilio, "Not a Simple Matter: Gay History and Gay Historians," in *Making Trouble: Essays on Gay History, Politics, and the University* (New York: Routledge, 1992), 138–47; Duggan, "The Discipline Problem," *GLQ: A Journal of Lesbian and Gay Studies* 2 (August 1995): 179–91.

73. Philip Nobile, "Don't Ask, Don't Tell, Don't Publish: Homophobia and Lincoln Studies?" *History News Network* (June 10, 2001), http://historynewsnetwork.org/articles/article.html?id=97 (September 3, 2001).

74. Lloyd, "Was Lincoln Gay?"

75. David Thelen, "Memory and American History," *Journal of American History* 75 (March 1989): 1117–29.

76. Quoted in Robbins, "Writer Asserts Proof," 6. Burlingame implies that documentary proof is self-evident, obscuring the politics of interpretation that he exercises in other statements. The resiliency of ideology in the face of such "proof" can be witnessed in the controversy over Thomas Jefferson's memory. See Jan Ellen Lewis and Peter S. Onuf, eds., *Sally Hemings and Thomas Jefferson: History, Memory, and Civic Culture* (Charlottesville: University of Virginia Press, 1997).

77. Quoted in Robbins, "Writer Asserts Proof," 6.

78. Among the Lincoln scholars making these claims are Gabor Boritt, Douglas Wilson, Michael Burlingame, and Gene Griessman. See their testimony in Lloyd, "Was Lincoln Gay?"; Stephanie Simon, "Lincoln Country Aghast"; W. Scott Thompson, "Was Lincoln Gay?" *History News Network* (June 10, 2001), http://historynewsnetwork.org/article.html?id=96 (September 3, 2001); Boritt, *The Lincoln Enigma: The Changing Faces of an American Icon* (New York: Oxford University Press, 2001), xiv–xvi.

79. Hilary Shenfeld, "Lincoln's Love Life: A Lesson in Historical Interpretation," *Chicago Daily Herald*, July 8, 1999, 3.

80. Quoted in Lloyd, "Was Lincoln Gay?"

81. Michael Burlingame, *The Inner World of Abraham Lincoln* (Urbana: University of Illinois Press, 1994), 123–24.

82. Burlingame, *The Inner World of Abraham Lincoln*, 135–36. Douglas L. Wilson, "Abraham Lincoln, Ann Rutledge, and the Evidence of Herndon's Informants," in *Lincoln before Washington*, 74–98.

83. Schwartz, quoted in Simon, "Lincoln Country Aghast"; Rogin, quoted in Lloyd, "Was Lincoln Gay?"

84. Glenn Williams, "Gay Myths," *History News Network* (June 11, 2001), http://historynewsnetwork.org/articles/comments/displayComment.html?cmid=70 (September 3, 2001).

85. Boritt, *The Lincoln Enigma*, xv–xvi.

86. Quoted in Shenfeld, "Lincoln's Love Life," 3.

87. Quoted in Gumbel, "Abe Lincoln's Home Town Outraged at His 'Outing,'" 21.

88. Timothy Garton Ash, "The Life of Death," *New York Review of Books* (December 19, 1985), 39, quoted in Richard King, "The Discipline of Fact/The Freedom of Fiction," *Journal of American Studies* 25 (1991): 171–88.

89. Martin Bauml Duberman, "'Writhing Bedfellows' in Antebellum South Carolina: Historical Interpretation and the Politics of Evidence," in *Hidden from History*, ed. Duberman, Vicinus, and Chauncey, 168.

90. Among the gay scholars included in Donald's study are Jonathan Ned Katz and C. A. Tripp. David Herbert Donald, *"We Are Lincoln Men": Abraham Lincoln and His Friends* (New York, Simon and Schuster, 2003), 227. Although this essay was originally published before Tripp's *The Intimate World of Abraham Lincoln* (2005), I am well aware of the controversy it sparked, which I see as a connected but distinct battle in the ongoing memory war over Lincoln's sexuality. In a forthcoming essay I examine Tripp's book, its relationship to the Lincoln establishment, including Donald's *"We Are Lincoln Men,"* and the politics of evidentiary materiality. C. A. Tripp, *The Intimate World of Abraham Lincoln* (New York: Simon and Schuster, 2005); Charles E. Morris III, "Hard Evidence: The Vexations of Lincoln's Queer Corpus," in *Rhetoric and Materiality*, ed. Barbara Biesecker and John Lucaites (forthcoming).

91. Donald, *"We Are Lincoln Men,"* 35.

92. The weight of Donald's accumulated case is compelling, until each reason is scrutinized in turn. The reduction of "homoeroticism" to the "blunt" question, "Did they have sex together?," is a deceptively narrow definitional argument, courting a negative judgment by eliminating alternatives. Moreover, his presumption of sexual candor in the nineteenth century on the one hand, and apparent appeal to ignorance on the other, is conspicuous, to say the least: "no contemporary ever raised the question of sexual relations between Lincoln and Speed," "No one ever suggested that he and Speed were sexual partners," "There was no sexual implication in these [normative same-sex bed sharing] sleeping arrangements," "But such relationships [sodomy] were not merely infrequent; they were against the law." Further, Donald's claim that only young men engaged in romantic or homoerotic relationships is striking. We might consider Walt Whitman as a synecdoche for the trouble here with his hasty generalization. Finally, likening Lincoln's language found in his Speed letters to the generic affections of his professional correspondence is absurd. To claim that they are "totally lacking in expressions of warm affection" seems to deliberately ignore the intense emotional bond between these men that served as the context for their 1842 correspondence, as well as its unambiguous expression. Indeed, such a claim contradicts *his own conclusion*, offered later in this chapter when discussing their mutual comfort regarding *women*, that Lincoln's letters to Speed were "the most intimately personal letters that he ever wrote." Like other Lincoln scholars, Donald's interpretive reach grows more expansive, if not more coherent and judicious, when engaging Lincoln from a heteronormative perspective. Donald, *"We Are Lincoln Men,"* 35–51.

93. It would not be the first time a leading scholar responded in such a manner to a queer reading of a prominent American figure. See, for instance, Athan Theoharis, *J. Edgar Hoover, Sex, and Crime: An Historical Antidote* (Chicago: Ivan R. Dee, 1995).

94. Larry Kramer, "Yesterday, Today, and Tomorrow," 66.

95. Ibid. Lincoln's precise wording: "It is for us the living, rather, to be dedicated here to the unfinished work which they who fought here have thus far so nobly advanced. It is rather for us to be here dedicated to the great task remaining before us—that from these honored dead we take increased devotion to that cause for which they gave the last full measure of their devotion—that we here highly resolve that these dead shall not have died in vain." Quoted in Garry Wills, *Lincoln at Gettysburg: The Words That Remade America* (New York: Touchstone, 1992), 263.

96. As a heartening postscript, I offer two anecdotes. In February 2003, the National Park Service initially bowed to pressure from far-right Christian groups demanding that images

of the progay Millennium March be removed from an eight-minute tourist video shown at the Lincoln Memorial. After an outcry from the gay community, NPS decided to retain the queer images in the video (if, regrettably, also adding images of a Promise Keepers gathering and pro–Gulf War demonstration, events that did not occur at the Lincoln Memorial). In February 2004, Massachusetts governor Mitt Romney appropriated Lincoln to resist those "activist" courts threatening the institution of heterosexual marriage. By contrast, a Reuters photograph depicted a young San Francisco gay couple, fresh from city hall in the heady atmosphere created by Gavin Newsom's defiance of state-sanctioned homophobia, jubilantly displaying their marriage license. They were standing in front of a statue of Lincoln. "Censoring History," *Advocate*, February 3, 2004, 13; Mitt Romney, "A Citizen's Guide to Protecting Marriage," *Wall Street Journal*, February 5, 2004, A12; *China Daily News*, February 14, 2004, http://www.chinadaily.com.cn/English/doc/2004–02/14/content_306106 .htm (February 15, 2004).

on the Development of Counter-Racist Quare Public Address Studies

Julie M. Thompson

Black men loving black men a call to action, a call to action, an acknowledgment of responsibility, we take care of our own kind, when the nights
grow cold and silent. These days, the nights are cold-blooded and the silence
echoes with complicity.

Joseph Beam, "Brother to Brother: Words from the Heart,"
in *In the Life: A Black Gay Anthology*, ed. Beam

Those artifacts warranting inclusion in major anthologies of great speakers and
speeches still reflect the privileges of education, wealth, masculinity, whiteness, and
heterosexuality.[1] The voices that counter such privilege on multiple fronts—for
instance, the voices of counter-racist quare[2] activists—rarely catch our critical attention. In this chapter, I draw from E. Patrick Johnson's recent formulation of "quare"
studies to explore the theoretical, methodological, and textual considerations that
appear paramount to the process of "quaring" public address. As Johnson explains,
"quare" draws on various black vernacular practices to refer to nonheterosexual
identities and subjectivities. I will use "quare" instead of "queer" both to stand in
solidarity with members of contemporary black gay culture who perceive "queer"
as rife with whiteness and to further my interests in developing theory that is
explicitly counter-racist. I also acknowledge fully that usage of the word "queer"
poses numerous problems because of its history and current popular status (in various sectors and regions of the United States) as a homonegative epithet. Like other
impersonal referents, "queer" sometimes connotes maleness, masculinity, and, most
important for my purposes, whiteness. Disciplinary debates about canonicity are
not my primary concern in this chapter, nor do I feel compelled to rehash the
debates here. Rather I am concerned to theorize quare public address "from the
bottom up," using Marlon Riggs's *Tongues Untied* as the exemplar text from which
to do so.

I will argue that quaring public address entails a fundamental disruption of historical silences in rhetorical scholarship regarding human sexuality, race, gender, and
class. This disruption—this forcible separation—entails an elemental breaking apart

of the reified conceptualization of the representative homosexual speaking subject as "white," as well as a breaking apart of normalized imaginary representations of the racialized speaking subject as heterosexual. To quare public address, I will argue, is to render what I would call *homonormative* or *quarecentric* standpoints regarding human erotic desires, passions, and lived experiences intelligible and authoritative in various public spheres.

Any quare public address project should avoid the historical tendency for gay and lesbian studies to reflect a narrow range of human experiences marked by ostensibly shared oppression, on the one hand, and race, class, and gender privilege, on the other. Quare public address would not simply identify and valorize the rhetorical artistry or virtuosity of those great speakers who "happened to be gay." Deciding who is or was "gay" is difficult enough—if only because such decisions may fall prey to essentializing or totalizing impulses. In this sense, my orientation to rhetorical historiography resembles the "deviant historiography" theorized by Jennifer Terry, who argues that any project that seeks "to correct the historical record through locating great or even common homosexuals in the past in order to reconstruct their effaced stories" makes the erroneous supposition that gay, lesbian, bisexual, or transgendered identity and experience is "essentially transhistorical and transcultural."[3] "Quaring," to my mind, functions as a verb rather than an adjective—it is a particular type of action or a specific critical stance that one takes as a critical rhetorician.[4] In my conceptual scheme, artifacts can be quared in the reading (just as audiences and orators can be "quared"). Quaring public address, then, could be imagined as a process of proselytical invention, whereby the critic can "recruit" a text into quareness.[5]

In addition to disrupting historical silences in public address scholarship, quaring public address entails a reworking of the fundamental concepts central to the study of public address. By this, I mean to say that quare public address projects challenge the ways in which the concepts of and relationships between "speaker," "speech," "audience," "occasion," "context," "constraints," and "change" are imagined. Although I do not have the space here to treat each concept individually, the chapter will highlight the ways in which public address cannot be quared without a concomitant quaring of the fundamental concepts related to canonization. For instance, traditional public address studies tend to focus on speeches delivered by notable individuals in the interest of pursuing some sort of instrumental change or conservation of sociopolitical conditions and delivered to primary, secondary, and tertiary audiences on specific occasions. The project of quare public address explodes this conceptualization in the interests of blending the strengths of public address scholarship with the sensibilities of cultural studies and critical rhetoric. In that sense, my aims are similar to those suggested recently by Robert Hariman.[6] Hariman offers theoretical correctives to the terministic screens embedded in both neoclassical and poststructural approaches to public address studies by "alter[ing] their conception of rhetorical artistry."[7]

I enumerate the fundamental critical principles I have developed in relationship to the process of quaring public address. I use Marlon Riggs's 1989 documentary text *Tongues Untied* to illustrate these critical principles. In particular, I draw on Riggs's documentary as a text that quares our understandings of contemporary eloquence. Quare approaches to public address studies must confront how political economy shapes the very emergence of the representational speaking subject. More important, quare public address should question the category of the "representational speaking subject," by asking which voices "count" as representative: shall those voices be leaders of social movements? Vernacular voices? If we wish to resist the repressive forces of social stratification in our studies of eloquence, must we abandon the model of the representative individual voice?[8]

Tongues Untied: Articulating Black Gay Masculinities

In 1989, media activist and documentary filmmaker Marlon Riggs released *Tongues Untied*, a fifty-five-minute experimental film that explores the struggles of black gay men in contemporary American culture. Part autobiography, part documentary, part performance narrative, *Tongues Untied* was produced primarily for a black gay male audience by a small collective of black gay men working with the visionary leadership of Riggs, a self-identified black gay man. In an interview for *Jump Cut* magazine in 1991, Riggs described the documentary as an attempt to use poetry to place black gay men "within the overall historical context of black struggle in this country. . . . I was dealing with the weaving, in terms of our lives, where truth, fiction, fantasy, fact, history, mythology really interweave to inform our character, psyche, values and beliefs."[9] The film enjoyed critical acclaim on the film festival circuit and eventually was awarded numerous honors, including recognition as best video at the New York Documentary Film Festival, best documentary at the Berlin International Film Festival, best independent/experimental work by the Los Angeles Film Critics.[10]

In an article for *Art Journal* in 1991, Riggs recounted his multiple reasons for creating and producing the film: "The mythology of America, the myth of what it means to be an American, is facing, at last, its own inexorable fate. For what this myth required for too long, for too many of us, was the soul-crushing negation of our lives and our struggles, the silencing of our most intimate, deepest, life-sustaining truths. . . . And the reason America's mythic walls are finally crumbling is simply this: we are no longer willing to bleed, and hence, to pay."[11]

Riggs then recounts the multiple ways in which racism and heteronormativity silence millions of Americans: "no prophets of revolution spoke to me, spoke *of* me."[12] Multiple forms of political and social domination produce anguish, anger, and depression. The most damning effect of domination, Riggs suggests, is the silence about blackness and gayness: "I withdrew into the shadows of my soul: chained my tongue; attempted, as best I could, to snuff out the flame of my sexuality; assumed the impassive face and stiff pose of Silent Black Macho."[13] But the silence could not stop Riggs from searching for a sense of self, a community that reflected the complexity of his identity. The primary lesson for Riggs was that when "existing history and culture do not acknowledge and address you—do not see or talk to you—you must write a new history, shape a new culture, that will."[14] The film's title, then, symbolizes what Riggs considers the "most radical—as in fundamental—form of self-affirmation" for the "collective, marginalized, dehumanized Other": speaking. "As communities historically oppressed through silence, through the power of voice we continually find our freedom, realize our fullest humanity."[15]

PBS executives decided to include *Tongues Untied* in its 1991 *Point of View* series. This decision was not without controversy, however, in light of the film's inclusion of profane speech and erotic images of black men embracing one another. The *Economist* noted that more than 50 percent of public television stations in the United States declined to air the documentary, although it had "already been honored with 16 awards."[16] Nearly 40 percent of the nation's fifty largest media markets with PBS affiliates—eighteen stations total—declined to air the experimental documentary. The Kansas City, Missouri, PBS station, for instance, refused to air *Tongues Untied* on the grounds that its linguistic content would offend its audience's sensibilities: "the 'F' word is not a word that we schedule. The drawings of male genitals and scenes of men kissing are 'shocking,' but not necessarily the problem. . . . [However], if the 'fucks' were excised," the program could be included in the schedule.[17] Some PBS stations refused to air the program because it would not find much of an audience, or even particularly "sympathetic" audiences. Two broadcast managers who did decide to broadcast *Tongues Untied* did so even in light of its controversial point of view and subject matter.[18] Another *Current* article noted "some pubcasters knocked it because Riggs didn't hold back his anger in an attempt to win over the sympathies of mainstream viewers."[19] The fact that so many PBS stations declined broadcast raises a critical question: for a series designed to educate audiences about the diversity of human experience, why would a documentary that achieves this design constitute such a threat?

One possible answer emerges in the impulse to totalize characterizations of the public. Michael Warner explains that the "public" tends to be imagined as a "kind of social totality," a "concrete audience," and as an "entity that comes into being only in relation to texts and their circulation."[20] Warner explains further that the public's unity has a distinctly ideological character. Such unity is contingent on "institutionalized forms of power to realize the agency attributed to the public; and it depends on a hierarchy of faculties that allows some activities to count as public or general, while others are thought to be merely personal, private, or particular. Some publics, for these reasons, are more likely than others to stand in for *the* public, to frame their address as the universal discussion of the people."[21]

In this case, PBS member stations, critics, and newspaper columnists alike presumed that white heterosexual people almost exclusively comprised the viewing public. As Riggs himself observed subsequent to the controversy over public funding of the film, "Public television serves merely to consolidate the myths, power, and authority of the majority: minorities might be granted the right to speak and be heard, but only if we abide by the 'master codes' of courteous speech, proper subject matter, conventional aesthetics, and 'mainstream' appeal. Disobey this often unwritten rule and you risk banishment into cultural oblivion."[22] Riggs's refusal to cater to white heterosexual audiences angered legislators and reviewers alike. In a review for the *Washington Post*, Courtland Milloy proclaimed that *Tongues Untied* was "bold," but nevertheless ignor[ed] the "big picture." By "ignoring the heterosexual audience, the film misses a chance to contribute to changing the hostile climate that keeps black homosexuals in their closets. Achieving that goal should have been a priority."[23] Forcing oppressed groups to speak the "master's language," however, would undermine both Riggs's visionary voice and the voices of other oppositional groups.

The contestation of such master codes is central to the quare canonization project, and recent work in critical rhetoric provides a useful vocabulary for understanding and undertaking such contestation. In their work on the criticism of vernacular discourses, Kent Ono and John Sloop suggest that, whereas "uncovering" vernacular discourses is not necessarily an emancipatory enterprise, such efforts nonetheless help critics and audiences understand the dual capacity of language to affirm and negate, to unite and divide.[24] Vernacular discourses exhibit two primary characteristics in contradistinction to hegemonic or dominant discourses. First, vernacular discourses are culturally syncretic, in that speakers use the vernacular to both counter hegemony and affirm their sense of community.[25] Second, "vernacular discourse is constantly engaged in the process of pastiche, in constructing a unique discursive form out of cultural fragments. Pastiche fractures culture in the process of appropriating it through imaginative reconstructive surgery."[26] The common practice of "quoting" that jazz musicians employ, or the "sampling" of hip-hop and rap, are examples of pastiche.

Moreover, Riggs's reference to "master codes" deserves its own critical commentary. In the history of U.S. race relations, the word "master" was understood primarily in relationship to "slave," and enslaved populations were prohibited by law and in everyday life from obtaining education that would help them learn how to read and write King's English, the master code. Disallowing participation in hegemonic discourse communities guaranteed the development of at least two social conditions: first, that racial domination would continue and, second, that oppressed collectives would develop their own vernaculars as a means of cultural survival and resistance.[27]

Poets and critics including Adrienne Rich, bell hooks, Audre Lorde, and Mark McPhail have commented on the difficulties associated with oppressed peoples using what Lorde refers to as the "master's tools." In an essay on language, hooks observes that

> Initially, I resist the idea of the "oppressor's language," certain that this construct has the potential to disempower those of us who are just learning to speak, who are just learning to claim language as a place where we make ourselves subject. *"This is the oppressor's language yet I need it to talk to you."* Adrienne Rich's words. Then, when I first read these words, and now, they make me think of standard English, of learning to speak against black vernacular, against the ruptured and broken speech of a dispossessed and displaced people. Standard English is not the speech of exile. It is the language of conquest and domination. . . . Reflecting on Adrienne Rich's words, I know that it is not the English language that hurts me, but what the oppressors do with it, how they shape it to become a territory that limits and defines, how they make it a weapon that can shame, humiliate, colonize.[28]

The reflections offered by hooks remind us that members of historically dominated communities must often use the "oppressor's language" to contest domination; we must speak standard English to gain the ear of those with the power to improve social and material conditions. The language itself, however, often effaces, erases, or otherwise fails to capture or represent the lived experiences of the oppressed. It is for precisely this reason that vernacular discourses become so important, especially to the project of quare public address, since gay, lesbian, bisexual, or transgendered folk have developed our own vernacular discourses over the years. For instance, some quare people often engage in pastiche by using the word "family" with homonormative inflections. Speaking generally, gay folks use the word "family" to refer to both blood relations and (and this is significant) other members of the gay, lesbian, bisexual, and transgendered community.[29] Sexual attraction, dating, and romantic relationships are a popular topic of conversation among gay folks. Sometimes we try to figure out if RuPaul's latest love interest is "family," by which we mean to inquire about the sexual orientation of said interest. "Is Julie family?" one might ask. To the casual auditor, the question probably sounds innocent enough, but the "code" helps members of often invisible gay communities connect and communicate with one another without risking potentially homonegative or gay-bashing responses.

In the *Jump Cut* interview from 1991, Riggs specifies that his intended primary audience was black gay men: "I didn't mind if everybody got it. . . . Frankly, with *Tongues Untied* if white heterosexuals don't understand the reasons why black people are angry and just consider this piece militant, then so be it. I'm not going to take time to justify this for people for whom this experience is totally alien.

Tongues Untied is an affirmation of the feeling and experiences of black gay men, made for them by a black gay man, or actually black gay men because the piece has a number of voices. If others understand this, fine, but making sure everyone understands this was not my prerequisite in making this."[30] In Riggs's words, the "principal virtue" of the documentary is its "refusal to present a historically disparaged community begging on bended knee for tidbits of mainstream tolerance. What *Tongues* instead affirms and demands is a frank, uncensored, uncompromising articulation of an autonomously defined self and social identity. (SNAP!)."[31]

Riggs's refusal to follow the "master codes" that would at various turns distort and often silence the experiences of the black gay male community signifies a tenet central to quaring public address: the standards by which rhetorical critics evaluate "eloquence" should not automatically find fault with homonormative perspectives, since such fault-finding would preempt the fruitful examination of quare voices and quare perspectives. What I am suggesting, of course, is that critics investigate our own socialization within and biases toward heteronormativity, as such biases affect the ways in which we receive quarecentric discourses and experiences. The critical comments deriding Riggs's anger is a case in point of how quarecentric rhetoric is judged negatively in its failure to honor and voice heteronormative master codes. Riggs himself notes that "playing with traditional forms," "altering them," and "perhaps innovating them" because of an "infusion of a black gay expression" was central to the production of *Tongues Untied*. Riggs's emphasis on play, alteration, and innovation are at the core of quare public address studies. I premise my own quaring of public address on several critical principles, enumerated and explained below. The list is intended to be normatively suggestive rather than exhaustive and exclusive. The principles themselves grew out of multiple viewings/readings of *Tongues Untied;* I invite readers to add their own principles.

Critical Principle 1: A quare public address should include speakers from a multitude of races, genders, economic classes, sexualities, and ethnicities.

The first critical principle is perhaps rather apparent, in light of the reformations of rhetorical theory and criticism offered by scholars with critical perspectives ranging from liberal feminist approaches to critical race theory to postcolonial and Marxian approaches to discourse. Scholars who wish to quare public address should follow the examples of prior theoreticians who have posed significant challenges to the masculinist, racist, and elitist history of public address and argumentation. For instance, the works of Dana Cloud, John Lucaites and Celeste Condit, Philip Wander, Barbara Biesecker, and John Sloop and Kent Ono illustrate various approaches to the criticism of public discourse that transcends the traditional focus on presidential speech and other elite discourses.[32]

The ideological pressure placed on Riggs to speak with a different voice—one that would not discomfort white folk, heterosexuals, and nonblack gay people—

signifies one central problematic in the project of canonization: can cultural radicals ever measure up to canonical standards of eloquence, especially when such advocates occupy multiple positions of alterity? The failure of radical, oppositional, or dissenting voices to achieve "eloquence" in dominant public spheres, perhaps, says more about an audience's difficulty hearing than it does about a speaker's lack of ability to use the master's tools. Courtland Milloy's response to *Tongues Untied*, for example, implies that the boundaries of effective speech (if they are to be broadcast or mediated in any significant sense) must necessarily take up and reflect the voice of the white heterosexual majority. His critical comments deriding Riggs's anger exemplify how quarecentric rhetoric is judged negatively because it refuses to mimic or voice essentially heteronormative master codes. Marcos Becquer observed, "This glaring lack of our own inputs in the process of identity construction effectively bypasses the double bind in which many of us in positions of alterity find ourselves. 'Cornered by identities [we] never wanted to claim,' the conundrum of whether or not to speak in discursive systems which deem themselves natural and render you unnatural is displaced by the politically lifesaving need to counteract our reified and closed identities within those systems."[33]

Recent work in some multiracial feminist theory and in queer black studies might provide that cultural language, and might offer nonreductive approaches to identity. Multiracial feminisms, as Maxine Baca Zinn and Bonnie Thornton Dill explain, "emphasize race as a primary force situating genders differently."[34] Multiracial feminist theories recognize that inequalities exist within intricate webs or matrices. As such, the analysis of gender oppression can never be separated productively or usefully from simultaneous analyses of racial, class, and other forms of inequality. As Zinn and Dill put it, "Race, class, gender, and sexuality are not reducible to individual attributes to be measured and assessed for their separate contribution in explaining given social outcomes."[35]

What I am suggesting, of course, is that we follow the leadership of multiracial feminist scholars and activists in our attempts to quare public address. Our scholarly efforts must speak to the multiplicity and complexity of human life, for the speaking subject is never "simply" gay *or* black *or* working-class *or* Buddhist *or* transgendered. The speaking subject indeed occupies multiple positions in the social and cultural hierarchies that inform everyday lived experience. Dwight A. McBride writes of the "overwhelming weight and frustration of having to speak in a race discourse that seems to have grown all too comfortable with the routine practice of speaking about a 'black community' as a discursive unit wholly separate from black lesbians and gay men. . . . any critique that does no more than to render token lip service to black gay and lesbian experience" both "denies the complexity of who we are" and perpetuates the myth of hegemonic black heteronormativity.[36] Riggs himself sums up the twin concerns of multiracial feminisms and of quare black studies in his observation that "as gay men we're othered by the dominant straight society, as black men by white society."[37]

Quite simply, then, quare public address cannot focus exclusively on the inequalities produced and perpetuated along the binary axis of heterosexuality/homosexuality. Instead we must quare public address studies through explicit critical attention to the ways in which speaking subjects are simultaneously racialized, gendered, and positioned within socioeconomic class and other cultural/political hierarchies. Such a goal is imperative if the project is to enjoy relevance to the complicated quotidian.

It is by now a commonplace in many cultural sectors that many people imagine the "gay community," and indeed the "gay community" itself has been guilty of this, as highly educated, white, and male. The gay rights movement has been notorious for its enactments of racist exclusion—if not by "sidelining," minimizing, or denying the dynamic role racism plays in the oppression of gay folks of color, then by replicating racist structures within its own institutions. The "leaders" of the post-Stonewall gay liberation movement, for instance, have mostly been white men. As Essex Hemphill writes in "Does Your Mama Know about Me?" the contemporary "gay rights" movement of the 1980s and 1990s "was not seriously concerned with the existence of black gay men except as sexual objects. In media and art the Black male was given little representation except as a big, Black dick. . . . It has not fully dawned on white gay men that racist conditioning has rendered many of them no different from their heterosexual brothers in the eyes of Black gays and lesbians. Coming out of the closet to confront sexual oppression has not necessarily given white males the motivation or insight to transcend their racist conditioning."[38]

Indeed, though gay liberation rhetoric often holds itself out as inclusive and "community-based," Hemphill and countless others found that the "disparity between words and actions was as wide as the Atlantic Ocean and deeper than Dante's hell. There was no 'gay' community for Black men to come home to in the 1980s. The community we found was as mythical and distant from the realities of Black men as was Oz from Kansas."[39]

The "gay community," then, is not immune from the broader and deeper cultural trends that exclude African Americans and other people of color, for any co-cultural group will to some extent reflect the hierarchies of race, class, and gender politics at play in the majority culture.[40] *Tongues Untied* is significant "precisely because of our lived experiences of discrimination in and exclusion from the white gay and lesbian community, and of discrimination in and exclusions from the black community."[41] The first critical principle, then, refuses to replicate this history of racism, misogyny, and class privilege. This will be no easy task, but Riggs's documentary illuminates the path. Indeed the portrayals of identity in *Tongues Untied* are "complex and multivalent: gay men are also feminists; black civil rights workers and gay activists share convergent interests. The goal of recognizing these multiple identities, as Riggs has suggested elsewhere, is to find community across differences."[42]

Tongues Untied takes as its foundational premise the factual observation that racist, heteronormative culture silences black gay men. In the documentary's opening sequence, the audience hears the voice-over of men chanting softly "brother to brother, brother to brother, brother to brother" in a rhythm that resembles the human heartbeat. The viewer observes black and white shots of black men congregating in public spaces—at the park, playing basketball, and at a gay pride parade. The screen fades to white. The second scene depicts black gay male poet Essex Hemphill with three other men in a circle, shaking hands and joining hands. A male voice-over helps the viewer imagine what Hemphill might be thinking: "Silence is what I hear after the handshake and the slap of five, after I hear 'What's happenin'? Hey boy! What's up, cous'? How ya feel, girlfriend, blood, miss thang?' When talking with a girlfriend, I am more likely to muse about my latest piece or so-and-so's party at Club Shi-Shi than about the anger and hurt I felt that morning when a jeweler refused me entrance to his store because I am black and male and we are all perceived as thieves. I will swallow the hurt and should I speak of it I will vocalize only the anger, saying '"I shoulda bust out his fuckin' windows.'"[43]

As the narrator's ruminations about silence are heard, the audience witnesses a sequence of extreme close-up shots of individual black men on a blackscreen background, along with titles indicating the names of individual black men and/or incidents of racist violence. The viewer witnesses footage of riots, with citizens "looting" businesses while SWAT teams and police in riot gear chase the rioters. The on-screen titles remind the viewer of Howard Beach, Virginia Beach, the murder of Yusef Hawkins, and AIDS. Each of these titles is intercut with still shots that move slowly from a medium close-up to an extreme close-up of individual black men. The movement of the camera in this fashion reminds the viewer that each "incident" of racist violence affected a person, a human being. After the narrator says, "So have I learned to squelch my exclamations of joy. What remains is the wrath," the screen fades to black and the following titles emerge: "Black Men/fade/endangered species?/fade/Tongues Untied/by Marlon Riggs featuring Essex Hemphill."

The documentary title itself suggests that quare public address must engage multiplicity and unreflective conflations of queerness and whiteness. Counter-racist quare theory, as Rinaldo Walcott suggests, entails a "blackened queerness and queered blackness."[44] A brief sequence during the first third of the documentary illustrates the ways in which hegemonic whiteness can affect experiences living under racist conditions, even in terms of the production of erotic desire. As Riggs performs the voice-over, viewers are treated to a montage of white male beefcake photos, shots of men attending the Folsom Street Leather Fair, and other iconic images of ideal gay masculinity that are explicitly white. "In California," Riggs intones, "I learned the taste and touch of snow / cruising white boys I played out adolescent dreams deferred. Maybe from time to time a brother glanced my way; I never noticed. I was immersed in vanilla / I savored this single flavor, one deliberately not my own. I avoided the question: Why? Pretended not to notice the absence of black images in this new gay life in bookstores, poster shops, film festivals, even my own fantasies."

As Riggs continues the voice-over reflections of his own lived experiences in San Francisco, the camera cuts to a slow-motion shot of Riggs strolling down Castro Street between Market and Eighteenth streets. Riggs remembers that he "tried not to notice the few images of blacks that were most popular," and the viewer observes still shots of fat black mammies, hypermasculine and hypersexualized black men, and slaves: "Something in Oz and me was amiss, but I tried not to notice. I was intent on the search for my reflection/love/affirmation/in eyes of blue gray green. Searching, I discovered something I didn't expect, something that decades of determined assimilation could not blind me to: In this great gay mecca, I was an invisible man; I had no shadow, no substance, no place, no history, no reflection. I was an alien unseen, and seen, unwanted. Here, as in Hephzibah [Georgia], I was a 'nigger' *still*. I quit the Castro no longer my home, my mecca, and went in search of someplace better."

Critical Principle 2: Quaring public address can enrich and extend existing approaches to public address scholarship by focusing on speaking subjects as diverse collectives. Quaring public address can thus focus on collectively "authored" forms of public address.

I think that the critic necessarily must interrogate and renovate Aristotelian and other individualist assumptions regarding the speaker/speech/audience/occasion/context/change/constraint relationship. This suggestion, of course, is in keeping with Barbara Biesecker's claims regarding canonization (or not) of women's voices in the American rhetorical tradition.[45] To paraphrase Biesecker, critics interested in the rhetoric of the oppressed, dispossessed, and displaced must continue to recover those voices hidden in/from history while simultaneously interrogating the cultural, social, economic, and symbolic conditions that enable speaking subjects to emerge.[46] In developing a quare public address, we must be vigilant in our efforts to avoid tokenization of quare voices or engage in "supplementary" canonization that fails to revolutionize the standards by which critics judge eloquence.[47]

If we take a poststructuralist perspective on identity—that is, that individuated and group identities are constructed in and through complex discursive webs and that those webs are embedded in what Patricia Hill Collins has named the "matrix of domination"—we may begin to enact "praxes which reveal the guises of domination and may thus redefine our positions vis-à-vis representation through the acknowledgment of the heterogeneity of identity."[48] Collective representation of multiple identities poses a specific challenge to a quare public address project. That we focus on collective contestations of hegemonic conditions or on group-based rhetoric is not new—the 1970 Wingspread Conference on Rhetorical Criticism made a similar call.[49]

But the ways in which the voices of *individual* orators continue to be privileged as the site of critical interrogation needs further consideration.[50] Is the focus on the individual orator/advocate an intractable focus of public address studies? What assumptions are at stake in retaining the individual as a primary locus of critical attention? What will quare public address studies gain by retaining this focus? What might we lose, if the tendency to focus on individual voices leads to a neglect of collective rhetorics? Have we conceptualized sufficiently an apparatus for the analysis of collective rhetorics—analytical tools not premised on the individual speaking subject? Does the rhetorical theory of social movements provide an adequate conceptual vocabulary for the formation of quare public address studies or the theorization of models of collective public address?

Mercer's quare scholarship provides an important insight relative to my concern for the twin problems of individualism and representation: Our politics, Mercer argues, "should be seen as a hybridized form of political and cultural practice. By this I mean precisely because of our lived experiences of discrimination in and exclusion from the white gay and lesbian community, and of discrimination in and exclusions from the black community, we locate ourselves in the spaces *between* different communities—at the intersections of power relations determined by race, class, gender, and sexuality."[51]

Moreover, Mercer contends, "It is impossible for any one individual to speak as a representative for an entire community without risking the violent reductionism which repeats the stereotypical view within the majority culture that minority communities are homogenous, unitary, and monolithic because their members are all the same. It is impossible for any one black person to claim the right to speak for the diversity of identities and experiences within black society without the risk that such diversity will be simplified and reduced to what is seen as typical, a process which thereby reproduces and replicates the logic of the racist stereotype that all black people are, essentially, the same."[52]

These two observations raise the thorny issue of the putative link between a focus on the individual rhetor and the degree to which that individual will be received within the critical community (or even among popular audiences) as representative of the communities of which she or he is a part. Quare public address studies, I think, might problematize this link by distinguishing between speaking as an individual representative of a particular group and speaking "as one voice among others, each of which articulates different experiences and identities."[53]

Of course, it is the case that models of eloquence have accounted for the phenomenon of social movements. Many fine studies of civil rights oratory, feminist rhetoric, and various labor movements have been published, and other scholars have rightly launched critiques of some problematic assumptions that anchor the study of public address.[54] As others have already pointed out, exclusive focus on individual rhetors would necessarily overlook collective contestations of oppressive conditions. Liberal models of eloquence necessarily focus on the rhetorical virtuosity of individual orators. Although I would not suggest that scholars abandon those models, we would do well to take seriously Biesecker's suggestion to interrogate the conditions that enable individual and collective speaking subjects to emerge at particular moments in history.

The opening sequence of *Tongues Untied* contextualizes Riggs's polemic as a critical response to the racist and heteronormative silencing of black gay men in American culture. The balance of the documentary contains short vignettes depicting the lives, struggles, and loves of black gay men in the United States. The documentary contains fictional, poetic, and animated representations of these lived experiences. What is most important to recognize here is that the stories included in the narrative are not solely representative of Riggs's experiences. Although Riggs viewed his voice as an anchor, the experimental documentary included a multiplicity of voices. The stories include the search for romantic partnership, interpersonal conflict on a bus based on Hemphill's short story "Without Comment," a story about black gay men denied entrance to a dance club by a racist gay club employee, stories about growing up in the South during the 1960s and 1970s, gay bashing, and the subject of black men loving white men. Phillip Brian Harper observes in his analysis of visual representations of black gay men that "*Tongues Untied*'s most striking achievement is its collectivization of that voice through the incorporation of written work by a range of black gay men."[55]

Subsequent to Riggs's self-removal from the world of the Castro, the viewer bears witness to the journeys and lived experiences of many black gay men in their search for a social identity free from the racism of the "gay community" and free from the heteronormativity of contemporary black culture. Where to turn? The black church typically offers little sense of home, as we hear the passionate admonishments from a preacher that "homosexuality is an abomination." Nor is there comfort to be found in the black political community, as the loyalty of black gay men to the struggle against racism is questioned: "What are you first, gay or black?" Finally, men such as Riggs, Hemphill, and their contemporaries remain exiles in other sectors of the black community through the practices of name-calling: "punks" and "faggots" are disallowed community with their black brothers and sisters. Riggs observes in his *Afterimage* interview that speaking from a homonormative or nonassimilationist position to challenge the fact of stratification itself is often viewed with a jaundiced eye by funding foundations, arts patrons, and various audiences. "Even progressive funders don't want to touch this," Riggs observes, because "I'm dealing with black rage. I'm dealing with the disenfranchisement of black people and redemption through language and through images that are not part of the conventional wisdom of how we should go about our empowerment."[56] The bounds to which quare voices might "represent" therefore are also subject to contestation within the rhetorical milieu.[57]

Critical Principle 3: Our objects of study will be those voices that contest the (il)logic of heternormativity.

Heteronormativity, I will suggest, is less a pastiche of homonegative attitudes, policies, and practices—ranging from sodomy statutes to characterizations of quare identity as pathological, sinful, or criminal to prohibitions against same-sex marriage to everyday, garden-variety discriminatory practices against quare people—than a particular (il)logic that both demands loyalty to patriarchal systems of family, reproduction, and filial relationships and organizes itself around the dichotomous dualism of hetero/homo.[58] The ideological scheme of heteronormativity exercises its coercive powers by characterizing heterosexuality as a timeless, natural, and normal means of containing and organizing human desire. It does so by rewarding those individual citizens who buy into the dream of monogamous, long-term heterosexual marriage; it also exercises coercive power by punishing those who opt out of heteronormativity's regime by refusing to marry or by simply experiencing desire deemed illegitimate by the normative political economy.

If heteronormativity is conceptualized primarily as a coercive ideological illogic, how do advocates contest such illogic rhetorically? If heteronormativity tries to contain and channel human desire in certain directions and to certain ends (reproduction within patriarchal familial forms), is "quarecentricity" a simple matter of refusing to be co-opted by that illogic? Can an advocate embrace the quarecentric as a critical/activist stance that refuses, challenges, or otherwise contests the channeling of human desire into the heteronormative reproductive economy and without essentializing quareness? In other words, does challenging heteronormativity in all of its instantiations entail arguing from entirely different grounds that refuse the dichotomous dualism of hetero/homo? I would assert that quarecentricity embraces those representations of homosocial human desire that are fundamentally counter-hegemonic.

It is important to note that one need not necessarily identify as quare or gay, lesbian, bisexual, or transgendered to contest heteronormativity. As Johnson observes astutely, we "cannot afford to be armchair theorists. . . . quare theorists must make theory work for its constituency. Although we share with our white quare peers sexual oppression, gay, lesbians, bisexuals, and transgendered people of color also share racial oppression with other members of our community. We cannot afford to abandon them simply because they are heterosexual."[59] Finally, quare "studies must encourage strategic coalition building around laws and policies that have the potential to affect us across racial, sexual, and class divides."[60]

Although the "speaker" might not necessarily identify as quare, the rhetorical "text" and the circumstances under which such texts are produced could very well be so! What I am suggesting here is that we transcend the search for a gay past that is limited to the identification of historic actors who may or may not have experienced same-sex desire. Rather, if public address studies concerns the historical study of oratory, we can look beyond the speaker to focus on the speech, the occasion, or the circumstances that occasioned the utterances on which we sharpen our critical faculties. Quare circumstances offer the critic opportunities to explore modes of address that might otherwise be overlooked. By "circumstances," I am thinking of such occasions as gay pride festivals, poetry readings, and drag performances.

French feminist philosopher and language theorist Monique Wittig observes that "the straight mind cannot conceive of a culture, a society where heterosexuality would not order not only all human relationships but also its very production of concepts and all the processes which escape consciousness, as well."[61] Wittig's observation describes perfectly the conditions that constitute heteronormativity. Conditions are heteronormative when lived experience and social institutions are organized and constructed around the implicit norm that all human beings are (and must remain) heterosexual until proven otherwise. Heternormativity pervades contemporary American culture, ordering everything from the production of commercials for "I Can't Believe It's Not Butter" and Sealy Posturepedic mattresses to popular television programs—even NBC's *Will and Grace* is organized around heterosexual tropes and conventions.[62] But it is not merely popular or commercial culture that is organized through heteronormativity. Public policies, workplace policies (insurance and benefits), and education are heteronormative too. Failure to adhere to heteronormative conditions can result in discrimination and pervasive inequality. The clearest example of heteronormative public policy that I can identify is the 1996 United States Defense of Marriage Act (DOMA), signed into law by President Bill Clinton. DOMA allows states to pass laws prohibiting same-sex couples the right to marry; the legislation also allows states to ignore the full faith and credit clause of the Constitution by telling states that they do not have to recognize same-sex marriages allowed in other states. In effect, DOMA not only prohibits gay men and lesbians from accessing the constitutional right to marry, but also punishes them for their efforts to secure equality under the law by placing an extra tax burden on them if they do formalize their relationships publicly.[63]

Ignored and exiled in the hegemonic whiteness of the gay community, attacked and reviled in the black heterosexual community, these black gay men—and their experiences—led Riggs to narrate that "their jokes, their laughter form a chorus of contempt. Each joke levels us a little more, and we sit silently. Sometimes join in the laughter as if deep down we too believe we are the lowest among the low. No one will redeem your name, your love, your life, your manhood but *you*. No one will save you but you." The camera then focuses its gaze on poet Essex Hemphill:

"I know the anger that lies inside me like I know the beat of my heart and the taste of my spit. It is easier to be angry than to hurt / Anger is what I do best. It is easier to be furious than yearning/easier to crucify myself and you / than to take on the threatening universe of whiteness by admitting we are worth wanting each other." The camera draws back from the extreme close-up shot of Hemphill, and the viewer observes still shots of various black men. A heartbeat sound effect plays in the soundtrack, while various men provide voice-overs:

> I too know anger, my body contains as much anger as water. It is the mate-rial from which I have built my house, blood red bricks that cry in the rain. It is the face and posture I show the world. It is the way, sometimes the *only* way I am granted audience. It is sometimes the way I show affection. I am angry because of the treatment I am afforded as a black man. That fiery anger is stoked additionally with the fuse of contempt and despisal shown me by my community because I am gay. I cannot go home as who I am. When I speak of home I mean not only the familial constellation from which I grew, but the entire black community: the black press, the black church, black academicians, the black literati, and the black left. Where is *my* reflec-tion? I am most often rendered invisible, perceived as a threat to the family, or I am tolerated if I am silent and inconspicuous. I cannot go home as who I am and that hurts me deeply.[64]

The final shots in the documentary's third segment splice footage of gay rights activist marches with the civil rights marches of the early 1960s. The juxtaposition of gay black men with black civil rights activists contextualizes gay identity as a political matter, as a matter of social justice—and not a purely private or individ-ual matter. As the viewer witnesses this juxtaposition, she hears Riggs in voice-over narration: "Whatever awaits me, this much I know: I was blind to my brother's beauty, and now I see my own. Death to the voice that believed that we weren't worth wanting, loving each other. Now, I hear. I was mute, tongue-tied. Burdened by shadows and silence. Now I speak and my burden is lightened, lifted, free." The documentary ends the way it began, with a chorus of voices chanting softly "brother to brother, brother to brother." Against a blackscreen, the viewer reads the following: "Black men loving black men a call to action, a call to action, an acknowledgment of responsibility, we take care of our own kind, when the nights grow cold and silent. These days, the nights are cold-blooded and the silence echoes with complicity."

Riggs argues near the end of his interview with film critics Chuck Kleinhans and Julia Lesage that the montage of civil rights and gay struggle was crucial. "From my vantage point," he claims, "that montage was absolutely necessary. I had to move my experience out of just the personal realm and make it a communal and public experience. . . . not to remain personal and poetic but also to be hard-edged and muscular in clarifying the connection between civil rights black American struggles over three centuries and what we're doing now as black gay men."[65]

It is not immediately clear in the material quoted above how Riggs's documentary challenges heteronormativity—indeed the rhetorical problem of heteronormativity would at first glance appear to reside decidedly outside Riggs's topical focus in *Tongues Untied*. But the ways in which the documentary, as well as his later documentary entitled *Black Is . . . Black Ain't* challenge the presumptive heterosexuality embedded in blackness provide the quare-positive critic with a conceptual apparatus that explodes the category of heteronormativity beyond its currently rather narrowly construed bounds.[66] The documentary's third major segment tells the stories of black men learning to love one another. The segment begins with a still shot of Riggs cloaked in a dark wool blanket; this still shot is mixed with shots of a casket and funeral. The heartbeat sound effects set the meter of the segment. Riggs narrates the voice-over: "In search of self, I listen to the beat of my heart, to rhythms muffled beneath layers of delusion, pain, alienation, silence. The beat was my salvation. I let this primal pulse lead me past broken dreams, solitude, fragments of identity to a *new* place, a home: not of peace, harmony, and sunshine, *NO—but truth. Simple, shameless, brazen truth.*"

The documentary then turns to a critical and poetic examination of life within the black gay men's community—the audience watches a group of eight men enjoying themselves at a dinner party and discussing the practices of the "Snap!" and "vogueing" (black gay vernacular practices appropriated by and made popular in the white pop culture sphere by Madonna). The viewer observes several scenes from New York City drag balls while Essex Hemphill recites his poem "In the Life" in voice-over narration. The poem signifies the message that a black gay man might speak to his mother regarding gay identity and life in the gay community: "I learned there is no tender mercy for men of color / for sons who love men like me. / Do not feel shame for how I live. I chose this tribe / of warriors and outlaws."

The viewer then witnesses men dancing together in a public park, performing the electric slide to the heartbeat sound effects. The segment's next scene positions the spectator as voyeur, as she watches a group of men enjoying drinks together at a bar. An unnamed man exits the restroom and cruises Essex Hemphill. Hemphill returns the passionate gaze, and Hemphill's voice provides a poetic off-screen narration:

> I'm chocolate candy, a handful of cookies, the goodies you are forbidden to eat. I'm a piece of cake, a slice of pie, an ice cream bar that chills your teeth. Think of me as your favorite treat, a pan of popcorn kernels / waitin' for the heat. Exiting the john, I check the mirror for the face of naked lust / his eyes howl at me / coyote separated from the roving pack. / Love potions solve no mysteries / provide no comment on the unspoken. / Our lives tremble between pathos and seduction.

The camera then focuses its gaze on Hemphill's face while he completes the recitation of his poem against a blackscreen background: "Our inhibitions force us to be equal, we swallow hard black love potions from a golden glass. New language beckons us, its dialect present, intimate. Through my eyes, focused is pure naked light fixed on you like magic, clarity / I see risks. Regret, there will be none / let some wonder, some worry, some accuse. Let you and I know the tenderness only *we* can bear." The love that black men have for one another is infused with quarecentric and political meaning. As the audiences witnesses black men coming together to love, we also witness the camera panning a gay pride march where men carry a banner that reads: "Black Men Loving Black Men: A Revolutionary Act." What makes this love quarecentric and political, the spectator might inquire? Black men learning to love one another in the face of gay bashing, racism, and AIDS.

Critical Principle 4: The audiences addressed by quare rhetorics/rhetors or within quare circumstances include both hegemonic and counterpublics.

In elaborating this principle, I move away from consideration of the identity and subject position of the speaker, away from the text, to explicit consideration of the audiences for quare rhetorical performances. Such consideration is crucial for the process of bringing into focus those audiences "othered" through hegemonic discourse practices—those audiences relegated to the abject position of the "Third Persona," to borrow from Phil Wander's treatment of exclusionary ideological discourses.[67] For the purposes of my discussion, hegemonic publics are those audiences saturated with racial, gender, class, and/or hetero-privilege. Such publics in an election year may be hailed as "taxpayers," "constituents," "voters," or the "electorate." In U.S. foreign policy rhetoric, the hegemonic public is typically construed as "American." Privileged audiences are granted considerable rhetorical power by the tendency for advocates to characterize the public's concerns in monolithic or homogenized terms. Feminist political theorist Nancy Fraser offers a useful definition of "counterpublics" as "parallel discursive arenas where members of subordinated social groups invent and circulate counterdiscourses to formulate oppositional interpretations of their identities, interests, and needs."[68] Members of the Black Public Sphere Collective characterize the black public sphere as a "critical social imaginary" rooted in black vernacular practices, including "street talk," music, "church voices," and others; the primary rhetorical functions of the black public sphere include a "wider sphere of critical practice and visionary politics, in which intellectuals can join with the energies of the street, the school, the church, and the city to constitute a challenge to the exclusionary violence of much public space in the United States."[69] Again quare canonization must not neglect the multiple forms of exclusion that attend the facts of social stratification and the oppression(s) therein engendered.

The rhetorical division of audiences into hegemonic and counterpublics, how-ever, does more than both reproduce and contest the facts and character of social stratification. This rhetorical division functions also to quash and punish dissent; it also tries to establish the grounds on which oppositional discourses might be con-stituted. Thus, as queer theorist Michael Warner posited recently, counterpublics are more than "subalterns with a reform program." Indeed counterpublics are astutely aware of the dynamics of domination/subordination, and thus the "cultural horizon against which [a counterpublic] marks itself off is not just a general or wider public, but a dominant one. . . . The discourse that constitutes it is not merely a different or alternative idiom, but one that in other contexts would be regarded with hostility or a sense of indecorousness."[70]

My concern here for how audiences are both invested with and divested of rhetorical power (to participate in public deliberation and public address) relates to the processes and practices by which counterpublics are silenced and therefore find it difficult to contest hegemonic sociopolitical conditions. Subaltern counterpublics, in Joseph Beam's words, are "silenced" and "cornered by identities" they "never wanted to claim." Quare public address scholars, I think, would want to pay close attention to this process of investment/divestment or the division of audiences into hegemonic and subaltern publics.

The controversy over PBS's decision to air *Tongues Untied* illustrates how com-plicated and conflicted this process can be, for the boundaries between hegemonic/counterpublic is always subject to contestation. More precisely, the controversy illu-minates how a rhetor's construction of "audience" may not be acknowledged by media outlets, which tend to grant hegemonic public status to those groups already vested with some sort of privilege in the evil schemes of social stratification. Riggs produced his documentary for and by a black gay male public. From Riggs's per-spective, black gay men in particular and black folks in general constituted the pub-lic(s) to which he directed his rhetoric, even as the documentary simultaneously acknowledged that in a racist and heteronormative culture black gay men are both invisible and reviled (and therefore a potential counterpublic). Riggs, however, refused to concede this casting of black gay men—Indeed the documentary denied those very grounds.

The PBS decision to air the documentary illustrates the contestation of audience hegemony. The Kansas City, Missouri, PBS station's characterization of "drawings of male genitals" and "scenes of men kissing" as "shocking" presumes a different hegemonic public than Riggs had in mind, for it is doubtful that gay folk (and, perhaps, even straight-but-not-narrow types) would find such images "shocking" or problematic—especially given the paucity of gay-positive and antiracist images on television. The assertions by some station managers that audiences would be negli-gible in size or lacking in "sympathy" again casts the audience as presumptively white and heterosexual—an arguably arbitrary and shortsighted attribution.

Provisional Conclusions: On the Development of Quare Public Address Studies

My primary purpose here has been to identify and elaborate several key critical principles that could form the foundational premises of quare/queer public address studies. Although I do not presume to have identified all such principles, I would go so far as to argue that the conceptualizations offered herein, if considered thoughtfully and nondefensively, can open up additional terrain for scholarly reflection and analysis. One of my primary claims is that quaring public address is primarily a process of adopting a particular critical stance in relationship to public culture, to rhetorical artifacts, and to the fact of social stratification and political domination. Quaring public address necessitates an honest and forthright acknowledgment of the rhetorical conditions, limits, and possibilities occasioned by racist and homonegative domination. As *Tongues Untied* demonstrates so eloquently, racism and heteronormativity function synergistically to silence various audience constituencies and rhetors in an effort to maintain white supremacy and heteropatriarchy.

From where I stand, it would be impractical, imprudent, and ineffective to queer/quare public address without sustained attention to how domination affects the nature and functions of the rhetorical process itself. As such, quaring public address might blend "traditional" conceptualizations of the *functions* of public address with the political sensibilities of various counterracist, postcolonial, and feminist discourses; and with the orientation to discourse offered by key principles in the critical rhetoric project envisioned initially by Ray McKerrow and refined by Ono, Sloop, and Thompson, among others.[71] Quare public address studies reject a focus on "adding" gay, lesbian, bisexual, and transgendered voices to the preexisting public address canon. The additive model, as I hope is clear by now, fails to contest the elitist approaches to the rhetorical process and thus necessarily will misapply existing standards to vernacular and experimental forms of rhetorical activities.

Quare public address, then, tries to discern how and to what rhetorical end the artifact under critical examination "speaks" quarely. An artifact qualifies for quare analysis when the artifact's rhetorical functions include the contestation of heteronormativity, whiteness, class privilege, and/or hegemonic masculinities and femininities, for all such focuses contest the normal in American rhetorical culture. The radical potential of our project remains to be actualized—again I am interested in the emancipatory potentiality of human discourse. Such potential is seen most easily, I think, when the artifact engages in extensive tinkering with sedimented, hidden, or reified doxastic claims regarding the normal characterizations of eloquence: that our greatest speakers are normally or usually white, male, heterosexual, and highly educated. Quarecentricity, as I conceive it, has little to do with identifying an "essential" quareness or quare identity and more to do with a radical skepticism about the ability of current models of public address to address the problems of racist and homonegative domination.

One implication that deserves additional consideration here is the relationship of the critic to the artifact/discourse under analysis. It should be clear to the reader by now that I conceive of criticism as partial, situated, and provisional. Our very humanity, the various subject positions that we each occupy necessarily affect our critical relationships to rhetorical artifacts and to our assumptions about the rhetorical process. My own socialization within various lesbian-feminist cultures, for instance, has enabled me to understand heterosexuality as a discursive regime in Wittig's sense. My whiteness, if left uninterrogated, will lead me to ask some critical questions but to neglect others. In other words, our own positionalities within the matrix of domination will open up some avenues of exploration but might blind us to other possibilities. It would thus behoove the critic, I think, to take into account how one's positionality both enables and disables our critical readings of rhetorical artifacts and our orientation to the rhetorical process and public address.

I would imagine that some might argue that a white quare counter-racist feminist critic has nothing insightful to say about black gay male discourses and that racial and gender barriers make it impossible for the critic to understand the discourse of the "other." Such claims are premised on a mystification of the production of knowledge claims and the privileged position of mainstream scholars, who rarely face such attacks.[72] I wish to register my strong objections to such claims on the grounds that they serve the ends and means of domination by keeping the oppressed, dispossessed, disadvantaged, and dominated among us fighting with one another rather than fighting the systems of domination themselves.[73] Although I will never experience directly the pain of racist domination, I do experience on a daily basis the privileges of whiteness and am complicit in maintaining systems of domination regardless of whether I am fully conscious of such complicity. I also witness racial domination on a daily basis by virtue of my own social preferences.[74] One need not occupy a specific subject position in order to listen carefully and hear the concerns of those who occupy it—as long as we realize that there are limitations to what we might offer that critical process. It is possible, and again I think *Tongues Untied* demonstrates this, to stand in solidarity across differences and to cultivate critical perspectives that are not premised on the blind arrogance of privilege.

On the other hand, I do understand the skepticism and suspicion with which members of oppressed populations regard privileged folks when it comes to being the subjects of study—again because privilege has a tendency to blind the privileged to the everyday realities of racial domination, homonegativity, class warfare, and misogyny that many citizens of the world experience. I would like to develop orientations to rhetorical process that cultivate solidarity across difference—that contest and reject privilege—so that we might gain a fuller appreciation for the eloquence of tongues that have heretofore been shackled.

Notes

1. For instance, see James Andrews and David Zarefsky, eds., *American Voices* (New York: Longman, 1989); Ronald F. Reid, ed., *Three Centuries of American Rhetorical Discourse* (Prospect Heights, Ill.: Waveland Press, 1988); Andrews and Zarefsky, eds., *Contemporary American Voices* (New York: Longman, 1992); Halford Ross Ryan, ed., *Contemporary American Public Discourse* (Prospect Heights, Ill.: Waveland, 1992). Some anthologies do include multiple examples of voices "representative" of historically marginalized and oppressed groups. See, for instance, Maureen Harrison and Steve Gilbert, eds., *Landmark American Speeches*, vol. 3, *The 20th Century* (Carlsbad, Calif.: Excellent Books, 2001); and Richard Johannesen et al., eds., *Contemporary American Speeches*, 6th ed. (Dubuque, Iowa: Kendall/Hunt, 1988). A third category of anthologies is devoted specifically to female orators and/or orators from various racial and ethnic minority groups in the United States. See Robbie Jean Walker, ed., *The Rhetoric of Struggle: Public Address by African-American Women* (New York: Garland, 1992); Shirley Wilson Logan, ed., *With Pen and Voice* (Carbondale, Ill.: Southern Illinois University Press, 1995); W. C. Vanderwirth, comp., *Indian Oratory: Famous Speeches by Noted Indian Chieftans* (Norman: University of Oklahoma Press, 1971); Philip S. Foner and Robert J. Branham, eds., *Lift Every Voice: African American Oratory 1787–1900* (Tuscaloosa: University of Alabama Press, 1998); Alice Moore Dunbar, *Masterpieces of Negro Eloquence* (1914; New York: G. K. Hall, 1997); and the massive tome edited by Deborah Gillan Straub, *Voices of Multicultural America: Notable Speeches Delivered by African, Asian, Hispanic and Native Americans, 1790–1995* (New York: Gale Research, 1996).

2. E. Patrick Johnson, "'Quare Studies; or, Almost Everything I Know about Queer Studies I Learned from My Grandmother," *Text and Performance Quarterly* 21 (November 2001): 1–25.

3. Jennifer Terry, "Theorizing Deviant Historiography," in *Feminists Revision History*, ed. Ann-Louise Shapiro (New Brunswick, N.J.: Rutgers University Press, 1994), 284.

4. Raymie E. McKerrow, "Critical Rhetoric: Theory and Praxis," *Communication Monographs* 56 (June 1989): 91–111.

5. Thanks to Lisbeth Lipari for helping me phrase this point.

6. Robert Hariman, "Afterword: Relocating the Art of Public Address," in *Rhetoric and Political Culture in Nineteenth Century America* (East Lansing: Michigan State University Press, 1998), 163–83.

7. Hariman, "Afterword," 171. Hariman characterizes the neoclassical approach as follows: "Oratory remains the premier genre of public address and the basic object of analysis is the individual speech, which is understood to address a particular situation and to be oriented towards a tangible policy or definition of civic culture." Poststructuralist approaches, on the other hand, "challenges every assumption of authorial intention, textual practice, civic context, and political privilege that is embedded in the classical model. The basic object of analysis is the social structure controlling comprehensive processes of discourse production and reception, while the analysis emphasizes the fragmentary nature of all discursive practice, the limited role of individual human agency, and the dispensability of any particular text." Hariman, "Afterword," 167.

8. Recent work on counterpublics and vernacular rhetoric addresses such concerns. See, for instance, Robert Asen and Daniel C. Brouwer, eds., *Counterpublics and the State* (Albany,

N.Y.: SUNY Press, 2001) and Gerard Hauser, *Vernacular Voices: The Rhetorics of Publics and Public Spheres* (Columbia: University of South Carolina Press, 1999); see also notes 69, 70, and 71 below.

9. Chuck Kleinhans and Julia Lesage, "Listening to the Heartbeat: Interview with Marlon Riggs," *Jump Cut* 36 (1991): 120.

10. Frank J. Prial, "TV Film about Gay Black Men Is Under Attack," *New York Times*, June 25, 1991, B1.

11. Marlon T. Riggs, "Notes of a Signifyin' Snap! Queen," *Art Journal* 50 (fall 1991): 60.

12. Ibid., 61.

13. Ibid.

14. Ibid.

15. Ibid., 63

16. "Blackscreened," *Economist* (July 20, 1991): 108.

17. Jack Robertiello, "Many Stations Nix or Delay Film about Black Gay Men," *Current Online*, http://www.current.org/prog/prog112g.html (October 18, 2001).

18. "Ottinger and Kobin: Two of the Broadcast Managers Who Stood Up for Diversity of Viewpoints," *Current Online*, http://www.current.org/prog/prog123p.html (October 18, 2001).

19. Steve Behrens, "From P.O.V.: A Regular Supply of Irregular Humanity," *Current Online*, http://www.current.org/prog/prog123p.html (October 18, 2001).

20. Michael Warner, "Publics and Counterpublics," *Public Culture* 14 (winter 2002): 49, 50.

21. Ibid., 84.

22. Marlon Riggs, "Tongues *Re*-Tied," in *Resolutions: Contemporary Video Practices*, ed. Michael Renov and Erika Suderburg (Minneapolis: University of Minnesota Press, 1996), 187–88.

23. Courtland Milloy, "Film on Black Gays Is Bold, but Ignores the Big Picture," *Washington Post*, July 18, 1991, C3.

24. Kent A. Ono and John M. Sloop, "The Critique of Vernacular Discourse," *Communication Monographs* 62 (March 1995): 19–46.

25. Ibid., 21–23; cf. Jeannette L. Dates and William Barlow, eds., *Split Image: African Americans in the Mass Media*, 2d ed. (Washington, D.C.: Howard University Press, 1993); Ed Guerrero, *Framing Blackness: The African American Image in Film* (Philadelphia: Temple University Press, 1993); Herman Gray, *Watching Race: Television and the Struggle for "Blackness"* (Minneapolis: University of Minnesota Press, 1995).

26. Ono and Sloop, "Critique," 23.

27. Cf. James C. Scott's notion of "hidden transcripts" in *Domination and the Arts of Resistance* (New Haven, Conn.: Yale University Press, 1990). Scott contends, for instance, "Slaves and serfs ordinarily dare not contest the terms of their subordination openly. Behind the scenes, though, they are likely to create and defend a social space in which offstage dissent to the official transcript of power relations may be voiced." Scott, xi. *Tongues Untied*, then, is remarkable in the sense that Riggs and his collaborators refused to hide their opposition or bite their tongues in the face of oppressive regimes. The rhetorical genius of *Tongues Untied* is indeed its refusal to function as a "hidden transcript."

28. bell hooks, "Language: Teaching New Worlds/New Words," in *Teaching to Transgress* (New York: Routledge, 1994), 168.

29. Cf. Kath Weston, *Families We Choose: Gays, Lesbians, Kinship* (New York: Columbia University Press, 1997).

30. "Listening to the Heartbeat," 122.

31. Riggs, "Tongues *Re*-Tied," 188.

32. See, for example, Dana L. Cloud, "The Null Persona: Race and the Rhetoric of Silence in the Uprising of '34," *Rhetoric & Public Affairs* 2 (summer 1999): 177–209; Celeste M. Condit and John L. Lucaites, *Crafting Equality: America's Anglo-African Word* (Chicago: University of Chicago Press, 1990); Philip Wander, "The Third Persona: An Ideological Turn in Rhetorical Theory," *Central States Speech Journal* 35 (winter 1984): 197–216; Barbara Biesecker, "Coming to Terms with Recent Attempts to Write Women into the History of Rhetoric," *Philosophy & Rhetoric* 25 (1992) 140–61; and Karlyn Kohrs Campbell, *Man Cannot Speak for Her*, 2 vols. (New York: Praeger, 1989).

33. Marcos Becquer, "Snap! Thology and Other Discursive Practices in Tongues Untied," *Wide Angle* 13, no. 2 (April 1991): 7.

34. Maxine Baca Zinn and Bonnie Thornton Dill, "Theorizing Difference from Multiracial Feminism," *Feminist Studies* 22 (summer 1996): 321–32.

35. Ibid.

36. Dwight A. McBride, "Can the Queen Speak? Racial Essentialism, Sexuality, and the Problem of Authority," *Callaloo* 21 (spring 1998): 365.

37. Lyle Ashton Harris, "Cultural Healing: An Interview with Marlon Riggs," *Afterimage*, March 1991, 8.

38. Essex Hemphill, "Does Your Mama Know about Me?" in *Ceremonies* (San Francisco: Cleis Press, 1992), 42, 43–44.

39. Hemphill, "Does Your Mama Know about Me?" 44.

40. Cf. Phillip Brian Harper, "Walk-On Parts and Speaking Subjects: Screen Representations of Black Gay Men," *Callaloo* 18 (spring 1995): 392.

41. Kobena Mercer, "Dark and Lovely Too: Black Gay Men in Independent Film," in *Queer Looks: Perspectives on Lesbian and Gay Film and Video*, ed. Martha Gever, Pratibha Parmar, and John Greyson (New York: Routledge, 1993), 239.

42. Maurice Berger, "Too Shocking to Show?" *Art in America*, (July 1992): 39.

43. *Tongues Untied*, 1989, directed by Marlon Riggs.

44. Vincent Woodard, "Just as Quare as They Want to Be: A Review of the Black Queer Studies in the Millennium Conference," *Callaloo* 23 (fall 2000): 1279.

45. Biesecker, "Coming to Terms," 140–61.

46. Ibid., 148.

47. Cf. ibid., 142–44.

48. Bequer, "Snap! Thology," 7.

49. Lloyd Bitzer and Edwin Black, eds., *The Prospect of Rhetoric: Report on the National Development Project* (Englewood Cliffs, N.J.: Prentice-Hall, 1971).

50. Cf. Catherine Helen Palczewski's critique of Gerard Hauser's *Vernacular Voices:* "The book purports to expand studies of publicity beyond the official discourse that comes from powerful voices located in 'institutional forums' (36). . . . Although such a shift in focus is one I applaud, the case studies presented in the book do not actualize this shift." See Palczewski, review of *Vernacular Voices, Rhetoric and Public Affairs* 3 (winter 2000): 683.

51. Mercer, "Dark and Lovely Too," 239.

52. Ibid., 243.

53. Ibid., 244.

54. See, for instance, Lisa A. Flores, "Creating Discursive Space through a Rhetoric of Difference: Chicana Feminists Craft a Homeland," *Quarterly Journal of Speech* 82 (May 1996): 142–56; Amy R. Slagell, "The Rhetorical Structure of Frances E. Willard's Campaign for Woman Suffrage, 1876–1896," *Rhetoric and Public Affairs* 4 (spring 2001): 1–23; Robert Terrill, "Protest, Prophecy, and Prudence in the Rhetoric of Malcolm X," *Rhetoric and Public Affairs* 4 (spring 2001): 25–53; John C. Hammerback and Richard J. Jensen, "Ethnic Heritage as Rhetorical Legacy: The Plan of Delano," *Quarterly Journal of Speech* 80 (February 1994): 53–70; and Lester C. Olson, "On the Margins of Rhetoric: Audre Lorde Transforming Silence into Language and Action" *Quarterly Journal of Speech* 83 (February 1997): 49–70.

55. Harper, "Walk-On Parts and Speaking Subjects," 392.

56. Harris, "Cultural Healing," 8.

57. Cf. Philip Brian Harper, *Are We Not Men? Masculine Anxiety and the Problem of African-American Identity* (New York: Oxford University Press, 1996).

58. Cf. The 1917 Collective, "Capitalism and Homophobia: Marxism and the Struggle for Gay/Lesbian Rights," in *The Material Queer: A LesBiGay Cultural Studies Reader,* ed. Donald Morton (Boulder, Colo.: Westview, 1996), 369–79; Eve Kosofsky Sedgwick, *Epistemology of the Closet* (Berkeley: University of California Press, 1990).

59. Johnson, "Quare," 18.

60. Ibid.

61. Monique Wittig, *The Straight Mind and Other Essays* (Boston: Beacon Press, 1992).

62. See Kathleen Battles and Wendy Hilton-Morrow's excellent essay "Gay Characters in Conventional Spaces: *Will and Grace* and the Situation Comedy Genre," *Critical Studies in Media Communication* 19 (March 2002): 87–105.

63. There is a considerable tax disincentive for enrolling for domestic partner benefits, whereas married heterosexual couples can participate in one another's health plans without the federal government treating the cash value of those benefits as taxable income. I learned of these effects when I attended a domestic partner benefits orientation session at a former place of employment, whose nondiscrimination clause includes gay men and lesbians and which offers health benefits to employees registered as domestic partners.

64. Riggs quotes the work of Joseph Beam in this passage.

65. "Listening to the Heartbeat," 126.

66. Cf. Johnson, "Quare," 14–18.

67. Wander, "The Third Persona," 197–216.

68. Nancy Fraser, "Rethinking the Public Sphere: A Contribution to the Critique of Actually Existing Democracy," in *Habermas and the Public Sphere,* ed. Craig Calhoun (Cambridge, Mass.: MIT Press, 1992), 123; rhetorician Erik Doxtader extends Fraser's analysis to include attention to the rhetorical functions of counterpublics and counterpublicity and to consider the "problem of how (subaltern) counterpublics speak." See "In the Name of Reconciliation: The Faith and Works of Counterpublicity," in *Counterpublics and the State,* ed. Asen and Brouwer, 75.

69. The Black Public Sphere Collective, *The Black Public Sphere: A Public Culture Book* (Chicago: University of Chicago Press, 1995), 2–3.

70. Warner, "Publics and Counterpublics," 86.

71. For instance, see McKerrow, "Critical Rhetoric," 91–111; Kent A. Ono and John M. Sloop, "Commitment to Telos: A Sustained Critical Rhetoric," *Communication Monographs* 59 (March 1992): 48–61; Norman Clark, "The Critical Servant: An Isocratean Contribution to Critical Rhetoric," *Quarterly Journal of Speech* 82 (May 1996): 111–25; John M. Murphy, "Critical Rhetoric as Political Discourse," *Argumentation and Advocacy* 32 (summer 1995): 1–16; Julie M. Thompson, *Mommy Queerest: Contemporary Rhetorics of Lesbian Maternal Identity* (Amherst: University of Massachusetts Press, 2002).

72. The claims that one can only study one's own kind are solipsistic. If such claims were true, scholarship of any kind would be unnecessary; we really would have to limit ourselves to contemplating our navels.

73. In some senses, of course, this identity-politics-based critique has passed, at least within the academy. I am not so sure, however, that the critique has died in various nonacademic publics.

74. For instance, I have witnessed directly the racist profiling of two former significant others by retail clerks, security guards, and police.

Part Two

queer
FIGURATIONS

Lucy Lobdell's Queer Circumstances

John M. Sloop

I made up my mind to dress in men's attire to seek labor, as I was used to
men's work . . . and I was capable of doing men's work, and getting men's
wages.

Narrative of Lucy Ann Lobdell

Lucy Lobdell wrote to her uncle in 1852, explaining that her husband, Mr. George
Washington Slater, had left her "in rather queer circumstances." To modern ears, her
phrasing is archaic, but only partially so.[1] The Lobdell story, ultimately involving a
romance that begins in a New York almshouse and blossoms in lean-tos and hovels
that witness the transformation of Lucy Lobdell into the Reverend Joseph Israel
Lobdell, remains a queer one a century and a half later. Despite the relative paucity
of discourse—we have Lobdell's autobiographical narrative of the first portion of
her life and a smattering of newspaper articles, medical reports, and family newslet-
ters—it remains fertile ground for historical understandings of medical, moral, and
psychiatric jurisdictions over sexuality and identity, as well as contemporary uses of
historical figures in our own understandings of sexual and gendered practices.

Moreover, given that the Lobdell story provides one of the first known published
medical/psychiatric uses of the term "lesbian" and is a narrative that now might well
fit comfortably within the pages of Leslie Feinberg's *Transgendered Warriors*,[2] it is a
story worth recounting and clearly worthy of critical attention. That is, both the historic and contemporary articulations of Lucy Lobdell's story are grounds on which
one could provide a critical understanding and troubling of gender categories and
sexual practices, a troubling that illumines the past—that in some sense queers the
study of public address[3] and works to encourage a rethinking, or queering, of present categories.

The Lobdell Narrative

I begin with my own version of Lucy Lobdell's life story, a version stitched together
from my reading of published accounts of the case.[4] Lucy Ann Lobdell was born on
December 2, 1829, in Albany County, New York, and was raised in the lumbering
community of Long Eddy. A bright, hardworking, and contrary child, Lobdell not

only raised and cared for the family's poultry and livestock but also learned to play the violin and was so successful in her primary and secondary schooling that she was able to take a job as a teacher in a small community near Long Eddy. In addition to her many skills, or perhaps due to them, Lobdell was also highly sought after as a romantic partner by many men in her community. After having dismissed several young men who courted her, Lobdell married George Slater, a union that took place in part because she felt sympathy for Slater, a man whose entire nuclear family had died by the time they met. Such pity, however, did not serve well as a strong basis for a lasting marriage, as it quickly became evident that the two were ill-suited for one another. While Slater felt threatened by Lobdell's intelligence, Lobdell found herself annoyed by Slater's attempts to control her. Slater ultimately abandoned Lobdell and then spread rumors to the larger community that Lobdell was unfaithful during the marriage. Lobdell, pregnant at the time and finding it difficult to quell Slater's rumors, was forced to move back in with her mother and father. Because her parents were aging and ill, Lobdell not only had to return to her work as a farmhand, but she also developed skills as a hunter as another way to provide food for the family. During one of her hunting trips, dressed in "manly hunting clothes," Lobdell encountered and charmed a man who ultimately published a local news story about her—a story that gave Lobdell some degree of regional fame—entitled "Lucy Ann Lobdell, the Female Hunter of Delaware and Sullivan County."[5]

Regardless of the fame, and although a worthy farmhand, Lobdell was unable to provide adequately for her child and ill and aging parents. Secretly passing as a man, Lobdell disappeared once more, reasoning that, able-bodied in male guise, she would be "capable of doing men's work, and getting men's wages."[6] Indeed, over the next several years, Lobdell seems to have found a number of jobs, living as a man in a variety of communities, although never able to maintain steady work. Lobdell ultimately returned destitute to her parents after having been discovered to be "really" a woman at one job site.

We know almost all of the story thus far from the publication of Lobdell's autobiography, a narrative that ends in a mid-nineteenth-century liberal feminist prayer for equal pay for equal labor (published "by the authoress," on the basis of her local fame as "The Female Hunter of Delaware County," as an attempt to secure adequate financial support for her family). After recounting her childhood, her life with Slater, and her local fame as a hunter, Lobdell turns the autobiography into a manifesto of sorts, beginning by criticizing an economic order in which "we behold her [woman] married for the sake of getting a home," a home that eventually, Lobdell warns, will house a woman, her children, and an unhappy drunkard husband.[7] In light of the dire state of such a life, Lobdell asserts that women should have the right to different circumstances: "Help, one and all, to aid woman, the weaker vessel. If she is willing to toil, give her wages equal with that of man. And as in sorrow she bears her own curse, secure to her rights, or permit her to wear the pants, and breathe the pure air of heaven."[8] Wedding equal-pay arguments to a biblical hermeneutics that articulates all humanity as of equal value, Lobdell's autobiography crafts an engaging, if fairly standard, feminist treatise.[9]

If the Lobdell story ended here, it would either have been confined to the annals of the Lobdell family or, at best, raised as a curiosity in the history of feminist discourse (as it is, only three original copies are known to exist). Lobdell's life, however, took a number of twists and turns after the publication of the autobiography, ultimately leading to her insertion in the matrix of psychiatric, medical, and gender discourses. In 1856 Lobdell placed her daughter in an Almshouse at Delhi, New York, avowing that she would find well-paying work before returning. In Minnesota, dressed as a man and now identifying himself as "La-Roi"[10] Lobdell, he took several hunting, logging, and prospecting jobs, oftentimes sleeping in beds with men who never suspected that Lobdell "was actually female."[11] In Wayne County, Pennsylvania, Lobdell took on the title "professor of dance" and the name Joseph I. Lobdell, opening a school in Dyberry. Of this period of Lobdell's life, folklorist Robert Pike notes that "this slim, agile-good-looking gentleman, with his buckskin gloves and stovepipe hat, was warmly welcomed . . . and his gallant manners and appearance captivated the heart of more than one lass whom he led out in the mazes of the waltz."[12] After becoming engaged to the daughter of one of Dyberry's leading lumbermen, Lobdell was revealed to be "really" a female when a Long Eddy lumber salesman came to town and recognized Joseph as Lucy. Physically threatened and chased out of town, Lobdell wandered in the region for seven years, living in lean-tos and hovels she built, appearing in settlements only to sell wares and buy hunting supplies.

After this seven-year period, Lobdell returned home, one of Pike's witnesses tells us, "physically broken and all trace . . . of femininity itself destroyed."[13] A burden to his parents, Lobdell moved into the same almshouse that held his daughter. There, in 1868, a wealthy and educated young woman—Marie Louise Perry of the Boston Perrys[14]—arrived at the almshouse, having run out of money while chasing her husband, who had escaped Boston with another woman. When Perry and Lobdell met, Pike reports, "a strange and inexplicable affection sprang up," and the two of them escaped when the almshouse refused to permit them to marry.[15] The two proceeded to move from town to town, appearing as a married couple, Methodist minister "Joseph Israel Lobdell" and his wife, Marie Louise. After being imprisoned several times for vagrancy and released on the appeal of Marie Louise, Lobdell was eventually moved back into the Delhi almshouse, then, by state law, moved into the Ovid Asylum in Seneca County, New York, and, finally, into the Willard Psychiatric Center, where he was observed for the remainder of his life and where several "psychiatric" essays were written about him. As for Marie Louise Perry, having refused to leave Lobdell's side, she was informed that Lobdell had died long before he actually had. Marie Louise then left town, referring to herself as a widow, and disappeared to history. Whereas various news accounts reported Lobdell's death in the late 1890s, psychiatric reports place her death in a state hospital in Binghamton on May 28, 1912.[16]

This narrative, as told through a variety of sources, obviously provides a rich body of discourse that was interesting to Lobdell's lay contemporaries as well as to an emerging group of "sexologists" who were attempting to understand sex and sexuality through a medical lens. Hence the discourse about Lobdell and her relationship with Perry emerges through a number of different existing, and emerging, matrices. As a result, we are given the chance to interrogate these discourses for underlying cultural (that is, both widespread culture and medical culture) assumptions about gender, sexuality, and normative behaviors.

In this chapter, I will make three inquiries of this body of discourse, the first concerning the semiotics of gender—the signifiers of "proper" masculinity and femininity. That is, in view of the story's retelling, we cannot help but see some of the same questions asked, and answered, that are routinely asked in cases when a body or style troubles the semiotics of gender: How did Lobdell successfully "appear" as a man? How did "she" perform it convincingly in public and in the bedroom? What did "she" wear? How did "she" style her hair? I do not mean to look here, of course, for phenomenological answers to these questions. Rather I assume that the very existence of these questions, and the types of answers given, are manifestations of the ways in which gender's signifiers are crystallized at the level of popular culture and/or at the level of psychiatric discourse in any given temporal-cultural context.[17]

Second, because the historical period of the late nineteenth century is one in which psychiatric discourses were laying claims of jurisdiction in cases that would now be called homosexuality,[18] I want to highlight and discuss those aspects of Lobdell's behavior and self-identity that are interpreted through a medical/psychiatric lens. What behaviors, what evidence, mark Lobdell as sane or insane? What behaviors could Lobdell exhibit and still fit within cultural codes of morality and mental health? What evidence did psychiatric experts provide for their claims?

Third and finally, in terms of contemporary politics of sexuality and gender, I want to highlight and trouble the ways Lobdell is being remembered as an historical figure. Through what contemporary identificatory categories is Lobdell's body filtered, and which categories are erased? With what evidence is such a hermeneutics performed? Finally, what are the costs and benefits of such readings to contemporary culture?

The Semiotics of Gender

In wide-ranging work concerning a variety of ways in which gender is troubled— from recent discussions of the rhetoric of intersexuality to discussions of the public representations of transgenderism—an understanding of gender as performative is repeatedly invoked.[19] Such work explicitly or implicitly works to some degree on the shared assumption that gender is understood and performed through a cultural grammar that is cited and recited within, as Judith Butler puts it, "a forced reiteration of norms."[20] From such a perspective, one could look at any case in which the understood and assumed "language" of gender is transgressed and find the multiple ways that public discourse acts as an ideological frame through which bodies and bodily actions are disciplined back into accepted grammar (either by making the bodies relearn that grammar or through explanations of why troubled bodies are "aberrations"). Whereas the "grammar" of gender and sexuality changes incrementally over time, and whereas there are always linguistic communities with accepted slang and transgressive grammatical structures, the logic of mass-mediated or "public" address necessarily works to reflect and "clawback" commonsense assumptions.[21] Hence, in looking at the discourse surrounding the Lobdell case, one would expect to find a reemployment of the cultural grammar of gender as writers attempt to make "bigendered" sense of Lobdell and Perry. Moreover, because all conversations take place within larger cultural understandings, one would also expect that medical discourses would reflect some of those same commonsense assumptions if they also hold to a bigendered understanding of humanity.[22]

Historically, as Terry notes, the Lobdell case, and its eventual publication and discussion in medical journals, occurred during a period in which homosexuality was being rearticulated as transgressive in a physical and psychiatric manner rather than in a religious one.[23] Terry observes that debates over the meaning of homosexuality took place on the grounds of three primary assumptions: first, that only two sexes existed; second, that males and females were fundamentally different; and, third, that males were positioned as superior on the basis of their inherent gift of reason.[24] Although I will turn in the next section to assumptions made by sex theorists Richard von Krafft-Ebing and Karl Ulrichs in terms of the "causes" and moral status of same-sex lovers, here I more simply underline the common assumption—an assumption often still commonly held—that in a same-sex pairing of two female-bodied women, one of the two would behave, for all intents and purposes, as a man.[25] That is, in couple, one of the two would have to be sexually inverted. For the relationship to be recognizable, then, an assumption must be that we have a clear and shared understanding of the grammar of masculinity and femininity. Hence, in the discussions about Lobdell and Perry, we should be able to see a fairly solid historical drawing of what makes one a man and the other a woman.

While both Lobdell and Perry are described in various reports to have behaved as tomboys as children[26] (given both Krafft-Ebing and Ulrichs's belief that sexual inversion was somewhat inborn),[27] as a couple we find a stronger stress on the ways Lobdell signified the male and Perry the female within their adult relationship. Not only does there seem to be an urgency in such a semiotics to maintain a bigendered logic (that is, there is a male and a female in any sexual relationship), but, as I will illustrate below, there is also a simultaneous stress on both the fact that Lobdell was indeed successful in his performance or enactment of masculinity and, at the same time, that there are always semiotic "leaks" that allow us to see through her "impersonation." These representations, by illustrating how Lobdell is a successful performer of masculinity, work to explain how so many people were fooled, and also that ultimately, because there will always be so many exposures of the "true" gender, a lifelong impersonation is difficult, if not impossible, to pull off. As a whole, then, it is as if the discourse of the cultural imaginary is explaining that ultimately one would be able to detect gender trouble (for example, "Oh, that's not a man. The voice shows me that this is a woman in man's clothes") so that, as Marjorie Garber puts it, we might "guard against a difference that might otherwise put the identity of one's own position in question."[28]

In 1846, for example, we find an article in the *Bridgeport Connecticut Standard News* in which the author relays a story of an accidental meeting with Lucy Lobdell, the "female hunter of Delaware and Sullivan County."[29] The essay is interesting not only because it describes the clothing Lobdell wore on her body and the movements she made with her body when she hunted, but also because Lobdell herself reprinted it in her autobiography, inviting us to read her as being pleased with the report of her success in drag. The author, a Mr. Talmage, begins by noting that one day, while approaching Sullivan County, he was "overtaken by what I at first supposed was a young man, with a rifle on his shoulder."[30] After chasing down the hunter because he thought the voice he heard when exchanging greetings had sounded female, Talmage spends enough time with Lobdell to observe that she was a most unusual woman. Lobdell's manner of dress is described thus: "The only article of female apparel visible was a close-fitting hood upon her head, such as is often worn by deer hunters; next, an India-rubber overcoat. Her nether limbs were encased in a pair of snug-fitting corduroy pants. . . . She had a good looking rifle upon her shoulder, and a brace of double-barreled pistols in the side-pockets of her coat, while a most formidable hunting-knife hung suspended by her side."[31] Talmage goes on to report, and Lobdell quotes him, that she proved her prowess with the rifle through target shooting and, through a number of chores, illustrated her ability to labor as hard as a man. Talmage sets a pattern, then, in which Lobdell's performance of masculinity is adept, with only the signifier of the voice acting as a leak through which the "true" gender is expressed.

A combination of a description of Lobdell's handsome physical features and traditionally masculine clothing repeatedly comes into play in explaining Lobdell's initial successes "portraying" a man. For example, folklorist Robert Pike notes that when Lobdell introduced himself as a "professor of the dance" witnesses remembered him as a "slim, agile-good-looking gentleman, with his buckskin gloves and stovepipe hat."[32] In a retelling of this same story by a different (anonymous) author, Lobdell appears as "a dashing, good looking young fellow" in similar attire.[33]

Further, and perhaps predictably given its function as a phallus, Lobdell's ability with a gun is raised several times to explain the successful male performance.[34] For example, Mindy Desen relies on witnesses contemporary with Lobdell in noting that when provisions fell short one winter and Lucy had to use a gun to procure food, "her" performance as a hunter, better than that of the others in her company, reified "her" male performance.[35] In a narrative concerning this same period, Pike and another anonymous author observe that Lobdell could handle both an axe and a gun better than any men in the region.[36] Finally, the *National Police Gazette* story observes that Lobdell "was known far and wide for her wonderful skill with the rifle, not only in target-shooting, but in hunting deer and other game."[37]

In addition to her clothing and her skills, Lobdell's physical appearance, first as a female and then as a male, also works to reaffirm her ability to pass, while simultaneously stressing the perils of passing. Hence Robert Pike notes via an interview with an "old timer" in 1913 that Lobdell, as a woman, appeared thus: "her hair, which she kept cut sort, was dark, while her clear, cold, dark gray eyes added something to her appearance that made all the young lumbermen in the settlement fear her."[38] Pike also notes that when Lobdell returned home after her first attempt to live as a male in Pennsylvania, her physical look as a female had been erased and her "femininity destroyed." When they arrived in Monroe County, Pennsylvania, as the Reverend Joseph Lobdell and wife, not only was femininity erased, but Lobdell was now "a tall, gaunt, ragged man" with a rifle and a "mass of matted hair" that he no longer seemed to take care of.[39] Further, P. M. Wise, Lobdell's psychiatrist at Willard, notes that, on admittance, not only was Lobdell dressed in male attire, but she also had a coarse voice and "her features were masculine."[40]

It is useful when turning to the signifiers that highlight Perry's role as the "normal" woman in this relationship to observe with Terry that, "from 1880 to 1920, homosexuality was appraised by American physicians as a troubling effect of modernity that posed a threat to the nation's welfare."[41] Having associated homosexuality largely with the lower classes, who were represented as lazy and slovenly, public discourse provided a configuration in which homosexuality was a danger to upper- and middle-class families, which suggests that mixing with lower classes (a category that was also articulated with race) could be dangerous to the upper classes because it encouraged women to upset the expected domestic order. As Lisa Duggan argues, the "normal" woman (here, Marie Louise Perry) was troubling precisely because, though she appeared "conventionally feminine," her actions illustrated that she could not be fully known or controlled.[42] The discourse—both public and medical—surrounding Perry indeed articulates some of these concerns.[43]

Again, although Perry is described in medical reports as appearing as a tomboy while a child (a necessary part of the same-sex equation), when she is with Lobdell, as the "normal woman" in the bigendered relationship, descriptions of her "femininity" take over.[44] Hence she is always described as being in a dress, as attractive, and as having grown into "graceful womanhood."[45] Moreover, one particular repeated story crystallizes and highlights both Perry's femininity and her status as a higher-class and traditionally feminine woman. When Lobdell was arrested in 1876 and committed to jail in Honesdale, Pennsylvania, Perry is said to have written a letter beseeching authorities to release him. Repeatedly authors make note that the letter she wrote was "strikingly neat in chirography," even though she had to use "pokeberry" juice to write it.[46] Indeed Wise notes that in the pokeberry note, "The chirography is faultless and the language used is a model of clear, correct English."[47] Underscoring this point, an anonymous author notes that Perry's ability to write such a beautiful note was evidence that she was "still showing in her manner traces of culture strangely antagonistic to this pariah life" she was forced to live because of her attraction to Lobdell.[48]

Finally, not only do highlighted signifiers point to Perry's role as the "normal" (that is, not inverted but feminine and beautiful)[49] middle- or upper-class woman, but one particular story seems to serve as a warning of the dangers that await "normal" women who fall sexually for lower-class women.[50] In several narratives of their relationship, we learn that toward the end of their lives together the estate of Marie Louis Perry's mother was settled and that Perry was informed that a sizeable property, "valued at several thousand dollars," had been left to her by her mother. For unexplained reasons, however, Perry never claimed the property and ultimately wandered away "leading her curious and most remarkable life."[51] Regardless of which version of the couple's life we are reading, in every telling Perry is a "normal" woman who was brought to a ruin of sorts through her interactions with Lobdell.

Taken as a whole, the discourse concerning Lucy Lobdell and Marie Louise Perry works to reify the articulation between homosexuality and inversion as well as the crystallized link between male or female and their respective signifiers. Moreover, in the midst of the reaffirmation of these links, we also see a story that highlights the combination between poverty and homosexuality and the perils faced in modernity by normal women.

"Science Purifies Everything"

In *Madness and Civilization*, Michel Foucault argues that at the turn of the nineteenth century medical experts and psychiatrists, as a result of new categories that they were developing and implementing in their analyses and conversations, began expressing outrage that those criminals who were morally culpable for their behavior and the insane—who were not—were being housed together. As a result, they argued that new categories were needed to alter ways of understanding and treating people with such different needs.[52] It is important, however, even given the assumption that an insane individual was not as morally responsible for his or her actions, to bear in mind that the concept of insanity continued to operate as a rhetorical tool through which those outside the norm might be disciplined. Foucault argues, "With the new status of the medical personage, the deepest meaning of confinement is abolished: mental disease, with the new meanings we now give it, is made possible."[53] What these new meanings provide, of course, as Philippe Riot illustrates in his analysis of the Pierre Rivierre case, is that the narrative of any "insane" or "criminal" case is told differently, with different signifiers coming to the fore, based on the perspective of the storyteller in terms of the notions of sanity and insanity.[54]

This changing notion of "insanity" or madness is particularly important during the era surrounding the Lobdell case, especially in cases of sexual and gender ambiguity, because it was during this period that Krafft-Ebing was first being read in the United States and that the pathological condition involving same-sex love and cross-sex behavior was being described in medical journals. Hence this case offers a look at early articulations between homosexuality and "an inborn constitutional defect that manifested in overall degeneracy."[55] Similar to Duggan's observation that such stories often worked to protect the middle-class domestic structure, "madness," as Charles Morris argues in his study of the discourse "around" Abigail Folsom, "was a malleable and highly gendered trope" that was often used against female (and feminist) abolitionists who did not follow middle-class roles of gender decorum.[56] More specifically, however, madness allowed an explanation of improper behavior while also allowing the observer to express a benevolent and non-judgmental concern (at least as a guise), because "madness" implied that the offender was not under the control of her own free will. Morris notes, for example, William Lloyd Garrison's judgment of Folsom: "The unfortunate woman alluded to in the present article is not a fit object of ridicule or denunciation, but of compassion and charity."[57] Garrison's "compassion," as we shall see, is the same brand of compassion to be directed toward people such as Lobdell and Perry as psychiatry begins to turn its gaze on their behavior—a slightly bemused and slightly indifferent compassion that implies that such behavior is a perversion of nature's design without forcing a moral judgment.[58]

It seems clear that, whereas "common-sense" morally condemned and excluded Lobdell and Perry, the changes in "medical sense" led experts to isolate but not condemn the pair. Although we have only reported witnesses from the communities from which Joseph Lobdell and his wife were driven, general reports tell us that their members "taunted and jeered" Lucy for falsely impersonating a man and chased her out of town when she was "exposed."[59] Specifically, we learn that the couple was driven away from Monroe County, Pennsylvania, imprisoned for vagrancy (a criminal act) in Stroudsburg, and when Lobdell was discovered to be female while in prison, the two were driven away from town.[60] Hence while Lobdell was imprisoned or jailed several times for vagrancy (and once for entering a schoolhouse and demanding to teach), Lobdell was banished, seen as unfit to live in a community, only after being identified as a male impersonator. When we move from the phenomenological level of what happened to Lobdell when he interacted with "the public" to the level of psychiatric writings about "her," however, we see Lobdell rearticulated as the agent of a partially amoral act that resulted from the interaction of "her" congenital condition with the demands of the surrounding culture.

In one of his two published statements on the case, James Kiernan of the Chicago Academy of Medicine draws on the work of Karl Ulrichs, who theorized by drawing on his own sexual desires for men.[61] First, expressing concern that some might read his discussion of the Lucy Lobdell–Marie Louise Perry pairing to be rather prurient, Kiernan notes that there is no cause for censor because "in medicine, the prurient does not exist, since, 'science like fire purifies everything.'"[62] After noting Ulrichs's belief that "urnings" (his name for "fellow sufferers" of his condition) could all recognize one another, Kiernan made special note of Ulrichs's theory of how same-sex love developed. For men, Ulrichs hypothesized that the desire for same-sex love was caused by what amounted to a birth defect in which a male body housed "the soul of a woman."[63] While noting that he was not armed to discuss the theological issue of the soul (he is, after all, a scientist), Kiernan endorses the overall Ulrichs thesis by hypothesizing that, rather than a female soul, Ulrichs and others like him housed a female brain in a male body. Just as hermaphrodites are often born with ambiguous or "wrong" genitalia, he notes, so might one be born with such a brain in that the brain "is as much an organ of the body as the sexual apparatus."[64] Such a hypothesis does come with a judgment—albeit a physical one rather than a moral one—as Kiernan says, "It should also be remembered that the lowest animals are bisexual and that the various types of hermaphrodism are instances of more or less complete reversion to the ancestral type."[65] Hence, he goes on to note, even if we did not know homosexuals to exist, our theories of the body would have to invent them because "urnings" are "to be expected *a priori*" (and hence they are natural reversions to lower species).[66] Such a claim is especially important when we recall that the same psychiatric lines of thought "mapped populations onto a teleological vector of development from primitive to civilized, and hence expected more homosexuality in non-white and lower class populations" who were clearly articulated as being reversions to ancestral type.[67]

Of both Lobdell and Perry, as evidence of their hermaphroditic minds, Kiernan provides stories of their lives that represent both as somewhat "manly" from birth (namely, if both love women, both must to some degree have male brains). Moreover he observes that the tendency toward hermaphroditism is also a form of insanity. And, as evidence of their insanity, he offers familial instances of other forms (that is, other than homosexuality) of insanity. The underlying assumption is that although the parents may not have been homosexual, any form of insanity led one to be open to sexual perversion, especially during an era in which the traditional domestic order was being threatened. As Terry notes, "What was inherited was a predisposition to engage in immoral acts of various sorts."[68] Hence Perry's mother is said to have been insane, while Perry displayed "a great liking for boyish games and attire and a repugnance to suitors" throughout her life.[69] Lobdell too is said to have "an insane ancestry on the maternal side and to have preferred muscular sports and labor. She was averse to the attentions of young men and preferred the society of her own sex."[70] While the two ultimately settled into the assumedly natural gender roles of male and female, they both apparently were born with a predisposition toward same-sex perversion.

Finally, the notes of the doctor's logbooks at the Willard Psychiatric Center illustrate some of the same problematic alliances between insanity and behavior. Lobdell was admitted in 1880 at age fifty-six, the book notes, with a history of insanity for more than twenty years.[71] Moreover, in providing the evidence of insanity, H. A. Gates, M.D., and John Calhoun, in their respective "Certificate(s) of Insanity," list as the first cause that Lobdell "is uncontrollable indecent & immoral & insists on wearing male attire calling herself a huntress."[72] Further, when admitted, the report notes that her conversation was "silly" and that she dressed in "male attire." At the end of this claim is one word: "dementia."[73] On January 7, 1882, however, we find that Lobdell is said to call herself Joseph only "when she is excited and when composed Lucy," which indicates a belief that there is a sane side of her that knows herself as Lucy. Lobdell's dementia is her male identification.[74]

The search for an explanation of Lobdell's condition went beyond a discussion of hermaphroditism of the mind and toward a search for masculine manifestations on the body. In the scant evidence we have, we witness Lobdell claiming to the doctors that "she" had an unusual clitoris which acted as a penis.[75] Hence both Kiernan and Wise note that, after being admitted in the Willard Hospital for the Insane, "Joe" Lobdell attempted "normal" sexual intercourse with nurses and others at the hospital. Moreover they report that Lobdell claimed to have normal—and satisfactory—male-female sexual relations only with her wife (never with her husband).[76] Further, in the logbook maintained at the Willard Psychiatric Center, we learn that Lobdell is said to have an enlarged clitoris, an observation that reappears in several medical/psychiatric reports after Wise made his inspection.[77] As Duggan observes of this same impulse to locate the "perversion" of Alice Mitchell in her "abnormal genitalia," this equation of ambiguous or odd genitalia with ambiguous or odd sexuality was a centuries-old assumption.[78] Indeed, in Wise's comments on the case, Lobdell claims that she did not have so much an abnormally large clitoris as she had a hidden penis that could arise out of her clitoris when needed, much like the head of a turtle out of its shell. Hence Wise claims that Lobdell thought herself a man because she had "peculiar organs that make me more a man than a woman."[79] While Wise reports that he never saw this penis, the appearance of a clitoris that could seemingly act like a penis helps make culturally acceptable the question of how Lobdell passed to others and perhaps to "herself," answering the ever-imagined question, "What did they do in bed?" In this way, the bigendered heteronormativity that is still largely expected, and that was strongly assumed in the medicalized sexuality of the late nineteenth century, is maintained.

In this discussion of the enlarged clitoris or hidden penis, we see both an assertion of a series of semiotic codes on the surface of the body that explain how others could believe Lobdell to be a man, and, as if to satisfy those who wondered about the level of "deception" that Perry must have experienced, we also find a semiotics of depth. Regardless of Lobdell's "actual body," the discourse supplies a description of gestures and appearances on the body that explains Lobdell as masculine and a real or imagined phallus that helps both explain her "perversion" and Perry's mistaken attachment. It is worth noting that this description of the overgrown clitoris is one that works along the lines of race, class, and sexuality. Sander Gilman points out, for example, that descriptions of "larger than normal" clitorises were used in discussing the "abnormal" sexual appetites of African American women and lesbians,[80] and Roderick Ferguson has noted the ways in which the political economy has functioned in the United States to create material and discursive links between lower classes and nonheteronormative subject positions.[81] Once again this signifier worked to warn middle- and upper-class women to stay away from the ruin that could be brought on if one socialized with lower-class white women or black women in general.

In the end, although Kiernan and Wise might not necessarily agree on the cause of Lobdell or Perry's "behavior," they both ultimately take a position toward Lobdell that claims an enlightened neutrality toward her sexual behavior but does so at the cost of framing Lobdell as an atavistic being, open for inspection at the desire of science. Despite Kiernan's invocation of Ulrichs, who saw homosexuality as a benign inborn anomaly that was simply one of many possible human aberrations, both instead move, like Krafft-Ebing, to posit Lobdell's behavior as evidence of insanity. Lobdell is framed as a human being with a degenerative constitution.

Hence, although neither found homosexuals necessarily morally at fault or lacking (that is, "science, like fire, purifies everything"), both see cause to keep them separated from heterosexuals. As Wise notes, "It would be more charitable and just if society would protect them from the ridicule and aspersion they must always suffer, if their responsibility is legally admitted, by recognizing them as the victims of a distressing monodelusional form of insanity. It is reasonable to consider true sexual perversion as always a pathological condition and a peculiar manifestation of insanity."[82] Similarly, Kiernan sees the condition, because it almost always results from a "neurotic ancestry," as something that cannot be removed, and he proposes with Krafft-Ebing that "these patients should be excepted from legal penalties and allowed to follow their inclinations when harmless and not violating public decency."[83] While the public would tar and feather Lobdell, then, the medical and psychiatric establishments, though not knowing where to place the problem (body, brain, modernity), purify the subjects, leaving their morality intact. In other words, it is a "scientific acceptance" of a degenerative and atavistic condition, an "acceptance" in the realm of science that simultaneously continued to encourage ridicule in the realm of the public.

"A Terribly Consequential Seizure": The Corpse of a Lesbian

Of attempts to hoist identities onto others, or to deny identities to others that they adapted or may have chosen for themselves, Eve Sedgwick warns, "To alienate conclusively, definitively, from anyone on any theoretical ground the authority to describe and name their own sexual desire is a terribly consequential seizure."[84] When we are dealing with a corpse, especially one with so little discursive record from which to speak, the ability to arrange such a seizure is perhaps easier while the consequences, especially for those still "in the flesh," are no less severe. Indeed, whether it be an historical case such as this or a more contemporary one, we are well advised to be wary of the ways in which critics and historians remember the corpse, using concepts such as denial, repression, fear, or internalized shame, in ways that, as C. Jacob Hale argues, "tend to dismiss the agency of the subject once animated in that dead flesh."[85] Moreover, and perhaps more important, such dismissals of identificatory categories often marginalize or culturally devalue positions claimed by the animated subject for all others who would wish to identify with it.

In the case of Lucy Lobdell (or others from his era), however, we have a different situation than with a contemporary case if only because we are dealing with a context in which none of the more obvious current identity categories were available for Lobdell to claim. That is, Lucy could neither claim lesbianism nor transgenderism, because neither was a commonly uttered identity; in some sense, Lobdell's was truly an unspeakable "perversion," at least in terms of a contemporary discursive frame. Nonetheless Lobdell reportedly did make claims about his identity both implicitly and overtly, and, in the present, others continue to make claims for "her." As far as we can tell, Lobdell spent the greatest portion of his life dressed "as a man," living "as a man," considering "herself" to be a man, specifically, the husband of Marie Louis Perry. If we stop Lobdell's story at the point of the autobiography, however, we have a subject who claims that "she" had "made up my mind to dress in men's attire to seek labor as . . . I was capable to doing men's work and getting men's wages,"[86] a woman who just thereafter is reported to have called "herself" La-Roi Lobdell and worked as a man solely to better her financial position.[87] Which Lobdell do we choose—the charming and talented former schoolteacher turned feminist advocate who dressed as a man for financial motives; a lesbian so closeted that she claims to be a man so that she might be able to avoid self-confession; the transgendered Lobdell who not only dressed "as a man" but reportedly claimed to be more man than woman, romantically pursuing women for traditional heterosexual romance? Since the categories available to Lobdell are unsatisfactory in the current cultural context, how has her identity been "seized," and what are the consequences of that seizure?

Obviously, the perspective I am taking tells us that all categories of identity are contingent and historical. Even if some of the same words are employed (for example, "man" or "woman"), their cultural and medical meanings are different. So, in a sense, of course, we do not need to "choose" or label Lobdell in any particular way (even though many historical and contemporary writers do label Lobdell, and their labeling deserves attention and criticism). Nonetheless I want to suggest that even when one takes a discursive or cultural approach to identity categories, there is value in "collecting" particular individuals for genealogical histories that help construct a safer discursive space in the present. That is, although it is clear that Lucy Lobdell could not be "transgendered" because no such category existed, I am putting in a bid here to collect him as transgendered, to place him in Leslie Feinberg's canon, if simply for the purpose of helping provide "transgenderism" in the present with an historical lineage.

To point, then: given that Lobdell's life as the Reverend Joseph Israel Lobdell, husband of Marie Louise Perry, was not one that was financially rewarding—he was forced to live in lean-tos, hovels, and almshouses throughout his life if he chose to dress and perform as a man—Lobdell's maintenance of an identity as a man would seem more indicative of a transgendered identity than that of a lesbian. Though I realize that the life of a same-sex couple would have had its own difficulties and would certainly not have led to financial rewards, Lobdell's claims to be "more man than a woman"[88] while under observation and his continued insistence on this identity certainly allow us to at least posit transgenderism as a likely candidate. Almost all versions of Lobdell's story during his life and since then, however, have consistently denied that one category either implicitly or overtly.

As I have illustrated throughout this chapter, articles and essays written during Lobdell's lifetime, in light of the absence of a transgendered category and the negative status of same-sex lovers, consistently move Lobdell into the category of a mad or insane *woman*. On the surface level, this is performed through the use, as Judith Halberstam would have it, of "misgendered pronouns" and other descriptions of Lobdell as a woman.[89] That is, in all examples of discourse about Lobdell throughout his life, both public and medical or psychiatric, Lobdell is referred to as a woman and through the use of the pronoun "she." Indeed, when the name "Joseph" or the label "husband" are employed, they are always qualified through quotation marks or other indicators to be clear that the author is referring to Lucy Lobdell, a woman, acting *as if* she was a man.[90] Further, whereas the "popular" and public discourse about Lobdell simply assumes that "she" is mad, we have seen not only that the psychiatrists tightly articulated lesbianism with insanity, but we also might return to the following note, inscribed in the doctor's logbook at Willard, to see how tightly bound gender identity was with sanity and insanity: "When she is excited she calls herself Joseph and when composed Lucy."[91]

Although contemporary accounts have for the most part disarticulated Lobdell's sexual and gender performances from her sanity, they have fared little better in recognizing her identity as a man. Through the omission of information[92] or the practice of supplying Lobdell with unconscious motives, Lobdell is generally either remembered as a feminist who dressed as a man to advance liberal feminism or as a lesbian who was simply unable, or unwilling, to admit to same-sex desires. Of the first order, we witness the words of Ernest James, the recent compiler of the autobiography of Lucy Lobdell and a dossier of relevant information, who, in personal conversation noted that Lobdell was most certainly a lesbian but ignores even this aspect of "her" identity in introducing the autobiography. In his telling, Lucy's story is that of a woman who was held back by a society that did not allow woman proper job opportunities. Ultimately James sees Lobdell as heroic and imagines "her" as a productive member of society had "she" lived in our era. "Today," James notes, "Lucy Ann would have been the CEO of a corporation, a well known educator or a politician. Discrimination of the type experienced by Lucy Ann and others like her has been a loss to this great country."[93] Similarly, a 1992 retelling of the story in a Lobdell family newsletter erases Lobdell's life with Marie Louise Perry (while acknowledging that Lobdell had dressed as a man to get work) and contends that Lucy's mental problems were in fact caused by an inability to find meaningful labor and that "years of hardship had evidently done irreparable damage to Lucy's psyche."[94] Nonetheless, we are told, Lobdell's feminist efforts were not in vain. In a variation of James's placement of Lobdell in the present, Desens writes, "I've spoken to members of the Crawson family in Long Eddy. One of Lucy's great-great-great-grandchildren is also named Lucy. She is an Air-Traffic controller with the military in Hawaii."[95] Here again Lobdell's sexuality and gender identity are erased in favor of highlighting "her" role as mold-breaking feminist.

Recent historical work in gay and lesbian studies also tends toward an erasure of the transgendered possibility in Lobdell's case. Such work ranges from generic "gay and lesbians in history" websites to scholarly/critical work. I want to be very clear here that I am neither claiming sinister motives in any of these cases nor denying that the authors themselves might personally posit Lobdell as transgendered. Rather it is more the case that these histories, focusing on the historical constraints on identity within a given era or place, simply have no need to discuss Lobdell in any way other than that used by discourse contemporary with Lobdell's life. Hence, if the context did not have a category for transgenderism or the like; the works do not mention those categories.[96]

The numerous websites that feature Lobdell almost uniformly do so by situating Lobdell as a lesbian and/or a cross-dressing female, reaffirming the "Lucy Lobdell as woman" equation. For example, on the "Sear's Queer Southern Century (or so) Timeline," Lobdell is named a "cross-dresser"[97] and the Lesbian History Project's "Notable Lesbians" list archives Lobdell among its members as a "passing woman."[98] Both Perry and Lobdell are listed together on "Historical Lesbian Couples" site,[99] whereas "Swade's Tribal Chant Lesbian History" repeatedly refers to Lobdell as "she," noting that she dressed as a man "to earn more money" and fits the Perry-Lobdell relationship into "lesbian history" as well.[100] In each of these cases, we see a "claw-back" of both Lobdell and Perry into a female-female lesbian relationship rather than a queered heterosexual one.[101]

Recent scholarly work that draws on the case as an historical example also often articulates the pair as a lesbian couple. For example, in her analysis of the Alice Mitchell–Freda Ward case, Duggan includes a reprint of a *National Police Gazette* story about Lobdell and Perry as an example of the type of sensational news stories that were published about lesbian lovers during that era. Indeed the story sees Lobdell's behavior as a "passing strategy" meant to allow her to have a relationship with Perry.[102] Similarly, Jennifer Terry draws forth the case several times to mention its employment in psychiatric writing as an example of same-sex love.[103] Moreover, after providing a thorough history of Lobdell's life in his *Gay American History*, Jonathan Ned Katz ultimately erases Lobdell's claims to maleness. To point, after briefly discussing Lobdell's final institutionalization, observation, and death, Katz concludes that "the key to understanding Lobdell's difficulties and later decline into madness seems to lie in the conflict of this assertive, intelligent, proud female with that behavior her society declared proper and improper for women."[104] In Katz's phrasing, Lobdell's madness is phenomenon rather than meaning, a fact rather than an interpretation. Indeed, in this articulation, there is no allowance for the idea that the very labeling of Lobdell as "mad" was itself a result of the institutional inability to identify Lobdell as male. That is, rather than Lobdell being "mad," we could read the category of "madness" from an institutional perspective as part and parcel of Lobdell's self-identification as male.

Finally, and perhaps most explicitly in terms of "seizing" an individual's identity, Beverly Greene authored two essays in *Oasis* in 1997 that were, respectively, a history of "women loving women" and a history of "transgendered"[105] individuals in history. In the June issue focusing on lesbians, Greene observes that the term "lesbian" was employed for the first time as an "official" category in P. M. Wise's 1883 *Neurologist and Alienist* essay focusing on Lobdell. As Greene notes, the term was used to describe Lobdell, "a woman who left her husband and children behind after a rocky marriage to live as a man and marry another woman."[106] Here, although evidence suggests that Lobdell was abandoned by her husband and then lived alone for years before meeting Perry, Greene represents Lobdell as a woman who actively left her marriage to pursue Perry and live as a man. Though acknowledging Lobdell's self-identification as male, Greene expresses doubts about this identity: "While her statements might make it seem to the reader that Lucy was in fact transgendered, I do not believe that this was the case. I think that she was a butch dyke looking for an acceptable outlet for her all too natural feelings towards woman, a search which proved to be more than many women could handle considering . . . pressures to the contrary."[107]

Several months later, in the October issue, Greene includes Lobdell in her "transgender" history on the basis of Lobdell's claim to be male and to have a clitoris that functioned as a penis. Here too, however, Greene immediately expresses doubt as to Lobdell's claims (and by extension to all other historical cases of transgenderism) by observing, "Even these stories leave us scratching our head as we have no way of knowing how many were in fact f2m [female to male] persons, simply liked to cross dress, or felt that they had to pass as a man in order to live out their life as a woman loving woman."[108] No way of knowing, one might respond, save Lobdell's own reported words while living with Perry and his words when entering the asylum for the final time. Although no one has access to Lobdell's mind, Greene works to reclaim the Lobdell corpse beyond that corpse's reported desires "when animated in the flesh." Again, then, we find a consequential seizure of meaning that denies one form of identity in place of others.

I am not claiming knowledge of Lobdell's own "feelings" but am more simply advocating critical pause, reflecting on what it means to advocate for any particular reading of Lucy Lobdell's identity. What does it mean for those in the present to doubt a transgendered or transsexual identity from the past? What does it mean to ignore the reported words and desires of what is now a corpse? What does it mean to import one's politics and desires directly on another body when the discourse said to have emerged out of that body resists one's politics? In short, what are the costs and benefits in the present of advocating one category at the expense of another in the past?

Conclusions

The discourse surrounding the queer circumstances of Lucy Lobdell—historical and contemporary, "public" and psychiatric/academic—and the analysis of this discourse provide fodder and example for what it might mean to queer public address studies, especially if we want this to mean something more than simply the inclusion of "queer" voices in the public address canon.[109] First, taking a performative perspective on gender, one that understands that the constraints on the "proper" performance of gender are constituted in and by the discursive assumptions of any given temporal-linguistic culture, encourages us to understand the Lobdell case as one nodal point where disciplinary mechanisms expose themselves in public and institutional address. By understanding the ways that Lobdell's gender performance troubled cultural assumptions and brought into play a variety of linguistic and institutional "taming" mechanisms, we are able to help build one part of the larger mosaic of historical studies that allow us to understand the meaning of gender and sexuality at the turn of the nineteenth century. Moreover, in the manner of Foucault, we are encouraged to see the ways new institutions were gaining the power of definition over same-sex desire, over gender identity. The value in using "public" address in such a manner is not, of course, simply to solely understand the past and the meanings of the past. Rather the value in such a queering of public address studies is to continue the larger project of understanding the ways in which the discursive material of the past continues to constrain and give weight to meanings and constraints in the present. In queering public address, in understanding the contingent articulations of gender and sexuality, we encourage a stronger sense of flexibility in contemporary definitions. That is, if queering public address allows us to understand the contingency of definitions and performative constraints in the past, it forces us to understand the same about the present.[110]

Second, and related, to queer public address is to come to understand that the application of the grammar of the present to explain and describe bodies and subjects from the past necessitates a queer fit of language to bodies and desires. That is, whatever terms we apply over the bodies of Lucy Lobdell and Marie Louise Perry, those are terms that either literally could not be employed by those subjects in self-identification or could not be applied with their current meanings. While at a basic level this is an obvious point, as critics and activists we must diligently remind ourselves that the names we apply to such subjects, the ways in which we animate the various corpses we bring to life, are also enabling and constraining in the present. Taking a page from Foucault, when we queer public address—when we write about "queer circumstances"—we should be well aware that one part of our task is the writing of a (queer) history of the present.[111]

Notes

1. Lobdell, 5–38. In this essay, as in all essays concerning transsexuals or transgendered individuals, pronouns are somewhat "troubling." Here, I will use "she" or "her" when referring to Lobdell up until the point that Lobdell reportedly "marries" Marie Louise Perry, and I will use "he" or "his" thereafter. When I quote others, I will of course retain the pronouns that they use. Because I side with reading Lobdell as a transgendered man, my attempt is to use pronouns and signifiers (for example, quotation marks) that signify this representation.

2. Leslie Feinberg, *Transgender Warriors: Making History from Joan of Arc to Dennis Rodman* (Boston: Beacon Press, 1996).

3. While what it means to "queer public address" is still a matter of debate and contention, I agree with Dana Cloud ("The First Lady's Privates: Queering Eleanor Roosevelt for Public Address Studies," present volume) that it cannot simply mean going back to include "queer" figures and their discourse in the public address canon, which would simply be a matter of a "traditional" public address study of a queer person. In this essay, I hope to look at a queer figure and the public address surrounding that figure to understand the constraints on gender/sexual performance in a particular historical/cultural moment and then think about

how an analysis of this discourse operates in the present. To be clear, part of "queering public address" is the "queering" of contemporary concepts and identities. This should become clear as one works toward the conclusion of this essay. In a way, then, this essay is an attempt to experiment in queering public address. As I think should be clear from reading this essay and the sources I employ, I would take both Jennifer Terry, *An American Obsession: Science, Medicine, and Homosexuality in Modern Society* (Chicago: University of Chicago Press, 1999), and Lisa Duggan, *Sapphic Slashers: Sex, Violence, and American Modernity* (Durham, N.C.: Duke University Press, 2000), as examples of this type of work.

4. The various documents from which I draw the narrative will be cited throughout this essay. I would, however, point first to Jonathan Ned Katz, *Gay American History* (New York: Discus, 1976), 325–42. Katz's history, and his encouragement of other historians/critics, has been responsible for a great deal of the current interest in the case. Second, anyone interested in the case owes a great debt to Ernest James, a Lobdell descendant. Not only has James privately republished Lobdell's autobiography, but he has also compiled a short dossier of material on the case. James directed me to his collection and provided me with a number of ideas for other sources. See Ernest C. James, ed., *Narrative and Publications Relating to Lucy Ann Lobdell, the Female Hunter of Delaware and Sullivan Counties,* New York (Sacramento, Calif.: E. C. James, 1996).

5. Mr. Talmage, "Lucy Ann Lobdell, The Female Hunter of Delaware and Sullivan County," *Bridgeport Connecticut Standard News Story,* February 2, 1856. Reprinted in James, ed., *Narrative,* 39–40.

6. James, ed., *Narrative,* 36. For a history of gender "passing" during this period, see J. S. Thompson, *The Mysteries of Sex: Women Who Passed as Men and Men Who Impersonated Them* (New York: Causeway, 1974).

7. James, ed., *Narrative,* 37.

8. Ibid.

9. For a discussion of such treatises and ideas, see Sara M. Evans, *Born for Liberty: A History of Women in America* (New York: Free Press, 1997).

10. Carolyn Dever has pointed out to me in conversation that this name is interesting in that it works as a pseudo-French translation of "the female king." Although I have not seen this mentioned elsewhere and also have no clue as to Lobdell's purpose in creating this name, it is an intriguing signifier.

11. Mindy Desens, "The Wild Woman of Manannah," *Lobdell Lines* 5 (1992). Reprinted in James, ed., *Narrative,* 42.

12. Robert E. Pike, "Lucy Ann Lobdell, The Female Hunter of Delaware and Sullivan County," *New York Folklore Quarterly* (autumn 1959). Quoted in James, ed., *Narrative,* 46.

13. Pike, "Lucy," 47–48.

14. Ibid., 49. I want to emphasize this "family title" as it indicates some of the class issues that we see arise in the Lobdell-Perry story. Further, although I think it is coincidental, I want to at least briefly mention that the description of Perry as "of the Boston Perrys" certainly works to help call forth the signifier of the "Boston marriage," a term, Lillian Faderman observes, that "was used in late nineteenth-century New England to describe a long-term monogamous relationship between two otherwise unmarried women." See Lillian Faderman,

Surpassing the Love of Men: Romantic Friendship and Love between Women from the Renaissance to the Present (New York: Quality Paperback Book Club, 1981), 190.

15. Pike, "Lucy," 49.

16. Actually, the date of death is something of a mystery, as various dates are given by different sources, from October 7, 1879, to 1912. The website "Swade's Lesbian Tribal Chant" briefly discusses this. See http://www.swade.net/lesbian/tribal_chant/les_hist.html (August 15, 2005).

17. While the "and/or" would be appropriate if my subject were contemporary discourse, given that there is great overlap between these realms of conversation, in the case of the late nineteenth century, it is even more appropriate because, as Jennifer Terry points out, psychiatric "experts" often wrote about these cases solely on the basis of the reports they read in newspapers or given by other psychiatrists. Although meetings with the subjects were preferable, they certainly were not required. See Terry, *American*, 40–73. See also Duggan, *Sapphic*, 25–26.

18. Terry, *American*, 40.

19. See, for example, Kate Bornstein, *Gender Outlaw: On Men, Women, and the Rest of Us* (New York: Routledge, 1994); Marjorie Garber, *Vested Interests: Cross-Dressing and Cultural Anxiety* (New York: Routledge, 1992); Alice Domurat Dreger, *Hermaphrodites and the Medical Invention of Sex* (Cambridge, Mass.: Harvard University Press, 1998); Suzanne J. Kessler, *Lessons from the Intersexed* (New Brunswick, N.J.: Rutgers University Press, 1988); Judith Butler, *Undoing Gender* (New York: Routledge, 2004), especially chap. 4; and Judith Halberstam, *In a Queer Time & Place: Transgender Bodies, Subcultural Lives* (New York: NYU Press, 2004).

20. Judith Butler, *Bodies That Matter: On the Discursive Limits of "Sex"* (New York: Routledge, 1993), 95.

21. As I am using it here, see John Fiske and John Hartley, *Reading Television* (New York: Methuen, 1978), 87.

22. That is, whereas medical or psychiatric discourses were clearly witnessing an emergent discourse about the "causes" of "sexual perversion," the signs of "male" and "female" behavior can be expected to be relatively stable.

23. Another strong take on the history of homosexuality in medical and sociological circles, especially male homosexuality, is found in Robert Alan Brookey, *Reinventing the Male Homosexual: The Rhetoric and Power of the Gay Gene* (Bloomington: Indiana University Press, 2002).

24. Terry, *American*, 33.

25. Jennifer Terry notes that for Swiss neurologist August Forel and many others, "sexual relations between women were interpreted according to a two-sex model whereby the seducer was cast as fundamentally masculine by virtue of her manly taste in clothing, her desire to be virile, and her predatory pursuit of the passive (i.e., feminine) woman." Terry, *American*, 64.

26. On the same page of an essay, James Kiernan notes both that "Perry displayed a great liking for boyish games and attire and a repugnance to suitors" and that Lobdell is said to "have preferred muscular sports and labor" and was "averse to the attentions of young men," 202. See Jas. G. Kiernan, "Psychological Aspects of the Sexual Appetite," *Alienist and Neurologist* 12 (1891): 202.

27. Terry, *American*, 42.

28. Garber, *Vested*, 130.

29. Talmage, *Lucy Ann Lobdell*, 39.

30. Ibid.

31. Ibid.

32. Pike, "Lucy."

33. This anonymous essay, published in 1913, is one of many included in Ernest James' "Ancestors" collection. "Life of Lucy Ann Lobdell," 56.

34. In *Sapphic Slashers*, Duggan includes two articles back to back that were published in the tabloid-like *National Police Gazette* in the late nineteenth century as examples of lesbian love stories. The first is the Lobdell-Perry story, which discusses briefly Lobdell's hunting abilities. The second, a tale focusing on Lily Duer and Ella Hearn, notes that Duer, the "manly" one of the pair, "carried a pistol and was an expert shot," *Sapphic*, 131. One's skill with a pistol works in both stories as a signifier of masculinity.

35. Desens, "Wild."

36. Pike, "Lucy."

37. Quoted in Duggan, *Sapphic*, 125.

38. Pike, "Lucy." 45.

39. Ibid.

40. P. M. Wise, "Case of Sexual Perversion," *Alienist and Neurologist* 4 (1893): 87–91.

41. Terry, *American*, 116. While I often cringe at the usage of ambiguous terms such as "modernity," here Terry uses it because physicians themselves employed the term. When they did, they were concerned that new "freedoms" enjoyed by women (for example, more schooling) might lead to attachments that threatened traditional heteronormative households.

42. Duggan, *Sapphic*, 29–30.

43. For a fascinating account of the materialist intersections of class, sexuality, and race, see Roderick A. Ferguson, *Aberrations in Black: Toward a Queer of Color Critique* (Minnesota: University of Minnesota Press, 2004). Although this case has less little to do with race overtly, Ferguson's discussion of the always already queerness of lower-class populations would be telling in the Lobdell case as well, at least in terms of how the public articulation of class and sexuality is configured.

44. This stress on the masculinity of one and the femininity of the other is, according to Duggan, a common trait of all the public stories of "lesbian love" from this period. *Sapphic*, 52–53.

45. "Life," 58–59.

46. This story appears in many accounts of Lobdell's life. See, for example, "Life," 59; Pike, "Lucy," 44. A personal note of thanks goes to Roger Stahl for personal correspondence regarding the uses of "pokeberry juice."

47. Wise, "Case," 89. Almost the same wording is used in "A Curious."

48. "Life," 60.

49. Femininity and beauty are stressed in "Life," 55.

50. A source worth consulting on such issues is G. J. Barker-Benfield, *The Horrors of a Half-Known Life: Male Attitudes toward Women and Sexuality in Nineteenth Century America* (New York: Harper and Row, 1977).

51. Jas. G. Kiernan, "Original Communications. Insanity. Lecture XXVI: Sexual Perversion," *Detroit Lancet* 7 (1884): 483; see also Kiernan, "Psychological," 203.

52. Michel Foucault, *Madness and Civilization: A History of Insanity in the Age of Reason* (New York: Vintage, 1965), 221.

53. Ibid., 270.

54. Philippe Riot, "The Parallel Lives of Pierre Riviere," in *"I, Pierre Riviere, Having Slaughtered My Mother, My Sister, and My Brother . . ."*: A Case of Parricide in the 19th Century, ed. Michel Foucault (Lincoln, Nebr.: Bison Books, 1975), 229–50.

55. For a discussion of this articulation, see Terry, *American*, 42, and Duggan, *Sapphic*, 25–26. Although I want to emphasize that Karl Ulrichs's understanding of homosexuality's cause was different—it was not insanity but a benign and inborn predisposition, which I will touch on later—both Ulrichs and Krafft-Ebing saw the condition as congenital.

56. Charles E. Morris III, "'Our Capital Aversion': Abigail Folsom, Madness, and Radical Antislavery Praxis," *Women's Studies in Communication* 24 (2001): 62–89.

57. Morris, "Our," 80.

58. Hopefully, it is obvious that I would hold that any description implies "moral judgment" in the sense that all descriptions are discursive and therefore political. What I mean to imply here is that the formula employed by Garrison and scientists of the era gave the impression that their claims were neutral and therefore amoral.

59. Desens, "Wild," 42.

60. Pike, "Life," 49.

61. Kiernan "Original," 481.

62. Ibid. I want to draw special attention to this claim by Kiernan in light of Terry's claims that elsewhere Kiernan argued that, while perhaps not prurient, such cases represented a form of insanity that should not be sympathized with (81). As I will show in this essay, however, in this case, Kiernan implicitly endorsed the recommendations of Ulrichs and P. M. Wise, the physician/psychiatrist who worked with Lobdell at the Willard Asylum for the Insane.

63. Kiernan, "Original," 481.

64. Ibid.

65. Ibid.

66. Ibid.

67. See Duggan, *Sapphic*, 157.

68. Terry, *American*, 93.

69. Kiernan, "Psychological," 202.

70. Ibid.

71. Cited in Katz, *Gay*, 340.

72. Cited in ibid.

73. Cited in ibid.

74. Cited in ibid.

75. Although dealing with a different time period, Joanne Meyerowitz notes that it has been common for transsexuals to claim when dealing with members of the medical profession that they are hermaphrodites despite the appearance of their bodies (for example, they claim to have "hidden" testicles), much in the way that Lobdell made the claim about her "secret" penis. While we of course cannot "see" Lobdell's body today, I would assume that her

doctors' inspections would have enabled them to witness anything "unusual" about Lobdell's body. See Joanne Meyerowitz, *How Sex Changed: A History of Transsexuality in the United States* (Cambridge, Mass.: Harvard University Press, 2002), 139.

76. Kiernan, "Original," 203; these are cited in Wise, "Case," 90. It is interesting to note this discussion of inadequate sexual relations with George Slater is not highlighted in any of the reports given that Krafft-Ebing theorized that lesbians would mostly disappear if men were more sensitive to women's sexual and emotional needs. As Terry notes, "While Krafft-Ebing believed that 'true' female inversion existed in some cases, the majority of lesbians were drawn into perversion because of the absence or misdeeds of men." *American*, 63.

77. The logbook is quoted in Katz, *Gay*, 340–41. See also Kiernan, "Original," 483, and Psychological," 203; Wise, "Case," 89.

78. Duggan, *Sapphic*, 26, 106; Dreger's, historical work, *Hermaphrodites*, also deals with this same equation throughout.

79. Wise, "Case," 89–90.

80. Sander L. Gilman, "Black Bodies, White Bodies: Toward an Iconography of Female Sexuality in Late Nineteenth-Century Art, Medicine, and Literature," in *"Race," Writing and Difference*, ed. Henry Louis Gates, Jr. (Chicago: University of Chicago Press, 1985), 237.

81. Ferguson, *Aberrations*, 11–18.

82. Wise, "Case," 90.

83. Kiernan, "Psychological," 483.

84. Eve Kosofsky Sedgwick, *Epistemology of the Closet* (Berkeley: University of California Press, 1990), 26.

85. C. Jacob Hale, "Consuming the Living, Dis(re)membering the Dead in the Butch/FTM Borderlands," *GLQ: A Journal of Lesbian and Gay Studies* 4 (1998): 343.

86. James, ed., *Narrative*, 34.

87. Desens, "Wild," 49.

88. Wise, "Case," 89–90.

89. Judith Halberstam, *Female Masculinity* (Durham, N.C.: Duke University Press, 1998), 290.

90. To illustrate the power of ideological constraints in everyday practice, I have found my own attempts to reverse the punctuation process in this essay by placing "she" in quotation marks to be very awkward.

91. Quoted in Katz, *Gay*, 341.

92. One source that not only leaves out information but is riddled with misspellings and what can only be taken to be fictional information is Ethelyn Pearson, *It Really Happened Here!* (Gwinn, N.D.: McCleery & Sons). An excerpt from the Lobdell chapter entitled "Early Female Impersonator was Scandal of Minnesota!" can be found at http://www.jmcompanies.com/mccleery_sons/HTML/happened.html (March 10, 2002). In addition to the many typos and misspellings, the page depicts Lobdell as a wandering female "imposter" who died quickly after the "La-Roi Lobdell" story told by Desens, "Wild," 43. In this version, Lobdell dresses as a man, is discovered to be an imposter, and dies after living in a cave in Monroe County, Pennsylvania.

93. Ernest James, "Genealogy," in *Narrative and Publications Relating to Lucy Ann Lobdell, the Female Hunter of Delaware and Sullivan Counties, New York* (Santa Rosa, Calif.: Ernest

James, 1996), 2. I should also note a review of the film *The Ballad of Little J* by Linda Lopez McAlister on WMNF-FM, Tampa, Florida (November 13, 1993). Here, McAlister discusses Lobdell as a woman who took on a male person a "largely for economic reasons." In such an account, we basically see a repetition of the claims made by Lobdell in her autobiography. See http://www.inform.umd.edu/EdRes/Topic/Wom/FilmReviews/ballad-of-little-jo-mcalister (March 10, 2002).

94. Desens, "Wild," 43.

95. Ibid.

96. There are exceptions, of course. For example, the *History News Network* site contains a listing of marriage resisters and observes, "In upstate New York, Lucy Ann Lobdell became the Reverend Joseph Lobdell and lived for a decade with his wife, Maria Perry." See http://hnn.us/roundup/entries/6844.html (August 15, 2005).

97. Http://www.jtsears.com/histime.htm (August 15, 2005).

98. Http://www.women.it/les/storia/lhp-list.htm (August 15, 2005).

99. Http://niftynats.tripod.com/lesbians/ (August 15, 2005).

100. Http://www.swade.net/lesbian/tribal_chant/les_hist.html (August 15, 2005). The "Gay South Africa" website notes that this case denoted the "first time Lesbian is used to denote woman-loving-woman" behavior (http://www.gaysouthafrica.org.za/lesbian/history.asp. [August 15, 2005]), and this timeline/history is reprinted on the Mongolian Lesbian Community website at http://www.mongoldyke.org.mn/world_hist_eng.htm (retrieved August 15, 2005). Moreover, this information is a trivia question on "Beverly's Name That Notable Woman Loving Woman Contest" webpage (http://www.geocities.com/WestHollywood/1769/winners2.html [August 15, 2005]). The Kandiyohi County website notes in its history that Lucy was a woman who disguised herself "as a man" one winter (http://www.kandiyohi.com/stay/history.htm [August 15, 2005]).

101. In the most blatant and overt usage of this reinscription, one website utilizes the "lesbian histories" contained on previously cited webpages—including the story of Lucy Lobdell and Marie Louise Perry—and accompanies these stories with female-female nude images taken from a traditional male heterosexual fantasy perspective.

102. Duggan, *Sapphic*, 125–28.

103. Although I do want to note that Terry indexes the Lobdell case under the name "Lucy Slater," Lobdell's "married name." I mention this if only because it works against Lobdell's own practice. Not only did "she" use the name Lobdell both before and after her marriage to George Slater, but in "her" autobiography, Lobdell takes care to note that "she" informed Slater that "she" had returned to the maiden name Lobdell, a practice that evidently upset Slater. See Terry, *American*, 536, and Lobdell, *Narrative*, 33.

104. Katz, *Gay*, 342.

105. See Beverly Greene, "Notable Women Loving Women in History" *Oasis*, June 1997, http://www.oasismag.com/Issues/9706/column-greene.html (March 10, 2002), and Beverly Greene, "Transgendered Persons and Passing Men in History," *Oasis*, October 1997, http://www.oasismag.com/Issues/9710/column-greene.html (March 10, 2002).

106. Greene, "Notable."

107. Ibid.

108. Greene, "Transgendered."

109. See Cloud, present volume.

110. Although I hope this point is already clear, I want to stress that queering public address should help force us to understand that all descriptions of "speakers" from the past are always already political—not just those about cases like this one that deal directly with a case of gender and sexuality. Hence, a scholar who assumes "normal heterosexuality" in discussions of, say, Abraham Lincoln, is politically constructing—and working through interpretive categories—just as much as one who studies a case like this one. For an excellent analysis of descriptions of Lincoln and his gender/sexuality, see Charles E. Morris III, "My Old Kentucky Homo: Lincoln and the Politics of Queer Public Memory," in *Framing Public Memory*, ed. Kendall R. Phillips (Tuscaloosa: University of Alabama Press, 2004), 89–114.

111. Michel Foucault, *Discipline and Punish: The Birth of the Prison*, (New York: Vintage, 1979), 30–31. In addition to Jennifer Terry's reading of Foucault's "effective histories" in which she sees Foucault as studying the "process which takes stock of effects, or, in other words, of the accidents . . . that gave birth to those things that continue to have value for us," I would also want to stress that his comments in *Discipline and Punish*, in "Nietzsche, History, Genealogy," and elsewhere lead us to see that an "effective history" is also a "instrumentally more useful kind of history" because it is useful to highlight the politics and concerns of everyday life in the present. Terry, *American*, 20–21; Foucault, "Nietzsche, History, Genealogy," in *The Foucault Reader*, ed. Paul Rabinow (New York: Pantheon, 1984), 86–90.

queer harlem

Exploring the Rhetorical Limits
of a Black Gay "Utopia"

Eric King Watts

FIRE . . . flaming, burning, searing, and penetrating far beneath the super-
ficial items of the flesh to boil the sluggish blood . . .
FIRE . . . *melting steel and iron bars, poking livid tongues between stone aper-*
tures and burning wooden opposition with a cackling chuckle of contempt . . .
Fy-ah,
Fy-ah, Lawd,
Fy-ah gonna burn ma soul!

Wallace Thurman, foreword,
Fire!! Devoted to Younger Negro Artists

In a letter dated October 8, 1928, Alain LeRoy Locke advised Scholley Pace
Alexander, business manager of the soon-to-be-published literary magazine
Harlem: A Forum of Negro Life, about the new venture's proper place in the "New
Negro Movement" and warned Alexander about the influence of his partners and
friends, Wallace Thurman and Richard Bruce Nugent: "About the magazine, I can
only say try to keep it balanced—all of you are temperamental—do not exploit
that to the verge of eccentricity—for after all the eccentric is not beautiful."[1]
Locke expressed admiration for their collaboration on *Harlem*, alluding to the doctrine of African Americans "putting one's best foot forward"[2] to promote social
equality during the Harlem Renaissance, but the letter is both cautious and ironic.
Locke portrayed W. E. B. Du Bois as closed-minded and dogmatic in his attempts
as editor of the *Crisis* to regulate the ways in which black art served the ends of
civil rights. "Have controversies," Locke explained, but unlike Du Bois, who cultivated a "creed of me and my dog . . . give both sides."[3] Deterring Alexander and
friends in this letter from being "eccentric" and from giving in to the polemical,
Locke seems to be trying to mitigate the impact that extreme ideologies have on
black literature. Such counsel is consistent with the figure of the African American intellectual Locke sculpted two years earlier in his influential anthology *The*

New Negro: An Interpretation,[4] which presents the black savant as an arbiter of competing positions and a mediator of conflicting voices, ensuring that "both sides" get heard.

From the perspective of the "friends," Thurman and Nugent, however, nothing could be further from the truth. Locke's admonishment of the "eccentric" concerns something else, something unspoken, and something off center, unconventional, deviant—queer. The "temperamental" natures of Thurman and Nugent needed to be guarded against, for their lifestyles were perceived as indulgent and unhealthy, "decadent" and strange. To Locke, their "eccentricity" was a distraction from the aims of beauty and a corruption of the objects of beauty. Thurman's and Nugent's queerness were in part constitutive of the "culture of homosexuality"[5] that was cultivated among a coterie of young bohemian-styled black intellectuals migrating to upper Manhattan. Their desire to express their "eccentric" ways in black cultural forms therefore was unsettling to those who hoped that the Harlem Renaissance would produce a "mainstream" black American nationality, an ethos deemed worthy of social equality.

Furthermore, what is apparent in Locke's letter is that queer Harlem was a sort of "open secret," constitutive of a discourse of indirection and innuendo rather than candidly acknowledged.[6] In this sense, questions about the impact of queer desire on black literary production and a black rhetorical voice should not be limited to literary theory and practice; such queries must be understood as addendums to the public moral argument sponsored in 1926 by the *Crisis* literary editor, Jessie Fauset—"The Negro in Art: How Shall He Be Portrayed?"[7] This nearly year-long debate involved a consideration of the "proper" topics for the invention of an African American ethos and the "obligations" that black artists had toward the cultivation of a "positive" racial identity.[8] Such literary elites as Langston Hughes, Countee Cullen, Carl Van Vechten, and Sherwood Anderson, although taking up sometimes significantly different positions, expressed negative opinions about the debate's underlying proposition, that black artists ought to be "propagandists," that black cultural expression should be shaped by the explicit concerns of civil rights and "racial uplift." And so, Locke's letter is ironic, because he is not so much interested in a fair hearing of "both sides" as concerned with placing rhetorical limits on the inventive possibilities of queer imagination. Such boundaries were necessary, Locke believed, for the maintenance of a straight, middle-class, "respectable" ethos —the New Negro's "dwelling place."[9]

This chapter will explore the relationship between queer voice and African American ethos during the height of the Harlem Renaissance. I argue that, although Harlem was revered as an African American "homeland" that nurtured black artistic possibilities and was celebrated as an after-hours playground for Greenwich Village "decadents" seeking safe haven for experiments with the exotic, New Negro racial politics were inhospitable toward the cultivation of a black gay "home" and queer voices. This chapter examines the struggle over Harlem dwelling places and the conditions for inventing queer rhetorical voices. I will first situate these rhetorical struggles within the complex and intriguing milieu of mid-1920s Harlem and gay New York. Then, I will perform a textual analysis of Thurman's roman à clef novel *Infants of the Spring*. In this fictionalized account of Thurman's Harlem experiences, the younger generation of black artists tries to mediate an imposing racial consciousness with the "freedom" promised by bohemian living. Thurman dramatizes the "failure" of the New Negro Movement as, in part, resulting from the inability to negotiate a shared dwelling place for both queer and racial voices. Coolly received and harshly reviewed, the book, ironically, represents this "failure."[10] *Infants*, however, does make a queer sound; it interrupts the orthodoxy of New Negro discourse by confessing to the movement's "secret." It ushers out of the closet the manner in which queer "deviance" was constitutive of a preoccupation with a "respectable" African American ethos. By reflecting on queer homelessness and voicelessness, queer Harlem's "decadence" is posited as a function of the New Negro's obsession with race, forcing queer desire to be overindulgent in order to be acknowledged—portraying it literally and figuratively in excess of the racial bodies meant to contain it. *Infants* reveals such experiences through a utopian vision where black queer life may be "free" of racial boundaries and can imagine new ways in which folks can belong together, but queer life is also put out in the middle of "no where," "no place," subject to a tragic, silent death.

Staying In (Coming Out): Excess and Border Crossing in Queer Harlem

There are numerous accounts of the era known as the Harlem Renaissance. Although much disagreement exists as to the specific character or "worth" of the black artistry assigned to this period, the sheer volume of work about black writers and black writing testifies to its importance. In his autobiography *The Big Sea*, Langston Hughes observes that Harlem in the 1920s was a time and place where "the Negro was in vogue."[11] This observation can be made to shine a light on how the Harlem tourist trade became a spectacular industry; how it promoted dancing, music, and nonstop revelry as a commodity. If we turn toward this sheen, we see bright, flashy smiles and hear deep-throated laughter. Being "in vogue" is, of course, trendy and faddish and subject to staging. Hughes sees this too: "Harlem Nights became show nights for the Nordics," his story continues. "All of us know that the gay and sparkling life of the so-called Negro Renaissance of the '20's was not so gay and sparkling beneath the surface as it looked."[12]

The ethos of the New Negro can be understood, then, as one of Harlem's more prominent fabrications, but Harlem manufactured all sorts of productions for white consumption, and if we look "beneath the surface" our vision is swept "downtown" toward Greenwich Village. George Chauncey describes the transformation of the Village during Prohibition from a "backwater" working-class neighborhood into a thriving bohemian community of artists and intellectuals.[13] Villagers liberated themselves from the rigid norms and social practices of late-Victorian mores, flaunting nontraditional lifestyles that were considered "unmanly" because of the celebration of single "free-lovers and anti-materialists. . . . [Villagers] had forsaken many of the other social roles and characteristics prescribed for their class and gender in ways stereotypically associated with homosexuals." This Bohemia, then, protected homosexuality as one of its "queer tastes" but was often mistakenly identified with it. Hence the Village attracted scores of homosexual and heterosexual folks who sought escape from middle-class sexual and social repression: "Part of the attraction of an amusement district such as Greenwich Village . . . was that it constituted a *liminal space* where visitors were encouraged to disregard some of the social injunctions that normally constrained their behavior, where they could observe and vicariously experience behavior that in other settings—particularly their own neighborhoods—they might consider objectionable enough to suppress."[14]

Hedonists flocked to the Village to gawk at the "queers" and to play among them. Indeed, some residents "complained that their less scrupulous compatriots had begun to cater to the tourist trade, decking themselves out in the costumes visitors expected of bohemians, selling their verse and etchings to the unsophisticated, and offering tours of a fabricated 'Bohemia' to the gullible."[15] As queer performances by "'pseudo-Bohemians' interested . . . in a mindless escape from the conventions of bourgeois society" became increasingly commodified, vice squads stepped up the moral policing of most of New York. But because of racist neglect and disinterest, the moral authorities, such as the Committee of Fourteen, allowed the underground liquor, gambling, and sex trade to go largely unchecked in Harlem. Gay and lesbian Villagers, seeking refuge from what was becoming a queer stage show, ventured into Harlem, where "gay life was livelier and more open" than downtown.[16] It is precisely this queer "migration" that helped sponsor queer Harlem and set it in opposition to the orthodoxy of the New Negro. And so, what is of interest here is not just what lies beneath the veneer of raced and sexualized performances for the benefit of tourism and social activism, but also how attempts to reinvent queer rhetorical voices should be placed in relation to these practices.

To both Du Bois and Locke, the art of the "New Negro" could broker new civil rights. The invention of a race literature for social change is understandable when we consider that the late-Victorian social equation of "high" art and "civilization" was largely unquestioned by Harlem elite. Indeed, although the Harlem Renaissance is usually indexed to the early 1920s, its ideological tenets can be traced back to the nineteenth century and can be observed in letters such as the one that Charles W. Chesnutt penned to James Weldon Johnson in 1913, congratulating him on his "Emancipation Anniversary poem, 'Fifty Years.'" In the letter Chesnutt beams, "I can only add, after endorsing all [that the other critics] say, that it is the finest thing I have ever read on the subject, which is saying a good deal, and the finest thing I have seen from the pen of a colored writer for a long time—which is not saying quite so much. If you can find themes which will equally inspire you, why may you not become the poet for which the race is waiting?"[17]

Here we see how literary accomplishment is identified with an African American ethos. But Chesnutt's congratulatory remarks also reference the interpretive task of locating the proper topics—the themes that will inspire—for rhetorical invention. In a sense, it is not just the poet for whom the race is waiting, but there is also the anticipation of *kairos*, the right time and place enabling writers to find the right words to touch the hearts of readers; 1913 was not the time. Responding to a request in 1924 for a copy of *The Autobiography of an Ex-Colored Man*, Johnson explained that when he published it anonymously "fourteen years ago there was little or no interest in the Negro. In fact, we had reached the deepest depths of apathy regarding him so far as the general public is concerned."[18] Convinced that black social advancement was always overdue, Du Bois dedicated, as early as 1916, significant editorial space in the *Crisis* to the publication of black writing;[19] and by June of the same year he joyfully reported a substantial increase in the literary works received by his office.[20]

Positioned as one of Hazel Carby's "race men"[21] in Harlem, Du Bois collided with NAACP official policy privileging the legislative route to social equality. Convinced from the very start of the journal that racial prejudice was "unreasonable,"[22] a "viscous habit of mind,"[23] Du Bois formally acknowledged in editorial principle what his writing demonstrated all along. That is, racism could be neither erased nor transformed by force of law because dominant cultural logic makes it particularly pernicious.[24] Du Bois received invaluable assistance from Jessie Fauset when she joined the *Crisis* as its literary editor in 1919. By 1923 her keen eye and ear had already recognized the literary talent of Hughes and Jean Toomer, providing them both with a Harlem debut.[25] Despite Fauset's tutelage at the *Crisis*, in this struggle over cultural forms and social knowledge, the ethos of race occupied the primary ground of the hermeneutical situation of Harlem Renaissance intellectuals, marginalizing to different degrees class, gender, and sexuality.

By the time Thurman moved to Manhattan from California in September 1925, Harlem was enjoying a reputation as an African American mecca[26] but was on the brink of a significant controversy regarding the architecture of this "New Negro" home. I have detailed elsewhere some salient features of this problem facing black artistry.[27] For the purposes of this chapter, it is crucial to understand only that, with the publication of "the bible of the emerging Harlem Renaissance,"[28] *The New Negro*, artists were impelled to relocate African cultural forms within American modernist aesthetics. Locke posited that "pagan" topics and feelings allowed black folk to take advantage of the wealth of emotions that connected black Americans to their ancestral roots. To Locke, Africa's legacy offered a strictly defined topical structure for the sort of interpretive acts that make up writing. Locke's appeal to

African artistic classics to inspire and guide the younger artists was largely hailed as a monumental breakthrough in the philosophy of black aesthetics. It seized the advantage over Du Bois's mantra of "propaganda" by paying homage to the "higher" ideals of art; it was also in keeping with the spirit of "primitivism" at the bottom of much ravenous attention that white folks paid Harlem. And thus it posited racial experiences as legitimate resources for art. *The New Negro* therefore ushered in a full-fledged "advertisement" for Harlem and for the very idea of a modern black America. Locke was nearly prophetic when he proclaimed that the younger generation evidenced a "new psychology" regarding race consciousness, but in the case of Thurman, this new mentality fostered very little interest in the racial uplift mission at the heart of the "New Negro" ethos.

Underlying Thurman's rejection of "New Negro" racial philosophy was a complicated matrix of desire. Thurman wished to be free of racial constraints, free of middle-class values, free from the perceived ignorance of the masses, and free from dictates of authoritarian regimes in general.[29] He also yearned to be a writer, a *great writer*, and soon after he arrived in Harlem, he secured a job as utility man at a brand new little magazine called the *Looking Glass*, edited by his new friend, Theophilus Lewis. The magazine quickly collapsed, but Thurman's friendship with Lewis was to last a lifetime. Lewis, a part-time drama critic, returned to work at the *Messenger* and took Thurman with him. It was in the employment of the quasi-socialist, quasi-progressive magazine that Thurman was influenced by George Schuyler's conservatism and impressed with his creative resemblance to W. H. Mencken, whom Thurman studied at the University of Southern California. Schuyler's acid-dipped criticism of the Harlem Renaissance advanced the *Messenger*'s generally antagonistic posture toward black leadership's rear guard.

Taking up this iconoclastic temper, Thurman attempted to live out his "bohemian lifestyle and his self-defined outsider-critic status."[30] Encouraged by disapproval from members of the Talented Tenth generation and increasingly surrounded by young intellectuals who also "advocated emancipation from the demands of racial propaganda,"[31] Thurman embraced through his writing the notion "of an intellectual aristocracy . . . the Artist-Iconoclast [that] set the elite in opposition to the mob, the individual to the mass, the artist to society, rebellion to conformity, excellence to mediocrity, and scepticism [sic] to mindless assent."[32] Hence Thurman's critique of the constraints of group identity took shape as attacks on New Negro proponents, producing among a cadre of young black bohemians an antipathy toward "the black middle class as subject matter for the artistic interpretation of the African American experience."[33]

The problem with smashing idols is that it creates voids that beckon for new images and symbols for the constitution of meaning. Snubbing a range of topics made available by the New Negro ethos, artists such as Hughes, Nugent, Claude McKay, Zora Neale Hurston, Eric Walrond, Dorothy West, and Georgia Douglas

Johnson were encouraged by Thurman to try out in the *Messenger* new themes of free-spirited urban living. Such experimentation was met with dissension from Locke, but it was excited by the arrival of one of the most marketable and combustible works of this era, Carl Van Vechten's *Nigger Heaven*. With such an incendiary title, Hughes recalled later that most black folk didn't even have to read it to hate it.[34] Du Bois in particular thought it to be a betrayal of the generosity afforded Van Vechten by black folk.

But Thurman felt the book represented an odd sort of truth: that the Harlem Renaissance was a disturbingly shallow sensation made up of the trivial and the inane; he insinuated in his review that it captured the spectacle of Harlem revelry as experienced by a white ("Negro") spectator reporting his findings to whites. Thurman's review concluded with the speculation that the novel "should have a wide appeal and gain much favorable notice."[35] Not surprisingly, then, most of its favorable reviews came from white readers who, incidentally, after 1926, constituted the majority of readers of Harlem Renaissance works.[36] *Nigger Heaven* set Harlem on its edge, and Van Vechten seemed to be loving every minute of it; in a letter to James Weldon Johnson he called the attention "wonderful so far" while noting that Harlem was "seething in controversy."[37] Eric Garber argues that from the perspective of "downtown" this storm lit up the northern skies and had to be witnessed up close; thus the novel intensified the sexualized consumption of black bodies.[38]

Van Vechten had touched a raw nerve in Harlem's social body. How shall the Negro be portrayed? Should it be a prim and proper embodiment of the "dead conventional Negro-white ideas of the past," as Hughes put it,[39] or shall black bodies be shaped by their imagined excesses, as drunken, lewd, and violent creatures of Harlem's wild nights? Although this dichotomy is a false one, Thurman and his fellow travelers, Nugent in particular, seemed caught up in its dialectical energies. When in 1926, Thurman, Nugent, Hughes, Hurston, and visual artist Aaron Douglas collaborated on the one and only issue of *Fire!!*, Thurman barred Du Bois and Locke from having any say in it. Apparently he believed that the propagandist and the "mother hen," as Hurston called Locke, would frustrate his efforts at cultivating truly new Harlem voices. Thus Thurman can be seen to embrace explorations into flawed and pathetic black individuals, even of the *Nigger Heaven* variety, precisely because his sharp pivot away from the obligations of racial uplift occurred in rhythm with the tempo of the "decadent" Jazz Age. "Freed" from the obligations constitutive of New Negro racial discourse, the editors of *Fire!!* set out to free other young artists by performing a vital rhetorical interruption.

The Voice and Voicelessness of *Infants of the Spring*

In exploring the conditions under which voice (or voicelessness) occurs in public moral argument, I have posited elsewhere that rhetorical voice is a phenomenon endowed by the public acknowledgment of the ethical and emotional dimensions of speech.[40] Voice is a dialogic event in which persons are reoriented toward one another by the shared acknowledgment of the obligations and anxieties incumbent in building dwelling places. There are two dimensions of public speech that require acknowledgment if voice is to be realized. First, the emotions associated with being-on-the-line, with publicly addressing an issue or event, need to be acknowledged so as to stimulate voice. Second, the ethical import of taking a position and representing it rhetorically demands acknowledgment to fulfill voice. Voice is essentially a phenomenon of public hearing in which speakers must often interrupt ongoing conversations that do not make room for them in order to be acknowledged. David Appelbaum suggests that the type of utterance that "unsettles the familiar cadence of taken for granted discourse"[41] can be perceived as a "cough" that can "interrupt."[42] Similarly, Michael J. Hyde and Kenneth Rufo characterize the "rhetorical interruption" as a positive moment, because it constitutes the temporal and spatial preconditions for voice, a moment when new possibilities for *addressivity* and *answerability* are brought into being.[43]

It is to such a moment that we now turn. *Infants of the Spring* was published in 1932, a few years after the crest of the rising tide of black artistry in Harlem. As such, its reception was tepid and the book seemed to be quickly forgotten. Although flawed by its laborious dialogue and narrative incoherence, *Infants* is the only novel about the Harlem Renaissance written by a black author during the movement. It is also noteworthy because the novel re-creates a dwelling place for homoeroticism. Thurman, however, places such strain on his characters that in the end nearly everyone in the book implodes from the pressure. We experience through the workings of Thurman's caustic imagination how a black queer utopian dream ends in a tragic half-life and how black queers who dare to dream otherwise pass away, out of blackness, out of Harlem, out of sight, and out of mind. But *Infants* is here to remind us of this passing by telling the story of queer housing, conviction, and eviction; our passage into *the* queer Harlem "home" should begin by keeping such passing in mind.

"Raymond opened the door with a flourish."[44] And with this grand gesture, the reader is escorted into the hub of black bohemian living. Raymond Taylor, Thurman's alter ego in *Infants*, is our tour guide and commentator throughout the novel, serving as both object and subject of Thurman's critical gaze. Through Raymond, Thurman invites us into his "home," his infamous studio at 267 West 136th Street, a house for indigent black artists nicknamed by Thurman and Hurston as the "Niggeratti Manor."[45] The Manor seems to represent a kind of crucible where unconventional black thought is applied to the exigencies of trying to live up to one's hopes of being a significant writer. Raymond immediately shows it to be a place where the vibrant and the "vulgar" radiate in red and black and where intellectual conversations about race and art are liberally lubricated by gin. Raymond's studio is also homoerotic, adorned with Paul Arbian's drawings of "highly colored phalli."[46]

Hence the first glimpse the reader gets of the Manor is framed by a composite of the signs of decadence and homoerotic "deviance." Thurman not only displays his home to us, but, by introducing us to the characters Samuel Carter and Stephen Jorgenson, he also instructs us on how white tourists often behaved while visiting. Sam, perhaps modeled after Leland Petit, a homosexual and a frequent visitor to the Manor, embodies gay white, paternal sentimentalism,[47] the "social service workers, reformed socialistic ministers, foreign missionaries . . . all so saccharine and benevolent."[48] Stephen symbolizes both Thurman's desire for his Canadian-born friend and lover, Harald Jan Stefansson, and Carl Van Vechten's rapacious appetite for black culture. As we get to know Raymond, Sam, and Stephen, we begin to appreciate how a queer ethos and voice are cultivated in *Infants* as well as how they are subject to destruction and dissipation.

Queer voice in *Infants* is instigated by the articulation of a bold rhetorical interruption. The Manor is not simply red and black; we are told that the colors are "loud."[49] Red and black allude to the aesthetic and ethical challenge made by Thurman and friends with the magazine *Fire!!* Aaron Douglas's red and black cover art stood in sharp contrast to the conservative literary designs of the *Opportunity* and the *Crisis*. Michael Cobb describes *Fire!!* as a "self-consciously asserted . . . aesthetic rupture" of New Negro discourse.[50] *Fire!!* was designed to be completely different and, since Thurman and Nugent decided to write stories about prostitution and homosexual love for the first issue, it was explicitly meant to shock. *Infants* reproduces this disruption of New Negro respectability and decency by beginning with a "loud," flamboyant, "striking" "sound."[51] Samuel is predictably annoyed by the vulgarity of this queer resonance, but Stephen is drawn to it. He closely inspects the "colored phalli," appreciating the artist's handling of color; this explicit interest establishes the foundation for the queer desire that will soon blossom between Raymond and Stephen.

Thurman and Nugent moved into the Manor in November 1926 and lived there until 1928, "forming the core of Harlem's black bohemia."[52] In the novel Raymond shares this space with Paul Arbian, Pelham Gaylord, and Eustace Savoy, each character signifying a form of dis-ease with the black body. Eustace is a struggling singer who believes that the spirituals are too "primitive" to be worth his time. Raymond "had no sympathy whatsoever with Negroes like Eustace, who contended that should their art be Negroid, they, the artist, must be considered inferior."[53] Pelham, on the other hand, has no talent to be corrupted by anxieties associated with blackness; but he yearns, nevertheless, to write like the others, to acquire "queer tastes," a desire that *is* corruptible. He wants to be *of* the "Niggeratti," someone who could sound like an eccentric. According to Ray, however, Pelham was born to be just a servant. Paul Arbian is the fictional counterpart to Nugent; the name "Arbian" sounds out Nugent's initials, "R," "B," "N." Because Thurman felt that Nugent epitomized bohemian living and because Nugent was openly gay while living at the

Manor, Paul Arbian is iconic; he stands for a range of possibilities and typifies a set of problems for a queer ethos.

For queer voice to be actualized, the rhetorical interruption that echoes through the first few pages of *Infants* must be accompanied by the acknowledgment of the ethical and emotional dimensions of queer speech. In *Infants*, the ethical dimensions of speech are disclosed by the challenges to New Negro racial philosophy offered by the inhabitants of the Manor. In particular, *Infants* dramatizes boundary crossings, the violation of social rules and conventions associated with interracial and homosexual communion. Similarly, queer ethos materializes as a black bohemian utopia, a dwelling place for those on the "fringe" of the New Negro movement.[54] Thurman uses characters' bodies and narrative action to destabilize the very idea of rule-bound behavior. When Paul enters the novel, his movement and body instigate queer voice and shape queer ethos.

"'Ain't he a beauty, Eustace?'" Paul announces, referring to Stephen. "'Have you ever been seduced?'" he asks the startled but amused newcomer. "'Don't blush. You just looked so pure and undefiled that I had to ask that.'"[55] Enamored with Stephen's white, virginal presence, Paul sits at his feet to gaze at the man "fashioned like a Viking" and offers him a tip on style: "Take that part out of your hair and have it windblown. The hair, not the part. Plastering it down like that destroys the golden glint."[56] Paul's performance is disruptive (he literally interrupts the ongoing conversation in the room), and despite the attention paid to Stephen, it is narcissistic; it brings notice to him. Thurman reinforces the idea that Paul's gaze is self-reflexive by concentrating on Paul's body: "Paul was very tall. His face was the color of a bleached saffron leaf. His hair was wiry and untrained. It was his habit not to wear a necktie because he knew that his neck was too well modeled to be hidden from public gaze. He wore no sox [*sic*] either, nor underwear, and those few clothes he did deign to affect were musty and dishevelled [*sic*]."[57] As an effeminate man, Paul, in contemporary terms, can be said to be "flaming"—that is, he is on fire.[58] As such his manner matches the shade of fire-engine red on the cover of *Fire!!* and splashed across Ray's studio walls. Couched within this signification system, Paul is at "home."

Paul's personal style is inspired by Nugent's distaste for what was considered the "proper" attitude and place for Harlem's black literati.[59] Hence Paul displays the bohemian's penchant for crossing over the lines. Indeed Nugent "cared not for any societal structure which dictated his behavior."[60] Liberated from social norms, the inhabitants of the Manor no longer needed to negotiate so intensely when and how they entered Harlem circles. The Manor was open all day and night, and in the book, such unencumbered access to others rapidly engenders a friendship between Raymond and Stephen that is described in the language of pastoral romance. "They had become as intimate in that short period as if they had known each other since childhood. In fact, there was something delightfully naïve and childlike about their frankly acknowledged affection for one another."[61] This fondness has been discussed by other critics as homoerotic, even though Thurman refers most directly to racial taboos associated with their friendship.[62] Despite the "potential for exploitation" when white folks "invaded" Harlem, Garber notes that "with its sexually tolerant population and its quasi-legal nightlife, Harlem offered an oasis to white homosexuals. . . . This identification and feeling of kinship . . . may have been the beginnings of homosexual 'minority consciousness.'"[63] I'll take up the character of this felicity in a moment when I explore the emotions of voice. What is important at this juncture is that Raymond and Stephen's "kinship" serves as the impetus for Stephen to move into the Manor.

While trying to convince Stephen that Harlem's charm is due to the fact that it is just "New York . . . black New York," Raymond challenges the logic of racial tourism: "[Negroes] have the same social, physical and intellectual divisions. You're only being intrigued, as I have said before, by the newness of the thing. You should live here a while."[64] The author's voice can be heard in Ray's words here. In *The World Tomorrow*, Thurman wrote that "in Harlem we find a community as American as Gopher Prairie or Zenith. . . . It permits of everything possessed by that stupendous ensemble—New York City—of which it is a part."[65] There are two concepts being posited here. First, Raymond's explanation of Stephen's consumptive habits ties them to the maintenance of Harlem's novelty, masking its "true" character. Since the moment of his arrival in New York, Thurman was a critic of the "artificial" character of the Harlem Renaissance and believed that it was the mission of intellectuals such as himself to debunk it.[66] *Infants* therefore explores the perils of "posing." For example, Stephen tries to understand Paul's need to be the center of attention and focuses on how racial consciousness produces his hyperbolic performances: "Paul has never recovered from the shock of realizing that no matter how bizarre a personality he may develop," Stephen tells Raymond, "he will still be a Negro, subject to snubs from certain ignorant people. . . . being a Negro, he feels that his chances for excessive notoriety à la Wilde are slim. Thus the exaggerated poses and extreme mannerisms. Since he can't be white, he will be a most unusual Negro."[67] Paul's queer excesses are in part precipitated by the containment field produced by his black body responding to both New Negro doctrine and white consumption. To be recognized as more than black, he is excessive.

Paul's posture is a counterpart to the New Negro pose. In perhaps the most widely studied chapter in the novel, Dr. A. L. Parkes, Alain Locke's character, asks Raymond to convene a distinguished salon so as to "establish the younger Negro talent once and for all as a vital artistic force." Artists in attendance include Langston Hughes as Tony Crews, Countee Cullen as Dewitt Clinton, and Zora Neale Hurston as Sweetie May Carr. The meeting begins with Dr. Parkes praising the group's potential, but as in the letter with which I opened this chapter, Dr. Parkes warns of "decadence" damaging the movement and suggests a return to African cultural forms as topics for invention. Commentators have taken the ensuing melee as a synecdoche for the Harlem Renaissance's debacle. I wish to note how Thurman uses this scene as a refutation of the claim made by Locke in the anthology *The New Negro*, that this new ethos was no longer a "pose" for the benefit of racial protest but rather that New Negro artists have attained "poise."[68] Thurman observes that Sweetie May Carr was popular to white folk because "she lived up to their conception of what a typical Negro should be."[69] "It's like this," she tells Raymond. "I have to eat. I also wish to finish my education. Being a Negro writer these days is a racket and I'm going to make the most of it while it lasts. . . . My ultimate ambition, as you know, is to become a gynecologist. And the only way I can live easily until I have the requisite training is to pose as a writer of potential ability. *Voila!* I get my tuition paid at Columbia. . . . I find queer places for whites to go in Harlem. . . . They fall for it. . . . Thank God for this Negro literary renaissance!"[70] In a sense, Sweetie May tells us she is wearing a mask, hiding from view the fact that the New Negro embodies strategies for individual and group advancement. Furthermore *Infants* shows us that it is the pressure to conform to this racial mission that harms queer speech.

Raymond and Stephen's relationship also testifies to the notion that to better understand Harlem's "real" self, one must live in Harlem. The Niggeratti Manor, as the place where such living is made possible, materializes queer ethos as an alternative social location with great "truth" value. The capacity for ways of life to provoke and sustain mutual understanding and affection among people perceived as different must be comprehended as *Infants*' chief ethical challenge to sexual and racial orthodoxy. The prime example of this confrontation in the novel is the donation party. Modeled after Harlem's infamous rent parties, the cost of admission to the Manor's donation party is food rather than rent money. The party starts slowly but, by midnight, is in full, hedonistic swing. Taking stock of the festivities, Raymond is encouraged by the interracial crowd's collective boundary crossing; the Manor seems to sway back and forth, coaxing lovers into embraces, singers into song, and writers into verse: "The party had reached new heights. . . . Color lines had been completely eradicated. Whites and blacks clung passionately together as if trying to effect a permanent merger. Liquor, jazz music, and close physical contact had achieved what decades of propaganda had advocated with little success."

The party in the Manor is both the time and the place for the birth of a new form of civic culture. "Here, Raymond thought . . . is social equality."[71] He notices how comfortable Paul seems, hand in hand with "Bud," his "bootblack" friend with "the most beautiful body I've ever seen."[72] Scholars have noted how rent parties "were the best place for Harlem lesbians and gays to socialize, providing safety and privacy."[73] But in *Infants*, the "liminal space" of this challenge to strict, rule-bound racial and sexual decorum is fragile and conflicted, because queer ethos here is constitutive of excesses and overindulgences, tendencies linked to the pressure of racial conformity and appetites for exotic "others." As such, dis-ease is also present and grows stronger as the party wears on. "The crowd confused [a group of school teachers] as it did most of the Harlem intellectuals who strayed in and who all felt decidedly out of place."[74]

In order for *Infants'* queer voice to be actualized, the emotional dimensions of its speech are in need of acknowledgment. To this end, Raymond describes a kind of euphoria (which is also the name of the woman who owns the Manor) that morphs into vertigo and then sickness. "Tomorrow," Raymond mumbles to himself as he surveys the crowd, "all of them will have an emotional hangover. They will fear for their sanity, for at last they have had a chance to do *openly what they only dared to do clandestinely* before."[75] Thurman's work suffers here from narrative incoherence but manages nevertheless to convey Raymond's nagging suspicion that, right before his eyes, the Manor has been transformed into a "sex circus," a place where spectators come for a scandalous show.[76] As Raymond's mood turns blue, we recognize that the Manor may no longer be a safe place for homosexual communion; rather than be "free" of social constraints about how one can be with racial and sexual others, the Manor is a kind of theater where Raymond and friends are prescribed to act outlandishly. And so, we see Raymond's "pleasure" vacated. At the precise moment when he is most giddy regarding his recognition of the gifts of black queer living, Raymond notices that Stephen has left him. He dashes throughout the house searching for his roommate and constant companion, and he has intruded on "the fanciful aggregation of Greenwich Village uranians Paul had gathered in Raymond's studio to admire his bootblack's touted body, and irritated and annoyed two snarling women who had closeted themselves in the bathroom."[77] He interrupts others' sexual delights while his own disappears. "Raymond felt nauseated. The music, the noise, the indiscriminate love-making, the drunken revelry began to sicken him. . . . It is going to be necessary, he thought, to have another emancipation to deliver the emancipated Negro from a new kind of slavery."[78]

Thurman is not clear here, but his disorientation and disgust are triggered by the recognition that Harlem's queer ethos is constitutive of an oppressive body politics. Dr. Parkes demands that one wear a New Negro mask, while the bohemian utopia of the Manor offers an orgy of flesh and drink. On the one hand, one's blackness makes one an instrument of the race. During a visit to the Manor, Dr. Parkes lectures Raymond about the donation party fallout: "This is a new day in the history of our race. Talented Negroes are being watched by countless people, white and black, to produce something new, something tremendous. . . . Scandal stories in the newspapers certainly won't influence the public favorably."[79] On the other hand, one's blackness is a consumable commodity in the tourist trade. Either way, one's body is not one's own. Rejecting the demands of the racial body therefore seems impossible. Stephen later confesses to Raymond in a letter that he had to leave the Manor on the night of the party because he too was feeling ill; rather than consuming the other on visitations to the Manor like the partygoers, Stephen is especially queasy because he has overeaten. "I am fed up on Harlem and on Negroes," Stephen writes. "I can stomach them no longer." He is sick of blackness and no longer feels at home in the Manor.

The promise of their homoerotic love is scuttled in *Infants* by explosive body politics. The naive and innocent character of Raymond and Stephen's friendship is despoiled by the harsh reality of "race business." Stephen explains in his letter, "I have no prejudices, you know; yet recently my being has been permeated with a vague disquiet. I feel lost among Negroes . . . the major thing is not my disquiet, but my growing dislike and antipathy. . . . I have lived recently in a suddenly precipitated fear that I had become unclean. . . . So complex and far reaching has this fear become that I rushed in a panic to a doctor."[80] Although Thurman seems heavy-handed here, it is important to note that *Infants'* queer voice barely has an opportunity to express love and joy before racial and sexual anxieties turn it into a bitter, fearful timbre. This tone can also be heard in Thurman's acrid commentary while with the *Messenger* regarding how black bohemia ultimately undermined the necessary discipline to cultivate truly gifted young writers.[81] The emotional character of *Infants'* voice is haunting precisely because we hear it faintly coming out of nowhere. In the book, Raymond and Paul create a queer "utopia," a no-place.[82] As a bohemian invention, this queer *ethos* is groundless, disorienting, and, in the end, the Niggeratti are dis-eased in it and displaced, that is, evicted from it.[83] As an object of spectacular consumption, the Manor is no longer a "closet" that protects and harbors; it is a stage on which black queer life is open to exploitation.

Euphoria Blake closes the Manor because of "gossip" that she is running a "Miscegenated bawdy house."[84] She fears that the "scandal" that worries Dr. Parkes is hurting her reputation. "I must make money," she explains to Raymond. "That's all a Negro can do. Money means freedom. There's nothing to this art stuff. . . . I only want to make money."[85] No longer feeling that the Manor would be a "monument to the New Negro,"[86] a symbol of "an intellectual aristocracy . . . engaged in the search for Truth (as opposed to money) as a means of social progress,"[87] Euphoria is depressed, and she is angry. Paul's surprise at his unexpected homelessness leads to insults directed at her materialism and her fear of social reprisal. She kicks him out of the Manor in a fit of rage.[88] The emotions that vivify queer voice in *Infants* rapidly descend from the heights of dreams and fantasies to the depths of despair. Raymond is alone and distraught about having to leave the Manor. In response, he suffers a mental breakdown and is bedridden. Thurman seems to struggle in the novel with his own morass and seems unsure how to make sense for the reader of the destruction of a utopian vision. Racial body politics consistently rise up to devour the homoerotic, but the reader cannot be entirely sure whether it is Thurman's anxieties about his own very dark skin or if this domination of race over sex in *Infants* conveys the pressure of New Negro doctrine. I will return to this ambivalence, but we must first examine Paul's fate in relation to the acknowledgment of voice.

In the novel's final chapter, Raymond is awakened in the middle of the night by a frightened voice on the phone telling him, "Paul's committed suicide."[89] Paul had left Harlem for Greenwich Village. Raymond catches the train there immediately; he is oddly detached from the death as a life-ending moment for a friend. The novel displaces the emotions of queer voice in favor of contemplating its acknowledgment. Raymond voices this contemplation: "Had Paul the debonair, Paul the poseur, Paul the irresponsible romanticist, finally faced reality and seen himself and the world as they actually were? . . . He had employed every other conceivable means to make himself stand out from the mob. Wooed the unusual, cultivated artificiality, defied all conventions of dress and conduct."[90] As the embodiment of queer ethos in *Infants*, Paul's "final stanza," his last-ditch effort at being endowed with queer voice, engages the reader. Thus Raymond recognizes the suicide as it is, as a manner of speaking, and is "not so much interested in the fact that Paul was dead as he was in wanting to know how death had been accomplished."[91]

Paul has staged his death to produce "delightful publicity" for the novel he has written, his self-murder acting as the trump card in a game of body politics pushing him farther out in the middle of nowhere. Posthumously published, his work would presumably be acknowledged; it would also be fueled by fascination sparked by the death scene: Paul locked himself in the bathroom, scattered the pages of his novel about the floor so that it could be immediately recognized in all of its glory; he lit incense and hung his art on the walls; he ran bathwater, dressed in a "crimson mandarin robe" and scarf, and slashed his wrists; "Paul lay crumpled at the bottom, a colorful, inanimate corpse in a crimson streaked tub."[92] *Infants* contemplates the conditions of queer voice and voicelessness. Paul's novel is in need of acknowledgment for the endowment of his voice, but he has written it in pencil and the tub has overflowed, rendering the novel illegible, save for the title page. On the title page of Paul's never-to-be-read novel is a sketch he made in black ink of the Niggeratti Manor collapsing because of a crumbling foundation. Raymond recognizes the irony: Paul's suicide "speech" drowns out his voice. His self-mutilation becomes his last word on the subject of how Harlem body politics affect black queer life. And so, Paul's voice is not as he wished it to be. What we finally hear is not the articulate soul of queer ethos, for it is forever erased by the flood caused by the inanimate corpse. Rather we hear finally the inarticulate exhalation made by Paul's bodily surrender.

Conclusions

Infants of the Spring is not a story that ends with the death of Paul Arbian; it testifies still to Thurman's attempts at cultivating his queer voice during the Harlem Renaissance. In the novel Thurman mocks both Harlem's literary establishment and its would-be saviors. Although Thurman has trouble maintaining any sort of stable footing in his staging of *Infants*, he dramatizes the limitations inscribed onto the black body as it was both claimed and consumed by racial and sexual politics. As Harlem responded to being in vogue, New Negro interpretive strategies were strengthened by the promise of racial advancement. Meanwhile the tourism industry that shifted into high gear by 1926 happily traded in those same black bodies. Thurman and friends discovered that their bodies were overvalued because their queerness was perceived as exceptional.

The Niggeratti Manor was the setting for the testing of these pressures; it was constitutive of a queer ethos and was the crucible for queer voices. I have argued that for queer voice to be actualized, its ethical and emotional dimensions must be acknowledged. *Infants* offered an ethical challenge to the New Negro's answer to the humanistic question "How shall I live?" Aesthetic theorists recognize this essential function of art as analogous to the ethos of rhetoric.[93] By this I mean that artworks capture and provide form to the imagination; this formation arises out of a complex context, a matrix of lived experience that allows viewers to understand those experiences precisely because they are made manifest in "readable" form. Such a work has the capacity to perform a rhetorical interruption by interceding in one's own ongoing life. I have attempted to clarify how Thurman's activities interrupted New Negro orthodoxy by positing alternative living arrangements. The production of *Fire!!* and *Harlem* were attempts to transform rhetorical interruptions into rhetorical forums for queer voice. Thurman realized that the failure of these magazines threatened voice. Friends of Thurman, such as Langston Hughes and Augustas Granville Dill, testify to the way that Thurman seemed to cover over his emotions in much of his writing.[94] The narrator of *Infants* favors the distant observation of the journalist to the sensual lyricism of the poet. And so the reader is told of emotions, not immersed in them. This detachment is most glaring when the reader is told of Paul's suicide. The reader has little sense of how Raymond feels about what he sees; indeed we are told that he does not feel, that he is mechanical.[95]

In addition to the sense that *Infants* is sort of numbing, the reader is made to ponder its voice and voicelessness. As a reader I was called by it. Thurman wrote after its publication that "The characters and their problems *cried out* for release. They intruded themselves into [my] every alien thought. And assumed an importance which blinded [me] to their true value."[96] Thurman was very disappointed with his writing of *Infants* and might have been embarrassed by its poor reception and criticism. This lack of acknowledgment by Harlem literati in general disconfirms its voice and can be linked to its "unspeakable" "true value."[97] *Infants* cries out still, but its voice has difficulty reaching us because of the dissipative energies also inscribed within it. Racial politics overwhelm same sexualities in the novel as Thurman's own racial anxieties colonize Raymond's social world.

Although West and Hughes understood the novel to be an "autobiographical" statement about Thurman's preoccupation with race, the Niggeratti Manor signifies a problematic of queer containment and shelter.[98] Siobhan Somerville discusses the "closet" as a space where queer living can be sustained precisely because it is hidden from view.[99] But in terms of the United States's racial history, such spaces for black folk are constitutive of racist systems in which the body can be disciplined.[100] Thurman registers disgust for the Manor because, despite intermingling with white folk, his body was subjected to a form of segregation; that is, the Manor's value as a queer harbor was directly related to the determination of his identity as a black queer. More than anything else, Thurman wanted to be a writer, but the Manor dispersed his desire in favor of the longing that others had for his black "deviance." This sort of excessive appetite for the "livelier" queer Harlem was predicated on passing over a racial boundary. As such, the boundary was delineated as a thing to be crossed after hours and under cover. The allure of these transgressions could not be maintained if Thurman got his wish. Queer Harlem must be peculiar even to gay New York.

Patriarchal heteronormativity, the novel suggests, is what is left standing as the Manor's walls come crumbling down. Put down in ink, Paul's drawing of the fall of the Manor survives the bloodbath. This is the queer sound of *Infants* and of Thurman: drifting to us over time and space, from the edges of no place, we hear a collapse. *Infants* can always produce that queer sound, and that is an important accomplishment. Thurman did not believe so; after its publication he wrote that there was "no excuse for having allowed [*Infants*] to be published."[101] Thurman's disavowal might be linked to his disclaimers to his wife in 1929 that he was ever a participant in queer Harlem's sexual experimentations.[102]

Despite their motivations, such attempts to reinvent self-identity are evident with other "queer" artists. For example, according to Charles Nero, Arnold Rampersad is guilty of exerting "herculean efforts" to show that Hughes was not gay in the biography *Life of Langston Hughes*. Nero posits that the persistent "mission" for black intellectuals to show racial figures and black history in general in their "best light" provokes the reinvention of African American ethos and the suppression of queer voices.[103] Henry Louis Gates, Jr., argues that black history is in dire need of cultural reclamation because the development of black nationality has negated black gay and lesbian narratives.[104] The character of rhetorical voice is uniquely suited for this task because it requires the critic to attend to the emotional and ethical dimensions of public address. Rhetorical voice itself issues a "call of conscience" where we must attempt to feel the joy and pain of our fellows. *Infants* may be anesthetizing in the end, but Thurman's voice is arousing to this day. If this assessment is true, Thurman must be mistaken about having "no excuse" for *Infants*. For if black queer voices are to be moved out of the recesses of the imaginary in African American public speech, our social body must not cease to hear such cries.

Notes

1. Alain LeRoy Locke, letter to Scholley Pace Alexander, October 8, 1928. James Weldon Johnson Collection (hereafter JWJ Collection), Box 1, Folder 28, Beinecke Library, Yale University.

2. Jennifer DeVere Brody and Dwight A. McBride, "Part 2: Plum Nelly: New Essays in Black Queer Studies," *Callaloo* 23 (2000): 329.

3. Locke, JWJ Collection.

4. Alain LeRoy Locke, *The New Negro: An Interpretation* (1925; New York: Arno Press, 1968).

5. George Chauncey, *Gay New York: Gender, Urban Culture, and the Making of the Gay Male World, 1890–1940* (New York: Basic Books, 1994); see also Seth Clark Silberman, "Looking for Richard Bruce Nugent and Wallace Thurman: Reclaiming Black Male Same-Sexualities in the New Negro Movement," *In Process: A Graduate Student Journal of African American and African Diasporan Literature and Culture* 1(1996): 53–73.

6. Michael L. Cobb, "Insolent Racing, Rough Narrative: The Harlem Renaissance's Impolite Queers," *Callaloo* 23 (2000): 335.

7. "The Negro in Art: How Shall He Be Portrayed, A Symposium," *Crisis* 31–32 (1926).

8. Eric King Watts, "African American *Ethos* and Hermeneutical Rhetoric: An Exploration of Alain Locke's *The New Negro*," *Quarterly Journal of Speech* 88 (2002): 19–32.

9. Ironically, Locke's private homosexual ambitions often led him to "aggressively pursue his favorites" among the "New Negro." See Eric Garber, "A Spectacle in Color: The Lesbian and Gay Subculture of Jazz Age Harlem," in *Hidden from History: Reclaiming the Gay and Lesbian Past*, ed. Martin Bauml Duberman, Martha Vicinus, and George Chauncey, Jr. (New York: New American Library, 1989), 327.

10. For example, Rudolph Fisher charged in a review that *Infants* was burdened by "so much expositional and argumentative prattle on race prejudice and communism that one can not be sure at the end just what the book started out to say." *New York Herald Tribune Books* 24 (February 21, 1932): 16.

11. Langston Hughes, *The Big Sea: An Autobiography* (New York: Hill and Wang, 1940), 223.

12. Ibid., 226–27.

13. Chauncey, *Gay New York*, 233.

14. Ibid. (emphasis added), 236.

15. Ibid., 233.

16. Ibid., 233, 244.

17. Charles W. Chesnutt, correspondence to James Weldon Johnson, January 18, 1913, JWJ Collection, Box 1, Folder 90.

18. James Weldon Johnson, correspondence to Heywood Broun, May 2, 1924, JWJ Collection, Box 1, Folder 62.

19. W. E. B. Du Bois, "Our Policy," *Crisis* 11 (1916): 133.

20. W. E. B. Du Bois, *Crisis* 12 (1916): 69.

21. Hazel Carby, *Race Men* (Cambridge, Mass.: Harvard University Press, 1998).

22. W. E. B. Du Bois, *Crisis* 1 (1910): 16.

23. W. E. B. Du Bois, *Darkwater: Voices from Within the Veil* (1921; New York: Kraus-Thornson, 1975), 73.

24. Du Bois, *Crisis* 3 (1911): 26.

25. David Levering Lewis, *When Harlem Was in Vogue* (New York: Oxford University Press, 1979), 122.

26. Steven Watson, *The Harlem Renaissance: Hub of African American Culture* (New York: Pantheon, 1995).

27. Eric King Watts, "Cultivating a Black Public Voice: W. E. B. Du Bois and the 'Criteria of Negro Art,'" *Rhetoric and Public Affairs* 4 (2001): 181–201.

28. Bruce M. Tyler, *From Harlem to Hollywood: The Struggle for Racial and Cultural Democracy, 1920–1943* (New York: Garland, 1992), 13.

29. Eleonore van Notten, *Wallace Thurman's Harlem Renaissance* (Amsterdam, Nebr.: Costerus New Series 93, 1994), 93–130.

30. Ibid., 94.

31. Ibid., 119.

32. Ibid., 109.

33. Ibid., 119.

34. Hughes, *Big Sea*, 227.

35. Wallace Thurman, "A Stranger at the Gates: A Review of *Nigger Heaven*, by Carl Van Vechten," in *The Collected Writings of Wallace Thurman*, ed. Amritjit Singh and Daniel M. Scott III (New Brunswick, N.J.: Rutgers University Press, 2003), 192; review originally appeared in the *Messenger*, September 1926.

36. Van Notten, *Wallace Thurman's Harlem Renaissance*, 127.

37. Carl Van Vechten, letter dated September 7, 1926, JWJ Collection, Box 1, Folder 497.

38. Garber, "A Spectacle in Color," 328.

39. Hughes, *Big Sea*, 235.

40. Eric King Watts, "'Voice' and 'Voicelessness' in Rhetorical Studies," *Quarterly Journal of Speech* 87 (2001): 179–96.

41. Ibid., 187.

42. David Appelbaum, *Voice* (Albany, N.Y.: SUNY Press, 1990), 4.

43. Michael J. Hyde and Kenneth Rufo, "The Call of Conscience, Rhetorical Interruptions, and the Euthanasia Controversy," *Journal of Applied Communication Research* 28 (2000): 1–23.

44. Wallace Thurman, *Infants of the Spring* (1932; Carbondale: Southern Illinois University Press, 1979), 11.

45. Watson, *The Harlem Renaissance*.

46. Thurman, *Infants*, 12.

47. Garber, "A Spectacle in Color," 329.

48. Thurman, *Infants*, 14.

49. Ibid., 12.

50. Cobb, "Insolent Racing, Rough Narrative," 330.

51. Van Notten, *Wallace Thurman's Harlem Renaissance*, 143.

52. Ibid., 179.

53. Thurman, *Infants*, 107.

54. Silberman, "Looking for Richard Bruce Nugent and Wallace Thurman," 56.

55. Thurman, *Infants*, 20.

56. Ibid., 21.
57. Ibid., 23.
58. Brody and McBride, "Part 2," 328.
59. Hughes, *Big Sea*, 237.
60. Silberman, "Looking for Richard Bruce Nugent and Wallace Thurman," 59.
61. Thurman, *Infants*, 34.
62. Cobb, "Insolent Racing, Rough Narrative," 335.
63. Garber, "A Spectacle in Color," 329.
64. Thurman, *Infants*, 39.
65. Thurman, in Singh and Scott, *The Collected Writings*, 35.
66. Van Notten, *Wallace Thurman's Harlem Renaissance*, 182, 286.
67. Thurman, *Infants*, 59.
68. Locke, *The New Negro*, 3.
69. Thurman, *Infants*, 229.
70. Ibid., 230.
71. Ibid., 186.
72. Ibid., 175.
73. Garber, "A Spectacle in Color," 321.
74. Thurman, *Infants*, 183.
75. Ibid., 186–87, emphasis added.
76. Garber, "A Spectacle in Color," 322.
77. Thurman, *Infants*, 184.
78. Ibid., 187.
79. Ibid., 198.
80. Ibid., 190–91.
81. Van Notten, *Wallace Thurman's Harlem Renaissance*, 200.
82. Biddy Martin, "Sexualities without Genders and Other Queer Utopias," *diacritics* 24 (1994): 104–21.
83. Thurman, *Infants*, 266–70.
84. Ibid., 267.
85. Ibid., 268.
86. Ibid., 57.
87. Van Notten, *Wallace Thurman's Harlem Renaissance*, 108.
88. Thurman, *Infants*, 270.
89. Ibid., 280.
90. Ibid., 280–81.
91. Ibid., 281.
92. Ibid., 283.
93. Karol Berger, *A Theory of Art* (New York: Oxford University Press, 2000), 3–12.
94. Van Notten, *Wallace Thurman's Harlem Renaissance*, 266.
95. Thurman, *Infants*, 280.
96. Van Notten, *Wallace Thurman's Harlem Renaissance*, 263, emphasis added.
97. Cobb, "Insolent Racing, Rough Narrative," 335.
98. Van Notten, *Wallace Thurman's Harlem Renaissance*, 267.

99. Siobhan Somerville, *Queering the Color Line: Race and the Invention of Homosexuality in American Culture* (Durham, N.C.: Duke University Press, 2000), 92–93.

100. Patricia Hill Collins, *Black Sexual Politics: African Americans, Gender, and the New Racism* (New York: Routledge, 2004), 95.

101. Van Notten, *Wallace Thurman's Harlem Renaissance*, 263.

102. Ibid., 208–9.

103. Charles I. Nero, "Re/Membering Langston: Homophobic Textuality and Arnold Rampersad's *Life of Langston Hughes*," in *Queer Representations: Reading Lives, Reading Cultures,* ed. Martin Duberman (New York: NYU Press, 1997), 194–95.

104. Henry Louis Gates, Jr., "Black Man's Burden," in *Fear of a Queer Planet: Queer Politics and Social Theory,* ed. Michael Warner (Minneapolis: University of Minnesota Press, 1993), 234–35.

speak up! i can't queer you!

Robert Alan Brookey

My analyst told me that I was right out of my head
The way he described it, he said I'd be better dead than live
I didn't listen to his jive
I knew all along he was all wrong
And I knew that he thought I was crazy but I'm not
Oh no!

Bette Midler, "Twisted," music
and lyrics by Wardell Gray

On August 29, 1867, Karl Hienrich Ulrichs rose to address the Congress of German Jurists in Munich.[1] Ulrichs had spoken for only a short time before the audience shouted him down and he voluntarily left the platform. Ulrichs was interrupted because his speech advocated rights for homosexuals. In fact, Ulrichs's speech may be the first recorded instance of a public speech advocating lesbian and gay rights. In light of the period, the fact that the speech was interrupted offers no real surprise; the incident could serve as an example of the way that queer voices have been treated in the public sphere. Indeed the silencing of queer voices has been an important theme in the history of the gay rights movement. As Barbara Gittings, a leader of the Daughters of Bilitis, observes, "It never occurred to us in those early days that we could speak for ourselves, that we had the expert knowledge on ourselves. We were the ones explored, but we thought we needed the intervention of experts to do the exploring."[2] The silence to which Gittings refers, however, seems more figurative and political than literal: gays and lesbians were "silenced" to the degree that their voices had no legitimacy in the public sphere.

This type of silence commonly characterizes the political conditions of the socially marginalized. In the study of rhetoric and public address, those scholars who have analyzed the discourse of marginalized groups have often had to consider conditions of silence.[3] Unfortunately, in an effort to recognize the voices of the marginalized, some rhetorical scholars have taken on what Bonnie Dow has described as a "celebratory" approach. Dow argues that some scholars have been so anxious to honor women speakers that they sometimes fail to engage the full political import of what these women say.[4] Although Dow's comments are specific to feminist rhetorical scholarship, they reveal an assumption rhetorical scholars often make about the relationship between power and discourse.

As Barbara Biesecker has pointed out, the study of rhetoric defines power in oppressive terms: those in power are allowed to speak, and those without power are silenced.[5] Drawing on Michel Foucault's study of sexuality, Biesecker argues that this approach to power does not comprehend how censorship actually produces discourse. For example, Foucault argues that the supposed repression of sex actually produced sexuality as an object of knowledge.[6] In the process of disciplining sexuality, queerness and queer sexuality emerged from a discursive production that incorporated voices as a necessary element. Undoubtedly power relations were involved in the production of this knowledge, but the study of sexuality nevertheless produced discourse about sexual minorities. In this way power can be productive. As Biesecker observes, power is also productive in that it creates opportunities for resistance; she argues that rhetorical scholars should investigate how discourse manifests these resistances.[7] Because Foucault's concept of productive power extends from his analysis of sexuality, perhaps the rhetorical engagement of queer voice should also consider such resistances.

This chapter is not about silence. Instead I want to investigate the ways queers have been allowed to speak and in what ways they have been impelled to speak. In fact, I will argue that the institutional study of sexuality has actually produced queer speech, and it was in this very same production of discourse that queers began to mount their resistance and advocate for their sexual rights. Granted, this discourse did not always work to the benefit of queers, but I believe the political ambivalence of this discourse is worthy of note. I will argue that a queering of public address should refigure the relationship between power and discourse and the rhetorical study of queer voice should reject easy associations between silence and oppression, speech and freedom.

In this chapter I will demonstrate how oppression does not necessarily exact silence, nor does speech necessarily signify freedom from institutional power. I begin by reviewing Foucault's theories about the emergence of sexuality as an object of study in psychological discourse. I give special treatment to Foucault's concept of the "confession" because it reveals how queer voices emerged in psychological "talk." I then examine psychological discourse, paying special attention to Freud and psychoanalytic theory to demonstrate how queer voices were produced in this discourse. I will then examine how this context of psychoanalytic and psychological discourse created opportunities for resistance, and how this resistance contributed to the removal of homosexuality from the American Psychiatric Association official list of mental disorders. Finally I examine how the current reparative therapy movement has mounted its own counterresistance to gay activism.

Though I do not deny that historically queers have been marginalized, I want to acknowledge that queers have spoken, and it is in the conditions of this speech that

I think we find can find a more textured understanding of queer resistance, speech, and power.[8] Specifically, I will illustrate how the production and expression of queer speech, particularly in the context of the confessions, requires a refiguring of rhetorical subjectivity and objectivity. From a traditional model, the rhetorical subject commonly speaks about an exigency that is the object of speech. Within the context of the confession, however, the queer becomes a speaking subject contained in a discourse in which he or she is an object of study. The emergence of the queer voice, however, challenges the established assumptions about the relationship between the rhetorical subject and the object of speech.

Making a Queer You Can Hear

In volume 1 of *The History of Sexuality*, Foucault traces the emergence of queer sexuality as an object of study. He argues that the concept of the homosexual as a distinct individual emerged out of psychological thought during the nineteenth century. Prior to this time, sodomy laws existed to codify behaviors that today would be deemed homosexual, but the notion that certain individuals were predisposed to these behaviors did not exist. Although sodomy laws have survived, the idea that all members of a society are equally capable of homosexual acts has been replaced by a "repression hypothesis." Informed by nineteenth- and twentieth-century sexual theories, this hypothesis maintains that sexuality is an essential part of an individual's psychological makeup, a psychological characteristic that has been repressed by social mores. By locating sexuality in the "soul" (psyche) of the individual, society can regulate behavior by condemning sexual practices and thereby exercise power over individuals. Consequently individuals who participate in homosexual sex are no longer merely having sex; they are displaying a mental disorder. Constructing homosexuality as a psychological pathology gives the analyst authority over the homosexual. The analyst is in a position to say what homosexuality means for the individual; and in this way, homosexuals have been rendered incapable of understanding or explaining their own experience.[9]

Although Foucault does not offer his comments as a specific indictment of Freudian theory, and he seems to be addressing the general study of psychology, some of his observations seem particularly relevant to the practice of psychoanalysis. For example, he argues that because the repression hypothesis hides sexuality in the body, speech becomes a necessary element in the study of sexuality. In spite of the cultural pressures that seem to censure discourse about sex, Foucault argues that the emergence of sexuality as an object of study produced an explosion of discourse about sex. In fact, the study of sexuality required what Foucault describes as "the confession." The confession is a practice originating in religious discourse, specifically Catholicism, which then moved into the practices of psychology and psychoanalysis. For the analyst to understand the sexual "problem," the patient must speak about sex, must talk so that the deep aspects of the subconscious are revealed. In this way the confession became a necessary part of the psychological examination, and a practice of religious discourse became a practice of scientific discourse. Because the confession is necessary, there emerged what Foucault described as "a clinical codification of the inducement to speak."[10] In other words, the confession required speech; it demanded that the "pervert" talk about perversion. In the psychoanalytic therapeutic model, the homosexual was a speaking subject, but one who through the act of speech constituted himself as an object of study.

Other scholars have drawn on the convention of the confession to analyze the speech acts of marginalized groups. For example, Linda Alcoff and Laura Gray argue that whereas "silence" has been an important metaphor in the "survivor discourse" of the victims of sexual assault, the proliferation of opportunities to speak about sexual assault on television talk shows has not yielded any discernable political change. As they argue, "One of the dangers of the confessional discourse structure is that the survivor speech becomes a media commodity that has a use value based on its sensationalism and drama that circulates within the relations of media competition to boost ratings and wake up viewers. In this way, a goal or effect probably not intended by the survivors is made the organizing principle for how the show gets arranged, produced, and edited. The results of this process may well have no positive effect on the production/reproduction of practices of sexual violence."[11]

These results may be attributed to what Larry May and James Bohman have identified as the conservative, hegemonic function of the confession. They argue that the confession, as it is manifest in Catholicism and the "Men's Movement," actually functions to legitimate aggressive and violent male sexual behavior.[12] In her analysis of *Ellen*'s "coming-out" episode, Bonnie Dow isolates a similar conservative hegemonic function, albeit in the form of a lesbian confession. Dow illustrates how the use of the confession in the television show facilitates a foreclosure on any political engagement of sexual norms.[13]

These analyses of the confession reveal that the relationship between power and speech can be complex and that the act of confessional speech does not always yield political progress. The political ambivalence of confessional speech acts can be attributed to the fact that these opportunities to speak are often contained in institutional contexts—namely, the media, the church, and the discipline of psychology. Therefore the confession is often an inducement to speak, imposed by an institution interested in reproducing and extending its authority. In the case of sexual psychology, confession was a form of speech over which the patient had little agency and authority, because it was speech that produced the patient as an object, not a subject. Yet it is also important to note that this practice did not silence queer voices; it produced them. In the sections that follow, I will trace the confession through the evolution of sexual theory. Although the confession originally produced the queer voice as an object of study, I will argue that this mode of discourse created important opportunities for resistance.

Freud and the Production of Queer Voice

Prior to the psychological construct of sexual deviance, there were few if any plat-forms for queer speech; Ulrichs's speech, mentioned earlier, was the exception that proves the rule. In addition to his work as a rights advocate, Ulrichs was one of the first individuals who attempted to theorize male homosexuality. Ulrichs believed homosexuals ("urnings," as he called them) were "individuals among us whose body is built like a male, and at the same time, whose sexual drive is directed toward men, who are sexually not aroused by women, i.e., are horrified by any sexual con-tact with women."[14] He believed that the embryo contained female and male "germs" and that as the embryo developed one of the germs became dominant, pro-ducing either male or female sex organs. According to Ulrichs, these sexed germs also produced the sex drive, and it was possible for a male body to possess a female sex drive. He imagined a similar process occurred to produce lesbians ("Urningin"), who possessed a male sex drive. Ulrichs's theories represented homosexuality as a biological departure from heterosexuality, and this portrayal would facilitate the pathological theories that would later emerge. For example, Ulrichs's theories informed the work of German neurologist Richard von Krafft-Ebing, whose book *Psychopathia Sexualis* became one of the most important early studies of human sexuality.[15] Krafft-Ebing defined homosexuality not as a set of sexual acts but as a sexual desire for the same sex, a desire brought about either by genetic or situa-tional factors. Krafft-Ebing contrasted situational homosexuality to a more innate form that he described as an abnormal congenital manifestation, a degenerative condition. In contrast to Ulrichs, Krafft-Ebing was not a gay rights advocate, so he explicitly defined homosexuality as a debilitating pathology, a view of homosexual-ity that dominated psychological theory for some time. In particular, his theories set the stage for those that would emerge in the field of psychoanalysis.

Admittedly, Freudian psychoanalysis has not been the only form of psychology to identify homosexuality as an object of study. Nevertheless psychoanalysis domi-nated the study of homosexuality for years and still retains some influence.[16] Freud's theories of sexuality take several forms, but certain elements remain fairly constant. He argued that the child is born into a state of bisexuality, an innate sex-ual instinct that he referred to as "polymorphous perversity."[17] The child's bisexual energy originally is directed toward the mother, who is the first sexual object for the child. This attraction creates psychological obstacles that differ for the male and the female child. Freud's theories, however, were primarily concerned with male sexual development.[18] He believed that the male child enters a pre-Oedipal stage in which his sexual energy becomes channeled into a competition with the father for the mother's attention and affection. If this stage is resolved correctly, the child's sex-ual development will proceed into heterosexuality. If the child is not able to recon-cile his relationship with his mother, his development will be arrested and his sexual drive will be directed toward a homosexual object choice.

Freud's theories on homosexuality were developed through the analysis of case studies, and his reports of these cases illustrate how the confession was used in the psychoanalytic method. For example, in his famous analysis of the "Wolf Man," Freud gave a great deal of time interpreting a dream that the patient reported:

> I dreamt that it was night and that I was lying in my bed. (My bed stood with its foot towards the window; in front of the window there was a row of old walnut trees. I know it was winter when I had the dream, and night-time.) Suddenly the window opened of its own accord, and I was terrified to see that some white wolves were sitting on the big walnut tree in front of the window. There were six or seven of them. The wolves were quite white, and looked more like foxes or sheep-dogs, for they had big tails like foxes and they had their ears pricked like dogs when they pay attention to something. In great terror, evidently of being eaten up by the wolves, I screamed.[19]

Although this dream has no overt sexual content, Freud interpreted the dream as evidence of a repressed homosexuality. As he wrote, "His anxiety was a repudiation of the wish for sexual satisfaction from his father—the trend which had put the dream into his head. The form taken by the anxiety, the fear of 'being eaten by the wolf,' was only the (as we shall hear, regressive) transportation of the wish to be copulated with by his father."[20] In addition, Freud recounted how the patient participated in the interpretation of the dream, determining for himself that the opening window signified a moment of self-awareness, and that the tree in the dream was a Christmas tree. Freud latter explained that Christmas signified the patient's "unsatisfied love" and subsequent rage.[21]

Although the "Wolf Man" case figured prominently in Freud's theories of homosexuality, the patient in question was not actually homosexual. In fact, Freud noted that the patient ultimately asserted his "masculinity" (read heterosexuality), albeit in a problematic way.[22] Nevertheless, he argued that the patient's homosexual object choice was repressed and then replaced in the dream (the regressive transportation that he told the readers "we shall hear"). In other words, Freud produced the patient's voice as a queer voice. He induced the patient to speak, to relate the dream and participate in its interpretation. He then relayed the voice to the readers so that they could "hear" what the patient had to say. He then took the voice of the patient, who apparently did not participate in homosexual behavior, and presented it as a voice of repressed homosexual desire. In this way the patient was invested with sexuality and spoke with a queer voice.

In *Analysis of a Phobia in a Five-Year-Old Boy*, Freud divined another queer voice from the case of "Little Hans."[23] Because "Little Hans" was only a five-year-old whose own sexuality had yet to materialize, it was difficult to define him as an actual homosexual. Yet Freud identified in this patient the early traces of a homosexual orientation because the boy fixated on his own genitalia. Freud related several conversations in which Hans would discuss his "widdler" with his mother and his father, for example:

> Another time he was looking on intently while his mother was undressed before going to bed. "What are you staring like that for?" she asked.
> Hans: "I was only looking to see if you'd got a widdler too."
> Mother: "Of course. Didn't you know that?"
> Hans: "No. I thought you were so big you'd have a widdler like a horse."

This expectation of little Hans's deserves to be borne in mind; it will become important later on.[24]

As indeed it did when Freud wove the conversation into an explanation of Hans's agoraphobia, his fear of entering the street because a horse might bite him. Freud interpreted this fear to be a repressed anxiety that Hans experienced due to his intense affection for his mother. The case of Little Hans is, of course, classic Freud in that the underlying assumption about the child's latent homosexuality is based on his relationship with his mother and a resentment of his father. Yet, as Freud noted, the boy's development did not lead to homosexuality, "but to an energetic masculinity."[25]

Here, too, we see the confession in practice, but it is important to note that Freud's use extended beyond his conversations with Little Hans. In the introduction of the case, Freud explained that notes made by the boy's father augmented his analysis. As Freud pointed out, "No one else, in my opinion, could possibly have prevailed on the child to make any such avowals; the special knowledge by means of which he was able to interpret the remarks made by his five-year-old son was indispensable."[26] Therefore Little Hans was made to confess not only to Freud, but also to his father, who in turn made his own confession by allowing Freud access to his notes. In this manner, we see the father participating, albeit perhaps unwittingly, in the queering of his son's voice. Although his son did not develop into a homosexual, we find the father caught up in a confession that Freud used to characterize the man's relationship with his son in homoerotic, Oedipal terms.

Parental relations were also at the core of Freud's "Leonardo da Vinci and a Memory of His Childhood."[27] This work contains perhaps the best example of how sexual expression is divined from a discourse that would seem to be void of sexual import. It does not reflect the confession in the sense that da Vinci did not speak to Freud directly; rather Freud extracted a confession from the historic record. For example, Freud noted that da Vinci kept meticulous records of the gifts that he would buy his pupils. He referenced a passage in which da Vinci itemizes the purchase of a cloak for "Andrea Salaino," listing the cost of the braid and the buttons.[28] Freud then noted that da Vinci kept a similar record of the cost of his mother's funeral. Here da Vinci notes the amount paid for the pallbearers, priests, and gravediggers. From these accounts, it would be easy to regard da Vinci as a tedious miser. Freud, of course, avoided such an obvious interpretation. Instead he offered this assessment:

> It does not seem a very extravagant step to apply what we have learnt from the funeral account to the reckonings of the pupils' expenses. They would then be another instance of the scanty remnants of Leonardo's libidinal impulses finding expression in a compulsive manner and in a distorted form. On that view, his mother and his pupils, the likeness of his own boyish beauty, had been his sexual objects—so far as the sexual repression which dominated his nature allows us so to describe them—and the compulsion to note in laborious detail the sums he spent on them betrayed in this strange way his rudimentary conflicts.[29]

Here Freud outlined another theme that would inform his theories of homosexuality. Not only does this passage make reference to da Vinci's relationship with his mother, comparing it to his relationship with his pupils, but it also suggests that these relationships are actually narcissistic in nature. Therefore we can see how Freud's theories of homosexuality emerged from the discourse produced by his subjects. These examples also reveal the repression hypothesis at work. Because these subjects have repressed their sexual desire (Freud made specific mention of this point in his discussion of da Vinci), their desire must be uncovered in the interpretation of the subjects' discourse, even when that discourse seems to have no sexual content: a dream about wolves, a fear of horses, a financial record. In each of the cases noted, we do not see the silencing of queer voice; on the contrary we see the production of the voice through the means of the confession and psychoanalytic interpretation. Therefore queer voices were not silenced, but they were not allowed to speak freely either. The same disciplining forces that produced these voices also placed limits on what they could report and what the reader was allowed to "hear." To understand these disciplinary forces and their impact, it is important to trace how the field of psychoanalysis developed its theories of homosexuality.

Homosexuality after Freud

Although Freud offered alternative theories of homosexuality, these theories often suggest that homosexuality is a state of arrested sexual development. In spite of this arrested state, Freud observed that there are some "inverts" who appear to be normal in every way except for their sexuality. He also suggested that some form of homosexuality is innate and may be biological.[30] In other words, Freud did not maintain that homosexuality was always the product of psychological pathology. Consequently he regarded efforts to change homosexuals into heterosexuals with great pessimism.[31]

After World War II, psychoanalysts in North America reinterpreted Freud's theories of sexuality particularly in regard to homosexuality. Sandor Rado led this movement when he rejected Freud's theory of innate bisexuality.[32] Rado argued that from a biological standpoint, bisexuality does not exist and that the only proper biological development is heterosexuality. Rado rejected the possibility of a biological homosexuality and argued that homosexuality can only be a product of mental pathology, a pathology that disrupts the normal sexual reproductive function. Furthermore Rado believed that because homosexuality was a mental pathology, the possibility for change was much greater than Freud supposed. This theoretical departure from Freud produced important advantages for the field of psychoanalysis.

First, the rejection of innate bisexuality moved the study of sexuality out of the realm of the biological sciences and placed it fully within the authority of psychiatry. This theoretical move allowed the field of psychoanalysis to define heterosexuality and homosexuality as discrete, dichotomous categories and to regard heterosexuality as biologically normal and homosexuality as a psychological dysfunction. By eliminating the possibility of bisexuality and establishing homosexuality as a discrete category, psychoanalysts isolated homosexuality as an object of study. By denying the possibility of a biological cause and determining homosexuality to be a psychological pathology, psychoanalysts were able to claim authority over the study of homosexuality. To maintain their authority, however, psychoanalysts also had to frame homosexuality as a disorder that they could cure. In other words, by eschewing any biological factors, psychoanalysts were able to locate the origins of homosexuality in the psyche and argue for the efficacy of a psychoanalytic cure. The claim of pathology therefore supported the view that homosexuality was a problem that psychoanalysts could identify and eliminate.

Second, the conclusion that homosexuality was always and only a mental pathology, and could therefore be effectively treated, certainly was more acceptable to conservative postwar social sensibilities. Kenneth Lewes argues this point quite well in *The Psychoanalytic Theory of Male Homosexuality*.[33] He believes that Freud's original theories regarding homosexuality were actually quite sympathetic and claims that the negative view of male homosexuality that emerged from Rado's work indicates how psychoanalysis came under the influence of social, cultural, and political pressures. In the post–World War II period, psychoanalysts were able to establish their authority by positioning themselves as heroes in the battle against a grave social threat: homosexuality.[34] Psychoanalysts who followed Rado therefore were quite eager to accommodate the pressures that Lewes identifies, and the work of Irving Bieber and Edmund Bergler would perpetuate the pathological view of homosexuality in the decades to follow.

In the 1950s the New York Society of Medical Psychoanalysts conducted an extensive study of male homosexuality; Bieber assumed the responsibility of publishing the findings. The primary purpose of the study was to investigate Rado's claim that homosexuality could be cured. Consequently Bieber began his discussion of the study with the claim that "all psychoanalytic theories assume that homosexuality is psychopathologic."[35] Although the objective of this study was to demonstrate the effectiveness of psychoanalysis in the treatment of homosexuality, only 19 percent of the "exclusively homosexual" subjects were coded as "exclusively heterosexual" as of 1960. In spite of these results, Bieber concluded by reiterating the psychoanalytic position that all humans are biologically heterosexual and that all homosexuals must be helped to realize their heterosexual potential. "Our findings are optimistic guideposts not only for homosexuals but also for the psychoanalysts who treat them. We are firmly convinced that psychoanalysts may well orient themselves to a heterosexual objective in treating homosexual patients rather than 'adjust' even the more recalcitrant patient to a homosexual destiny. A conviction based on scientific fact that a heterosexual goal is achievable helps both patient and psychoanalyst to take in stride the inevitable setbacks during psychoanalysis."[36]

Actually, Bieber's own scientific facts revealed that successful conversion was the exception and not the rule. It is surprising then, that Bieber would argue against helping the homosexual adapt to homosexuality. Yet, he seemed to argue that even the homosexual who does not want to change should also be directed into heterosexuality. His argument, however, reveals an important element in the psychoanalytic construction of homosexuality as pathology: homosexuals are sick, and homosexuals who refuse to acknowledge their sickness are the sickest of all.

At this point the production of the queer voice in psychoanalytic literature takes on a new purpose. In Freud's writings, the queer voice was used to evidence his theories of homosexuality. In the work of some of the psychoanalysts that would follow Freud, the queer voice is offered up to demonstrate that homosexuality is indeed pathological. This purpose is most evident when psychoanalysts described homosexuals who defied scientific authority or challenged the psychoanalytic claim of pathology. For example, Bergler recounted a session with a homosexual patient in which the patient argued about the pathology of homosexuality:

> "Well, we homosexuals are different and difficult people."
> "Don't be so proud of your sickness!"
> "To quote you: 'Objection please!' I resent your calling homosexuality
>   a sickness. That's pure unadulterated nonsense."
> "Would you suggest a synonym for sickness?"
> "It is a way of living, that's all."
> "It's a way of expressing a neurotic conflict to be precise."[37]

The dialogue continued for a few pages, and in the course of the conversation Bergler was able to introduce several themes to support his claim that homosexuality is a neurosis. He dismissed the possibility of bisexuality and made reference to homosexuals' promiscuity and their inclination to pedophilia. By Bergler's own account of the conversation, he won the debate on homosexual pathology, offering these concluding remarks: "This discussion with a patient has been quoted in detail to serve as a general approach to the complex problem of male homosexuality, and to show the chronic technique of defense among these *sick people:* high-pitched narcissism, combined with 'injustice collecting.' They are the opposite of good losers."[38] Bergler then mentioned that this conclusion in no way reflects any moralizing on his part; it is scientific opinion based on the "fact that homosexuality is an unconscious and trouble-making defense mechanism."[39] This fact, of course, is observable in the conversation just related. The patient was required to confess, and the resistance contained in the confession was presented as evidence of pathology. Yet, it is clear that this psychoanalytic discourse provided an opportunity for resistance, and it is indicative of a larger form of resistance that would prove more troubling for Bergler.

In 1951 Bergler published *Neurotic Counterfeit-Sex*, a book whose second edition was retitled *Counterfeit-Sex: Homosexuality, Impotence, Frigidity*. In the preface to the second edition, Bergler explained the need to specify homosexuality in the title. Between the publication of the first and second editions, the early gay rights efforts of the homophile movement began to gain some visibility; for example, the Mattachine Society and the Daughters of Bilitis expanded their efforts during this period.[40] Bergler believed that the emergence of the homophile movement could be attributed to Alfred Kinsey's work (for reasons that will become clear later), and he dismissed its efforts to change public attitudes: "Kinsey claimed that every third man one meets on the street has had some homosexual experiences, as an adult. Armed with these misleading and faulty statistics, homosexuals started to ask for parity with heterosexuals."[41] Later in this book, by outlining all that is defective in the homosexual psyche, Bergler explained why such parity is unreasonable. His motive for opposing the gay rights efforts may be conveyed, albeit indirectly, by the concluding paragraph of the chapter: "There is no longer any justification for the homosexual's claim that his problems entitle him to pity—and acceptance of the status quo. His unconscious make-up is now scientifically understood, and the problem of therapy has been solved. I am proud of having contributed a good deal to the solution."[42] Here Bergler is advocating the use of therapy to cure homosexuality, and he is positioning himself as a primary authority on this form of therapy.

The classification of homosexuality as a mental disease was very important to the field of psychoanalysis to maintain their authority over homosexuality. Therefore those that questioned this authority and challenged the label of pathology, those patients that offered resistance, were deemed a significant threat. Consequently psychoanalysts sought to dismiss the oppositional voices of "recalcitrant" homosexuals by producing these voices as if they demonstrated the depths of homosexual psychosis. In other words, the act of speech within the context of the confessional psychoanalytic discourse created the homosexual as an object of study. Just as the disciplinary practices of psychoanalysis produced the queer voice, however, it also produced an opportunity for resistance. Bergler's account of his patient shows how this resistance could be manifested. Although Bergler may have dismissed the resistance of his patient and the early gay rights movement, he could not contain the other forms of resistance that would emerge.

Scientific Resistance

The authority psychoanalysts held over the study of sexuality remained unchallenged until Alfred Kinsey published *Sexual Behavior in the Human Male* in 1948.[43] The Kinsey Scale, which placed sexual orientation on a graduated continuum, was the most influential product of this research. This scale reintroduced the concept of bisexuality and provided a model for quantitative data collection. The impact on the psychoanalytic approach to homosexuality was threefold. First, the psychoanalysts' systematic dismissal of bisexual orientation was challenged by Kinsey's empirical findings, which indicated that a significant number of adults had experienced sexual intercourse with both sexes. Second, the quantitative methodology that Kinsey adopted to collect data seemed more scientifically rigorous and generalizable than the collection of anecdotal case studies that made up the psychoanalytic data. It is interesting to note, however, that the confession informed Kinsey's method as much as it did the psychoanalytic method. Kinsey took sexual "histories" from his subjects that required self-disclosure similar to the confession.[44] By changing the way the confession data were collected, collated, and interpreted, however, Kinsey was able to use the concept of the confession against the psychoanalysts. Kinsey was still requiring talk about sex, but he claimed that after enough people talked about their sexual practices homosexuality no longer seemed deviant.[45]

Kinsey's work is significant because it began to challenge the beliefs about homosexual pathology and thereby also questioned the assumption of clear distinctions between heterosexuals and homosexuals. Kinsey argued that the realities of sex are much more diverse and diffuse than the dual categories of homosexuality and heterosexuality suggest. Consequently the diverse and diffuse nature of sexual behavior called into question the abnormality of homosexuality: "Social reactions to the homosexual have obviously been based on the general belief that the deviant individual is unique and as such needs special consideration. When it is recognized that the particular boy who is discovered in homosexual relations in school, the business man who is having such activity, and the institutional inmate with a homosexual record, are involved in behavior that is not fundamentally different from that had by a fourth to a third of all of the rest of the population, the activity of the single individual acquires a somewhat different social significance."[46]

Indeed it does, because once homosexuality is recognized as being frequently practiced by a variety of individuals, it becomes difficult to imagine homosexuals as a distinctly deviant class. Furthermore Kinsey and his colleagues suggested that it also becomes difficult to call for the isolation and treatment of homosexuals when "at least one third of the male population would have to be isolated from the rest of the community, if all those with any homosexual capacities were to be so treated."[47] Kinsey's rejection of treatment for homosexuality would provide the third challenge to the psychoanalytic theories.

Kinsey's studies proved to be a significant threat; the psychoanalytic response to these challenges was either to dismiss Kinsey or to ignore his work altogether.[48] After Kinsey's study of female sexuality was published, Bergler and fellow psychoanalyst William Kroger found it necessary to author an entire book to rebut Kinsey's claims. In *Kinsey's Myth of Female Sexuality: The Medical Facts*, the authors warn that Kinsey *"put heterosexuality and homosexuality on an equal level as normal manifestations of the sex drive."*[49] They suggest that Kinsey had reached this conclusion because he simply did not understand Freud. Bergler and Kroger then reviewed psychoanalytic theory extensively in an attempt to "scientifically" prove that homosexuality is a "disease," all the while deriding what they perceived to be Kinsey's "ignorance." They wrote, "It is the opinion of the authors that Kinsey's conclusions on homosexuality are doing damage, and have in no way furthered the cause of scientific truth."[50]

Kinsey was not the only scientist opposing the psychoanalytic position on homosexuality. Evelyn Hooker's work was also instrumental in removing the mark of pathology from homosexuality. Her now famous article, "The Adjustment of the Male Overt Homosexual," reported results from her study that challenged many psychiatric assumptions about homosexuality.[51] Specifically, Hooker concluded that many homosexual subjects in her study did not suffer from severe mental disturbances and that homosexual subjects were just as diverse in their behavior and psychological profiles as heterosexual subjects. In addition, her study used two judges to evaluate the Rorschach tests of homosexual and heterosexual subjects. In a blind analysis, the judges found that the majority of both homosexual and heterosexual subjects were well adjusted, and, just as important, the judges could not distinguish between homosexual and heterosexual subjects.

Not only did Hooker publish her work in psychiatric journals, but she also published in the *Mattachine Review*, a publication of the Mattachine Society. In fact, the subjects of her study included volunteers from the Mattachine Society, and the society's collaboration with Hooker was not an uncommon practice in the early homophile movement.[52] The Mattachine Society sought out professors at UCLA and Berkeley, and often volunteered its members to serve as subjects in studies, in the hopes that the research would document the existence of normal homosexuals. As Ronald Bayer notes, "Homosexuals themselves could not affect the nature of social policy and the climate of opinion; they required the help of those who could speak in a disinterested fashion from the vantage point of scientific neutrality."[53] Bayer suggests that Hooker provided this needed help: "The appearance of Hooker's work in the mid-1950s was of critical importance for the evolution of the homophile movement. Her findings provided "facts" that could buttress the position of homosexuals who rejected the pathological view of their condition. She had met the psychiatrists on their own terms and provided their critics with clinical data with which to do battle."[54]

Bayer's observations reveal the importance of Hooker's work in the effort to legitimate the early gay rights movement. She presented a voice of scientific reason that lent her the type of credibility that gay rights advocates did not have. Hooker and Kinsey both helped to open up a space in the discourse so that the resistance offered by gays and lesbians could obtain legitimacy.

The practice of confession, however, was still in place. Kinsey's interviews required his subjects to provide an extensive disclosure of their sexual practices. In addition, although the members of the Mattachine Society may have had progressive motives when they offered themselves as subjects of study, they were still deferring to the authority of the scientists. As Gittings remarked, at this point in history lesbians and gays could not speak for themselves, so confessing to sympathetic scientists was one of the few forms of resistance available to them. Still these confessions were made to authorities associated with scientific disciplines, and thereby reproduced institutional power. Yet, because the queer voice operated as an object of scientific study, scientists such as Kinsey and Hooker could challenge the more denigrating theories of homosexuality.

Personal Resistance

In the 1960s social circumstances emerged that allowed a reconsideration of homosexuality. The civil rights movement placed issues of equality and social justice on the forefront of political debate. Consequently many oppressed groups began to examine how they had been subjected to discrimination and social prejudice. The second-wave feminist movement emerged during this period, as did the early gay rights movement.[55] Along with this political activism came new social attitudes, particularly in regard to sex. A sexual revolution had begun, in which all sorts of sexual norms and taboos were questioned and rejected. Although most of these norms had to do with heterosexuality (monogamy, premarital sex, birth control), the sexual revolution also refigured homosexuality. In terms of the gay rights movement specifically, these events culminated in the historic Stonewall riot. After Stonewall, gay activism blossomed, and the agenda of this new activism included challenging the way psychologists and psychiatrists classified and treated homosexuality.[56]

Martin Duberman's *Cures: A Gay Man's Odyssey* provides an interesting account of this period because he juxtaposes important advancements in gay rights with his own experiences in psychiatric therapy.[57] Duberman is an openly gay historian who has been instrumental in the rise of lesbian and gay scholarship in the academy. He was not always out, however, and as a young professor at Princeton he struggled with his sexuality and sought out psychiatric help. After some false starts with other therapists, Duberman met "Karl," a prominent psychoanalyst who promised to help him overcome his homosexuality. The early stages of his therapy took on familiar themes of psychoanalysis. For example, although Duberman made attempts to reconcile his relationship with his mother, Karl insisted that he break off contact altogether, arguing that she had manipulated Duberman to maintain a close bond. He claimed that, until Duberman severed this bond, he would never have an "adult" (read heterosexual) relationship.[58]

Karl also suggested that Duberman augment his individual sessions with group therapy sessions. Among the other patients in his therapy group was a man that Duberman referred to as "Dick." Dick, according to Karl, had successfully made the transition from homosexuality to heterosexuality. As in his individual sessions, Duberman was encouraged to confess to the group and discuss his homosexuality, and initially he was offered understanding. After one of his disclosures, Dick told Duberman, "I hope you'll get on the side of your own health."[59] Unfortunately, this understanding did not last, and, as the sessions progressed and Duberman continued to discuss his homosexuality, Karl lost his patience. During a session in which Duberman disclosed the promising aspects of a new relationship, Karl berated him for wasting the group's time and refusing to explore a possible relationship with a female group member. When Duberman responded to the woman in question, "I'm fond of you, but my feelings toward you don't go very deep, one way or the other," Karl replied, "You really won't take a chance, will you, you really won't move one inch out of your rut."[60] Later, Karl confronted Duberman with what he perceived to be his resistance to therapy and his resistance to Karl personally. Duberman replied that he resisted because he believed Karl had an agenda:

> "You want to turn me into somebody I'm not."
> "No," he said quietly, "I have no agenda, other than to make you more
>   comfortable in the world."
> "Precisely. The only way to be comfortable in this world is to be straight."
> "I believe that's so. Do you believe differently?"[61]

Duberman admitted to the reader that at the time he agreed with Karl, and did not see how he could be comfortable in a world that held homosexuals in such contempt.

Yet, as Duberman noted, the world was changing. Toward the end of the 1960s, the *Advocate* began to appear on newsstands, the Metropolitan Community Church emerged, and of course, the Stonewall riot occurred. He also noted that the National Institute of Mental Health issued a report that refuted many of the negative stereotypes about homosexuality, though he added that the report did not endorse homosexuality and advocated for reparative therapy. Still, the report was part of a larger movement to reclassify homosexuality, augmented by the work of Kinsey and Hooker. Perhaps emboldened by these events, Duberman became more defiant of Karl and his beliefs about homosexuality. After a group therapy session in which Dick, the supposedly "cured" homosexual, disclosed that he still had sex with men, Duberman raised some serious questions: "Was a comparison between the quality of my relationship with Larry and Dick's relationship with his wife valid? How did I know? How did one measure such things, and who was qualified to do the measuring? Clearly Karl, and the rest of the psychiatric fraternity, felt confident that they were qualified. But were they? It was all beginning to unravel."[62]

While this episode marked a beginning for Duberman, the culmination of his resistance would come after a conversation with Karl about the Gay Liberation Front. Duberman explained to Karl that the group made a compelling argument about how social oppression can explain the misery of homosexuals. Karl dismissed the argument as an easy excuse. When Duberman averred that he, himself, had trouble embracing the message, Karl responded, "Maybe it's your healthy side that resists such an easy out," to which Duberman replied: "No, I suspect it's the extent of my brainwashing—too many years hearing about my 'pathology,' and believing it."[63] Shortly after this exchange, Duberman withdrew from therapy.

Cures is an important book because it documents the personal struggles of a man who would later become a leader in the field of lesbian and gay scholarship. For my purposes, however, the book takes on another significance. Duberman's account illustrates in specific terms not only how he was subjected to the disciplining force of psychoanalysis, but also how he was able to obtain resistance by confronting his therapist specifically and the psychoanalytic view of homosexuality generally. From a rhetorical standpoint, the book is interesting because Duberman was able to use the method of confession against the psychoanalysts and as an opportunity to question this authority in personal terms. Duberman took this method used by psychoanalysts, adapted it to the form of autobiography, and then interpreted his own confession in a manner that challenged psychoanalytic authority. In this way Duberman not only challenged the theories of psychoanalysis, but also co-opted the confession to obtain his resistance. His own objectification became the substance of his resistance when in the act of authoring the book he adopted the more traditional role of a rhetorical subject. Duberman's resistance is significant because he helped establish a discipline that developed as an alternative authority in the study of sexuality. Yet, his accomplishments were due, in no small part, to his own exercise of institutional power. Duberman has enjoyed a distinguished academic career, and at the time of the publication of *Cures*, his reputation as an authority on gay history was firmly established. In other words, Duberman helped open new academic spaces for the study of homosexuality because his scholarship was still sanctioned by institutional authority.

Public Resistance and the APA Decision

In 1973 the American Psychiatric Association voted to remove homosexuality from its list of mental diseases. As would be imagined, this decision was not reached without a great deal of controversy. The conflict has been described as more of a battle than a debate, and the lines were drawn between revisionists such as Robert Stoller and Judd Marmor and classical psychoanalysts such as Bieber and Charles Socarides. The actual battle itself, however, was precipitated by gay activists who demanded the APA revise its assessment of homosexuality. Bayer's account of the battle is very detailed, and he describes how the new post-Stonewall militancy of the gay rights movement began to challenge the authority of psychiatric science. In fact, gay rights activists began to claim authority over homosexuality, arguing that it was a lifestyle choice and not a mental disorder; an argument similar to the one offered by Bergler's resistant patient.[64] While Duberman was more private in his resistance, other gays and lesbians publicly criticized the psychiatric therapy that they had received, and their resistance began to achieve some success.[65] For example, after gay activists had protested at the 1970 and 1971 APA conventions, a homosexual psychiatrist was allowed to speak at the 1972 convention in Dallas, though he did wear a mask to hide his identity.[66]

These protests led to the APA's board of trustees' 1973 decision, and as Howard Brown observes, "The board's vote made millions of Americans who had been officially ill that morning officially well that afternoon."[67] This decision, however, did not include ego-dystonic homosexuality, a condition experienced by homosexuals who wanted to change their sexual orientation.[68] This exception remained so that those who opposed the decision, and the opposition included many psychiatrists who practiced "curative" therapy, could continue their practices. Even this exception was rendered immaterial in 1997, however, when the APA determined that psychological therapies could not cure homosexuality.[69]

The APA's decision to declassify homosexuality was a watershed event in the gay rights movement. Many oppressive and discriminatory practices were justified by the official classification of homosexuality as a mental disease. Not all of these practices disappeared with the decision, but gay rights advocates could now credibly question the legitimacy of them. Furthermore gay rights advocates themselves enjoyed new legitimacy. This new legitimacy was not the product of silence. On the contrary, it was the product of several resistant discourses, many of which found their foothold in the confession. Although the psychoanalytic theories of homosexuality argued for pathology and therapy, and psychoanalytic advocates were vocal opponents of gay rights, resistant discourse formed two responses to psychoanalytic discourse. First, new theories of homosexuality questioning the psychoanalytic position that homosexuality was a mental pathology were produced. Second, personal and political resistance was mounted in the gay and lesbian rights movement, as Duberman demonstrates. Although psychoanalysts such as Bergler and Socarides attempted to stem both of these forms of resistance, their failure is well documented in the APA decision. But no failure is complete, at least if we follow Foucault's model of power, and sexuality still remains an object of institutional study. Just as the advocates of gay rights were able to mount a successful campaign of resistance to the psychoanalysts, the opponents of gay rights are mounting their own counterresistance.

The NARTH Situation

Psychoanalysts found the opportunity for counterresistance in the emergence of a politically activated religious fundamentalism, symbolized by such groups as the Christian Coalition and Focus on the Family. These groups argued that homosexuality is not an identity but a behavioral choice and, as such, law should not protect it. From this logic these religious groups argued that homosexuality is an immoral choice and that homosexuals are seeking special protections ("special rights") for their dangerous lifestyles. Ironically, these arguments demonstrate a rhetorical reversal of the same argument that was once used to challenge the classification of homosexual as a pathology: it is a lifestyle choice, or as Bergler's patient put it, "a way of living."[70]

It is from this political context that the reparative therapy movement began to gain greater visibility. Exodus, a religious organization devoted to converting homosexuals to the heterosexual lifestyle, had been around for several years. Recognizing a unique opportunity, psychoanalysts who had never accepted the APA decision on homosexuality decided to join the reparative therapy movement. In 1992 the National Association for Research and Therapy of Homosexuality (NARTH) was founded with Socarides as its first president. Although Socarides and NARTH claimed that their primary interest was the pursuit of scientific truth about human sexuality, a closer examination reveals a much more politicized agenda.

After forming NARTH Socarides published an anti–gay rights book entitled *Homosexuality: A Freedom Too Far.* The book was written in the form of a pseudo-Platonic dialogue, in which Socarides poses questions to himself that he then answers. For example: *"Isn't this 'men-loving-boys' business just a stereotype?* Those trying to normalize homosexuality often use the word, 'stereotype,' these days. They use the word to wave off any challenge at all about the kinkier proclivities of those involved in same-sex sex."[71] In this polemic (the book contains neither references nor a bibliography), Socarides argues in favor of sodomy laws and then reproduces the conservative arguments that homosexuals are a threat to society and the family and that gays and lesbians are after "special rights." It would seem that Socarides had a political agenda that extended beyond scientific curiosity.

As for NARTH, the organization claimed that it wanted to maintain its scientific objectivity and therefore would avoid taking any position on gay rights issues. Yet the organization also claimed that it would not forgo the opportunity to "editorialize" about these issues:

> We respect others' right to differ with us. We do not support coercive therapy—indeed the basic human rights of dignity, autonomy and free agency require that it be the client who chooses whether to embrace life as gay or lesbian, or to work toward change. But the fact that we respect and welcome intellectual diversity does not mean that we have no opinions—or that we consider all conflicting viewpoints to be equally valid. Toleration of difference does not require intellectual apathy. A respect for pluralism does not mandate relativism. And so on these pages, we will make our case for what we believe to be the truth—as indeed gay advocates also do, with equal intensity and conviction—in the public forum. During the last 25 years, powerful political pressures have done much to erode scientific study of homosexuality. As a result, there is now great misunderstanding surrounding this issue. Because of the angry tenor of the debate, many researchers have been intimidated, we believe, into trading the truth for silence."[72]

If this statement reflects the opinions of Socarides and other psychoanalysts involved in NARTH, it would seem that the organization and its membership were not scientifically disinterested. In fact, it would seem that the members of NARTH had a personal investment to the extent that they saw themselves not as the former oppressors of lesbians and gays, but now as the victims. According to NARTH's purpose, "When gay advocates reframed the public debate as a discussion about 'who one is' rather than 'what one does,' they successfully intimidated dissenters by casting them as personally bigoted and hateful. As a result, most people who defend the reality of male-female design have been embarrassed into public silence. NARTH stands ready to advise government, educational, and mental-health agencies as well as the media and religious groups on issues pertaining to homosexuality."[73] Here, too, the advocates of reparative therapy wanted to portray themselves as victims, forced into silence by the advocates of gay rights. In this way, NARTH characterized the gay rights issue as a zero-sum game. Any gain for gay rights comes at the expense of those advocating for reparative therapy, and any advance in gay rights undermines the authority of psychoanalysis. It is no accident that psychoanalysts hold leadership roles in NARTH.

As with Bergler, Socarides and the members of NARTH believed that advocating therapy for homosexuality entailed opposition to gay rights. Perhaps the best indication that NARTH placed politics high on its agenda was provided in the brochure for their 2001 annual conference. The keynote speaker was not a scientist, or even a psychoanalyst or psychologist; instead the speaker was political columnist Cal Thomas, a noted opponent to gay rights. Although the other speakers included individuals working in the field of psychology, the roster also included the Reverend Russell Waldrop, who was scheduled to discuss how "inclusion and diversity are used as buzz words to exclude NARTH from the debate" on gay rights, and how the clergy were "threatened with the possibility of not being licensed—or of losing their license—as professional counselors if they do not support gay affirming therapy."[74] Another speaker, Alan Cummings, a reformed homosexual, was scheduled to speak about how the media provided a distorted picture of homosexuality. Again members of the reparative therapy movement portrayed themselves as victims of an effort to silence opposition to gay rights and misrepresent the "truth" about homosexuality. In other words, an organization representing those once responsible for oppressing homosexuals now positions itself among the oppressed, the silenced, and the disempowered.

Conclusion

In this chapter I have tried to problematize the assumptions that are often made about the relationship between power and speech. As I have shown, the queer voice has seldom been silenced; in fact, it has been produced through the practice of the confession. The confession provides a rare opportunity to consider how queering public address requires the reconsideration of the rhetorical subject; it is a discursive space where a subject's speech can render them an object. My analysis reveals how the scientific discourse on homosexuality allowed for the oppression of homosexuals and the resistance that produced the modern gay rights movement. Therefore we can see that silence is not necessarily the product of oppression, speech does not necessarily denote subjectivity, and resistance is not necessarily complete. Although the APA declassified homosexuality as a mental disease, homosexuality has never escaped the institution, and organizations such as NARTH continue to challenge gay rights efforts and call for the reclassification of homosexuality as a pathological disease. Therefore resistance that is obtained within institutional discourse does not translate into absolute freedom, and we need to reexamine the assumptions that equate speech with power and silence with powerlessness.

When an antigay rights organization such as NARTH can claim it has been silenced, clearly a reexamination is in order. In light of the power enjoyed by the opponents to gay rights and the great visibility of Laura Schlessinger, Ann Coulter, and Rush Limbaugh, it would seem absurd to suggest that the opponents of gay rights have been "silenced." Although homosexuality was removed from the APA list, sexuality still remains an object of institutional study. When the members of NARTH say they have been silenced, what they really mean is that their view of homosexuality no longer dominates academic study. The work of sexologists and scholars in the humanities has repositioned the study of homosexuality in the academy and has allowed research to proceed without the assumptions of pathology that informed psychoanalysis. When NARTH claims to have been silenced, they are

correct to the extent that their theories of homosexuality have fallen out of institutional favor where the academy is concerned. Anti–gay rights activities, however,
have not been silenced, and their views are favored by some governmental and
political institutions.

Although it is popular to think of marginalized voices as silenced, and indeed
some have been denied speech, I wonder whether this approach is truly productive
to the project of queering public address. Whereas understanding the conditions of
victimage is important, and the celebration of the marginalized voice is attractive,
assuming that speech leads to freedom may be counterproductive. As long as
human sexuality remains under the authority of powerful institutions, we should
be reluctant to celebrate speech as resistance without recognizing how speech acts
may actually reproduce institutional power.

As 2004 began, we witnessed public acts of lesbian and gay resistance that Ulrichs may have never imagined: many lesbian and gay couples challenged existing
laws by obtaining marriage licenses. The media provided daily reports of couples
resisting marriage laws in California, Massachusetts, and Oregon. As I watched these
reports, my admiration for these couples was tempered by my recognition that these
acts of resistance also operated as confessions. First, because of the presence of the
media, many of these couples were making public confessions about their relationships. While the public confession of love often carries with it a sense of romance,
within the frame of these media reports these romantic gestures were rendered as
extreme instances of political controversy. In other words, these confessions of love
were quickly subsumed by legal concerns regarding government institutions and the
political exigencies of the two-party system. Pundits continually argued about the
constitutionality of gay marriage law and which party the issue would hurt more:
Republicans or Democrats.[75] In view of the outcome of the 2004 election, it would
seem that the issue hurt both Democrats and gay rights advocates.

Of course, these are important points, but they demonstrate how these couples'
resistant acts were immediately contained by institutional practices, and this leads
me to a greater concern about these confessions: the act of obtaining a marriage
license required these couples to confess to the state, and this confession was not
just a declaration of love, it was an admission of homosexuality. It is in this confession to the state that I see the danger of gay marriage. Although these marriages
may seem to be a form of resistance, they do not challenge the power of the state
institution. In fact, the demand for gay marriage actually reproduces the power of
the state to identify and recognize these relationships as legitimate and extends that
power to encompass a whole new set of relations. These couples have important
reasons to seek out this legitimization, but it is also important to recognize the risks.
Karlyn Kohrs Campbell was mindful of these risks when she discussed the issue
of gay marriage at the 2004 Public Address Conference.[76] Speaking from her own
experience with the early second-wave feminist movement, Campbell reminds us

that marriage, historically, is an institution of ownership, articulated by gendered roles of dominance and obedience. She also notes that marriage has always functioned as an instrument with which the government has been able to oversee and intervene into personal relationships.

Because these acts of resistance actually reproduce the power of the state, these newly married couples are at the mercy of the custodians of the state and may be subject to similar government oversight and intervention. Conservative politicians who have been very vocal about their opposition to gay rights dominate our federal government and many of our state governments. In fact, George W. Bush embraced a constitutional amendment to ban gay marriage as a central issue in his reelection campaign. In light of the recent failures of the gay marriage movement, it is quite clear that these conservative custodians would like to nullify these marriages. But what else might they do? How might these confessions be used? How will the state treat these couples that are now officially registered as homosexuals?

These are difficult questions. Yet, if we recognize that the relationship between power and speech is, at best, ambivalent, these are the sorts of questions we should be asking. In other words, queering public address should not just be about the celebration of queer speech and resistance. We need to recognize the unique conditions that confront sexual minorities and how these conditions create complex and sometimes confounding rhetorical situations. We can assume neither that silence is the product of oppression nor that speech produces freedom. We need to be mindful that discourse, and particularly discourse on sexuality, is often produced in respect to institutional conditions and that these conditions can be marshaled for and against the advancement of sexual rights. Although this vigilance may seem daunting, it should not be beyond the grasp of rhetorical scholars. It merely requires the rhetorical acumen that should come with the knowledge that every argument has more than two sides and a strong commitment to comprehend each of them.

Notes

1. Hubert Kennedy, *Ulrichs: The Life and Work of Karl Heinrich Ulrichs* (Boston: Alyson, 1988).

2. Jonathan Katz, *Gay American History* (New York: Thomas Y. Crowell, 1976), 426.

3. Karlyn Kohrs Campbell, *Man Cannot Speak for Her*, vol. 1 (New York: Praeger, 1989). Houston and Olga Idriss Davis, "Introduction: A Black Women's Angle of Vision on Communication Studies," in *Centering Ourselves: African American Feminist and Womanist Studies of Discourse*, ed. Houston and Davis (Cresskill, N.J.: Hampton Press, 2002), 1–20.

4. Bonnie J. Dow, "Feminism, Difference(s), and Rhetorical Studies," *Communication Studies* 46 (1995): 106–17.

5. Barbara Biesecker, "Michel Foucault and the Question of Rhetoric," *Philosophy and Rhetoric* 25 (1992): 351–64.

6. Michel Foucault, *The History of Sexuality,* vol. 1, *An Introduction,* trans. Robert Hurley (New York: Vintage, 1978).

7. Biesecker, "Michel Foucault," 357.

8. I should note that my investigation is limited to the study of homosexuality. There are other forms of queerness, by which I mean marginalized forms of sexual expression, that are not directly addressed in this chapter. I would add, however, that many of these forms of queerness have been commonly associated with homosexuality and that understanding the construction of homosexuality as a mental pathology is a project not completely divorced from understanding the marginalization of these other forms of queerness.

9. Foucault, *The History of Sexuality.*

10. Ibid., 65.

11. Linda Alcoff and Laura Gray, "Survivor Discourse: Transgression or Recuperation," *Signs: Journal of Women in Culture and Society* 18 (1993): 279.

12. Larry May and James Bohman, "Sexuality, Masculinity, and Confession: [Parts 1 & 2]," *Hypatia: A Journal of Feminist Philosophy* 12 (1997): 138–46, 146–54.

13. Bonnie J. Dow, "*Ellen,* Television, and the Politics of Gay and Lesbian Visibility," *Critical Studies in Media Communication* 18 (2001): 123–40.

14. Karl Hienrich Ulrichs, *The Riddle of "Man-Manly" Love: The Pioneering Work on Male Homosexuality,* vol. 1, trans. Michael A. Lombardi-Nash (Buffalo: Prometheus Books, 1994), 34.

15. Richard von Krafft-Ebing, *Psychopathia Sexualis,* trans. F. J. Rebman (Brooklyn: Physicians and Surgeons Book, 1922).

16. Kenneth Lewes, *The Psychoanalytic Theory of Male Homosexuality* (London: Quartet Books, 1988)

17. Sigmund Freud, *Three Essays on the Theory of Sexuality,* trans. James Strachey (London: Imago, 1949).

18. Freud's attempt to theorize lesbianism suggested that females develop a disrupted relationship with their father. Little was done with lesbianism in subsequent psychoanalytic theory. This oversight is not unique to psychology; other scientific studies of sexuality tend to favor men over women. See Robert Alan Brookey, *Reinventing the Male Homosexual: The Rhetoric and Power of the Gay Gene* (Bloomington: Indiana University Press, 2002).

19. Sigmund Freud, "From the History of an Infantile Neurosis," in *The Standard Edition of the Complete Psychological Works of Sigmund Freud,* vol. 17, trans. and ed. James Strachey (London: Hogarth Press, 1955), 29; first published in *Sammlung kleiner Schriften zur Neurosenlehre* 4 (1918): 578–717.

20. Ibid., 46.

21. Ibid., 36.

22. Ibid., 47.

23. Sigmund Freud, "Analysis of a Phobia in a Five-Year-Old Boy," in *The Standard Edition of the Complete Psychological Works of Sigmund Freud,* vol. 10, trans. and ed. Strachey, 3–149; first published in *Jahrbuch fuer Psychoanalytische und Psychopathologische Forschungen* 1 (1909): 1–109.

24. Ibid., 9–10.

25. Ibid., 110.

26. Ibid., 5.

27. Sigmund Freud, "Leonardo da Vinci and a Memory of His Childhood," in *The Standard Edition of the Complete Psychological Works of Sigmund Freud*, vol. 11, trans. and ed. Strachey, 59–137; first published in *Gesammelte Schriften* 9 (1910): 371–454.

28. Freud, "Leonardo da Vinci and a Memory of His Childhood," 103.

29. Ibid., 106.

30. Freud, *Three Essays on the Theory of Sexuality*, 14–26.

31. Henry Abelove's analysis of Freud's correspondence with American psychoanalysts reveals that Freud argued with those who sought to correct homosexuality. Freud opposed these efforts because he viewed them as a misuse of his theories motivated by a moralistic imperative. Henry Abelove, "Freud, Male Homosexuality, and the Americans," in *The Lesbian and Gay Studies Reader*, ed. Abelove, Michele Aina Barale, and David M. Halperin (New York: Routledge, 1993), 381–93.

32. Sandor Rado, *Psychoanalysis of Behavior*, vol. 1 (New York: Grune & Stratton, 1956).

33. Lewes, *The Psychoanalytic Theory of Male Homosexuality*, 173–75.

34. Jennifer Terry, *An American Obsession: Science, Medicine, and Homosexuality in Modern Society* (Chicago: University of Chicago Press, 1999), 310.

35. Irving Bieber, *Homosexuality*, rev. ed. (Northvale, N.J.: Aronson, 1988), 18.

36. Ibid., 319.

37. Edmund Bergler, *Counterfeit-Sex: Homosexuality, Impotence, Frigidity*, 2nd ed. (New York: Grune & Stratton, 1958), 186–87.

38. Ibid., 191 (emphasis in original).

39. Ibid.

40. John D'Emilio, *Sexual Politics, Sexual Communities: The Making of a Homosexual Minority in the United States, 1940–1970* (Chicago: University of Chicago Press, 1983).

41. Bergler, *Counterfeit-Sex*, vii–ix.

42. Ibid., 122.

43. Alfred C. Kinsey, Wardell B. Pomeroy, and Clyde E. Martin, *Sexual Behavior in the Human Male* (Philadelphia: W. B. Saunders, 1948); Jonathan Gathrone-Hardy, *Sex: The Measure of All Things* (Bloomington: Indiana University Press, 2000).

44. For a discussion of these histories, see George Corner, "The Origin, Methods, and Findings of the Report," in *Problems of Sexual Behavior*, ed. Charles Walter Clarke (New York: American Social Hygiene Association, 1948), 1–19.

45. Some statisticians believed Kinsey's sampling and analysis were faulty. See A. H. Hobbs and R. D. Lambert, "An Evaluation of 'Sexual Behavior in the Human Male,'" *American Journal of Psychiatry* 104 (1948): 758–65; Lewis M. Terman, "Kinsey's 'Sexual Behavior in the Human Male': Some Comments and Criticisms," *Psychological Bulletin* 45 (1948): 443–59.

46. Kinsey, Pomeroy, and Martin, *Sexual Behavior in the Human Male*, 663.

47. Ibid., 665.

48. Lewes, *The Psychoanalytic Theory of Male Homosexuality*.

49. Edmund Bergler and William Kroger, *Kinsey's Myth of Female Sexuality; the Medical Facts* (New York: Grune & Stratton, 1954), 117 (emphasis in original).

50. Bergler and Kroger, *Kinsey's Myth of Female Sexuality*, 141.

51. Evelyn Hooker, "The Adjustment of the Male Overt Homosexual," *Journal of Projective Techniques* 21 (1957): 18–31.

52. Both Hooker and Kinsey were asked to join a board of the Mattachine when the organization was in its early stages; both declined. See Stuart Timmons, *The Trouble with Harry Hay* (Boston: Alyson, 1990), 163.

53. Ronald Bayer, *Homosexuality and American Psychiatry: The Politics of Diagnosis* (Princeton, N.J.: Princeton University Press, 1987), 72.

54. Ibid., 53.

55. Abe Peck, *Uncovering the Sixties* (New York: Pantheon, 1985). See also John Laoghaire, *The Other Side of Silence: Men's Lives and Gay Identities: A Twentieth-Century History* (New York: Henry Holt, 1998).

56. Martin Duberman, *Stonewall* (New York: Dutton, 1993).

57. Martin Duberman, *Cures: A Gay Man's Odyssey* (New York: Dutton, 1991).

58. Ibid., 104.

59. Ibid., 97.

60. Ibid., 119.

61. Ibid., 139.

62. Ibid., 157.

63. Ibid., 193.

64. W. Herbert, "Politics of Biology," *U.S. News and World Report*, April 21, 1997, 72–80.

65. Christopher Z. Hobson, "Surviving Psychotherapy," in *Out of the Closets*, ed. Karla Jay and Allen Young (New York: NYU Press, 1972), 147–52.

66. Howard Brown, *Familiar Faces, Hidden Lives* (New York: Harcourt Brace Jovanovich, 1976).

67. Ibid., 200–201.

68. S. Morin and E. Rothblum, "Removing the Stigma: Fifteen Years of Progress," *American Psychologist* 46 (1991): 947–49.

69. "Psychologists Vote to Discredit 'Conversion' Therapy for Gays," *Star Tribune*, 15 August 1997, A9.

70. Herbert, "Politics of Biology."

71. Charles Socarides, *Homosexuality: A Freedom Too Far* (Phoenix: Adam Margrave, 1995), 33.

72. National Association for Research and Therapy of Homosexuality, *NARTH's Purpose*, 2001, http://www.narth.com/menus/statement.html (May 21, 2002).

73. Ibid.

74. National Association for Research and Therapy of Homosexuality, *NARTH Presents 2001 Annual Conference*, 2001, http://www.narth.com/docs/page2.pdf. (November 28, 2001).

75. Adam Nagourney and Janet Elder, "The 2004 Campaign: The Poll; Nation's Direction Prompts Voters' Concern, Poll Finds," *New York Times*, March 16, 2004, A24.

76. Karlyn Kohrs Campbell, "Civil Unions for All!: A Response to Martin Medhurst," paper read at 2004 Public Address Conference, October 7–10, Washington, D.C.

THE RHETORIC OF INTERSECTIONALITY

Lorraine Hansberry's 1957 Letters to the *Ladder*

Lisbeth Lipari

I have suspected for a good while now that the homosexual in America would ultimately pay a price for the intellectual impoverishment of women, and, in this instance, of homosexual women. . . . Men continue to misinterpret the second-rate status of women as implying a privileged status for themselves; heterosexuals think the same way about homosexuals; gentiles about Jews; whites about blacks; haves about have-nots.

Lorraine Hansberry,
unpublished letter to *ONE* magazine, April 18, 1961

Poetry is not only dream and vision; it is the skeleton architecture of our lives. It lays the foundations for a future of change, a bridge across our fears of what has never come before.

Audre Lorde, *Sister Outsider: Essays and Speeches*

One of the challenges of queering historical public address is to resist the impulse to produce an account of a "real" queer figure that in the end simply produces yet another discursive formation. Public address scholars such as Morris have articulated the ambiguities of the queer rhetorical persona who evades easy identification.[1] An interesting example of this can be seen in the discursive construction of Lorraine Hansberry, who, while widely regarded as a signifier for racial justice for close to fifty years, was not constructed as a queer signifier until after her death in 1965. That "revelation" came about in 1976 when Barbara Grier, former editor of the lesbian periodical the *Ladder*, publicly identified Hansberry as the author of two public letters published in the *Ladder* in 1957.[2] Excerpts from the letters were then published in Katz's 1976 edition of *Gay American History*.[3] Three years later in a 1979 special issue of *Freedomways* dedicated to Hansberry, the lesbian poet and critic Adrienne Rich referred to the letters in a critical interrogation of the silences surrounding Hansberry and her work.[4] Since then, Hansberry has been increasingly identified as a lesbian in lesbian and gay, African American, and other literary biographies.

But whereas from one perspective much has been made of the two *Ladder* letters—the fact of her speaking and the concurrent silencing of that speaking—relatively little has been made about what Hansberry actually says in the letters or in her other writing that addresses sexuality.[5] Few critics link the *Ladder* letters to Hansberry's other writings or address how Hansberry also wrote about gay experience and politics in two of her plays: *The Sign in Sidney Brustein's Window* and *Les Blancs*. In this chapter I will read the letters in their historical context as well as in relation to a number of her key texts across a range of genres, including plays, political speeches, letters and essays. My aim is to deepen our understanding of Hansberry's rhetorical vision and her commitments to social and political transformation. Thus I will not investigate Hansberry's "private" self in search of her "true" sexual identity. Rather I follow the path of cultural and queer studies that view identities as, in Stuart Hall's phrase, "necessary fictions."[6] As Scott Bravmann describes it, identities are seen as "temporary but compelling fabrications that are remade through the actively inventive projects of political mobilization and social movements, rather than as antecedent, immutable, essential truths."[7] My argument, however, is not that Hansberry or her sexual life did not exist: history is, and lives happen. The heavily occluded historical record suggests that Hansberry did articulate and theorize lesbian experience and that she had women lovers.[8] Rather than undergo a search for evidence of Hansberry's personal identity, however, I will instead explore Hansberry's publicly constructed rhetorical voice for its articulations of counterhegemonic perspectives on sexuality, race, gender, and class. For, in spite of her decision to stay closeted throughout her short life, Hansberry nevertheless articulated a vital lesbian political ethos.[9] Her passing as heterosexual can be understood as an example of what Morris calls a rhetorical tactic of resistance. "For certain individuals, passing constitutes the public expression of homosexual double consciousness, a measured and strategic form of straight masking employed to resist, and not merely survive, homophobic oppression."[10]

By interpreting the *Ladder* letters in relation to Hansberry's other writing, as well as their historical context in the 1950s homophile movement, I endeavor to read Hansberry as a major political rhetor and public intellectual of her time who, twenty years before the Combahee River Collective's landmark "Black Feminist Statement,"[11] and thirty years before critical interrogations of identity occupied the center of major intellectual debates, explored the complex interlocking intersections of race, class, gender, and sexuality from antiracist, postcolonial, feminist, antiessentialist, lesbian, and Marxist perspectives. Considering her peers—she was one year older than Toni Morrison, four years older than Audre Lorde, two years younger than Maya Angelou, and one year younger than Adrienne Rich—one can only imagine the contribution Hansberry might have made had she lived longer.

Personal History

Biographically, Hansberry was a complex and even contradictory figure who personally straddled multiple class, race, and sexual cleavages. She was born in 1930 in Chicago to a middle-class African American family in a South Side ghetto and experienced firsthand the structural violence of Jim Crow education and the physical violence of racism. In 1938 her father, a Republican businessman and U.S. deputy marshal, moved the family to a white neighborhood to deliberately contest racial restriction clauses. Carl Hansberry's suit was ultimately successful, and the events of the case created the background for what was to become, twenty years later, her critically acclaimed Broadway hit *Raisin in the Sun*.[12] Hansberry briefly attended the University of Wisconsin.

After moving to New York City in 1950, Hansberry soon joined with radical black and communist activists (including her future husband, Robert Nemiroff), and in 1951 began working at the progressive black paper founded in 1950 by Paul Robeson, *Freedom* (with Louis Burnham as editor), first as reporter then as associate editor. In 1953 she married Nemiroff, a white Jewish songwriter, and quit her job at the paper to focus full time on playwriting. In the late 1950s she wrote the two letters to the *Ladder*, clandestinely dated women, and attended meetings of the New York Chapter of the Daughters of Bilitis, the nascent organization for lesbians. In March 1959 *Raisin* opened on Broadway, and Hansberry won the New York Drama Critic's Circle Award for best play of the year, becoming the first black playwright and fifth woman to win this prestigious award. In 1961 the film version of *Raisin* won the Gary Cooper Award for "outstanding human values" at Cannes.

Battling severe illness that was to be diagnosed as cancer only shortly before her death, Hansberry divorced Nemiroff in the spring of 1964 and three months later named him her literary executor. Throughout the late 1950s and early 1960s she wrote and spoke widely against racism, sexism, and the burgeoning Vietnam War. In October 1964, three months before she died, *The Sign in Sidney Brustein's Window* opened and ran for 101 days. Despite its lukewarm critical reception, friends from the theatrical, literary, and political communities kept the play running until her death on January 12, 1965. Malcolm X and other intellectual and theatrical luminaries attended her funeral, and the Reverend Dr. Martin Luther King, Jr., sent a letter to be read aloud. Julius Lester notes the irony of Hansberry's death falling a little more than a month before Malcolm X's assassination: "Somehow it seems like more than a coincidence that the two should die within less than a month and a half of each other and scarcely nine months before the 'deferred dream' exploded in the streets of Watts."[13]

As a public rhetor, Hansberry was prolific: in addition to her plays she wrote public letters to the *Ladder*, the *New York Times*, the *Village Voice*; she wrote essays and journalism for *Freedom*, *Monthly Review*, *Black Scholar*, *Ebony*, *Liberation*, and the *Village Voice*; she gave speeches at New York Town Hall, the American Academy of Psycho-Therapists, the American Society of African Culture, the United Negro College Fund, and, at age twenty-two, to the Inter-Continental Peace Congress in Uruguay. In 1963 she took part in a historic meeting between civil rights leaders and Bobby Kennedy. According to James Baldwin, Hansberry ended the meeting after Kennedy denied her request for a "moral commitment": "The meeting ended with Lorraine standing up. She said . . . 'I am very worried about the state of the civilization which produced that photograph of the white cop standing on that Negro woman's neck in Birmingham.'"[14]

Yet in spite of these contributions, Hansberry remains a marginalized figure in that she has yet to be acknowledged as the public intellectual she was. Even luminaries of black culture sympathetic to gender and sexuality issues, such as Cornel West, tend to leave Hansberry out of the equation when listing black intellectuals and those who "championed the struggle for freedom and justice in a prophetic framework of moral reasoning."[15] Those who have written about Hansberry voice this frustration. For example, Doris Abrams wrote, "Not enough has been said about her as an American (black) intellectual leader. Her essays presaged the concerns of the 1960s. She had strong connections to Africa. Her writings provide a challenge to black and white America."[16] More recently, Jewell Gomez noted, "Because we have not studied Hansberry as a cultural worker and thinker but only as a dramatist, we have lost touch with the urgency of her political message and the poetry of her writing."[17] Even Amiri Baraka, who was part of the Black Arts movement that loudly criticized *Raisin* as bourgeois melodrama in the early 1960s, in 1995 wrote, "The truth is that Hansberry's dramatic skills have yet to be properly appreciated—and not just by those guardians of the status quo who pass themselves off as drama critics."[18]

Hansberry's marginality comes at least in part from the failure to read her as a political writer, specifically as a black, feminist, Marxist, lesbian thinker. As Barbara Smith has noted, "When black women's books are dealt with at all, it is usually in the context of Black literature which largely ignores the implications of sexual politics. When white women look at Black women's works they are of course ill-equipped to deal with the subtleties of racial politics."[19] Documenting the omission of black lesbian writers in many anthologies of black women's criticism and literature such as those by Wallace, Washington, and hooks, Cheryl Clarke writes, "Black bourgeois female intellectuals practice homophobia by omission more often than rabid homophobia."[20] Thus, in spite of her ostensible acclaim, Hansberry's rhetorical voice and vision have not been sufficiently critically addressed.

Thinking Politicially: Intersectionality and the Simultaneity of Oppression

Perhaps one of Hansberry's most significant contributions to the public discourse of her era may have been her comprehensive grasp of what Sojourner Truth first publicly articulated in her 1851 "Ain't I a Woman?" speech, what Barbara Smith theorized in 1983 as the "simultaneity of oppression," and what Kimberlé Crenshaw further developed in 1989 as the concept of "intersectionality."[21] As Smith describes it, "The concept of the simultaneity of oppression is still the crux of Black feminist understanding of political reality and, I believe, one of the most significant ideological contributions of Black feminist thought. . . . we saw no reason to rank oppressions or, as many forces in the Black community would have us do, to pretend that sexism, among all the 'isms' was not happening to us."[22] According to Patricia Hill Collins, "Intersectionality thus highlights how African American women and other social groups are positioned within unjust power relations, but it does so in a way that introduces complexity to formerly race-, class-, and gender-only approaches to social phenomena."[23]

That Hansberry thought intersectionally is evident in all her writings, regardless of genre—whether it be in the full-blown critiques of racism, sexism and capitalism in *Raisin*; of racism, homophobia, and colonialism in *Les Blancs*; or of capitalism and racism in her documentary text *The Movement*. Describing her early relationship with Louis E. Burnham, she says, "The things he taught me were great things: that all racism was rotten, white or black, that everything is political."[24] Hansberry's grasp of intersectionality is evident in *The Movement*, for example, a book that narrates documentary photographs of the civil rights movement. In the book Hansberry attends to race-class intersectionality in several places where she links racism to wider systems of economic and social exploitation: "The [white police] men in helmets are from a class of Southerners who are themselves victims of a system that has used them and their fathers before them for generations."[25] And beneath a photograph of an industrial slum, she writes, "The coming of industry into the Southland has not changed the problems of many of its people—white or black—for the better."[26]

In fact, Hansberry took on an astonishing range of political issues, all inflected with an intersectional perspective, including racism, colonialism, sexism, capitalism, heterosexism, and black nationalism. She articulated a critique of the "exotic" as "other" two decades before Edward Said, and three before Stuart Hall.[27] Her deconstruction of political "illusions" in her 1959 speech to the Society for African Culture could provide the curriculum for any contemporary course in cultural studies, which includes critiques of "a year's steady diet of television, motion pictures, the legitimate stage and the novel."[28] Among the illusions Hansberry takes on in this speech: "Most people who work for a living are executives, women are idiots, people are white, negroes do not exist . . . sex is very bad, sex is very good . . . war is inevitable, so are armies . . . any form of radicalism (except conservativism) is latent protest against Mom, toilet-training, or heterosexuality."[29] Later in the speech she asserts, "And as of today, if I am asked abroad if I am a free citizen of the United States of America, I must say only what is true: *No*."[30]

Further, Hansberry's political imagination included all cultural formations, and most especially theater, as a forum for political expression. In a letter responding to a note from a theater enthusiast, she writes, "That is—'thesis plays' and 'social plays' are supposed to be, by this reasoning, plays which plead a cause. We have grown so accustomed to this abuse of language and ideas that most people try to explain *why* that is so and do not understand that there are *no* plays which are not social and no plays that do not have a thesis."[31] Hansberry's political imagination is perhaps most comprehensively sketched in her 1959 speech, in which she outlines her theory of art as deeply political: "There is a desperate need in our time for the Negro writer to assume a partisanship in what I believe has been the traditional battleground of writers of stature for centuries, namely the war against the illusions of one's time and culture."[32] As a careful reading of her texts, including those published in the *Ladder*, reveals, some of the most unacknowledged cultural illusions Hansberry battled against were heterocentrism and homophobia.

Subaltern Counterpublics: The Daughters of Bilitis and the *Ladder*

In spite of what Eric Garber and other historians document as a flourishing homosexual subculture for African American gays and lesbians during the Harlem Renaissance (1920–1935),[33] the witch hunts of World War II and subsequent homophobic persecution and gay-baiting of the McCarthy period had driven much of New York's African American and white gay and lesbian subcultures underground by the 1950s. The period was, according to Lillian Faderman, "perhaps the worst time in history for women to love women."[34] In contrast to earlier decades, in the 1950s gays and lesbians were subject to what John D'Emilio calls systematized oppression, which included frequent police arrests and harassments; FBI harassment and infiltration; expulsion from the military, government employment, teaching positions, and university study; and job discrimination. "From 1947 through mid-1958, 1,700 job seekers were denied employment because of homosexuality. After that period, the government expanded its screening procedures."[35] Gay and lesbian bars were routinely raided, and patrons were not only arrested on morals charges, but also had their names and addresses published in the next day's newspaper. According to D'Emilio, "[Arrests] in the District of Columbia exceeded 1,000 per year during the early 1950s. Washington police frequently resorted to entrapment by plainclothesmen in Lafayette Park and downtown movie houses to arrest male homosexuals. In Philadelphia during the 1950s, misdemeanor charges against gay men and women averaged 100 per month."[36]

Ironically, however, it was during this same period that the self-titled "homophile movement" first took shape in the form of three different gay and lesbian organizations based in California: the Mattachine Society (founded in 1951 by and for gay men), the Daughters of Bilitis (DOB; founded in 1955 by and for lesbians), and One (an organization that began as a magazine started by Mattachine but split off, becoming its own organization around 1953). Each of these organizations built subaltern counterpublics to resist and find respite from oppressive social and discursive conventions of the ostensibly mainstream public. The notion of subaltern counterpublics derives from work by postcolonial, feminist, and critical theorists seeking to describe the existence of multiple (rather than singular) subordinate (rather than dominant) publics in democratic societies; the centrality of these publics to the development of subaltern political voice, critique, and identity; and how ostensibly democratic societies appropriate, marginalize, and occasionally accommodate the voices of oppressed minority groups who comprise subaltern counterpublics.[37] The1950s homophile organizations built previously nonexistent communities through face-to-face semipublic social interactions, public meetings, and national publications. In 1957, the organization One also undertook both an undergraduate and graduate school as well as a homosexual news service. Although each of the three organizations emphasized different aspects of and strategies for liberation, each was committed to overcoming the isolation and persecution of gay men and lesbians.

DOB was founded in 1955 by eight women from San Francisco "with a vague idea that something should be done about the problems of Lesbians, both within their own group and with the public."[38] One year later, they began publishing the *Ladder*, the first national lesbian publication.[39] The circulation of the first issue in October 1956 was 100, growing to 400 by the end of the first year and 3,800 by the last issue in 1972. As Alisa Klinger notes in a survey of lesbian activist writing, "The use of print by multicultural lesbian activists to establish strategic political identities and affinities and to articulate passionately their aspirations for civil rights and elemental social change has been the crux of lesbian liberation politics."[40]

The DOB statement of purpose, published in the first issue of the *Ladder*, indicates a mixture of both emancipatory and assimilationist aims: "Education of the variant, with particular emphasis on the psychological and sociological aspects," by establishing a library, sponsoring public discussions, educating the public, participating in research projects, investigating the penal code, and "advocating a mode of behaviour and dress acceptable to society." It was in relation to this last assimilationist aim in particular that Hansberry addressed her first letter to the *Ladder*. The early issues of the *Ladder* included essays, book reviews, fiction, poetry, letters from readers, calendars of meetings and events, and reports about public discussions held by DOB and other homophile organizations, which often included panels of "experts" debating psychological and legal perspectives on homosexuality. For example, the March 1957 issue contained a report of a panel of male psychologists, psychiatrists, pastors, and attorneys discussing the topic of "The Homosexual Neurosis."

The *Ladder* reporter wrote, "The crossfire period was delightful. A highlight for the homosexuals present occurred when someone asked Dr. Doebler why he felt that all homosexuals were neurotic. He answered that he'd never known any 'happy' homosexuals. The audience rocked with laughter [when] the next questioner asked Dr. Doebler if he'd ever had any 'happy' heterosexual patients. Dr. Doebler squirmed but answered forthrightly that he never had."[41] Other public discussions and articles reported in the *Ladder* concerned raising children in "a deviant relationship," lesbians and fear, psychotherapy versus public opinion, job hunting, criticism of mainstream media depictions of homosexuality, and the psychological dimensions of self-acceptance.

As part of its public advocacy and educational role, the DOB and the *Ladder* also organized and promoted impromptu actions in response to oppressive public actions against lesbians. For instance, the second issue included an article on a San Francisco police raid of the Alamo club, a lesbian bar, which resulted in the arrest of thirty-six women. The article focused on the question of civil rights and advocated public education for lesbian civil rights: "At the hearing the following Monday we understand that only four of those arrested pleaded not guilty. We feel that this was not due to actual guilt on the part of those so pleading but to an appalling lack of knowledge of the rights of a citizen in such a case."[42] The article concluded with an announcement of a DOB-sponsored public meeting with a San Francisco attorney who would discuss "The Lesbian and the Law."

Thus many of the public discussions and some of the writing featured the opinions of "expert" authorities, reflecting the values, aims, and perspectives of the largely middle-class constituency of the organization—particularly the value of what Faderman identifies as the aspiration for integration.[43] Further, in addition to the organization's conservative stance on assimilation and the politics of accommodation, the DOB took several perplexing positions during the late 1950s. For example, an article based on the "expertise" of psychologists in the March 1957 issue claimed that "the only thing a homosexual has to fear when looking for a job is whether his or her ability matches the job applied for—the problem of homosexuality per se does not enter the employment picture."[44] This is a fairly bewildering claim in light of the antigay persecutions occurring in plain sight in the fields of government and education. Even more mystifying, in the same issue, the DOB commended the "ACLU for its fine work in the defense of civil rights for all citizens." The article then quoted from the ACLU's newly published stand on homosexuality, which tacitly condoned homophobic laws: "It is not within the province of the Union to evaluate the validity of laws aimed at the suppression or elimination of homosexuals."[45]

The DOB, however, was aware of and even apologetic about its largely middle-class constituency. In the fourth issue of the *Ladder,* the editors described the DOB membership: "College students, saleswomen, dental technicians, photographers, stenographers, teachers, traffic management people. Some are home-owners, some are saving for a home, some are just living. . . . We aren't 'bar-hoppers' but people with steady jobs, most of them good positions. . . . At the moment we are all what might be termed 'white-collar' workers, but we want all kinds—those who want help and those who wish to help."[46]

Despite the editors' recognition of class and the ostensible desire to include lesbians from the working and upper classes, the concomitant remark distancing DOB members from "bar-hoppers" should be understood in its class and racial context. According to contemporary work in lesbian history, the 1950s lesbian bar culture was an important public arena for the creation of lesbian community. In their oral history of lesbians in Buffalo during the 1950s, Madeline Davis and Elizabeth Lapovsky Kennedy argue that "this public bar community was a formative predecessor to the modern gay liberation movement. These bars not only were essential meeting places with distinctive cultures and mores, but they were also the central arena for the lesbian confrontation with a hostile world. Participants in bar life were engaged in a constant, often violent, struggle for public space. Their dress code announced them as lesbians to their neighbors, to strangers, on the streets, and of course to all who entered the bars."[47]

Significantly, however, the 1950s lesbian bar culture was a largely white working-class space.[48] Oral histories, biography, and autobiography suggest that in many if not most U.S. cities, the bar culture by and large did not include black lesbians. In her autobiography *Zami*, for example, Audre Lorde describes thinking she and her friend were the only black lesbians in New York's Greenwich Village: "It seemed that loving women was something that other Black women just didn't do. And if they did, then it was in some fashion and in some place that was totally inaccessible to us, because we could never find them."[49] Similarly, in Rochella Thorpe's oral history of black lesbians in Detroit in the 1950s, African American lesbians describe both overt and covert incidents of racism that left them feeling unwelcome or invisible in predominantly white bars. Thorpe's history documents how Detroit black lesbians created semipublic spaces in the form of house parties to circumvent the racism of the white lesbian community and the homophobia of the black community. She writes, "One reason historians of lesbians have not been successful locating lesbians of color might be that they have assumed bars have been the center (both theoretical and actual) of lesbian communities."[50]

It was, however, to the *Ladder*'s discursive community, the only national lesbian counterpublic in existence at the time, that Hansberry addressed herself in 1957 while she was writing the play *A Raisin in the Sun*. Her first letter was published in May 1957, the eighth issue of the nascent publication, and her second three months later in August. The letters are actually more akin to essays and are longer than most of the other letters published in the *Ladder*: the May letter is approximately 840 words and the August letter roughly 1,340 words. Following the *Ladder*'s editorial conventions, neither letter is addressed or signed by name; the May letter is signed with the initials L.H.N., New York, and the August letter signed simply L.N., New York. This is in contrast to the rhetorical persona Hansberry used in her other writing (that is, the name "Lorraine Hansberry"); however, in public letters to the *Village Voice* and the *Ladder* she instead employed her married initials.[51] What we are to make of this is unclear, but it raises an interesting question about the constraints on Hansberry's public voice. Hansberry apparently wrote no other letters to the *Ladder*, though in 1961 she did write a letter to *One*, which was never mailed.

The *Ladder* Letters

A letter is a relational act of address: to write a letter is to place oneself in a dialogue with an explicitly acknowledged addressee. To write a public letter is to situate oneself in relation to a public, a real or imagined community of auditors who share, at the very least, the experience of the address. As Robert Fulkerson notes in his analysis of King's "Letter from Birmingham Jail," writers of public letters can address more than one audience simultaneously, and moreover, those audiences are, at the time of writing, "always a fiction."[52] Yet in contrast to other forms of the public letter, such as Cesar Chavez's "Letter from Delano," which explicitly drew on Mexican American historical traditions of public letters,[53] the anonymous public letters of the *Ladder* are not only without historical rhetorical heritage, but are also at once both public and private. The anonymous public letters of the *Ladder* thus occupy a liminal space—not quite public and not quite private, yet at the same time both public and private. Privacy is accorded to both writer and reader, each of whom remains unnamed and indirectly addressed. Yet the address is shared by a multiplicity of readers, who are an assumed public audience of interlocutors. In fact, letters to the *Ladder* were a central part of the periodical's textuality—sometimes even constituting intertextual dialogue.

Rhetorically then, this form of anonymous public letter invites us, the unimagined audience, to attend differently. As in other forms of the public letter, by making explicit their relation to prior speech acts, the letter writer engages in conversation still ongoing and unfolding; that is, they belong equally to the future as to the past. A letter is also an elicitation, an invitation for response. It anticipates, expects, and even demands a response. When Hansberry wrote to the *Ladder*, it was both a call as well as a response, a "here I am," to other lesbians. Thus her letters both acknowledge and construct a relationship between hidden writers and hidden readers who made up the secret subaltern public of the lesbian nation.

Hansberry begins the May letter with a request for as many back issues of the journal that $2.00 would cover, adding a promise of future "sizeable (for me, that is) donations" and then moves into four of what she calls "off-the-top-of-the-head reactions": (1) a brief exposition on the importance of separate publication venues for lesbians; (2) a longer disquisition in support of the DOB declaration of purpose that advocates modes of "acceptable" behavior and dress; (3) two sentences applauding the journal; and (4) a suggestion for overseas communication. Hansberry ends her letter with an elicitation for thoughts on the comparative dearth of gay and lesbian organizations on the East Coast: "Would like to hear speculation, light-hearted or otherwise." Hansberry's tone conveys warmth and a personal connection to her interlocutors; she uses informal, personal, and idiomatic expressions, such as "I'm glad as heck that you exist"; "Would it be presumptuous or far-fetched to suggest?"; and "Just a little afterthought."[54] Here, in contrast to her other published letters, Hansberry projects a kind of comfort and familiarity with her readers, as if, perhaps, she were writing to friends.

Despite its somewhat breezy and informal tone, the first two points of the letter resonate with Hansberry's elsewhere-articulated political vision. Before developing her argument for why women need "their own publications and organizations," Hansberry begins by denying any intention to "foster strict *separatist* notions, homo or hetero." This caveat comports both with the kind of coalition politics Hansberry advocates in other writing as well as her critiques of racial separatism. As to the former, for example, in her speech to New York's Town Hall Hansberry urges whites to stop being liberals and work side by side with African Americans in the struggle for civil rights. "The problem is we have to find some way with these dialogues to show and to encourage the white liberal to stop being a liberal and become an American radical."[55]

Hansberry's critique of separatism in this letter also resonates with her rejection of the kind of racial separatism advocated by black nationalism as expressed in her plays *A Raisin in the Sun* and *Les Blancs* and her other writings. For example, in *The Movement* she writes: "The Black Muslim movement represents a potluck nationalism that looks backward, not to the wonderful of black African civilization of medieval and antique periods, but to Arabic cultures. Muslim 'separation' is not a program, but an accommodation to American racism."[56] This idea is also developed in *A Raisin in the Sun* when, for example, the Younger family daughter, Beneatha, argues with her friend, an African student named Asagai, about racial reasoning.

> Beneatha: I know that's what you think. Because you are still where I left off. You with all your talk and dreams about Africa! You still think you can patch up the world. Cure the Great Sore of Colonialism with the penicillin of Independence!
> Asagai: Yes!
> Beneatha: Independence and then what? What about all the crooks and thieves and just plain idiots who will come into power and steal and plunder the same as before—only now they will be black and do it in the name of the new Independence—WHAT ABOUT THEM?!![57]

This critique of race-based separation also emerges in *Les Blancs*, in which an African expatriate living in England returns home for his father's village funeral to experience imminent anticolonial revolution. On encountering a white American journalist, the young man, Tshembe, soundly critiques separatist racial thinking: "Race—racism—is a device. No more. No less. It explains nothing at all. . . . It is simply a means. An invention to justify the rule of some men over others."[58] To sense how progressive these ideas were in the 1950s one need only read the words of Cornel West, thirty years later, as he critiques the ideas of black authenticity and racial reasoning. "In short, blackness is a political and ethical construct. Appeals to black authenticity ignore this fact. . . . The claims to black authenticity that feed on the closing-ranks mentality of black people are dangerous precisely because his closing of ranks is usually done at the expense of black women. It also tends to ignore the divisions of class and sexual orientation in black America. . . . In this way black nationalist and black male-centered claims to authenticity reinforce black cultural conservatism."[59]

In this brief opening to her May letter Hansberry also articulates her developed feminist consciousness. "Our problems, our experiences as women are profoundly unique as compared to the other half of the human race. Women, like other oppressed groups of one kind or another, have particularly had to pay a price for the intellectual impoverishment that the second class status imposed on us for centuries created and sustained."[60] This point echoes, for example, to arguments she makes in an unfinished essay, "In Defense of the Equality of Men," where she articulates a strong feminist argument and celebrates nineteenth-century feminists who "set a path that a grateful society will undoubtedly, in time, celebrate."[61] The point is also echoed two years later when, in an interview with Studs Terkel, she states, "Obviously the most oppressed group of any oppressed group will be its women who are twice oppressed."[62]

The bulk of Hansberry's May letter, however, engages a debate about the politics of accommodation, respectability, and conformity just beginning to unfold in the *Ladder*. As I mention above, one of the DOB statements of purpose was to "promote" acceptable dress and behavior among lesbians. This statement reflects both tactical and class tensions that were already present in the homophile movement before DOB was born. In its early years (1951–1954) the Mattachine Society challenged mainstream views of homosexuality "as an individual problem, as evidence of moral weakness, criminality, or pathology," with the view that homosexuals were an oppressed minority group, akin to other oppressed minorities.[63] This perspective reflected the views of the group's founder, Harry Hay, who, like Hansberry, was a communist.

But tensions produced in large part by anticommunist persecution led to a change of Mattachine's leadership in 1954, resulting in the organization's more assimilationist ethos. This new perspective was shared by the DOB leadership and was elaborated in a message from the president, D. Griffen, in the November 1956 issue of the *Ladder*, where she writes, "Let me again state that this is a homosexual *and* heterosexual organization that wishes to enlighten the public about the Lesbian and to teach them that we aren't the monsters that they depict us to be."[64] The president then quotes a letter from a so-called "lass" who writes, "But the kids in fly-front pants and with the butch haircuts and the mannish manner are the worst publicity we can get." "Very true," the president writes. "Our organization has already touched on that matter and has converted a few to remembering that they are women first and a butch or fem secondly, so their attire should be that which society will accept."[65]

But whereas the lesbian community's antiassimilationist perspective was not reflected in DOB, it did in fact exist. According to lesbian historians such as Davis and Kennedy, Faderman, and Joan Nestle, the "butch" persona emerged largely in response to sex, class, and gender oppression. "In the fifties, with the increased visibility of the established gay community, the concomitant postwar rigidification of sex roles, and the political repression of the McCarthy era, the street dyke emerged. She was a full-time 'queer,' who frequented the bars even on week nights and was ready at any time to fight for her space and dignity."[66] As Faderman discusses, however, the lesbian subcultures of the 1950s were as class-stratified as the rest of society: "Class mixing was extremely rare. Working-class lesbians tended to socialize only with other working-class lesbians. While some wealthy lesbians would occasionally have times among middle-class lesbian groups, more often those groups tended to be made up exclusively of women who earned their livings in professions as teachers, librarians, or social workers."[67]

Hansberry's second and more fully elaborated point in the May letter involves a thoughtful reflection on this debate that includes both a qualified endorsement of the assimilationist position and an engaging political explication of what "acceptable" dress and behavior mean for lesbians and other minorities. Thus, whereas several writers, such as Neil Miller and Joan Nestle, have cited this passage from Hansberry's letter as evidence that she disapproved of butch/femme role-playing and advocated assimilationist and conformist politics,[68] a closer reading of the letter in the context of her other work offers a different interpretation.

Hansberry begins her discussion on dress by disclaiming the moral high ground for her position by stating, "Rightly or wrongly (in view of some of the thought-provoking discussions I have seen elsewhere in another homosexual publication) I could not help but be encouraged and relieved" by the DOB policy. Hansberry then continues her equivocation by outing herself as "a Negro" and quickly dispatching the "shallowness" of lecturing one's "fellows about how to appear acceptable to the dominant social group."[69] She proceeds to offer an the argument against assimilation by drawing an analogy to racism: "The most splendid argument is simple and to the point. Ralph Bunche,[70] with all his clean fingernails, degrees, and of course undeniable service to the human race, could still be insulted, denied a hotel room or meal in many parts of the country. (Not to mention the possibility of being lynched on a lonely Georgia road for perhaps having demanded a glass of water in the wrong place)."[71] This statement reflects not just a counter-assimilationist argument, but also Hansberry's recognition of larger structures underlying antigay oppression that would not be obviated by mere or mindless conformity. "What ought to be clear is that one is oppressed or discriminated against because one is different, not 'wrong' or 'bad' somehow. This perhaps the bitterest of the entire pill."

After offering this eloquent critique of assimilation, however, Hansberry turns toward the brighter sun of pragmatism by offering a "critical view of revolutionary attitudes which . . . may tend to aggravate the problems of a group" and thus returns to her argument in favor of assimilation: "I have long since passed that period when I felt personal discomfort at the sight of an ill-dressed or illiterate Negro. Social awareness has taught me where to lay the blame. Someday, I expect, the 'discreet' Lesbian will not turn her head on the streets at the sight of the 'butch' strolling hand in hand with her friend in their trousers and definitive haircuts. But for the moment, it still disturbs. It creates an impossible area for discussion with one's most enlightened (to use a hopeful term) heterosexual friends."

As with her plays, Hansberry here offers a dialogic approach to her argument; she explicates contending perspectives in a way that vivifies and strengthens her argument, but she is also willing to acknowledge that her perspective may not be "right." Thus Hansberry's moral imagination, while set on a focused set of liberatory ends, is not unyielding with regard to questions of means. She wants to discover the "way" collectively, in dialogue with others of her community (as, she remarks, her enlightened friends cannot). Her equivocation, however, speaks not just to her moral imagination, but also to the fact that Hansberry's "double-consciousness" was not nor could ever be only, or even primarily, as a lesbian, but as an African American woman. Here, as for other African American queers, the complexities of intersectional politics come to the foreground. The communist- and gay-baiting of the McCarthy period exacted a steep price for not just for queer radicalism, but also for radicals in the civil rights movement, gay or straight.[72] In fact, an interview with early founders and members of DOB archived in the Lesbian Herstory Archives speaks directly on this point. According to Marion Glass, an early member of the New York chapter of DOB, one of the first activities of the new chapter was to contact Hansberry. "In her cordial discussion with us, Miss Hansberry reaffirmed her view that personal freedom and freedom from discrimination for the homosexual as well as for blacks would continue to receive her support. However, her business agent had advised her that open support of the homosexual would adversely affect the black civil rights movement and would be most untimely. Miss Hansberry felt that there was about to be a major development in the civil rights movement. She asked us to be patient."[73] This point is echoed in DOB founders when they write, "Many Black women who had been involved earlier in the homophile movement found themselves forced to make a choice between two 'causes' that touched their lives so intimately. One of them wrote a play that was a hit on Broadway."[74]

Thus Hansberry's approach to and critique of assimilation is markedly different than the kind of depoliticized conformity advocated by other DOB writers, including the well-known science fiction writer Marion Zimmer Bradley, who interestingly also wrote a proassimilationist letter published in the same issue of the *Ladder.* It states, in part, "I think Lesbians themselves could lessen the public attitudes by confining their differences to their friends and not force themselves deliberately upon public notice by deliberate idiosyncrasies of dress and speech; . . . the so-called normal does not consider that his private life is of concern to the general public; whatever he does in private, in public he makes an attempt to be courteously inconspicuous, and I believe that homosexuals and Lesbians might well do the same."[75]

But whereas Bradley situates the question of sexuality in the depoliticized context of "private life," Hansberry acknowledges the political dimensions of sexuality as it pertains to minority group oppression (at the same time as she is willing to sacrifice revolutionary politics to the pragmatics of political expediency). Hansberry rejects the notion of sexuality as a nonpolitical and private issue in several other texts, including *The Sign in Sidney Brustein's Window,* her unpublished letter to *One,* and her August letter to the *Ladder.* In the letter to *One,* for example, Hansberry explicates her notion of political intersectionality and explicitly links homosexuality to other forms of political oppression. She writes, "It is true that all human questions overlap and while our understanding of a trial in Israel or an execution in Vietnam may not momentarily be rapid-fire, life has a way of showing up why we should have cared all along. Men continue to misinterpret the second-rate status of women as implying a privileged status for themselves; heterosexuals think the same way about homosexuals; gentile about Jews; whites about blacks; haves about have-nots."[76] Further, whereas *Sign* includes two characters who express outright homophobia toward the play's single gay character, the otherwise radical protagonist Sidney reveals his heterocentrism through an entirely depoliticized view of sex:

> Sidney: And you, David, you have now written 14 plays about not caring, about the isolation of the soul of man . . . when what you really want is to say that you are ravaged by a society that will not sanctify your particular sexuality! If you don't like the sex laws, attack 'em, I think they're silly. You want to get up a petition? I'll sign one. Love little fishes if you want. But, David, please get over the notion that your particular 'thing' is something that only the deepest, saddest, the most nobly tortured can know about. It ain't—it's just one kind of sex—that's all. And in my opinion, the universe turns regardless.[77]

In reading this passage out of context, Miller cites this speech as a reflection of "Hansberry's own viewpoint."[78] But reading this speech in the context of Hansberry's *Ladder* letters and other writing allows an interpretation of Sidney's trivilization of homosexuality ("love the little fishes" and "just one kind of sex") as an error of misrecognition. That is, Sidney, by failing to see the social and political dimensions of homosexual persecution, falls prey to one of the cultural "illusions" of his time.

Although Hansberry does not take up the issue of lesbian assimilation elsewhere in her published writing, she does acknowledge briefly in her August letter a June *Ladder* essay on "Transvestism," which deepens the political analysis Hansberry had begun. "I am now pleased to see that there are those who have given and are giving good attention to the question in a most serious way." In the essay entitled "Transvestism: A Cross-Cultural Survey," Barbara Stephens sketches both political and psychological dimensions of women's cross-dressing, including what she calls "defensive transvestism," as resistance to sexism and the sexual objectification of women. In other words, by shifting the discursive ground about lesbian dress from the terrain of "passing" as straight to an issue of gender conformity as compliance with gender oppression, Stephens thus articulates the centrality of sexism to lesbian experience.[79] And this, to Hansberry—twenty years before lesbian-feminism emerges as a movement—is a laudable move. It is unclear from Stephens's essay whether or to what extent she is responding to Bradley's or Hansberry's May letters—she directly refers to neither letter—but she does write that "conformity has been recommended as a solution, but too often forced conformity is the mother of further neuroses."[80] I found no other writing in the *Ladder* on the topic of dress conformity for another year.

Like her May letter, Hansberry's August letter again opens with matters financial: an enclosure of $5.00 to "make good a so far neglected earlier promise of financial support." The tone of this letter is somewhat less breezy than the May letter, though it is still quite informal. Further, although Hansberry does not number her points as she did in May, she moves very quickly to her argument. The vast majority of this longer letter addresses a discussion on married lesbians initiated in the June issue by Nancy Osbourne in an article entitled "One Facet of Fear" and then further developed by Marion Zimmer Bradley in an essay in the July issue entitled "Some Remarks on Marriage." Whereas Osbourne recommends that the heterosexually married lesbian might best "keep her secret," Bradley recommends the lesbian divorce unless she can say to herself, if not her husband, "I find other women interesting; that does not in any way affect our relationship."[81]

Hansberry opens with an acknowledgment of Osbourne's letter, though she spends most of the text responding to two of Bradley's points by sketching, in opposition to Bradley's preferred psychosexual analysis of married lesbians, her own analysis of lesbian sexuality, politics, economics, and ethics. In this letter Hansberry again begins with a caveat, confessing that, although she was interested in Bradley's essay, "I understood what she was saying far less." Hansberry next goes on to rebut one of Bradley's premises: that if a married lesbian takes her marriage vows seriously "her interest in other women will affect her marriage no more than the heterosexual woman's healthy interest in other men."[82]

Hansberry's initial move is to distinguish Bradley's depiction of lesbians as having an "interest" in women from "the homosexual impulse," which Hansberry defines as having one's "most intense emotional and physical reactions toward other women."[83] Hansberry then advances a line of argument that examines the social context of married lesbians:

> Further, to assert that such women ought to be able to put genuine truth in the statement that her interest in other women will affect her marriage no more than the heterosexual woman's interest in other men is making an equation of two decidedly different social circumstances that simply have no equality in life. A woman of strength and honesty may, if she chooses, sever her marriage and marry a new male mate and society will be upset that the divorce rate is rising so—but there are few places in the United States, in any event, where she will be anything remotely akin to an "outcast." Obviously this is not true for a woman who would end her marriage to take up life with another woman.

Hansberry then suspends this line of argument for a paragraph to reflect briefly on the ethics of violating marriage vows, which she does not condone. "Not so much because of any sacredness of our dubious social morality, but rather because it involves the deception of another human being—and that, as always, is intolerable."[84] She then returns to the main line of her argument, adding both an economic and gender dimension to her analysis, before turning back to ethics:

> I suspect that the problem of the married woman who would prefer emotional-physical relationships with other women is proportionally much higher than a similar statistic for men. This is because the estate of woman being what it is, how could we ever begin to guess the numbers of women who are not prepared to risk a life alien to what they have been taught all their lives to believe was their "natural" destiny—AND—their only expectation for ECONOMIC security. It seems to me that this is why the question has an immensity that it does not have for male homosexuals. We must, as noted above, take a dim view of anyone who treats a married partner without respect; but at the same time I should imagine that we would have a particularly sensitive and sympathetic awareness of the nature of the "social trap" (I cannot think of a better set of words at the moment) which the fundamental position of women as a sex is likely to force many women into—homosexual or heterosexual.

Here Hansberry's analysis of marriage and its implications for women's sexuality reflects her sophisticated intersectional politics—she not only goes far beyond a privatized and psychological framing of marriage, but also explicates a feminist and political-economic understanding of the specific historical particularity of women's and particularly lesbian (as opposed to homosexual) experience. This understanding critiques the ideology of "naturalized femininity" first articulated by Simone de Beauvoir in *The Second Sex* (here I refer to her famous claim "that one is not born but is made a woman"). Thus, when Hansberry challenges what women "have been taught all their lives to believe was their 'natural' destiny," she is both joining and extending a feminist dialogue about the ideology of gender begun with de Beauvoir and continuing today.[85]

Further, Hansberry's aphoristic but compelling sketch of women's "social trap" is echoed in *The Sign in Sidney Brustein's Window,* where she explores the economic dimensions of race and gender oppression through the ill-fated relationship between the play's sole black character, Alton, and his white fiancée, Gloria, a prostitute. Hansberry first explores the intersectional problematics of race and gender oppression through Alton's eyes in a scene where he tells Sidney his reasons for breaking his engagement to Gloria.

> Alton: Someone who has coupled with my love . . . used her like . . . an . . .
> inanimate object . . . a thing, an instrument . . . a commodity. . . . Don't
> you understand, Sidney? Man, like I am spawned from commodities . . .
> and their purchasers. Don't you know this? I am running from being a
> commodity. How do you think I got the color I am, Sidney? Haven't you
> ever thought about it? I got this color from my grandmother being used
> as a commodity, man. The buying and the selling in this country began
> with me.[86]

But, whereas Alton recognizes the particular price paid by African and African American women slaves—he castigates the sexual commodification of slaves—he is oblivious to the commodification of women symbolized by heterosexual marriage. Hansberry explores this linkage in a conversation between Gloria and Sidney when she rehearses what she will say to Alton to explain her prostitution in a monologue that includes the "rationale" that, "the *real* prostitutes are everybody else; especially housewives and career girls."[87]

Hansberry returns to the question of ethics in the next full paragraph of her August letter, when she articulates a call for women intellectuals:

> For instance, the whole realm of morality and ethics is something that has
> escaped the attention of women by and large. And it needs the attention of
> intellectual women most desperately. I think it is about time that equipped
> women began to take on some of the ethical questions which a male domi-
> nated culture has produced and dissect and analyze them quite to pieces in

a serious fashion. It is time that "half the human race" had something to say about the nature of its existence. Otherwise—without revised basic thinking—the woman intellectual is likely to find herself trying to draw conclusions—moral conclusions—based on acceptance of a social moral superstructure which has never admitted to the equality of women and is therefore immoral itself. As per marriage, as per sexual practices, as per the rearing of children, etc.[88]

What is especially interesting about this letter is how Hansberry responds to Bradley's vaguely Freudian psychoanalytic framing of the question of married lesbians, which foregrounds questions of maternal desires. Hansberry's response instead foregrounds the social and economic contexts in which desire is rendered meaningful, or even possible. It is as if here, if for only a moment, the Hansberry-Bradley dialogue anticipates, if only in sketchy outline, pending debates between historical materialists and poststructuralist Lacanians. What Bradley presented as a psychological issue (she refers to lesbianism as a "psychosexual orientation") Hansberry reconfigured as a historically material experience grounded in social and political context. Hansberry did not respond to the psychological issue at all, brushing off the entire question with "I am afraid that homosexuality, whatever its origins, is far more real than that, far more profound in the demands it makes."[89]

Also remarkable is how Hansberry locates the sphere of the ethical. In contrast to first-wave feminists and contemporary civil rights activists who predicated ethical claims on notions of Christian or universalized morality, Hansberry predicates her political imagination not on a universalized morality that ignores, flattens, or obliterates distinctions, but in a historical-materialist context that recognizes questions of both the universal and the particular. That is, in contrast to abolitionist/feminist foremothers such as Angelina Grimké, who argued that women were equally capable of moral reasoning as were men, Hansberry argues that, because of historical and material conditions, women had different contributions to make—contributions that would expand the boundaries of moral thinking. Stephen Howard Browne, for example, summarizes Grimké's abiding principles of human rights as, "All human beings possess rights because they are moral beings; All human rights are essentially the same because moral nature is essentially the same. . . . Sex, being incidental, is subordinate to the primary and essential rights of moral being."[90] Hansberry is moving beyond the ethico-political domain of rights claims and into the ethico-political domain of moral possibility and imagination—a move from deontic spheres of moral duty and obligation to epistemic spheres of radical moral possibility. Thus Hansberry is not to be understood as essentialist—she is not arguing that women are different because of biological difference, but rather because of historically specific social location, in particular the social context of oppression.

This argument echoes the debates Hansberry engaged about *A Raisin in the Sun*, where she was accused of (or lauded for, depending on the audience) celebrating a depoliticized and decontextualized transcendent universality. But to Hansberry, historical specificity is, paradoxically, the ground and basis of universality. For example, in her 1959 speech, after riffing on the glorious potentialities of "man," she sets herself personally in historical context of extraordinary specificity: "I was born on the South Side of Chicago, I was born black and a female. I was born in a depression after another. While I was still in my teens the first atom bombs were dropped on human beings at Nagasaki and Hiroshima, and by the time I was twenty-three years old my government and that of the Soviet Union had entered actively in the worst conflict of nerves in human history."[91] Similarly, when Studs Terkel asks how she responds to the claim that *A Raisin in the Sun* "is not really a Negro play," she says,

> I believe one of the soundest ideas in dramatic writing is in order to create the universal, you must pay very great attention to the specific. Universality, I think, emerges from truthful identity of what is. In other words, I have told people that not only is the play about a Negro family, specifically and culturally, but it's not even a New York family or a southern Negro family—it is specifically Southside Chicago. To the extent we accept them and believe them as who they're supposed to be, to that extent they can become everybody. So I would say it is definitely a Negro play before it is anything else.[92]

The search for truth—historical, embodied, particular—is therefore central to Hansberry's political and moral imagination.

Hansberry's August letter to the *Ladder* closes with a tentative exploration of the link between homophobia and sexism: "In this kind of work [women's intellectual labor] there may be women to emerge who will be able to formulate a new and possible concept that homosexual persecution and condemnation has at its roots not only social ignorance, but a philosophically active anti-feminist dogma."[93] This theme is recapitulated in her letter to *One*, in which she also links the oppression of homosexuality to the oppression of women. "The relationship of anti-homosexual sentiment to the oppression of women has a special and deep implication. That is to say, that it must be clear that the reason for the double standard of social valuation is rooted in the societal contempt for the estate of womanhood in the first place. Everywhere the homosexual male is, in one way or another, seen as tantamount to the criminal for his deviation; and the woman homosexual as naughty, neurotic, adventurous, titillating, wicked or rebellious for hers."[94]

Not all black lesbian scholars, however, agree that lesbian sexuality is privileged over gay male sexuality "everywhere"—particularly in black communities. Ann Allen Shockley, for example, describes the special hostility directed toward black lesbians in the black community during the 1960s and earlier. "Combining with the stereotypical concepts and Black male power thrust of the 1960s was the sexism displayed by non-Lesbian Black females toward their Black Lesbian sisters. 'Fags' to

Black women are cute, entertaining, safe, and above all tolerated. Males are expected to venture sexually from the norm."[95] Although she is careful to contest the idea that black communities are more homophobic than other communities, hooks echoes Shockley: "In the particular black community where I was raised there was a real double standard. Black male homosexuals were often known, were talked about, were seen positively, and played important roles in community life, whereas lesbians were talked about solely in negative terms, and the women identified as lesbians were usually married. Often acceptance of male homosexuality was mediated by material privilege. . . . They were influential people in the community. This was not the case with any women."[96]

This point is echoed by Garber, who writes that during the Harlem Renaissance, "For Black lesbians, whose social options were more limited that those of their male counterparts, the support offered by the black entertainment world for nontraditional lifestyles was especially important."[97] Although each of these writers shares with Hansberry the interstitial connection of sexism to lesbian experience, the differences between Hansberry's and these other analyses raise questions both about Hansberry's experiences with gay and lesbian communities of color as well as her imagined audiences of the *Ladder* and *One*.

Hansberry's letter ends with a caveat that is also an indirect solicitation for dialogue. "But that is but a kernel of a speculative embryonic idea improperly introduced here." It is as though the dialogic form that serves as the underlying structure of Hansberry's dramatic writing is also central to her correspondence to the *Ladder.* For whatever reason, however, the August letter was Hansberry's last to the *Ladder,* and her 1961 *One* letter was never mailed. Hansberry never again publicly returned to issues of sexuality and sexism, focusing her remaining time and energy instead on the increasingly pressing battles against racism.

Conclusion

To deepen our understanding of the significance of Hansberry's letters to the *Ladder,* I have engaged in an intertextual reading of Hansberry's work within both her own textual context and the historical context of the period. Though perhaps unusual in blending literary texts and political discourse, the study offers a first step toward what Thompson describes as "queering" the discipline.[98] Morris, for example, writes, "Against the reasonable objection that such a 'literary' case study falls beyond the disciplinary pale of critical practice, I submit that recognizing and understanding various and complex responses to homophobic oppression which predate the Stonewall revolution often require critics, by necessity, to explore unorthodox texts."[99]

In addition, this chapter also attempts to resist one of the commonly received narratives about Hansberry articulated in both African American and lesbian and

gay contexts—that she was an assimilationist playwright of little political importance except biographically (that is, as an African American lesbian). As I have tried
to show in my analysis, this shortsighted narrative demands reinterpretation if not
outright contestation. A careful reading of her work in its historical context, as well
as in the context of her entire corpus of writing, reveals Hansberry as a writer
whose acumen and breadth clearly distinguish her as one of the foremost public
intellectuals of her time. Moreover, in the context of queer studies of public
address, Hansberry's contributions to the *Ladder* exemplify a distinctive and frequently omitted perspective in contemporary debates over race, gender, and sexuality.

The point of this chapter, however, is not to celebrate Hansberry as a heroic individual figure cut from the cloth of "great man" historiography. Critical historiography has rightly challenged the kind of rhetorical history that does no more than
celebrate status quo assumptions and ideologies, particularly those of heroic individualism. Yet at the same time black women's voices, particularly black lesbian
voices, still have yet to receive the critical attention and recognition their contributions warrant. It is long past time that we, scholars of public address, remedy that
omission. As Gomez writes, "As a Black woman, a writer, and a lesbian-feminist, I
need Lorraine Hansberry so that her brilliant vision lights my path. . . . She has
lately become an insurgent again, inside of me."[100] Thus studying the contributions
of black lesbian voices such as Hansberry's does not merely replicate the simplistic
formulations of liberal individualism that serve to valorize mythic individuals who
flourish without regard to context, community, or contest. In fact, critical interrogations of marginalized rhetors will in the end serve to contest such easy and reductive celebrations. As Nestle writes about African American lesbian Mabel Hampton,
"Ms. Hampton's lesbian history is embedded in the history of race and class in this
country; she makes us extend our historical perspective until she is at its center. The
focus then is not lesbian history, but lesbians in history."[101]

Thus, while valuable, the contributions of critical historiography that appropri-
ately destabilize notions of the mythic individual are misappropriated when used
to further erase or silence the contributions of marginalized speakers. Similarly, critiques of identity politics fail us when they are used to foreclose inquiry into the
rhetorical formation and historical production of queer discourse, despite the myriad theoretical problematics of the category "queer." For example, in discussing the
dual tensions between the political necessity of recognizing and articulating the
lived materiality of queer experience on the one hand, and the insufficiency of
identity categories such as "queer" on the other, Judith Butler asks us "to affirm the
contingency of the term [queer] so that it can become a discursive site whose uses
are not fully constrained in advance."[102] To affirm the contingency of the term "lesbian" in this case would be to recognize the complexity of Hansberry's historicity

as both a rhetor witnessing political persecution and as a person of history experiencing it. Further, affirming the contingency of Hansberry's *Ladder* letters means reading Hansberry the way she read the world—from a historically grounded intersectional perspective that denies no question its due.

Notes

1. See Charles E. Morris III, "Contextual Twilight/Critical Liminality: J. M. Barrie's *Courage* at St. Andrews, 1922," *Quarterly Journal of Speech* 82 (1996): 207–27; Morris, "'The Responsibilities of the Critic': F. O. Matthiessen's Homosexual Palimpsest," *Quarterly Journal of Speech* 84 (1998): 261–82.

2. Sharon DeLano, "An Interview with Barbara Grier," *Christopher Street* (October 1976), 41–46. In the interview, Grier states, "We got a lot of early work from writers who went on to be very well known. . . . we had work from Muriel Spark, Lorraine Hansberry."

3. Jonathan Katz, *Gay American History: Lesbians and Gay Men in the U.S.A.* (New York: Thomas Y. Crowell, 1976), 425.

4. Adrienne Rich, "The Problem with Lorraine Hansberry," *Freedomways* 19 (fourth quarter 1979): 247–55.

5. One important exception is Barbara Smith's introductory essay to the 1983 *Home Girls*, which quotes from one of the letters as a means to critique what she calls "anti-feminist myths." Smith writes, "I would like a lot more people to be aware that Lorraine Hansberry, one of our most respected artists and thinkers, was asking in a Lesbian context some of the same questions we are asking today, and for which we have been so maligned." Barbara Smith, introduction to *Home Girls: A Black Feminist Anthology*, ed. Smith (New York: Kitchen Table, Women of Color Press, 1983), xxxi.

6. Stuart Hall, "Cultural Identity and Cultural Diaspora," in *Colonial Discourse and Post-Colonial Theory: A Reader*, ed. Patrick Williams and Laura Chrisman (New York: Columbia University Press, 1994).

7. Scott Bravmann, *Queer Fictions of the Past: History, Culture, and Difference* (Cambridge: Cambridge University Press, 1997), 23.

8. According to Elise Harris, Hansberry had several affairs with women in New York in the late 1950s and early 1960s, the longest with a woman named Dorothy Secules, a secretary who lived in Hansberry's building in Greenwich Village. Elise Harris, "The Double Life of Lorraine Hansberry," *Out* (September 1999): 96–101, 174–75.

9. An intriguing but unexplored acknowledgment of this is offered in a critical analysis of Hansberry's drama that quotes Robert Nemiroff stating that "Hansberry's 'homosexuality' was not a peripheral or casual part of her life but contributed significantly on many levels to the sensitivity and complexity of her view of human beings and of the world." Steven R. Carter, *Hansberry's Drama: Commitment amid Complexity* (Ubana: University of Illinois Press, 1991), 6.

10. Morris, "'The Responsibilities of the Critic,'" 263.

11. This radical black feminist statement reads, "The most general statement of our politics at the present time would be that we are actively committed to struggling against racial, sexual, heterosexual, and class oppression and see as our particular task the development of

integrated analysis and practice based upon the fact that the major systems of oppression are interlocking." Combahee River Collective. "A Black Feminist Statement," in *This Bridge Called My Back: Writings by Radical Women of Color*, ed. Cherríe Moraga and Gloria Anzaldúa (Watertown, Mass.: Persephone Press, 1981), 210.

12. The case, *Hansberry v. Lee* (311 U.S. 32), was upheld by the U.S. Supreme Court.

13. Julius Lester, introduction to *Les Blancs: The Collected Last Plays of Lorraine Hansberry*, ed. Robert Nemiroff (New York: Random House, 1972), 3.

14. James Baldwin, "Lorraine Hansberry at the Summit," *Freedomways* 19 (1979): 272.

15. Despite the fact that he does not name her, West's phrasing aptly describes Hansberry's work. Cornel West, *Race Matters* (New York: Vintage, 1994), 48.

16. This quote was omitted from the published version but is contained in Abrams's notes held in the Lesbian Herstory Archives, Brooklyn, New York. Doris Abrams, notes for "Lorraine Hansberry," in *Notable American Women, The Modern Period*, ed. Barbara Sicherman et al. (Cambridge, Mass.: Belknap Press of Harvard University Press, 1980), 310–12.

17. Jewelle L. Gomez, "Lorraine Hansberry: Uncommon Warrior," in *Reading Black, Reading Feminist*, ed. Henry Louis Gates, Jr. (New York: Meridian Book, 1990), 314.

18. Amiri Baraka, "A Critical Reevaluation: *A Raisin in the Sun*'s Enduring Passion," in *A Raisin in the Sun and The Sign in Sidney Brustein's Window*, ed. Robert Nemiroff (New York: Vintage, 1990), 10.

19. Barbara Smith, "Toward a Black Feminist Criticism," in *Black Feminist Cultural Criticism*, ed. Jacqueline Bobo (Malden, Mass.: Blackwell, 2001), 6–23.

20. Cheryl Clarke, "The Failure to Transform: Homophobia in the Black Community," in *Dangerous Liaisons*, ed. Eric Brandt (New York: New Press, 2000), 38. See also Clarke, "Lesbianism: An Act of Resistance," in *This Bridge Called My Back: Writings by Radical Women of Color*, ed. Moraga and Anzaldúa, 128–37. In fact, hooks mentions Hansberry twice in her 1981 *Ain't I a Woman*, but, as Clarke notes, she fails to mention lesbian subjects or subjectivity anywhere in the book. bell hooks, *Ain't I a Woman: Black Women and Feminism* (Boston: South End Press, 1981). This omission is corrected in a later book, where hooks not only critiques homophobia in black communities, but also describes a double standard that often valued male homosexuals while deriding lesbians. bell hooks, *Talking Back: Thinking Feminist, Thinking Black* (Boston: South End Press, 1989).

21. "Dat man ober dar say dat womin needs to be helped into carriages and lifted ober ditches, and to hab de best place everywhar. Nobody ever helps me into carriages, or ober mud puddles, or gibs me any best place! And a'n't I a woman." Sojourner Truth, "A'n't I a Woman?" in *Let Nobody Turn Us Around: Voices of Resistance, Reform, and Renewal*, ed. Manning Marable and Leith Mullings (Lanham, Md.: Rowman and Littlefield, 2000), 67–68. Barbara Smith, *Home Girls*. Kimberlé Crenshaw, "Mapping the Margins: Intersectionality, Identity Politics, and Violence against Women of Color," in *Critical Race Theory: The Key Writings That Formed the Movement*, ed. Crenshaw, Neil Gotanda, Garry Peller, and Kendall Thomas (New York: New Press, 1995), 357–83.

22. Smith, *Home Girls*, xxxii.

23. Patricia Hill Collins, *Fighting Words: Black Women and the Search for Justice* (Minneapolis: University of Minnesota Press, 1998), 205.

24. Lorraine Hansberry, *To Be Young, Gifted, and Black*, ed. Robert Nemiroff (New York: Vintage, 1995), 79.

25. Lorraine Hansberry, *The Movement: Documentary of a Struggle for Equality* (New York: Simon and Schuster, 1964), 68.

26. Ibid, 13.

27. For example, in an essay published in the *Village Voice* in 1959 she wrote, "For in the minds of many, Walter remains, despite the play, despite performance, what American racial traditions *wish* him to be: an exotic. Some writers have been astonishingly incapable of discussing his purely *class* aspirations and have persistently confounded them with what they consider an exotic being's longing to 'wheel and deal' in what they further consider to be (and what Walter never can) 'the white man's world.'" Lorraine Hansberry, "An Author's Reflections: Willy Loman, Walter Younger, and He Who Must Live," in *Women in Theatre: Compassion and Hope*, ed. Karen Malpede (New York: Limelight Editions, 1985), 167.

28. Lorraine Hansberry, "The Negro Writer and His Roots: Toward a New Romanticism," *Black Scholar* 10 (March–April 1981): 4 (originally presented to a major black writers conference convened by the American Society of African Culture on March 1, 1959).

29. Ibid., 4.

30. Ibid.,10.

31. Hansberry's letter is published without a date, but it is addressed to a Mr. Ashworth. Hansberry, *To Be Young, Gifted, and Black*, 119.

32. Hansberry, "The Negro Writer and His Roots," 3.

33. Eric Garber, "A Spectacle in Color: The Lesbian and Gay Subculture of Jazz Age Harlem," in *Hidden from History: Reclaiming the Gay and Lesbian Past*, ed. Martin Bauml Duberman, Martha Vicinus, and George Chauncey, Jr. (New York: New American Library, 1989), 318–31.

34. Lillian Faderman, *Odd Girls and Twilight Lovers: A History of Lesbian Life in Twentieth Century America* (New York: Penguin, 1991), 157.

35. John D'Emilio, *Sexual Politics, Sexual Communities: The Making of a Homosexual Minority in the United States, 1940–1970* (Chicago: University of Chicago Press, 1983), 44.

36. Ibid., 49–50.

37. See, for example, Nancy Fraser, "Rethinking the Public Sphere: A Contribution to the Critique of Actually Existing Democracy," in *Habermas and the Public Sphere*, ed. Craig Calhoun (Cambridge, Mass.: MIT Press, 1994), 109–42; Robert Asen and Daniel C. Brouwer, *Counterpublics and the State* (Albany: SUNY Press, 2001); Michael Warner, *Publics and Counterpublics* (New York: Zone Books, 2002).

38. The *Ladder* (October 1956): 2. The founders of DOB took the organization's name from the title of a fictitious ancient Greek lesbian love poem written by Pierre Louys in 1894.

39. In 1947, however, a woman using the anagrammatic pen name Lisa Ben self-published a monthly magazine called *Vice Versa*, which was then passed from hand to hand. The magazine ceased publication after nine issues. See the *Ladder* (December 1956): 5.

40. Alisa Klinger, "Writing Civil Rights: The Political Aspirations of Lesbian Activist-Writers," in *Inventing Lesbian Cultures in America*, ed. Ellen Lewin (Boston: Beacon Press, 1996), 69.

41. Sten Russell, "The Searchers Probe 'The Homosexual Neurosis,'" *Ladder* (March 1957): 14.

42. "San Francisco Police Raid Reveals Lack of Knowledge of Citizen's Rights," *Ladder* (November 1956): 5.

43. Faderman, *Odd Girls and Twilight Lovers*, 180.

44. "Job Hunting Doesn't Need to Be a Problem," *Ladder* (March 1957): 5.

45. "The ACLU Takes a Stand on Homosexuality," *Ladder* (March 1957): 8. As mentioned above, however, DOB did take some moderately progressive political positions. For example, in the June 1957 issue the *Ladder* published an editorial supporting *One*'s Supreme Court case defending its right to publish, and DOB encouraged readers to contribute as much money as possible to the suit.

46. Del Griffin, "President's Message," *Ladder* (January 1957): 9.

47. Madeline Davis and Elizabeth Lapovsky Kennedy, "Oral History and the Study of Sexuality in the Lesbian Community: Buffalo, New York, 1940–1960," in *Hidden from History*, ed. Duberman, Vicinus, and Chauncey, 427.

48. See Davis and Kennedy, "Oral History"; Faderman, *Odd Girls and Twilight Lovers*; and Rochella Thorpe, "'A House Where Queers Go': African-American Nightlife in Detroit, 1940–1975," in *Inventing Lesbian Cultures in America*, ed. Lewin, 40–61.

49. Audre Lorde, *Zami: A New Spelling of My Name* (Freedom, Calif.: Crossing Press, 1982), 180.

50. Thorpe, "'A House Where Queers Go,'" 41.

51. Lorraine Hansberry, "On Strindberg and Sexism," in *Women in Theatre*, ed. Karen Malpede (New York: Limelight Editions, 1985) (originally published as a letter to the *Village Voice* in February 1956).

52. Robert P. Fulkerson, "The Public Letter as a Rhetorical Form: Structure, Logic, and Style in King's 'Letter from Birmingham Jail,'" *Quarterly Journal of Speech* 65 (1979): 121–36.

53. "To understand the letter and thus the debate between Chavez and the growers, it is crucial to understand the rhetorical history of Mexican Americans, of the public letter and other written documents as a rhetorical form of historical significance for those of Mexican descent, and of the discourse and person of Cesar Chavez." John C. Hammerback and Richard J. Jensen, "History and Culture as Rhetorical Constraints: Cesar Chavez's Letter from Delano," in *Doing Rhetorical History: Concepts and Cases*, ed. Kathleen J. Turner (Tuscaloosa: University of Alabama Press, 1998), 208.

54. Lorraine Hansberry, "Readers Respond," *Ladder* (May 1957): 26–28.

55. Lorraine Hansberry, "The Black Revolution and the White Backlash," in *Black Protest: History, Documents and Analyses: 1619 to the Present*, ed. Joanne Grant (New York: Fawcett, 1968), 447 (originally delivered as part of a forum sponsored by the Association of Artists for Freedom at Town Hall, New York, June 15, 1964).

56. Hansberry, *The Movement*, 48.

57. Lorraine Hansberry, *A Raisin in the Sun* (New York: Vintage, 1995), 133–34.

58. Lorraine Hansberry, *Les Blancs* (New York: Random House, 1972), 121.

59. West, *Race Matters*, 39–42.

60. Hansberry, *Ladder* (May 1957): 26.

61. Lorraine Hansberry, "In Defense of the Equality of Men," in *The Norton Anthology of Literature by Women*, ed. Sandra M. Gilbert and Susan Gubar (New York: Norton, 1985), 2062. Was this ironic title inspired by Wollstonecraft's first and initially most famous book, *A*

Vindication of the Rights of Men? Hansberry's essay contains an ironic exposition on the ways sexism presupposes "that men are in reality inferior human beings who have to be 'propped up.'" Elsewhere Hansberry mentions both William Godwin and Mary Wollstonecraft, though not the text in question.

62. Lorraine Hansberry, "Make New Sounds: Studs Terkel Interviews Lorraine Hansberry," *American Theatre* (November 1984): 6 (the article is a transcript of a radio show that originally aired in Chicago, May 12, 1959).

63. D'Emilio, *Sexual Politics, Sexual Communities,* 9.

64. Del Griffin, "President's Message," *Ladder* (November 1956): 2.

65. Ibid., 3.

66. Davis and Kennedy, "Oral History," 428.

67. Faderman, *Odd Girls and Twilight Lovers,* 178.

68. See Joan Nestle, "Butch-Femme Relationships: Sexual Courage in the 1950s," in *Lesbian Culture: An Anthology,* ed. Julia Penelope and Susan Wolfe (Freedom, Calif.: Crossing Press, 1993); Neil Miller, *Out of the Past: Gay and Lesbian History from 1869 to the Present* (New York: Vintage, 1995).

69. Hansberry, *Ladder* (May 1957): 27.

70. Ralph Bunche, scholar, activist, Africanist, and world statesman, was awarded the Nobel Peace Prize in 1950 for his United Nations mediation work, which led to armistice agreements in the Middle East. Bunche was the first black person to be awarded a Nobel Peace Prize. Benjamin Rivlin, *Ralph Bunche: The Man and His Times* (New York: Holmes and Meier, 1990).

71. Hansberry, *Ladder* (May 1957): 27.

72. Bayard Rustin, John Lewis, Paul Robeson, and Josephine Baker are a few that come to mind. See John D'Emilio, "Homophobia and the Trajectory of Postwar American Radicalism: The Career of Bayard Rustin," in *Modern American Queer History,* ed. Allida M. Black (Philadelphia: Temple University Press, 2001). Neil Miller also describes some of the tensions around Rustin's homosexuality in the civil rights movement. Miller, *Out of the Past,* 360–62. Garth Pauley describes how concessions to pragmatism led to the revision of John Lewis's historic speech. See Garth E. Pauley, "John Lewis's 'Serious Revolution': Rhetoric, Resistance, and Revision at the March on Washington," *Quarterly Journal of Speech* 84 (August 1998): 320–40. For a thorough explication of these issues, see Mary L. Dudziak, *Cold War Civil Rights: Race and the Image of American Democracy* (Princeton, N.J.: Princeton University Press, 2000).

73. Lesbian Herstory Archives, "Oral History of Daughters of Bilitis: Glass, Revised DOB Script, 10/9/95," 13.

74. Del Martin and Phyllis Lyon, *Lesbian/Woman* (San Francisco: Glide, 1972), 122.

75. Marion Zimmer Bradley, "Readers Respond," *Ladder* (May 1957): 21.

76. Lorraine Hansberry, "Unpublished Letter to *One,*" in Carter, *Hansberry's Drama,* 6.

77. Lorraine Hansberry, *The Sign in Sidney Brustein's Window* (New York: Samuel French, 1965), 57.

78. Miller, *Out of the Past,* 331

79. For example, Stephens lists the uses of transvestism as a "barrier against possible sexual assault" and "the rejection of the 'super-sex cult'. . . . In this day of the glorified pin-up girl

there are some who would rather be rated on their character and intellect than on hypertrophied anatomy." Barbara Stephens, "Transvestism: A Cross-Cultural Survey," *Ladder* (June 1957): 10–14. Stephens's political analysis of nonconforming women's dress was supported by two subsequent letters published in July—one of which stated, "We consider dresses, high heels and stocking holders the most uncomfortable contraptions men have invented to restrict the movements of women so they cannot walk very far, lift many things, or sit with their legs apart in warm weather" (A.C., N.Y., N.Y., "Readers Respond," *Ladder* [July 1957]: 28). Another writer critiqued dress conformity in the lesbian community from a different perspective: "The cult of conformity itself remains to be questioned. . . . Those who depart from the rules are punished for the 'crime' of not behaving like a typical Negro, professional worker, or feminine woman. The homosexual world is as guilty as the rest, when they would confer the straitjacket of 'Butchhood' upon its embryo members" (B.S., San Leandro, "Readers Respond," *Ladder* [July 1957]: 29).

80. Stephens, "Transvestism," 13.

81. Marion Zimmer Bradley, "Some Remarks on Marriage," *Ladder* [July 1957]: 14.

82. Ibid., 15.

83. Lorraine Hansberry, "Readers Respond," *Ladder* [August 1957]: 27.

84. Ibid., 28.

85. Hansberry was apparently influenced by *The Second Sex* and left at her death an unpublished essay on Simone de Beauvoir. Lorraine Hansberry, "Simone De Beauvoir and *The Second Sex:* An American Commentary," in *Words of Fire: An Anthology of African American Feminist Thought*, ed. Beverly Guy-Sheftall (New York: New Press, 1995), 128–42.

86. Hansberry, *The Sign in Sidney Brustein's Window*, 84.

87. Ibid., 106.

88. Hansberry, *Ladder* (August 1957): 30.

89. Ibid., 29.

90. Stephen Howard Browne, *Angelina Grimké: Rhetoric, Identity, and the Rhetorical Imagination* (East Lansing: Michigan State University Press, 1999), 108.

91. Hansberry, "The Negro Writer and His Roots," 11.

92. Hansberry, "Make New Sounds," 6.

93. Hansberry, *Ladder* (August 1957): 30.

94. Quoted in Carter, *Hansberry's Drama*, 6–7.

95. Ann Allen Shockley, "The Black Lesbian in American Literature: An Overview," in *Home Girls*, ed. Smith, 85.

96. hooks, *Talking Back*, 121.

97. Garber, "A Spectacle in Color," 325. Also see Gregory Conerly, "Swishing and Swaggering: Homosexuals in Black Magazines during the 1950s," in *The Greatest Taboo: Homosexuality in Black Communities*, ed. Delroy Constantine-Simms (Los Angeles: Alyson, 2001), 384–94. Conerly documents the qualified acceptance of black homosexuals and intolerance of black lesbianism in the magazines *Ebony* and *Jet* in the 1950s.

98. Julie Thompson, "On the Development of Counter-Racist Quare Public Address Studies," present volume.

99. Morris, "'The Responsibilities of the Critic,'" 279

100. Gomez, "Lorraine Hansberry: Uncommon Warrior," 316.

101. Joan Nestle, "I Lift My Eyes to the Hill: The Life of Mabel Hampton as Told by a White Woman," in *Queer Representations*, ed. Martin Duberman (New York: NYU Press, 1997), 258–75.

102. Judith Butler, *Bodies That Matter* (New York: Routledge, 1993), 230.

Traumatic Styles in Public Address

Audre Lorde's Discourse as Exemplar

Lester C. Olson

Of what I move
toward and through
and what I need
to leave behind me
for most of all I am
blessed within my selves
who are come to make our shattered faces
whole.

Audre Lorde, "Outside,"
The Collected Poems of Audre Lorde

This chapter identifies salient features of what I am tentatively characterizing as traumatic styles in American public address. One such feature consists of advocates' remarks concerning shattered illusions of invulnerability after fundamental assumptions about safety, trust, and communal life have disintegrated during an ordeal. Another feature is the rhetorical immediacy in advocates' narrative depictions of past traumatic experiences as abiding timelessly in the present such that their vivid memories are located outside of ordinary narrative time. In addition, certain characteristic emotive dynamics suffuse the public discourse, oscillating among numbness, disbelief, fear, anger, and rage. Another recurrent element of the styles is the advocates' calls for vigilance in coping with the hatred of oppressive adversaries and betrayals by similarly situated people seeking to survive. Finally, advocates typically depict a dichotomous and polarizing moral view of the world while seeking the support of onlookers in a dramatic struggle between rival groups, often portrayed as an agonistic struggle between good and evil. Taken together, I will argue, these characteristics constitute the synthetic core of highly variable traumatic styles.

For the purposes of the chapter, rhetorical style will be understood not simply as word choice and sentence structure, but rather as a distinctive way of holding and advocating beliefs in public discourse. By referring to this sense of style, I have in mind Richard Hofstadter's scholarship on the "paranoid style," which he claimed was a recurrent, pervasive pattern of advocacy in American political life. Referring to style, he said, "It is, above all, a way of seeing the world and of expressing oneself."[1] Like Hofstadter, I am not diagnosing an individual's psychology, but rather identifying a typical mode of advocacy in public discourse. I am less concerned with exploring an individual's sensibility than I am with examining recurrent public manifestations of traumatic styles in advocates' attempts to persuade participants in public forums.[2] Traumatic styles recur in speeches, essays, and even poems addressed to audiences to influence beliefs and actions. But unlike Hofstadter, who frankly admitted that he intended his naming of the paranoid style to be pejorative,[3] I would instead call for a critical attitude of compassionate understanding for the human frailties evidenced by public discourses depicting unspeakable experiences.

Since Hofstadter's widely influential 1968 essay, style has been explored as a sensibility in terms of rhetoric and politics. In 1978, for instance, Edwin Black explored what he called the "sentimental style" employed by Daniel Webster, whose public speeches endeavored to instruct audiences concerning what they should feel about his ideas even as he conveyed them. Black observed, "What I want most to note about this style is the detail with which it shapes one's response. No scintilla of reaction is left for the auditor's own creation. Every nuance of his response is suggested by the speech."[4] More recently, Robert Hariman's award-winning 1995 book, *Political Style: The Artistry of Power*, has identified and analyzed what he calls realist, courtly, republican, and bureaucratic political styles employed by four powerful figures, all men who exerted considerable influence extending beyond their lifetimes: Machiavelli, Kapuściński, Cicero, and Kafka.[5] Both explorations of style have concentrated on the sensibilities of privileged and powerful men to the exclusion of vulnerable populations of the varieties that Audre Lorde embodied as a black, lesbian, feminist, socialist, and mother. By shifting the critic's focus to center attention on political advocates who, like Lorde, spoke from relatively vulnerable political positions, this chapter will complement the previous scholarship concerning powerful men's style, while calling awareness to limitations that may result from generalizing about style from speeches only by the powerful and privileged.

In the process, this chapter's shift of focus to the styles of relatively vulnerable populations entails attention to a wealth of typically omitted or peripheral concepts in previous explorations of style, concepts that are nonetheless useful for a critic's analysis of traumatic styles. Such concepts include silence and silencing, discursive amnesia and public memory loss, symbolic matrices and intersectionality, identification and essentialism, symbolic fragmentation and appropriation, double and multiple consciousness, marginality and centrality, embodiment, performatives, and enactment, complicity or collusion, and double binds, paradoxes, and quandaries. Because these concepts have been neglected or omitted altogether from earlier treatments of style, this essay suggests that studies of rhetoric could be significantly enriched both conceptually and substantively by attention to traumatic styles and, more generally, by meaningful engagement with the speeches of politically vulnerable populations.

This chapter concentrates on identifying the recurring, synthetic features of traumatic styles in the complex rhetorical processes of advocates and listeners. The first section provides a general orientation to traumatic styles. The sections that follow then detail the public advocates' unspeakable speech, the audiences' experiences of unlistenable speech, and rhetorical depictions of recovery, reintegration, and communal healing through political actions both for advocates and their audiences. Throughout I will draw on excerpts from several of Lorde's public speeches, essays, and poems to illustrate salient features of traumatic styles and to suggest how her discourse tends on the whole to evince these styles, though she emphatically placed recovery, empowerment, and political engagement in the foreground. Lorde's public speeches and essays exemplify what biographer Elaine Maria Upton called "an intense engagement with modern urban traumas, with racism, wars, poverty, and political and social injustice throughout the world."[6] This chapter contributes to the scholarly literature in rhetoric and public address by identifying features of traumatic styles and by providing a sustained examination of several discourses by an important black, lesbian, feminist, mother, poet, and speaker who was reflexive and explicit about the liabilities and possibilities of her rhetorical style.

"Audre Lorde lived two lives," her authorized biographer, Alexis De Veaux, observed in the opening sentence of the biography *Warrior Poet*. Lorde was diagnosed with breast cancer in 1978, shortly after her speech concerning "The Uses of the Erotic." She had a mastectomy, a profoundly life-altering experience for her, evidenced throughout her subsequent discourse. Envisioning herself not as a victim suffering but as a warrior battling her condition, she drew on images of the Amazons of Dahomey, one-breasted women warriors, in her writings. Eventually, however, she was diagnosed with liver cancer, treatments for which she traveled in 1984 to Germany, where she gave poetry readings and interviews. De Veaux claimed, "Lorde's second life began after she was diagnosed with breast cancer and underwent a mastectomy in 1978."[7] Only one year before that, shortly after Lorde had been diagnosed at the time with a benign tumor, she began a fifteen-year career as a prominent public speaker. During this period of her second life, she addressed the topics of age, race, sex, sexuality, and economic class in a wide range of forums and publication outlets. Themes in her numerous speeches include silence and silencing; the habitual complicity of subordinated peoples with dominant groups; being an outsider as a position of both vulnerability and strength; the erotic as distinct from the pornographic in human relationships as well as commercial products; difference and anger as resources for collaboration and social change rather than divisiveness, capricious bias, and hatred; and survival in a hostile society. In general, her speeches, essays, and interviews are difficult for most readers and listeners because she dealt with sensitive and taboo topics ranging from rape, sexual assault, and pornography to harassment, various bias crimes, and other forms of abuse and violence.

Consequently Lorde is well known for her contributions to the women's movement during the 1970s and 1980s, especially her courageous struggle with breast cancer as recorded in her *Cancer Journals*, which were published in 1980. Her reputation among feminists and women's studies scholars continues to grow such that her photographic image has become an icon designating a strand of feminist thought devoted to equity across multiple differences among people. Lesbian, transgender, and queer communities have likewise taken increased interest in Lorde over the years, sometimes coupling her image as a warrior against breast cancer with images of gay men battling the AIDS pandemic, at other times evoking her maxim "Your silence will not protect you" to counter the closeting of same-sexuality. Entire organizations have been named for her or her writings, as exemplified by health and community centers bearing her name in San Francisco and New York. *Zami*, the title of her "biomythography," is also the name of a center for black lesbians located in Atlanta, Georgia. Even so, Lorde's socialism, sex, and race have been factors diminishing her appeal to socially and economically conservative gay men and lesbians. Her critical reception has been as diverse as the extraordinary range of audiences she addressed, opinions ranging from heartfelt hostility to deep appreciation and gratitude for her work.

An Orientation to Traumatic Styles

To characterize traumatic styles, I have referred to the plural "styles" rather than the singular "style" for several reasons. First, there are doubtless variations and changes in traumatic styles over time and place, as well as diverse patterns of socialization and histories of specific social groups or communities. In the case of some public advocates, such as rape survivor Andrea Dworkin,[8] black feminist Angela Davis,[9] and Jewish Hungarian survivor of the German Holocaust Elie Wiesel,[10] traumatic styles characterize many public pronouncements. In other cases, such as Oscar Wilde in *De Profundis*, an exemplar that emerged late in his life, the style marked a fundamental change in the Irish playwright's public voice after his ordeal during three trials and his imprisonment by the British government.[11] As the examples of Wiesel and Wilde suggest, traumatic styles are not limited only to American public discourse, however much cultural factors may vary it elsewhere. Few, if any, traumas rise to the proportions of the Holocaust, but individuals and groups experience recurrent, significant ordeals nonetheless. In addition, a plural reference to "styles" is warranted in that the discourse may be inflected differently by advocates depicting recovery than for those portraying recent injuries. Beyond this, the naming of a type, even if accurate for several advocates, can easily become a stereotype. This use of a type as a stereotype may be resisted, in part, by pluralizing the styles and differentiating within and across specific social groups.

It would be a serious blunder for rhetoric scholars to consider traumatic styles as merely a personal or psychological sensibility expressed in discourse, because such a characterization would deflect attention from a recurrent pattern of public address in a wide range of public forums and, more important, from the political, social, and economic practices that may discipline the styles into being. If traumatic styles are mistaken as only individual or psychological, attention may be diverted from minority communities' disproportionate experiences of homicide, physical assault, sexual violence, menacing, severe harassment, discrimination in housing, employment and services, and other overt acts literally using the bodies of those who are different to inscribe and to convey messages of contempt, hatred, and oppression. In addition, as others have suggested, psychiatry is an institution that has had a disgraceful history as an individuating, isolating, and silencing mechanism for disciplining and discrediting the voices of sexual minorities.[12] Recognizing traumatic styles as recurrent in public address has ramifications for professional critics' interpretations of such discourses and for other audiences, because listening to such discourse is arduous. Traumatic styles place atypical demands on audiences.

Exemplars of traumatic styles tend on the whole to be reactionary, confrontational, and adversarial, concerned as public advocates tend to be with agonistic conflict among entire categories of social groups across differences in sex, race, sexuality, economic class, religion, and the like. Advocates whose discourses exemplify traumatic styles typically oppose symbolic acts such as sustained and severe harassment, physical violence, and countless homicides disrupting lives within subordinated communities throughout the United States. Examples of such recurring experiences in American history range from chattel slavery, lynching, and racial harassment, to family violence, sexual harassment, and sexual assault, to the vicious, public displays of openly antigay and antilesbian hatred, homicide, and other violence toward queer communities. Consequently, traumatic styles are commonplace among the public discourses by gay men and lesbians, people of color, and women, for instance, simply because members of these social groups routinely cope with violent and dehumanizing ordeals and their legacies. But traumatic styles are certainly neither unique to nor characteristic of discourse by gay men and lesbians, recurring as traumatic styles do with varying content in the discourse of several communities. In certain historical moments traumatic styles have been ubiquitous in American public life.

Traumatic styles are not emblematic of any subordinated community. Instead traumatic styles represent points of fracture, chasms, within and laterally across various subordinated communities. Audiences ordinarily may experience traumatic rhetorical styles as unlistenable speech in part because of complexities that attend understanding experiences that are, at once, both individual and systemic. Audiences of the styles may simply refuse to listen, because they have the power or authority to do so. Or audiences may employ a complex and highly variable range of defensive ways of listening as a means to preserve their own illusions of invulnerability or false beliefs in a fundamentally just world. Examples of such defense mechanisms include caricaturing, infantilizing, or blaming the victims of traumatic experiences through an exaggerated and unrealistic assignment of the victims' responsibility for having had the experience. This cluster of defensive, symbolic practices is deeply rooted in myths of individualism in that they differentiate each targeted person's dubious decision making from those made by the rest of the group rather than recognize disproportionate risks to everyone within the group regardless of decisions made. At stake in refusing to listen or amplifying the victim's responsibilities for the harms that he or she has ostensibly brought onto himself or herself is each listener's heartfelt need for assurance that this ordeal or personal disaster cannot happen to him or her. Consequently, even though it may seem counterintuitive, blaming the victim can be especially pervasive among people similar to the targeted person or group because a commonplace desire for reassurance complicates listening to messages disrupting listeners' sense of safety and security. Additional challenges in listening result from the two commonplace distortions of either excessive identification or nonidentification with the harmed person or people. These patterns of distortion can result alternatively in falsely appropriating the injuries as one's own, or altogether discounting the experiences as too foreign to pertain to one's self.

Advocates exemplifying traumatic styles have made risky decisions in negotiating multiple double binds understood as lose-lose options.[13] For instance, depicting specific acts of victimization risks reproducing invidious stereotypes for entire groups as victims. At the same time, however, complicity in silence entails colluding with concealing the devastating harms, that disproportionately injure members of these groups. Whichever "choice" speakers and their audiences may make in response to unwelcome messages concerning yet another sexual assault, yet another violent act, yet another of the homicides affecting one of "us"—however "us" is understood—the decision entails significant losses. Hostile audience reactions likely come not only from those who dominate but also from those most at risk for similar harms, because of fear, listeners' faith that the right "choices" can reduce the risks of harms, and other factors sustaining the hearers' illusions of their own invulnerability or false faith in a fundamentally just world.

There reside yet additional double binds hidden beneath the first. There are, for instance, practical problems of political inexpediency. The acknowledgment of

victims and victimization may deflect attention from forward-looking agenda setting by members of subordinated communities. In addition, the public discourse
may strip people, who need some measure of personal agency, of the belief that
they possess the capacity to make any meaningful changes in society, especially if
the sources of the harms are deeply rooted in entire systems, as advocates sometimes suggest. This last bind may be buttressed by the quandaries posed in making
systemic claims about groups both collectively and as diverse individuals. There is
even a double bind in characterizing traumatic styles in this chapter, because attention to its features in discourse may deflect attention from the political, social, and
economic pathologies in the acts of extreme hatred that may contribute to some
targeted people's use of the styles. Consequently, in the predictable, ensuing acts of
silence and silencing, discursive amnesia and public memory loss, denial, dismissal,
devaluation of harms, and other seemingly endless varieties of vertical and horizontal hostility, to quote Audre Lorde's remark addressed to members of diverse subordinated communities, "we rob ourselves of ourselves and each other."[14]

Drastically divergent understandings of human fragility rooted in paradoxically
impersonal personal experience may become a crevasse separating speakers of traumatic styles from their audiences and complicating any meaningful communication
between them. Traumatic experiences may seem to be profoundly personal, especially when they result from having had an aspect of one's personhood targeted by
violent or dehumanizing others. But, on inspection, because the stereotypes and
myths actuating the hatred were pervasive in American life even before the targeted individual was born, the experiences are transparently impersonal. For some
practitioners of hatred, any member of the targeted group will do. Confronted with
this reality, audiences have an immense array of means for not listening, not heeding messages that, if comprehended and accepted, may call into question one's own
safety, one's own well being, one's own mortality. For audiences, ordinarily it is easier simply to forego the experience of listening to such discourse. As Carol Gilligan said concerning overt acts of sexism, "If you have power, you can opt not to
listen. And you do so with impunity."[15] Listening with empathy to traumatic styles
may be a profoundly transformative activity.[16] Let us turn next, then, to examine
synthetic elements, that, taken together, instantiate the styles: shattered illusions
of invulnerability, rhetorical immediacy in narrative time, abruptly fragmented
selves, emotive dynamics, vigilance, and a dichotomous symbolic world of agonistic struggle.

Unspeakable Speech

Traumatic experiences are unspeakable. As one consequence, at the outset, there is
a paradox. Some people do speak the unspeakable in public. In her landmark book
Trauma and Recovery, Judith Herman wrote, "The ordinary response to atrocities is
to banish them from consciousness. Certain violations of the social compact are too

terrible to utter aloud: this is the meaning of the word *unspeakable*." She added, "The conflict between the will to deny horrible events and the will to proclaim them aloud is the central dialectic of psychological trauma."[17] Conflicts between speech and silence, between declaration and denial, between recognition and invisibility permeate the rhetorical process, with quandaries for audiences as well as advocates. As a prominent black, lesbian, feminist, socialist poet and mother of two, Lorde belonged to several communities that deal routinely with dehumanization and violence.

Despite the distorting myths characterizing traumatic styles as self-indulgent, self-centered, or self-absorbed, advocates speak the unspeakable in public for an immense variety and range of reasons. Often the motivation is to ensure that the trauma does not repeat itself, that there are no additional targets of severe harassment, menacing, violence, or homicide.[18] Other times the speakers' goals are to transform entire political, social, and economic systems so that they become less supportive of perpetrators and more supportive of the victims, and generally, as Lorde once put it, to sustain "a world of possibility for us all."[19] Still other times, paradoxically, speakers remember in public precisely to forget, to be able to heal and to recover. The narrative recounting of traumatic experiences may locate them within an historic, narrative moment, an act that may enable survivors to place the events or deeds firmly into the past so as to move into the future. The speakers' objectives, however, are not always so honorable or oriented toward recovery. Some speakers seek revenge through publicly humiliating their victimizers. Others seek a public apology and acts of atonement from the perpetrators or those who aided and abetted the perpetrators. Still others seek compensation, not necessarily materialistic, for harms that can never adequately be compensated.[20] More often than not, the speakers' objectives can be multiple and shifting among a conflicted range of outcomes, some of which are improbable, if not impossible, to attain.

Shattered Illusions of Invulnerability

At the heart of traumatic styles is a symbolic world inhabited by victims, perpetrators, and bystanders, a world suffused with firsthand accounts usually from either the target or the witness of violence, terror, or extreme vulnerability and helplessness.[21] These advocates have few, if any, illusions of invulnerability, having had them shattered by lived experience: sometimes a single, overpowering moment; other times, an unending ordeal that day after day consumes the utmost energy. As Lorde observed in a 1977 speech to the Modern Language Association (MLA), "For to survive in the mouth of this dragon we call america, we have had to learn this first and most vital lesson—that we were never meant to survive."[22] Lorde's poem "A Litany for Survival" can be understood as addressed to "those of us who cannot indulge / the passing dreams of choice." She concluded that poem with insights concerning false choices among lose-lose options: "When we speak we are afraid / our words will not be heard / nor welcomed / but when we are silent / we are still afraid. / So it is better to speak / remembering / we were never meant to survive."[23] Elaine Upton observed that a "major theme of Lorde's writing is the theme of survival."[24]

Certainly, a great deal of the socialization of lesbians and gay men, like that of other sexual, racial, and religious minorities, has emphasized being extremely vulnerable to harm and dependent on others for support or protection. It is accurate to say that the illusions of invulnerability vary in some measure and, in specific cases, may reflect privilege in economic class, sex, race, sexuality, and the like, as well as confidence in individualism's myths, even among people who experience serious forms of discrimination. The substance of these illusions varies with the patterns of socialization and diverse histories of specific groups.[25]

Lorde regularly addressed the obstacles posed by her audience members' illusions of invulnerability. For instance, in a speech at Amherst College in April 1980, she generalized, "For white women there is a wider range of pretended choices and rewards for identifying with patriarchal power and its tools." Lorde amplified a few mechanisms that, despite the evidence, sustain the illusions: "Today, with the defeat of ERA, the tightening economy, and increased conservatism, it is easier once again for white women to believe the dangerous fantasy that if you are good enough, pretty enough, sweet enough, teach the children to behave, hate the right people, and marry the right men, then you will be allowed to co-exist with patriarchy in relative peace, at least until a man needs your job or the neighborhood rapist happens along." Focusing on race, she affirmed, "But Black women and our children know the fabric of our lives is stitched with violence and with hatred, that there is no rest. . . . For us, increasingly, violence weaves through the daily tissues of our living."[26]

Yet, despite the nation's history of chattel slavery, lynching, and assassinations of black leaders, the illusions surface in most minority communities, including black communities, buttressed as the illusions may be by individuating rhetorical processes such as blaming the victim.[27] This rhetorical process may help to preserve such illusions for some members of minority communities, since the harms seem to stem from each individual's failings, not a systemic situation facing the entire group. To circumvent such responses Lorde queried a predominantly black audience during Malcolm X Weekend at Harvard University in 1982: "Can any one of us here still afford to believe that efforts to reclaim the future can be private or individual?" She later asserted, "Nothing neutralizes creativity quicker than tokenism, that false sense of security fed by a myth of individual solutions."[28] Such comments suggest that Lorde recognized as problematic investments in individualism that sustained illusions of safety among black audiences.

Rhetorical Immediacy in Narrative Time
Survival may have been at stake during the traumatic experiences recollected with crystal clarity years later, perhaps even decades later, as though they had just

happened, here and now, in the present location and the present place. This rhetorical quality of timeless immediacy recurs again and again, season after season, year after year, because traumatic experience is located outside of ordinary narrative time, deeply embedded in the present. "Long after the danger is past, traumatized people relive the event as though it were continually recurring in the present," wrote Herman. She added, "It is as if time stops at the moment of trauma. The traumatic moment becomes encoded in an abnormal form of memory, which breaks spontaneously into consciousness, both as flashbacks during waking states and as traumatic nightmares during sleep."[29] In some cases, when the memory resulted from a single, highly dramatic event, the anniversary of it may become a time of vivid recollection.[30] Although almost all of Lorde's speeches depicted deplorable deeds, those deeds recurred in her rhetoric without reference to time and place, with few exceptions.[31] Lorde's public speeches are remarkably free of specific dates and locations for hostile actions, which recur timelessly again and again in the present moment.

With respect to public memory and narrative time, advocates whose rhetoric exemplifies traumatic styles may negotiate dilemmas while speaking the unspeakable in public. The act of speaking about ordeals necessarily entails reliving and reexperiencing by remembering the past yet again in the present, however anxious some advocates may be to place the experiences in the past. Yet silence may result in allowing perpetrators to prevail and persist in yet additional cases. Whichever "choice" advocates may make in negotiating the double bind, the decision will be attended by significant losses.

Lorde's decision was evident in the whole of her oeuvre. Elaine Upton remarked, "Along with the reality of cancer survival is the global challenge of survival in an ecologically degenerating world, and in a world of racism, sexism, and homophobia, as well as survival of the poor and of those who are abused in many ways. Lorde's poetry images forth a vast wreckage and wrenching concrete detail of racist, sexist, homophobic, and otherwise inhuman events."[32] Yet the range and complexity of the rhetorical obstacles to speech, exemplified by so many double binds, may place silence in the foreground for other people. Lorde regularly addressed that silence directly. For instance, she commented to the MLA, "I remind myself all the time now that if I were to have been born mute, or had maintained an oath of silence my whole life long for safety, I would still have suffered, and I would still die. It is very good for establishing perspective."[33]

Abruptly Fragmented Selves

In some cases, trauma results in what psychologists label "dissociation"—that is, the experience of seeming to move outside of one's own body, observing as it is acted on by another, a momentary severing of one's mind from one's own body. Although early research on trauma "viewed the capacity to disconnect mind from body as a merciful protection," such people are most likely to "relive in their bodies the moments of terror that they can not describe in words."[34] Consequently, characteristic of the traumatic styles are declarations concerning the processes of reintegrating a suddenly fragmented self "to make shattered faces whole," to quote Lorde's suggestively titled poem "Outside."[35]

These fracturing pressures may come from within communities where advocates may have expected to secure encouragement or support. Lorde remarked at Amherst College in 1980, "As a Black lesbian feminist comfortable with the many different ingredients of my identity, and a woman committed to racial and sexual freedom from oppression, I find I am constantly being encouraged to pluck out some one aspect of myself and present this as the meaningful whole, eclipsing or denying the other parts of self. But this is a destructive and fragmenting way to live." She emphasized, "My fullest concentration of energy is available to me only when I integrate all the parts of who I am, openly, allowing power from particular sources of my living to flow back and forth freely through all my different selves, without the restrictions of externally imposed definition."[36]

Double or multiple consciousness is a symbolic phenomenon in subordinated communities that may be related to seeing one's body from the outside as it is acted on by another, though both double and multiple consciousness certainly extend beyond the specifics of psychological dissociation. First articulated by W. E. B. Du Bois in *The Souls of Black Folks* (1907), the idea of "double consciousness" has been elaborated by many intellectuals from minority communities. "Double consciousness," as James Darsey noted, "implies a complexity of vision, the necessity for members of subordinate subcultures always to know the rules of the dominant culture as well as of their subculture."[37]

Accordingly, as a black person, Lorde needed to be familiar not only with how members of black communities represented themselves, but also how members of white communities represented them. As Lorde argued in an essay published by the *Black Scholar* in 1978, "For Black women as well as Black men, it is axiomatic that if we do not define ourselves for ourselves, we will be defined by others—for their use and to our detriment."[38] "Multiple consciousness" extends the idea of double consciousness by underscoring that, as a lesbian, Lorde needed to know the rules of dominating heterosexual and subordinated lesbian cultures. Moreover, as a woman, she needed to know the rules of dominating male and subordinated female cultures.[39] In "Who Said It Was Simple," Lorde wrote, "But I who am bound by my mirror / as well as my bed / see causes in colour / as well as sex / and sit here wondering / which me will survive / all these liberations."[40]

Emotive Dynamics

Some exemplars of traumatic styles are the result of natural disasters, such as earthquakes, tornadoes, or floods. Other times, the natural disaster can be located within an individual, as in a cancer diagnosis. This was in some respects the case for Lorde, whose *Cancer Journals* chronicled her experiences after an initial biopsy for a benign tumor and a subsequent biopsy for a malignant one. She inquired, "What is there possibly left for us to be afraid of, after we have dealt face to face with death and not embraced it? Once I accept the existence of dying as a life process, who can ever have power over me again?"[41] But when traumatic experiences have been the result of other people's deliberate deeds, as with Lorde's childhood and adult experiences,[42] speakers of traumatic styles have been forced to confront the human capacity for sadistic cruelty or for evil. Consequently, fundamental assumptions about living in community may have collapsed beneath the speakers' feet. Safety is only one casualty.[43] The capacity to feel may be another. Speakers of traumatic styles may oscillate among rage, anger, fear, disbelief, and numbness, "a world of flattened effect," to use Lorde's language.[44]

As for commonplace emotions of anger and rage that may suffuse manifestations of traumatic styles in public discourse,[45] speakers may depict these emotions as appropriate and perhaps even necessary resources, sharply distinguished from the hatred practiced by oppressive adversaries. In Lorde's speech to the National Women's Studies Association during 1981, for instance, she devoted the entire speech to "The Uses of Anger." She referred to "the anger of exclusion, of unquestioned privilege, of racial distortions, of silence, ill-use, stereotyping, defensiveness, misnaming, betrayal, and co-optation." In this speech, Lorde distinguished between the "hatred" of hostile people and women's legitimate "anger," which, she claimed, "are very different." She explained, "Hatred is the fury of those who do not share our goals, and its object is death and destruction. Anger is a grief of distortions between peers, and its object is change. . . . Every woman has a well-stocked arsenal of anger potentially useful against those oppressions, personal and institutional, which brought that anger into being. Focused with precision it can become a powerful source of energy serving progress and change."[46]

"Power" likewise concentrated on her experiences of anger and rage while seeking social justice. In a public comment about the poem, she acknowledged rage so intense that she needed to stop driving her car so that she would not run over the next white person she saw. She described her own furious response to an unjust verdict, which had just acquitted a police officer for his deliberate killing of a black youth while uttering the words, "Die you little motherfucker."[47] Lorde's poem confronted the insight that people who identify with the victims of hatred can experience hatred in reaction, however momentary. By doing so, such people may reproduce deplorable ways of relating across human differences. Upton commented, "One of the prominent feelings to which the reader must respond in Lorde's writing is anger and often rage."[48]

In a later essay initially published in an abbreviated form in *Essence* in October 1983, Lorde commented on the limitations of anger. Even while she affirmed that "sometimes it seems that anger alone keeps me alive; it burns with a bright and undiminished flame," she emphasized that "anger, like guilt, is an incomplete form of human knowledge." Perhaps this acknowledges that quandaries attend the uses of anger for audiences and for advocates in the rhetorical processes complicating traumatic styles.[49] To call awareness to a double bind that confronts advocates who express authentic emotions, Lorde elsewhere alluded to a white woman who remarked, "Tell me how you feel but don't say it too harshly or I cannot hear you." Lorde asked, "But is it my manner that keeps her from hearing, or the threat of a message that her life may change?"[50]

In exemplars of traumatic styles, speakers may depict relationships of trust that have been upended, as when members of vulnerable groups experience revictimization by failures in the criminal justice system.[51] Herman observed, "Traumatic events have primary effects not only on the psychological structures of the self but also on the systems of attachment and meaning that link individual and community. . . . Traumatized people feel utterly abandoned, utterly alone, cast out of the human and divine systems of care and protection."[52] Abandonment, betrayal, deceit, lies, and hypocrisy may appear normative to the speakers as a moral drama between rival groups extends into the larger community, where it may be depicted as an agonistic conflict between good and evil.

Several of Lorde's poems touch directly on deceit, betrayal, and treachery from close quarters.[53] Among the most disquieting is "Between Ourselves," in which she described her experiences of alienation within community: "Once when I walked into a room / my eyes would seek out the one or two Black faces / for contact or reassurance or a sign / I was not alone / now walking into rooms full of Black faces / that would destroy me for any difference / where shall my eyes look? / Once it was easy to know / who were my people."[54]

In another complicated, layered example, Lorde condemned black men's acts of intimidation toward black women who had considered entering into a feminist coalition with white women to combat sexism. She argued that if "threats of labeling, vilification, and/or emotional isolation are not enough to bring Black women docilely into camp as followers, or persuade us to avoid each other politically and emotionally, then the rule by terror can be expressed physically." She added, "Phone calls were made to those Black women who dared to explore the possibilities of a feminist connection with non-Black women. Some of these women, intimidated by threats and withdrawals of Black male approval, did turn against their sisters."[55]

Fear is one salient emotional legacy of seeking to survive the betrayals by similarly situated members of subordinated communities and the hatred by members of dominating groups.[56] Lorde's effort to place fear "into a perspective that gave [her] great strength" was a theme in her public speeches. In her 1977 MLA speech she observed, "In the cause of silence, each of us draws the face of her own fear— fear of contempt, of censure, or some judgment, or recognition, of challenge, or annihilation. But most of all, I think, we fear the visibility without which we cannot truly live." In the conclusion, Lorde urged, "We can learn to work and speak when we are afraid in the same way we have learned to work and speak when we are tired. For we have been socialized to respect fear more than our own needs for language and definition, and while we wait in silence for that final luxury of fearlessness, the weight of that silence will choke us."[57] The whole speech may be understood as a sustained confrontation with silence, fear, and complicity to transform them.

Vigilance

Under the circumstances of betrayal by similarly situated members of subordinated communities and hatred by members of dominating groups, vigilance is necessary to survive. Lorde affirmed at Amherst in 1980, "For in order to survive, those of us for whom oppression is as american as apple pie have had to be watchers, to become familiar with the language and the manners of the oppressor, sometimes adopting them for some illusion of protection."[58] This vigilance extends to not just the hateful actions of others, but also one's own complicity and even to language insofar as it may perpetuate racism, sexism, and the like. In Lorde's MLA speech, for instance, she claimed, "It is necessary to scrutinize not only the truth of what we speak, but the truth of that language by which we speak it."[59] Lorde elsewhere remarked in 1982, "Revolution is not a one-time event. It is becoming always vigilant for the smallest opportunity to make a genuine change in established, outgrown responses."[60]

A Dichotomous Symbolic World

In traumatic styles, the symbolic world may have become dichotomous. All men have oppressed all women. The masculine has disciplined the feminine. Whites have exploited blacks. Heterosexuals have annihilated gays and lesbians. Discernment concerning symbolic others evaporates, if only for a time. Moral subtlety disintegrates. Sweeping and hyperbolic generalizations depicting others may recur in a much too tidy depiction of society. If only in myth, the victims are altogether innocent, the perpetrators embody arbitrary and capricious malevolence, and bystanders are either allies or accomplices. There is no neutral ground. In some instances, the generalizations and hyperboles may serve strategic purposes for those who evince traumatic styles in that their claims may emphasize harms that do disproportionately affect entire groups. It may also help advocates to make it difficult for audiences to individualize the traumas inflicted disproportionately on certain groups. But, in another rhetorical double bind attending the complexities of combining systemic and individual analysis, it does so at the cost of failure to individuate and stereotyping.[61]

Perhaps the most emphatic instance of a bifurcating style in Lorde's public discourse was her 1978 speech "Uses of the Erotic: The Erotic as Power," in which she presented dichotomous relationships between women and men. Lorde's 1977 essay "Poetry Is Not a Luxury" likewise constructed agonistic oppositions between men and women: "The white fathers told us: I think, therefore I am. The Black mother within each of us—the poet—whispers in our dreams: I feel, therefore I can be free."[62] In a momentarily tidy symbolic world, there are no feminist men, no antiracist white males, no men accepting and perhaps even fearlessly loving lesbians. All men are patriarchs, if only in fantasy or momentary amnesia.

On the whole, most of Lorde's subsequent public speeches depicted bifurcations so characteristic of traumatic styles; she commented on white women and men's racism toward black women and men, and heterosexual women and men's antigay and antilesbian hatred. In Lorde's later rhetoric, the agonistic conflicts among social groups cut across multiple social divisions with invisible hierarchies concealed under simple terms: women, black, lesbian. Lorde asserted in 1980, "There is a pretense to a homogeneity of experience covered by the word *sisterhood* that does not in fact exist."[63] As a black, lesbian, feminist, mother, and socialist, she did not have the luxury of treating the oppositions simply. The complexity of her discourse depicting multiple social divisions is evidenced in her later speeches such as "The Master's Tools Will Never Dismantle the Master's House" (1979), "Age, Race, Class, and Sex: Women Redefining Difference" (1980), and "Learning from the 60s" (1982).[64]

Ultimately, in her subsequent speeches after "Uses of the Erotic," Lorde criticized the symbolic oppositions—between white and black, male and female, capitalist and socialist, heterosexual and homosexual, master and slave—as simplistic and useful to dominant groups for exploiting subordinated communities. In "Learning from the 60s" she claimed, "There is no such thing as a single-issue struggle because we do not live single-issue lives. . . . Each one of us here is a link in the connection between antipoor legislation, gay shootings, the burning of synagogues, street harassment, attacks against women, and resurgent violence against Black people."[65] In this respect, there was in a brief period of only a few years an extraordinary development in her rhetorical style representing social groups.[66]

Lorde went one step further in dismantling simplistic binaries, however, by collapsing the victim-perpetrator distinction within herself. In "Age, Race, Class, and Sex," she commented, "As Paulo Freire shows so well in *The Pedagogy of the Oppressed*, the true focus of revolutionary change is never merely the oppressive situations which we seek to escape, but that piece of the oppressor which is planted deep within each of us, and which knows only the oppressors' tactics, the oppressors' relationships."[67] In "Learning from the 60s" she remarked, "We must move against not only those forces which dehumanize us from the outside, but also against those oppressive values which we have been forced to take into ourselves."

Later in this speech, she encouraged her audience to ask, "In what way do I contribute to the subjugation of any part of those who I define as my people?"[68] Lorde did not entirely dismiss psychological work by individuals in bringing about social change, because of internalized practices and values, but she put political action in the foreground of her analysis.[69]

In traumatic styles, agonistic conflict between rival groups—sometimes depicted as a conflict between good and evil—may be locked in what usually seems like a mortal combat and, sometimes, actually becomes one.[70] Herman explained, "When the traumatic events are of human design, those who bear witness are caught in the conflict between victim and perpetrator. It is morally impossible to remain neutral in this conflict. The bystander is forced to take sides." Herman emphasized that in the struggle between perpetrator and victim, "It is very tempting to take the side of the perpetrator. All the perpetrator asks is that the bystander do nothing. He appeals to the universal desire to see, hear and speak no evil. The victim, on the contrary, asks the bystander to share the burden of pain. The victim demands action, engagement, and remembering."[71] Inactivity can result as much from bystanders' feeling helpless to do anything to stop the ordeal or being overwhelmed and distracted by the sheer range, magnitude, or complexity of the burdens as from any lack of concern about others.

In light of these dynamics of decision making, which are not necessarily conscious, bystanders may align themselves, not with the victims but rather with victimizers. In the general characteristics of traumatic styles, the bystanders' complicity with perpetrators compounds both moral and dichotomizing dimensions in speakers' accounts of traumatic experience rather than alleviates them.[72] In general, Herman observed, "The victim's greatest contempt is often reserved, not for the perpetrator, but for the passive bystander."[73] Lorde's rhetoric, however, often expressed anger rather than contempt. Thematically she called her audiences to transform silence and other forms of complicity with people who oppress others. In a sense, even the later audiences are witnesses or bystanders. Consequently anger, rage, and contempt evidenced in some manifestations of traumatic styles may contribute to making it unlistenable speech for the audiences who experience these styles. Public advocates who find themselves in moments of unspeakable speech may produce moments of unlistenable speech.

Unlistenable Speech

Speakers seeking to have audiences acknowledge their own vulnerability to harm and the need for active, political engagement find that, as one consequence, there are an immense variety of ways for audiences to respond to their claims. Patterns of audiences' interactions with traumatic styles are challenging to document, however, not only because the concept of audience has been under-theorized in general in public address scholarship, but also because the evidence is inevitably fragmentary, which tends to be suggestive rather than conclusive. Some patterns of human response are indicated in scholarship concerning resistance to claims about poverty, racism, sexism, and the like. Other patterns may be inferred, however fallibly, from patterns of response among psychiatrists who have specialized in dealing with trauma survivors.

Audiences of traumatic styles often refuse to listen, simply because they have the power to do so. Audiences may employ varied defense mechanisms to preserve some illusions of their own invulnerability or to sustain their false beliefs in a fundamentally just world. Examples of such defense mechanisms include caricaturing, infantilizing, or blaming the victims of traumatic experiences through an exaggerated and unrealistic assignment of the victims' responsibility rooted in myths of individualism, such as the belief that an individual can minimize the risk of harm by making the right "choices." If in specific cases victims may be in some respect partially responsible for the ordeals, so oftentimes are numerous others, whom audiences are able to ignore by concentrating intently on the victims' flawed performances. Lorde observed in the *Black Scholar* in 1979, "One tool of the Great-American-Double-Think is to blame the victims for victimization: Black people are said to invite lynching by not knowing our places, Black women are said to invite rape and murder and abuse by not being submissive enough, or by being too seductive."[74] Given sufficient faults, failings, or examples of bad judgment in the victims' sometimes fatally flawed performances, audience members can remain secure in the certain knowledge: this cannot happen to me.

Beyond the audiences endeavoring to maintain their own illusions of invulnerability, listeners may also seek to sustain their false faith in a fundamentally just world. Such patterns of human response to the styles even seem to recur among psychiatrists who specialize in treating trauma cases. Consequently speakers of the traumatic styles may be subjected by audiences to caricature as malingerers who cannot or will not move on, insufferable people seeking pity or sympathy or who are desperate for attention, even if speakers are articulate about systemic roots of their harms in laws, policies, and procedures. All such responses enable audiences to remain at a distance and safely above the speakers, however slightly. Classical considerations of ethos may undergo an inversion insofar as experience is concerned; prudence may be called into question; and decorum may disintegrate under public pressure, affronted by indiscretions and violated taboos.[75] Thus the speakers of traumatic styles may be infantilized. They may be said to have a penchant for wallowing. They may be depicted as too sensitive, too fragile, too delicate to cope with ordinary life experiences. They may be represented as having led sheltered lives. Failing that, some listeners may infer that surely victims were self-loathing masochists who must, after all, have been seeking suffering. Alternatively, some listeners may experience the advocates as embodiments of smoldering anger, rage, or vindictiveness—not, on inspection, all that distinguishable from the perpetrators whom they ostensibly deplore. These and other of the audiences' extensive array of defense mechanisms, which have surfaced even among trained psychiatrists, pose extraordinary rhetorical obstacles for speakers who would presume to depict ordeals in public.[76]

Among people who are compassionate and sympathetic in responding to trauma, there are a range of additional pitfalls, as Elizabeth V. Spelman has underscored. She identified three key paradoxes for people who are genuinely concerned about others' suffering, but who nonetheless appropriate that suffering, becoming ventriloquists of it as their own. By analyzing white women's uses of female slaves' suffering during the nineteenth-century women's movements, Spelman refers to the following paradoxes:

> The paradox in appropriation suggests that while a danger in assuming the experiences of others is that they as subjects of such experiences will be erased, a danger in *refusing* to do so is that one may thereby deny the possibility of a shared humanity. The paradox in identification reminds us that while the formula "women are slaves" tended to subvert white supremacy by denying differences between Black and white women, the formula sustained white supremacy insofar as it obscured white women's roles in supporting slavery. And the paradox in universality cautions that while calling on the experience of a marginalized group to represent "human experience" can be an important way of honoring that group's experience, it also can be a way of trivializing and thus further marginalizing them.[77]

It is not hard to see how such paradoxes may result in specific double binds for the listeners to traumatic styles, simply by rereading the excerpt replacing each "paradox" with quandary. In this case, because the relationship cut across subordinated communities, each paradox also underscored some difficulties in coalitions across demographic differences.

Ultimately, traumatic styles are not emblematic of any specific subordinated community, but rather constitute chasms within and among various communities. Members of subordinated communities who have been fortunate enough to elude physical harm or protracted ordeals may castigate those who have not been so fortunate. Rugged individualists within the community may fault others in highly variable acts that Lorde called "horizontal hostility." She generalized, "The tactic of encouraging horizontal hostility to becloud more pressing issues of oppression is by no means new, nor limited to relations between women. The same tactic is used to encourage separation between Black women and Black men."[78] Elsewhere, Lorde alluded to "those scars of oppression which lead us to war against ourselves in each other rather than against our enemies." Consequently, she claimed, "In the 1960s, the awakened anger of the Black community was often expressed, not vertically against the corruption of power and true sources of control over our lives, but horizontally toward those closest to us who mirrored our own impotence. . . . We were often far more vicious to each other than to the originators of our common problem."[79]

Rhetorical complexities attending traumatic styles do not end there, however, because public representations of traumatic experiences ordinarily occur under the surveillance of dominating others, who may seem eager to appropriate the remarks for their own ends. Although much of the dominating mythology of victimization concentrates on what the victims did to bring the trauma on themselves, and although audiences of the traumatic styles may have vested interests in adhering to the delusive myths, the realities of victimization can be much different than what the prevailing myths predispose audiences to believe. In the history of lynching, for instance, the most commonplace way statistically to become the targets of violence was not, as myth would have it, for a black man to make an inappropriate expression of sexual interest in a white woman, though some black men were lynched for that reason.[80] Recently, some have suggested that it was especially dangerous for black men to compete successfully against white male counterparts in business, though a difficulty with such claims is that direct competition may have been rare.[81] For members of subordinated communities, it can be dangerous—even deadly—to be successful in competition with ostensibly superior others. To maintain a sense of hierarchical place, some supremacists may encircle their targets to put them back in their place, lest there be any trace of living evidence to cast doubt on their superiority. Myth tends to be an ally not of the targets of violence but of the perpetrators.[82]

Because of the almost insurmountable rhetorical barricades that audiences erect to protect their own interests of maintaining some illusions of invulnerability or belief in a just world, explicit depictions of trauma in public address may be less commonplace than the indirect and fragmented manifestations of it. Herman wrote, "The psychological distress symptoms of traumatized people simultaneously call attention to the existence of an unspeakable secret and deflect attention from it."[83] For gay men and lesbians, the direct experience of being the target of severe harassment or violence can become a closet within a closet, precisely because the survivors of violence are often blamed for having had the experience, especially in cases of sexual violence or sexualized aggression.[84] But even the illusion of "the closet" is a myth deeply rooted in individualism, because sexuality is social, as can be confirmed by simple reflection on courtship: it is impossible to get a date, much less a mate, without communicating one's sexuality to the person being courted. Indeed some gay men's and lesbians' lifelong efforts to be invisible are a fallible sign of a hostile, abusive environment, the by-product of a silence enforced by violence and the threat of violence.

Recovery Discourse Reintegrating Self and Society through Political Action

Despite the extraordinary odds against being heard and understood, despite the "risk" of having ideas "bruised and misunderstood,"[85] the survivors of trauma can and do speak in public with an urgency and a depth of conviction reminiscent of true believers. Survivors bear witness. Advocates testify. Speakers remember in public. More important, speakers refuse to allow others to be silent or to forget. Some targets and witnesses of such violence, knowing that they, too, are worthy people or, in some instances, having felt safe and secure as contributing members of their communities, recount ordeals in public spaces. Having been made to feel extreme helplessness, as though vividly present traces of past ordeals would never end and could never be forgotten, the speakers concentrate on the process of reclaiming agency and public memory. Herman remarked, "Helplessness and isolation are the core experiences of psychological trauma. Empowerment and re-connection are the core experiences of recovery." Having experienced what psychologists label "dissociation," the speakers may concentrate on reclaiming inner directives, despite externally imposed demands. To some speakers of traumatic styles, it is vital to take pleasure simply in inhabiting one's own body, experiencing embodiment, and restoring a sense of trust and safety in community with others. Herman claimed, "Those who have survived learn that their sense of self, of worth, of humanity, depends on a feeling of connection to others. The solidarity of the group provides the strongest protection against terror and despair, and the strongest antidote to traumatic experience."[86] This final section comments on rhetorical depictions of recovery and communal healing for both advocates and their audiences in the aftermath, such as reintegrating self in society through political actions, restoration of appropriate trust in others, and reclaiming embodied pleasure within empowering communities.

As an exemplar, Lorde's "Uses of the Erotic: The Erotic as Power" is an eloquent call to recognize a broad range of traumatic experiences in the communal interest of recovery, social transformation, and political action. Lorde's speech enacted an endeavor to reconnect with community, as she affirmed recognition of harms and called for action to transform society. Herman generalized, "The response of the community has a powerful influence on the ultimate resolution of the trauma. Restoration of the breach between the traumatized person and the community depends, first, on public acknowledgment of the traumatic event and, second, on some form of community action." She further explained, "Once it is publicly recognized that a person has been harmed, the community must take action to assign responsibility for the harm and repair the injury. These two responses—recognition and restitution—are necessary to rebuild the survivor's sense of order and justice."[87]

Central to Lorde's call for individual and communal recovery was her endeavor to reclaim "the erotic." Conventional associations of "the erotic" specifically with sex acts complicate appreciating the meanings of Lorde's speech because, to her, "the erotic is the nurturer or nursemaid of all our deepest knowledge." Lorde did define the erotic to encompass sexual pleasure, as in her description of "moving into the sunlight against the body of a woman I love." But Lorde also defined the erotic as much more encompassing. For example, she asserted, "The erotic is a measure between the beginnings of our sense of self and the chaos of our strongest feelings. It is an internal sense of satisfaction to which, once we have experienced it, we know we can aspire." When Lorde identified examples of "erotically satisfying experience," she mentioned "dancing, building a bookcase, writing a poem, examining an idea." To Lorde, reclaiming work, not primarily for profit but rather as a deeply satisfying experience, was another meaning of the erotic. She acknowledged, "It is never easy to demand the most from ourselves, from our lives, from our work," explaining, "For as we begin to recognize our deepest feelings, we begin to give up, of necessity, being satisfied with suffering and self-negation, and with the numbness which so often seems like their only alternative in our society. Our acts against oppression become integral with self, motivated and empowered from within."[88]

"Uses of the Erotic" exemplifies several features of traumatic styles understood as a way of holding and advocating beliefs. She called on her auditors to acknowledge vulnerability in a hostile, symbolic world of men and economic exploitation. She sought to counter numbing, emotional responses to such hostility and, sometimes, physical harms by encouraging her audiences to reclaim the erotic and, in some measure, personal agency despite fear, disapproval, and "external directives" imposed by others and despite systemic obstacles in capitalism and patriarchy. Lorde concentrated on having her audiences reject such externally imposed demands while heeding "internal directives" or "internal knowledge and needs." Her concluding lines succinctly summarized this dynamic of symbolic rejection and acceptance: "Recognizing the power of the erotic within our lives can give us the energy to pursue genuine change within our world, rather than merely settle for a shift of characters in the same weary drama. For not only do we touch our most profoundly creative source, but we do that which is female and self-affirming in the face of a racist, patriarchal, and anti-erotic society."[89]

Despite a climate of hostile men and an imposing economic system, Lorde emphasized feeling embodied pleasure in self and in connection with others. When referring to how "the erotic" functioned for her in personal terms, she affirmed the role of feeling in community with others: "The sharing of joy, whether physical, emotional, psychic, or intellectual, forms a bridge between the sharers which can be the basis for understanding much of what is not shared between them, and lessens the threat of their differences. . . . That self-connection shared is a measure of the joy which I know myself to be capable of feeling, a reminder of my capacity for feeling." Her statement, "a reminder of my capacity for feeling," may be disquieting to audiences familiar with the numbing aftermath of trauma. She said, "In touch with the erotic, I become less willing to accept powerlessness, or those other supplied states of being which are not native to me, such as resignation, despair, self effacement, depression, and self-denial." These remarks cataloged commonplace legacies of traumatic experiences. She cautioned, "To refuse to be conscious of what we are feeling at any time, however comfortable that might seem, is to deny a large part of experience, and to allow ourselves to be reduced to the pornographic, the abused, and the absurd." Lorde appeared to allude to psychological dissociation during trauma when she commented on disconnections between mind and body while identifying the personal ramifications of sexism and capitalism for women's erotic lives: "When we live outside ourselves, and by that I mean on external directives only rather than from our internal knowledge and needs, when we live away from those erotic guides from within ourselves, then our lives are limited by external and alien forms, and we conform to the needs of a structure that is not based on human need, let alone an individual's."[90] Against the backdrop of such harms, Lorde called for recovery and reintegration in empowering communities by connecting her personal experiences to political actions. She generalized from her own life as a sustained example: "Another important way in which the erotic connection functions is the open and fearless underlining of my capacity for joy."[91]

In "Uses of the Erotic," Lorde situated these calls within a timeless narrative in a dichotomous symbolic world in which men oppress women. Lorde's shifting perspectives within this symbolic world can be illustrated by her comments concerning "the erotic." "As women, we have come to distrust that power which rises from our deepest and nonrational knowledge. We have been warned against it all our lives by the male world."[92] Notice how she shifted between how men and women defined "the erotic" and the "pornographic" in a subsequent passage: "The erotic has often been misnamed by men and used against women. It has been made into the confused, the trivial, the psychotic, the plasticized sensation. For this reason, we have often turned away from the exploration and consideration of the erotic as a source of power and information, confusing it with its opposite, the pornographic. But pornography is a direct denial of the power of the erotic, for it represents the suppression of true feeling."[93]

This passage articulated Lorde's double consciousness of the meanings and uses of the erotic in men's and women's lives. Yet, as is so often the case in traumatic styles, the dichotomizing depictions are reductive and much too tidy, as Lorde's later rhetoric explicitly recognized; she modified her language in subsequent speeches and essays. Yet there is reason to believe that her generalizations were strategic rhetorically in stressing a systemic rather than individual analysis; the audiotape of her included qualifiers such as "typically and historically" for men's role. Such qualifiers disappeared from the printed texts.[94] Intersectionality may emphasize an interaction among systemic structures informing social identity as they impinge on multiple consciousness.[95]

Yet she called on her hearers to recognize some dichotomies as "false." She affirmed, for instance, that "the dichotomy between the spiritual and the political is also false, resulting from an incomplete attention to our erotic knowledge."[96] Despite this gesture toward reintegration of such dichotomies, Lorde's rhetoric drew on and perpetuated a series of interconnected, binary oppositions—between men and women, between the dominant and the subordinate, between external and internal directives, between the political and the spiritual, and between the pornographic and the erotic. These oppositions relied on an underlying set of equations in which men were depicted as "the dominant," "the political," and "the pornographic." In contrast, women were portrayed as "the subordinate," "the spiritual," and the "erotic." The reproduction of these binary oppositions is unfortunate, because the binaries were often simplistic in comparison with Lorde's later speeches, which did emphasize sexism, but also considered intersecting factors of age, race, class, and sexuality. Although the bifurcating oppositions in Lorde's speech did contribute to its clarity and its rhetorical power, they were intellectually unsatisfying, as she herself seemed later to recognize. Yet, such polarizing dichotomies are commonplace in traumatic styles, perhaps because of a tendency, at least for a time, to overgeneralize in representing others as the sources of trauma or because of a strategic endeavor to stress systemic factors rather than merely individual ones.

In an interview with Adrienne Rich, Lorde acknowledged that feminists had criticized this speech for reproducing stereotypes of women, a criticism that her peers had also leveled at "Poetry Is Not a Luxury," which had been published in *Chrysalis* the previous year. In addition, both the speech and the essay reproduced invidious stereotypes of men. In the interview Lorde remarked, "After I published 'Uses of the Erotic,' a number of women who read it said that this is anti-feminist, that the use of the erotic as a guide is . . . reducing us once again to the unseen, the unusable. That in writing it I am returning us to a place of total intuition without insight." Rich interrupted, "And yet, in that essay you're talking about work and power, about two of the most political things that exist." Lorde replied,

> I try to say that the erotic has been used against us, even the word itself, so often, that we have been taught to suspect what is deepest in ourselves, and that is the way we learn to testify against ourselves, against our feelings. When we talk in terms of our lives and our survival as women, we can use our knowledge of the erotic creatively. The way you get people to testify against themselves is not to have police tactics and oppressive techniques. What you do is build it in so people learn to distrust everything in themselves that has not been sanctioned, to reject what is most creative in themselves to begin with, so you don't even need to stamp it out. . . . This turning away from the erotic on the part of some of our best minds, our most creative and analytic women, is disturbing and destructive. Because we cannot fight old power in old power terms only. The only way we can do it is by creating another whole structure that touches every aspect of our existence, at the same time as we are resisting.[97]

272   LESTER C. OLSON

This excerpt suggests that traumatic styles pose ramifications for careful listening. For example, traumatic styles make for arduous listening because of the complexity of listeners' attention to commentary about both individual and collective social conditions and concerns. What listeners may be tempted to dismiss as hyperbolic, sweeping, and simplistic generalizations may signal a need to adjust listening practices to situate the discourse as commentary on systems, not individuals, and to recognize the generalizations as having exceptions and complexities. Further, for listeners who feel unable to do much substantive to intervene, listening may embody a transformative practice by raising awareness that subsequently may inform political actions.

Still later in this interview, Lorde situated her speech in her own personal history with breast cancer. Although she had already experienced the diagnosis of a benign tumor and had described that experience at the MLA during 1977, she commented in the interview about the later diagnosis of a malignant tumor: "So much of the work I did, I did before I knew consciously that I had cancer. Questions of death and dying, dealing with power and strength, the sense of 'What am I paying for?' that I wrote about in that paper, were crucial to me a year later. 'Uses of the Erotic' was written four weeks before I found out I had breast cancer, in 1978." She added, "The existence of that paper enabled me to pick up and go to Houston and California; it enabled me to start working again. I don't know when I'd have been able to write again, if I hadn't had those words."[98]

In this connection, Lorde's comments at the outset of the interview situated the speech concerning the erotic well within the whole of her public speaking during the late 1970s and early 1980s. Rich inquired, "What do you mean when you say that two essays, 'Poetry Is Not a Luxury' and 'Uses of the Erotic,' are really progressions?" Lorde replied, "They're part of something that's not finished yet. I don't know what the rest of it is, but they're clear progressions in feeling out something connected with the first piece of prose I ever wrote."[99] One could infer from the interview that inchoate in the speech was the beginning of a dramatic series of developments in Lorde's philosophy, role, and techniques as a public speaker. These developments were a consequence, in part, of frank and difficult dialogues that ensued within the empowering communities that she actively sought to constitute and to re-envision radically. Consequently her later public speaking was much more sophisticated in its rhetorical artistry.

Conclusion

Lorde's rhetoric in "Uses of the Erotic" most clearly exemplifies traumatic styles, as Lorde sought to transform society by eloquently calling on her audiences to recognize and remember injuries, to experience recovery, and to reclaim embodied pleasure in living in intimate community with others. In general Lorde's speeches, essays, and poems enacted the integrity of her character in seeking to improve the lives of women and their children through empowering communities. Herman described such integrity in the wake of ordeals: "Integrity is the capacity to affirm the value of life in the face of death, to be reconciled with the finite limits of one's own life and the tragic limitations of the human condition, and to accept these realities without despair. Integrity is the foundation on which trust in relationships is originally formed, and on which shattered trust may be restored. The interlocking of integrity and trust in caretaking relationships completes the cycle of generations and regenerates the sense of human community which trauma destroys."[100] By endeavoring "to make our lives and the lives of our children richer and more possible," as Lorde put it in her speech concerning the erotic, she enacted these qualities of recovery, reintegrating self within community by calling for political actions reclaiming "the erotic."

At the outset of this chapter, I stressed that the identification of traumatic styles was tentative, because, although I believe my critical interpretation to be accurate, I also have misgivings about the potential misuses of such naming to deflect attention from the systemic, institutionalized roots of the hatred and intolerance. Traumatic styles are recurrent precisely because of their underlying systemic sources. It also concerns me that critics could misuse the naming of traumatic styles to interpret discourses or an individual's rhetorical style in public life without recognizing the pathological practices of domineering groups that discipline those discourses into being. There is a risk that the naming of the styles could be easily appropriated to perpetuate stereotypes in an ideology of domination, simply by isolating the discourse from its context. In any event, it would be important to resist using traumatic styles to focus on the individual speaker without attention to the cultural conditions imposing on lives in ways that produce the discourse. It would certainly be misleading to call it "post" traumatic, since racism, sexism, and other biases persist through invidious practices even today. They are ongoing, recurrent, practices that cannot accurately be relegated only to the past, even though "post" can mean "in response to" as well as a temporal relationship. Although Lorde acknowledged individual and collective harms, her public discourse emphatically kept politics and social engagement in the foreground: "I am not only a casualty, I am also a warrior."[101]

Morever, the naming of a type can easily become a stereotype. Certainly some survivors of trauma speak in other rhetorical styles. It would be unfortunate if attention to traumatic styles deflected attention from the voices of trauma survivors who do not speak in traumatic styles, because traumatic styles may frame critics' attention in a limiting way. There are also doubtless variations and changes in traumatic styles over time and place—hence the plural, styles. The testimonies of Holocaust survivors would add to an understanding of traumatic styles, though I worry that fixation on ordeals of such horrific scope and magnitude may result in ignoring mundane, daily acts of violence and intimidation. Although it extends beyond the scope of this chapter, it would be useful to examine how specific systemic factors, such as the legal system, discipline discourses into tidy binary relations in a dichotomous perspective on social relations. An example of this would be the legal system's procedural insistence on the distinctions between innocent victims and guilty perpetrators rather than the complexity posed typically by victim-perpetrators and mutual combatants. Another instance would be the notion that justice can be meaningfully realized by verdicts, when social transformation is much more fundamental than penal punishments or economic outcomes. It would also be useful to investigate how changes in these systems over time impinge on discursive shifts in the styles.

Some exemplars of traumatic styles can be found among speeches by members of typically dominant groups, such as combat veterans who have experienced the front lines of war or American people generally after traumas such as the Oklahoma City bombing. Although the earliest complete drafts of this chapter were finished before September 11, 2001, public comments on the recent attacks on the World Trade Center and the Pentagon evinced traumatic styles, though in some ways that differ significantly from discourse concerning the routine domestic terrorism disrupting lives in subordinated communities. Nobody in Congress has affirmed, for example, that, however deplorable the hateful deeds, the terrorists are entitled to their views that such killing exemplifies moral virtue. Nor has anybody in Congress held that commitment to freedom of expression, however well established in the United Nation's Universal Declaration of Human Rights, should circumscribe any responses to the terrorists' deeds or their teachings of hatred toward Americans, because they are deeds that convey meanings and the doers profess to be guided by religious dictates. Affirming such views would appear to be transparently what it is. Leaders in the United States have demonstrated that, if motivated, they can be quite skilled at discerning sham misuses of religion to mask hatred as spiritual virtue and violence as free speech. Yet some of the same prominent leaders display incomprehension in discerning blasphemous misuses of sacred texts to mask domestic terrorism whenever they consider how to curtail the bias crimes that so routinely produce traumatic experiences within some subordinated communities in the United States.

Finally, then, how does this chapter bear on projects to "queer" public address scholarship, which I take to be the activity of explicitly naming, analyzing, and interpreting ramifications of various sexualities in critical studies of authors, texts, critics, audiences, organizations and institutions (such as ACT UP), and ideologies (such as the Radical Fairies)? I hope that this chapter suggests my deep ambivalence about the pitfalls and promise of such projects, because they entail significant risks even as they advance exciting possibilities. Some risks in such projects are the usual, familiar problems attending identity politics. Among these are a deflection from the material conditions and social practices impacting queer people's lives exemplified by acts of hatred and bias, plus an oversimplification of the diversity among queer people, especially the hidden hierarchies of race, sex, economic class, age, and the like. There are risks of gaps, silences, omissions, and subordinations among queers as harmful consequences.

Along with those factors, there is a high probability that relatively privileged queers will endeavor to represent the rest, by speaking for and about others who inhabit this category with them. Although contributors to this volume have tried with varying degrees of success to be broad and inclusive in our work, it is the case that almost all of us are white, middle-class academics with sufficient age and experience to engage such scholarship without the overt likelihood of losing livelihoods or extensive networks of friends. Lesbian feminists have labored long and hard to engage combined sexist and antiqueer biases impacting their lives. So, although ordinarily gender neutrality in language usage is desirable, the gender neutrality of "queer" risks erasure and silencing, appropriation and invisibility with respect to sex as a factor intersecting with sexuality. So too with race, age, economic class, disability, religion, marital or parental status, political commitments, educational backgrounds, and other factors. Moreover it is almost always a mistake to isolate any communities materially or symbolically.

Yet to "queer" public address studies has extraordinary prospects for anyone concerned with accuracy, completeness, and complexity in public address scholarship, not to mention social justice. At the same time that it enacts a symbolic reversal of a pejorative term by reclaiming it in potentially life-enhancing ways for queers of all backgrounds, queer is also a useful term for a coalition among diverse sexualities, which terms such as *gay, lesbian, bisexual, transgender,* and *transexual* are also too simple to adequately name. Oversimplification of diverse queers seems linguistically inevitable and politically necessary to confer visibility on queer aspects of communication and society. Minimally, to queer public address scholarship embraces the prospect of centering intellectually on rhetorical practices and concepts that have been undervalued in dominant approaches to rhetoric scholarship. This is exemplified by previous research concerning style wherein key practices and concepts cannot be found or are peripheral, presumably because of a fixation on socially, politically, and economically powerful figures.[102] Examples of practices and concepts that are omitted or peripheral in traditional research on style but that are featured centrally in this chapter include silence and silencing; discursive amnesia and public memory loss; symbolic matrices and intersectionality; identification and essentialism; symbolic fragmentation and appropriation; double and multiple consciousness; marginality and centrality; embodiment, performatives, and enactment; complicity or collusion; and, of course, the usual paradoxes, quandaries, and double binds of varieties that scholars will need to confront directly in projects to "queer" public address by engaging the risks along with the extraordinary potential.

The implications of this stance on queering public address are extensive. Here I want only to share one brief example to illustrate how it can be creative and generative to queer public address, for instance, by valuing the First Amendment rights of gay men, lesbians, bisexuals, gender-bending, and trans-people. It begins, as all fantasies do, with an implausible premise, a dependable resource for humor such as camp, which sustains the spirit of queers whose laughter rises above oppressive circumstances. In this case, the FBI decides to conduct an undercover operation calculated to apprehend antigay attackers. To capture these violent offenders, the agency assigns teams consisting of pairs of handsome, well-dressed, muscular, fashionable men who endeavor to pass as gay. There is, of course, no need for wiretaps, spyware, surveillance devices, or the like. There is no need for camouflage gear of the sort that police have sometimes used to apprehend gay couples in remote, secluded woods. All these special agents need to do is walk down the street simply holding hands, or, better yet, to kiss in public. Let me assure you, the violence would come to them (especially if they learn to kiss each other well in secret practice sessions).

I freely admit that the likelihood of men in the FBI learning to passionately kiss each other in practice sessions may strain credulity. But this is, after all, a fairy's fantasy, one in which the federal government values the safety, the security of person, of gay men, not to mention freedom of expression. So, to get back to this fairy's tale, two such FBI agents stroll hand in hand past a construction site amid catcalls and the usual sorts of public verbal harassment. Epithets such as "cocksucker," "faggot," and "queer" sound out in tones that suggest that these are bad things for anyone to be. The special agents fearlessly continue on down the street, hand in hand. The number of annoyed onlookers swells to nine or possibly eleven men, who become increasingly vocal, unpleasant, and menacing in their behavior. One or another of the workers picks up a baseball bat, while another grabs a nearby tire iron and blocks the two FBI agents' way. An appreciative crowd starts to surround them while shouting epithets, catcalls, and such.

Perhaps at this moment one or another of the special agents remembers a statistic: ordinarily, in a gay-bashing, there are three attackers against each victim. That figure seems a little low today. Perhaps the other agent reflects, however momentarily, on just who exactly in this scenario enacts the masculine value of "manly courage"—the two special agents passing as queers, or the large gang of publicly heterosexual men whose bravado seems so transparently false as their numbers swell. At this moment, the special agents, being fearless, of course, as FBI agents are reputed to be, embrace each other in a long, passionate, French kiss. They are confident that the reinforcements are nearby. So, they kiss—one long, slow, erotic kiss. They have been practicing (as in *practicing* homosexual).

When I have told this fairy's tale in the past, at this moment in the story, one of my straight male friends interrupted, "Oh, I see, egg them on." (I pass over in silence any critical observations concerning the alacrity with which straight friends take control or revise a gentle fairy's tale.) "Oh, no, no, no, no," I replied emphatically. "Refuse to be bullied and intimidated into sacrificing their First Amendment rights."

Consider, for a moment, the generative insight to be gained from centering on gay men's expressiveness as worthy of public support and government protection, not just insights concerning courage and cowardice, or manliness and masculinity, but also concerning the very nature of bias crimes. It becomes apparent that bias crimes become clearly recognizable as First Amendment offenses, because bias crimes come into existence to suppress, to censor, to annihilate what the targeted individual(s) represent, stand for, symbolize, or express to the attackers. If there is no symbolic representation embodied in a person, there is no bias crime. From this standpoint, bias crimes become actionable as assaults on nothing less than the U.S. Constitution, specifically on the First Amendment, because they undermine freedom of expression, not to mention freedom of association, security of person, and other fundamental human rights specified in the United Nations Universal Declaration of Human Rights. From this standpoint, the political use of the First Amendment to enable the perpetrator's "expressive" violent deeds becomes transparently a ruse employed ironically to undermine the First Amendment rights of the assaulted queers. At least, that is one fairy's tale.

Notes

Earlier portions of this essay were presented at conferences of the National Communication Association in November 2001, the Rhetoric Society of America in May 2002, and the Women's Studies Program at the University of Pittsburgh in November 2002. I am grateful to Robin R. Means Coleman, Lisbeth Lipari, Carol A. Stabile, Julie Thompson, and Jennifer K. Wood for constructive criticisms of preliminary drafts. In addition, I would like to thank the Women's Studies Program and the Faculty of Arts and Sciences at the University of Pittsburgh for grants supporting research for this essay at the Lesbian Herstory Archives in Brooklyn, New York, in May 2002.

1. Richard Hofstadter, "The Paranoid Style in American Politics," in *The Paranoid Style in American Politics, and Other Essays* (New York: Knopf, 1965), 3–40, quotation from 4.

2. Although these elements comport well with the diagnosis for "post-traumatic stress disorder" in the American Psychiatric Association, *Diagnostic and Statistical Manual of Mental Disorders IV*, 4th ed. (Washington D.C.: American Psychiatric Association, 1994), 424–29, it is the appearance of the styles in discourse addressed to audiences that interests rhetoric scholars.

3. Hofstadter, "The Paranoid Style in American Politics," 5.

4. Edwin Black, "The Sentimental Style as Escapism, or the Devil with Dan'l Webster," in *Form and Genre: Shaping Rhetorical Action*, ed. Karlyn Kohrs Campbell and Kathleen Hall Jamieson (Falls Church, Va.: Speech Communication Association, 1978), 75–86, quotation from 78.

5. Robert Hariman, *Political Style: The Artistry of Power* (Chicago: University of Chicago Press, 1995).

6. Elaine Maria Upton, "Audre Lorde (1934–1992)," in *Contemporary Lesbian Writers of the United States: A Bio-Bibliographical Critical Sourcebook*, ed. Sandra Pollack and Denise D. Knight (Westport, Conn.: Greenwood, 1993), 318.

7. Alexis De Veaux, *Warrior Poet: A Biography of Audre Lorde* (New York: Norton, 2004), xi.

8. For example, Andrea Dworkin, "I Want a Twenty-Four-Hour Truce during Which There Is No Rape," in *Transforming a Rape Culture*, ed. Emilie Buchwald, Pamela Fletcher, and Martha Roth (Minneapolis, Minn.: Milkweed Editions, 1993), 11–22.

9. For example, Angela Davis, "We Do Not Consent: Violence against Women in a Racist Society," *Women, Culture, & Politics* (New York: Vintage, 1990), 35–52.

10. For example, Elie Wiesel, "The Perils of Indifference," April 12, 1999, Millennium Lecture Series, wysiwyg://11/http://www.historyplace.com/speeches/wiesel.htm (May 4, 2004).

11. Oscar Wilde, *De Profundis and Other Writings* (London: Penguin Books, repr. 1986).

12. On this point, see Robert Brookey's and John Sloop's essays in this volume as well as chapter 4 of Julie M. Thompson, *Mommy Queerist* (Amherst, Mass.: University of Massachusetts Press, 2002). For a general treatment of this concern, see Dana L. Cloud, *Control and Consolation in American Culture and Politics: Rhetoric of Therapy* (Thousand Oaks, Calif.: Sage, 1998).

13. Kathleen Hall Jamieson, "The Binds That Tie," in *Beyond the Double Bind: Women and Leadership* (New York: Oxford University Press, 1995).

14. Audre Lorde, "The Transformation of Silence into Language and Action," in *Sister Outsider: Essays & Speeches by Audre Lorde* (Freedom, Calif.: Crossing, 1984), 44. On discursive amnesia, see Wen Shu Lee and Phillip C. Wander, "On Discursive Amnesia: Reinventing the Possibilities for Democracy through Discursive Amnesty," in *The Public Voice in a Democracy at Risk*, ed. Michael Salvador and Patricia M. Sias (Westport, Conn.: Praeger, 1998), 152–53.

15. Carol Gilligan as discussant in "Feminist Discourse, Moral Values, and the Law: A Conversation," *Buffalo Law Review* 34 (1985): 62.

16. For a sustained example of radical listening drawn from nineteenth-century American life, see Susan Zaeske, "The 'Promiscuous Audience' Controversy and the Emergence of the Early Woman's Rights Movement," *Quarterly Journal of Speech* 81 (1995): 198.

17. Judith Herman, *Trauma and Recovery: The Aftermath of Violence: From Domestic Abuse to Political Terror* (1992; New York: Perseus, 1997), 1.

18. Herman, *Trauma and Recovery*, 208.

19. Audre Lorde, "The Master's Tools Will Never Dismantle the Master's House," in *Sister Outsider*, 112.

20. Herman, *Trauma and Recovery*, 70, 175, 177, 189, 190, 190–91.

21. Ibid., 92.

22. Lorde, "Transformation of Silence," 42.

23. Audre Lorde, "A Litany for Survival," *Collected Poems*, 255, 256.

24. Upton, "Audre Lorde," 319.

25. In the case of women, for instance, see Davis, "We Do Not Consent," 37, 41, 42. Davis's speech detailed how specific myths and patterns of human response, such as blaming the individual victim, sustain an individual's illusions of safety, despite the statistics for the group.

26. Audre Lorde, "Age, Race, Class, and Sex: Women Redefining Difference," in *Sister Outsider*, 119.

27. William Ryan, *Blaming the Victim*, revised, updated ed. (New York: Vintage, 1976). This book is primarily about poverty, but some generalizations in it are applicable to other situations.

28. Audre Lorde, "Learning from the 60s," in *Sister Outsider*, 142.

29. Herman, *Trauma and Recovery*, 37.

30. For example, John Jay Chapman, "Coatesville Address," *Harper's Weekly* (September 21, 1912), discussed in Edwin Black, *Rhetorical Criticism: A Study in Method* (New York: Macmillan, 1965), 79–82.

31. One exception would be the reference to Patricia Cowen in Audre Lorde, "Scratching the Surface: Some Notes on Barriers to Women and Loving," in *Sister Outsider*, 52. But the date does disappear from subsequent mentions of Cowen's murder, for instance, in Lorde's, "Sexism: An American Disease in Blackface," in *Sister Outsider*, 61, 64.

32. Upton, "Audre Lorde," 320.

33. Lorde, "Transformation of Silence," 43.

34. Herman, *Trauma and Recovery*, 43, 239, 238–39.

35. Lorde, "Outside," in *Collected Poems*, 227, 280. On this aspect of Lorde's rhetoric, see Ann Louise Keating, "Making 'Our Shattered Faces Whole': The Black Goddess and Audre Lorde's Revision of Patriarchal Myth," *Frontiers* 13, no. 1 (1992): 23.

36. Lorde, "Age, Race, Class, and Sex," 120–21.

37. James Darsey, "'The Voice of Exile': W. E. B. Du Bois and the Quest for Culture," in *Rhetoric and Community: Studies in Unity and Fragmentation*, ed. J. Michael Hogan (Columbia: University of South Carolina Press, 1998), 97.

38. Lorde, "Scratching the Surface," 45.

39. Scholarship that discusses the implications of layering, matrixing, and compounding variables in social identity include Patricia Hill Collins, "Learning from the Outsider Within: The Sociological Significance of Black Feminist Thought," *Social Problems* 33 (December 1986): 514–32; Collins, "Knowledge, Consciousness, and the Politics of Empowerment," in *Black Feminist Thought: Knowledge, Consciousness, and the Politics of Empowerment* (New York: Routledge, 1990), 221–38; Nancy A. Hewitt, "Compounding Differences," *Feminist Studies* 18, no. 2 (summer 1992): 313–26; Deborah K. King, "Multiple Jeopardy, Multiple Consciousness: The Context of Black Feminist Ideology," *Signs* 14, no. 1 (1988): 42–72; Maxine Baca Zinn and Bonnie Thornton Dill, "Theorizing Difference from Multiracial Feminism," *Feminist Studies* 22, no. 2 (summer 1996): 321–31.

40. Audre Lorde, "Who Said It Was Simple," in *Collected Poems*, 92.

41. Audre Lorde, *The Cancer Journals* (San Francisco: Spinsters, Ink, 1980), 25. For a detailed comment on her emotional responses at the outset, see Lorde, "Transformation of Silence," 40–41.

42. For detailed, numerous examples of this, see Lorde, "The Uses of Anger: Women Responding to Racism," in *Sister Outsider*, 125–26, and "Eye to Eye: Black Women, Hatred, and Anger," in *Sister Outsider*, 147–48.

43. Herman, *Trauma and Recovery*, 7, 51, 154, 162. The struggle between good and evil is thematic in Wiesel's discourse, for example.

44. Audre Lorde, "Uses of the Erotic," in *Sister Outsider*, 56.

45. On anger and rage, see Herman, *Trauma and Recovery*, 138, 143.

46. Lorde, "Uses of Anger," 124, 129, 127.

47. Audre Lorde, "Power," in *Collected Poems*, 215, 319.

48. Upton, "Audre Lorde," 319.

49. Lorde, "Eye to Eye," 152.

50. Lorde, "Uses of Anger," 125.

51. For example, Mary Cavanaugh, "Statement on Sexual Harassment in the Veterans Administration," 1997, which may be found at http://gos.sbc.edu/c/cavanaugh.htm (January 4, 2001). This entire speech is another exemplar of traumatic styles.

52. Herman, *Trauma and Recovery*, 51, 52. Abandonment and isolation are not necessarily individual experiences. For instance, Elie Wiesel, "This Honor Belongs to All the Survivors," in *Representative American Speeches*, ed. Owen Peterson (New York: H. W. Wilson, 1987), 59–73.

53. Examples of such poems include "Learning to Write," "To the Poet Who Happens to Be Black and the Black Poet Who Happens to Be a Woman," and "Conversation in Crisis," in Lorde, *Collected Poems*, 402, 360, and 50, respectively.

54. Audre Lorde, "Between Ourselves," in *Collected Poems*, 223.

55. Lorde, "Scratching the Surface," 47.

56. Even so monumental a figure as Martin Luther King devoted a sermon to "Antidotes to Fear," in *A Testament of Hope*, ed. James Melvin Washington (New York: Harper Collins, 1991), 509–17. In "Perils," Wiesel likewise portrayed himself as "carried by profound fear and extraordinary hope" (5).

57. Lorde, "Transformation of Silence," 41, 42, 42, 43, 44.

58. Lorde, "Age, Race, Class, and Sex," 114.

59. Lorde, "Transformation of Silence," 43.

60. Lorde, "Learning from the 60s," 140–41.

61. For instance, Andrea Dworkin's speech, "I Want a Twenty-Four-Hour Truce," implicated all men in women's experience of rape. But she did so in a way that stereotyped both men and women. She failed to recognize that most women have not and will not be sexually assaulted, even though, as a group, women do live with disproportionate risk. Further, some men in her audience may have been sexual assault survivors, who, as a consequence of her generalizations, were forced to confront her distorting stereotypes of such assaults.

62. Audre Lorde, "Poetry Is Not a Luxury," 38.

63. Lorde, "Age, Race, Class, and Sex," 116.

64. Lorde, "The Master's Tools," 110–13; "Age, Race, Class, and Sex," 114–23; and "Learning from the 60s," 134–44.

65. Lorde, "Learning from the 60s," 138, 139.

66. This development was not unique to her as a public speaker, because a similar development is discernable in Malcolm X's speeches, especially near the end of his life. Malcolm X, *The Final Speeches*, ed. Steve Clark (New York: Pathfinder, 1992); *Malcolm X Speaks*, ed. George Breitman (New York: Pathfinder, 1989). In "Learning from the 60s," Lorde explicitly distanced herself from Malcolm X's earliest public discourse, while commending the evolutions in evidence toward the end of his life.

67. Lorde, "Age, Race, Class, and Sex," 123.

68. Lorde, "Learning from the 60s," 135, 139.

69. Lorde's partner for nineteen years, Francis Louise Clayton, was a psychologist. Upton, "Audre Lorde," 316.

70. Wiesel, "Perils," 2.

71. Herman, *Trauma and Recovery*, 7–8.

72. For example, Wiesel, "Perils," 4.

73. Herman, *Trauma and Recovery*, 92.

74. Lorde, "Sexism," 60.

75. For an alternative view of the breadth of *ethos, prudence,* and *decorum* as concepts in public address scholarship, see Robert Hariman, "Afterword: Relocating the Art of Public Address," in *Rhetoric and Political Culture in Nineteenth-Century America* (East Lansing: Michigan State University Press, 1997), 163–83, esp. 171. This essay endorses scholarship that has been ongoing for at least two decades now on vernacular discourse and a broad range of media, though without citations here.

76. I base the suggestions in this paragraph on Herman's chapter concerning psychotherapists' commonplace responses in therapeutic settings to victims of traumatic experiences. Herman, *Trauma and Recovery*, 133–54.

77. Elizabeth V. Spelman, *Fruits of Sorrow: Framing Our Attention to Suffering* (Boston: Beacon, 1997), 131–32. Additional insightful essays that address this vexing problem include Linda Alcoff, "The Problem of Speaking for Others," *Cultural Critique* 20 (winter 1991–1992): 5–32; Michael Awkward, "Negotiations of Power: White Critics, Black Texts, and the Self-Referential Impulse," *American Literary History* 2 (winter 1990): 581–606; Kenneth W. Warren, "From under the Superscript: A Response to Michael Awkward," *American Literary History* 4 (spring 1992): 97–103; Awkward, "The Politics of Positionality: A Reply to Kenneth Warren," *American Literary History* 4 (spring 1992): 104–105; and Joan W. Scott, "Experience," in *Feminists Theorize the Political*, ed. Judith Butler and Scott (New York: Routledge, 1992), 22–40.

78. Lorde, "Scratching the Surface," 48, 51. Lorde reiterated this idea in "Uses of Anger," 131 and "Learning from the 60s," 135.

79. Lorde, "Learning from the 60s," 135, 135–36, 136.

80. Ida B. Wells devoted much of her public life to substantiating that claim in the face of stiff resistance. For examples of Wells's public speeches, see Ida B. Wells, "Southern Horrors: Lynch Law in All Its Phases," in Karlyn Kohrs Campbell, *Man Cannot Speak for Her*, vol. 2 (New York: Greenwood, 1989), 385–420; Ida M. Wells-Barnett, "Lynching, Our National Crime," in *Rhetoric of Struggle*, ed. Robbie Jean Walker (New York: Garland, 1992), 97–102. For background on Wells's speaking, see Campbell, "The Heavy Burdens of Afro-American Women: Sex, Race, and Class," *Man Cannot Speak for Her*, vol. 1 (New York: Praeger, 1989), 145–56; Campbell, "The Power of Hegemony: Capitalism and Racism in the 'Nadir of Negro History,'" in *Rhetoric and Community: Studies in Unity and Fragmentation*, ed. J. Michael Hogan (Columbia: University of South Carolina Press, 1998), 97; Gail Bederman, "Civilization, the Decline of Middle-Class Manliness, and Ida B. Wells' Anti-Lynching Campaign (1892–94)," in *Gender and American History since 1890*, ed. Barbara Melosh (London: Routledge, 1993), 207–39; Mary M. Boone Hutton, "Ida B. Wells Barnett (1862–1931), Agitator for African American Rights," in *Women Public Speakers in the U.S., 1925–1993*, ed. Campbell (Westport, Conn: Greenwood, 1994), 462–75.

81. Lu-in Wang, "The Transforming Power of 'Hate': Social Cognition Theory and the Harms of Bias-Related Crime," *Southern California Law Review* 71, no. 1 (1997): 47–135.

82. Diane Hope, "Communication and Human Rights: The Symbolic Structures of Racism and Sexism," in *Speech Communication in the Twentieth Century,* ed. Thomas W. Benson (Carbondale: Southern Illinois University Press, 1985), 63–89. This may also be the case for examples of bias exercised within subordinated communities, as when sexism recurs within black communities coping with a legacy of racism. For instance, in the sexual harassment case of Anita Hill and Clarence Thomas, myths made the discourse extraordinarily complex. For a detailed analysis of myth in relationship to credibility, see Kimberlé Crenshaw, "Whose Story Is It, Anyway? Feminist and Anti-Racist Appropriations of Anita Hill," in *Rac-ing Justice, Engendering Power: Essays on Anita Hill, Clarence Thomas, and the Construction of Social Reality* (New York: Pantheon, 1992), 402–40.

83. Herman, *Trauma and Recovery,* 1.

84. On blaming the victim in antigay and antilesbian violence, see Urvashi Vaid, *Virtual Equality: The Mainstreaming of Gay and Lesbian Liberation* (New York: Doubleday, 1995), 141.

85. Lorde, "Transformation of Silence," 40.

86. Herman, *Trauma and Recovery,* 197, 197, 155, 214.

87. Ibid., 70; see also 154, 197, 214.

88. Lorde, "Uses of the Erotic," 56, 59, 54, 57, 54, 58.

89. Ibid., 58.

90. Ibid.

91. Ibid., 56, 57, 58, 59, 58, 56.

92. Ibid., 53.

93. Ibid., 54.

94. The speech has been preserved on an audiotape entitled "Power and Oppression," which is held in drawer A 3 5 at the Lesbian Herstory Archive, Brooklyn, New York. The audiotape differs in noteworthy ways from all printed texts of the speech. On other strategic aspects of Lorde's representations of the erotic in her speech and poetry, see Sagri Dhairyam, "'Artifacts for Survival': Remapping the Contours of Poetry with Audre Lorde," *Feminist Studies* 18 (summer 1992): 237, 254, n. 18.

95. Kimberlé Crenshaw, "Mapping the Margins: Intersectionality, Identity Politics, and Violence against Women of Color," http://www.hsph.harvard.edu/grhf/WoC/feminisms; crenshaw.htp (August 6, 2000).

96. Lorde, "Uses of the Erotic," *Sister Outsider,* 56.

97. Audre Lorde and Adrienne Rich, "An Interview: Audre Lorde and Adrienne Rich," in *Sister Outsider,* 102–3. For an example of such criticism among the commentaries in print, see Kathleen M. Sands, "Uses of the Thea(o)logian: Sex and Theodicy in Religious Feminism," *Journal of Feminist Studies in Religion* 8 (1992): 10–11.

98. Lorde and Rich, "An Interview," 109.

99. Ibid., 81.

100. Herman, *Trauma and Recovery,* 154.

101. Lorde, "Transformation of Silence," 41.

102. For instance, see Hariman's otherwise admirable book, *Political Style.*

contributors

Robert Alan Brookey (Ph.D., University of Minesota, 1998) is associate professor of communication at Northern Illinois University. He is the author of *Reinventing the Homosexual: The Rhetoric and Power of the Gay Gene* (2002), and he has published widely on the politics of gender and sexuality in *Critical Studies in Media Communication, Western Journal of Communication, Communication Studies, Argumentation and Advocacy,* and the *International Journal of Sexuality and Gender Studies.*

Dana L. Cloud (Ph.D., University of Iowa, 1992) is associate professor of communication studies at the University of Texas–Austin. She has published numerous articles and book chapters focusing on critical analysis of the media, the elaboration and defense of Marxist theory in the field, queer theory, public sphere theory, and other topics. Her most recent work has explored visual rhetorics of empire in an essay published in the *Quarterly Journal of Speech* (2004). She has published one book, *Control and Consolation in American Culture and Politics* (1998), and has another in process, *The Dilemmas of Dissidents: Democratic Unionists at Boeing, 1989–1999.* She lives in Austin with her partner, Katie Feyh; her daughter, Samantha; and two dogs. In her spare time she engages in political activism in the areas of labor, GLBT rights, the justice system and the death penalty, antiracism, and other causes. She is a longtime member of the International Socialist Organization.

Karen A. Foss (Ph.D., University of Iowa, 1976) is professor of communication at the University of New Mexico in Albuquerque. She has taught at Humboldt State University and the University of Massachusetts, and she has served as director of women's studies at both Humboldt and the University of New Mexico. Her research and teaching interests include contemporary rhetorical theory and criticism, feminist perspectives on communication, the incorporation of marginalized voices into rhetorical theory and practice, and social movements and social change. She is coauthor of *Contemporary Perspectives on Rhetoric; Feminist Rhetorical Theories; Women Speak: The Eloquence of Women's Lives; Inviting Transformation: Presentational Speaking for a Changing World;* and *Theories of Human Communication.*

Lisbeth Lipari (Ph.D., Stanford University, 1996) is chair and associate professor in the Department of Communication at Denison University. She teaches courses in ethics and political discourse, and her work focuses on the relationship between language and ethics in the public sphere. Central to her research are questions involving the role of public communication in achieving just and equitable democratic practice. Her essays on language, politics, and ethics have appeared in the *Quarterly Journal of Speech, Communication Theory, Journalism and Mass Communication Quarterly, Journal of Communication, Argumentation and Advocacy*, and *Media, Culture, and Society*. She is currently working on a book project exploring ethics in the relation of alterity to listening, as well as a rhetorical history of the work of Lorraine Hansberry.

Charles E. Morris III (Ph.D., Pennsylvania State University, 1998) is associate professor in the Department of Communication at Boston College. He is coeditor, with Stephen Howard Browne, of *Readings on the Rhetoric of Social Protest* (2001, 2006). His essays have appeared in the *Quarterly Journal of Speech, Communication and Critical/Cultural Studies, Rhetoric and Public Affairs, Women's Studies in Communication*, and *Free Speech Yearbook*. For his work on queer rhetorical history, he has received the Karl Wallace Memorial Award (2001) and the Golden Anniversary Monograph Award (2003) from the National Communication Association.

Lester C. Olson (Ph.D., University of Wisconsin, 1984) is professor in the Department of Communication at the University of Pittsburgh. He is author of *Emblems of American Community in the Revolutionary Era: A Study in Rhetorical Iconology* (1991) and *Benjamin Franklin's Vision of America, 1754–1784: A Study in Rhetorical Iconology* (2004) and of numerous articles that have appeared in such journals as *Quarterly Journal of Speech* and *Philosophy and Rhetoric*. The National Communication Association has recognized his work with the Gerald R. Miller (1985), Karl R. Wallace (1986), and Winans-Wichelns (1992) Awards, and he was the recipient of the Rhetoric Society of America's 2005 Book Award and NCA's Marie Hochmuth Nichols Award for *Ben Franklin's Vision of American Community*.

John M. Sloop (Ph.D., University of Iowa, 1995) is professor and chair of communication studies at Vanderbilt University. Winner of NCA's Karl Wallace Memorial Award (1998) and Winans-Wichelns Award (2005), Sloop has published numerous articles, coedited two volumes, and authored three books, *The Cultural Prison* (1996), *Shifting Borders: Rhetoric, Immigration and California's Proposition 187* (2002, coauthored with Kent A. Ono), and *Disciplining Gender: Rhetorics of Sex Identity in Contemporary U.S. Culture* (2004).

Ralph R. Smith (Ph.D., University of Southern California, 1973) is emeritus professor of communication, Missouri State University. He is the author of *Nonverbal Communication* (1970) and coauthor of *Progay/Antigay: The Rhetorical War over Sexuality* (2000). He is also the author of articles in the *Quarterly Journal* *of Speech, Central States Speech Journal,* and the *Southern Speech Communication Journal.*

Julie M. Thompson (Ph.D., Indiana University, 1998) is director of the Writing and Oral Communication Programs at Hamline University. She is author of *Mommy Queerest: Contemporary Rhetorics of Lesbian Maternal Identity* (2002).

Eric King Watts (Ph.D., Northwestern University, 1995) is associate professor in the Department of Communication at the University of North Carolina, Chapel Hill. His articles on African American rhetoric and culture have been published in the *Quarterly Journal of Speech, Rhetoric and Public Affairs; Critical Studies in Media Communication, Communication Studies;* and *New Media and Society.* Watts received the 2002 New Investigator Award from the Rhetorical and Communication Theory Division of the National Communication Association.

Russel R. Windes (Ph.D., Northwestern University, 1959) is emeritus professor, City University of New York. He is the author of, among other books, *Argumentation and Advocacy* (1963) and coauthor of *Progay/Antigay: The Rhetorical War over Sexuality* (2000). As consulting editor in communication for Random House and Bobbs-Merrill, he edited fifty-two books. He is the author of many articles and monographs.

InDex

Connolly, William, 62
constitutive identity, 47
constraints, 75, 84, 89, 122, 163, 165,
    166, 179, 186, 229
constructionism, 56, 57, 60, 61, 62
contradiction, 8, 77, 78–79, 81, 83,
    85–86, 88
Cook, Blanche Wiesen, 26, 37, 38
Cook, Nancy, 27, 28, 29, 36
Cooper, Davida, 52
Coors, 79, 83, 85
Cosby, Bill, 25
Coulter, Ann, 214
counternostalgia, 96, 112n. 14
counterpublics, 138, 139, 145n. 68,
    225–26, 228
Crenshaw, Kimberlé, 224
Crisis, 174, 175, 178, 182
critical rhetoric, 5, 18n. 32, 122, 125,
    140
Crompton, Louis, 63
Cullen, Countee, 175, 184
cultural consumption, 176, 177
cultural performances, 1, 2
cultural production, 12
cultural studies, 3
culture wars, 27
Cummings, Alan, 214
Cures, 210
Current, 124
cyberspace, 1

D'Emilio, John, 5, 43n. 47, 48, 225
da Vinci, Leonardo, 201–2
Darsey, James, 259
Daughters of Bilitis, 19n. 34, 195, 205,
    222, 225–29, 232–34, 245n. 45. *See
    also* assimilationism
Daughters of the American Revolution
    (D.A.R.), 35, 93
Davis, Angela, 252, 278n. 25
Davis, F. James, 59
Davis, Madeline, 228
Dawidoff, Robert, 52

de Beauvoir, Simone, 237
de Helen, Sandra, 28
De Lauretis, Teresa, 89n. 1
De Veaux, Alexis, 251
Debs, Eugene, 23
decadence, 175, 176, 182
deconstruction, 3, 50, 56, 59, 60, 61,
    224
Defense of Marriage Act (DOMA), 53,
    72n. 137, 135
Degeneres, Ellen, 198
Deitcher, David, 6, 19n. 38
Deming, Bruce, 60
Democratic Party, 29, 76, 215
Depression, 34, 222
Desens, Mindy, 155, 163
Detroit, Mich., 228
deviance, 79, 85, 88, 122, 176, 182, 190,
    199
deviant historiography, 5, 8, 12, 122
Dickerman, Marion, 27, 36
Dill, Augustas Granville, 189
Dill, Bonnie Thornton, 128
disability, 13, 52, 58, 275
discursive amnesia, 250, 255, 275
disidentification, 1
dissociation, 258–59, 268, 270
Donald, David Herbert, 99, 109,
    119n. 92
double-consciousness, 233, 259, 275
Douglas, Aaron, 180, 182
Douglas, Georgia, 179
Douglas, Lord Alfred, 11
Douglass, Frederick, 94
Dow, Bonnie, 195, 198
drag, 135, 137, 154
Du Bois, W. E. B., 174, 177, 178, 179,
    180, 222, 259
Duberman, Martin, 95, 109, 208, 209,
    210, 211
Duggan, Lisa, 6, 26, 55, 155, 157,
    164
Dworkin, Andrea, 252, 280n. 61
Dynes, Wayne, 57

Georgia, 233
Gettysburg Address, 93, 110
Gilligan, Carol, 255
Gillon, Steven, 37, 38
Gilman, Sander, 160
Gittings, Barbara, 195, 208
Glass, Marion, 233
Gomez, Jewell, 223, 241
Goodman, Gerre, 55
Gray, Laura, 198
Greene, Beverly, 164–65
Greenwich Village, 13, 175, 176, 177,
    186, 188, 228
Grier, Barbara, 28, 220
Griffen, D., 232
Grimké, Angelina, 238
Gross, Larry, 39, 52
Gurewitsch, David, 37
Gusfield, Joseph, 46

Habermas, Jurgen, 53, 54
Hacking, Ian, 46
Halberstam, Judith, 162
Hale, C. Jacob, 161
Hall, Radclyffe, 31
Hall, Stuart, 221, 224
Halley, Janet E., 58–59, 71n. 107
Halperin, David, 54
Hampton, Mabel, 241
Hansberry, Carl, 222
Hansberry, Lorraine, 10, 11, 220–42
Hariman, Robert, 3, 122, 250
Harlem, 9, 13, 19n. 34, 174–90
Harlem: A Forum of Negro Life, 174, 189
Harlem Renaissance, 174, 175, 176, 177,
    179, 180, 181, 184, 185, 188, 225,
    240
Harper, Phillip Brian, 133
Harris, Elise, 242n. 8
Harvard University, 257
Hawaii, 63, 64
Hawkins, Yusef, 130
Hay, Harry, 231
Hay, John, 97

Hellmers, Norman, 108
Hemphill, Essex, 129, 130, 133, 135,
    136, 137, 138
Hennessy, Rosemary, 57
Henning, Fanny, 98, 99, 100, 109
Herman, Didi, 52
Herman, Judith, 255–56, 258, 261, 264,
    267, 268, 273
hermaphroditism, 158, 159, 170n. 75
Herndon, William, 97, 100
heteronormativity: 1, 16n. 17, 25, 44n.
    71, 109, 160, 190; and conventions
    of, 5, 7, 30, 39, 55; and discourse, 9,
    14n. 10, 127; and power, 62, 102,
    107; and race, 123, 128, 130,
    134–38
heterosexism, 49, 55, 225
heterosexuality, 134, 203, 209
Hetherington, Kevin, 47
Hickok, Lorena (Hick), 23–38
Hill, Anita, 282n. 82
historical materialism, 238
History News Network, 108
Hofstadter, Richard, 250
Holocaust, 34, 54, 109, 252, 253, 273
homoerotic, 182, 184
homophobia, 10, 30, 50, 78, 86, 101,
    105, 107, 221, 223, 224, 225, 228,
    239, 240, 258
homosexual panic, 103, 104, 105, 108,
    116n. 57
homosexuality, 152, 153, 155, 156, 158,
    175, 177, 186, 195, 196, 200, 209,
    217n. 8; and homophile movement,
    8, 48, 49, 221, 225–26, 231, 234;
    homosociality, 12; as a debilitating
    pathology, 199; as a psychological
    pathology, 197; as a pathology, 204,
    205, 214; and reparative therapy, 212,
    213, 214
Hooker, Evelyn, 207, 208, 210
hooks, bell, 82, 126, 223, 240
Hoover, J. Edgar, 37
Howard Beach, N.Y., 130

Lincoln Memorial, 35, 94, 120n. 96
Lipari, Lisbeth, 10, 11, 12
listening, 253, 254, 255, 272
Lobdell, Joseph I. (Israel). *See* Lobdell, Lucy
Lobdell, La-Roi. *See* Lobdell, Lucy
Lobdell, Lucy, 9, 11, 19n. 34, 149–66, 172n. 103
Locher, Barry, 104
Locke, Alain LeRoy, 174, 175, 177, 178, 179, 180, 185
Looking Glass, 179
Lorde, Audre, 10, 11, 126, 222, 228, 249–73
Los Angeles Film Critics, 123
Love, Heather, 6, 50
Lucaites, John, 127
Lucas, Stephen, 14n. 9
lynching, 233, 257, 265

Machiavelli, 250
Madonna, 137
Madsen, Hunter, 52
Malcolm X, 222, 257, 280n. 66
marginalized rhetors, 74, 78, 89, 241
Marmor, Judd, 211
Marxism, 45, 221, 223
masculinity, 12, 156, 159, 168n. 25, 200
Massachusetts, 64, 65, 120n. 96, 215
Massachusetts Gay Civil Rights Bill, 60
material culture, 3
Mattachine Review, 207
Mattachine Society, 19n. 34, 48, 205, 207–8, 226, 231
May, Larry, 198
McBride, Dwight A., 128
McCarthy, Joseph, 225, 232
McKay, Claude, 179
McKerrow, Ray, 140
McPhail, Mark, 126
Medhurst, Martin, 14n. 9
memory: and collective memory, 102, 104, 105, 108; and heteronormativity, 108; and history, 94; and gays, 95, 96,

105; and the public, 23, 39, 40, 95, 103, 104, 106, 250, 255, 275, 268; and queers, 8, 24; and vernacular, 117n. 64
Mencken, W. H., 179
Mercer, Kobena, 132
Mercer, Lucy, 32, 34, 38
Messenger, 179, 180, 187
metonymy, 2, 6, 96
Metropolitan Community Church (MCC), 209
Meyerowitz, Joanne, 170n. 75
militarism, 49
Milk, Harvey, 8, 11, 74–89
Millennium March, 93, 120n. 96
Miller, Diane Helene, 52, 55, 65
Miller, Earl, 36, 38
Miller, Neil, 27, 31, 232, 235
Milloy, Courtland, 125, 128
Minnesota, 151
misgendered pronouns, 162
Mitchell, Alice, 159, 164
mnemonic encounters, 94
mnemonicide, 9, 103, 104, 116n. 55
Modern Language Association (MLA), 256, 258, 261, 262, 272
Moghadam, Valentine, 46
Mohr, Richard, 53, 56
Monette, Paul, 93, 94
Monthly Review, 223
Moritz, Marguerite, 35
Morris, Charles, 8, 11, 12, 35, 157, 220, 221, 240
Morrison, Toni, 222
Moscone, George, 74, 75, 76, 82

Nagel, Joanne, 59
National Association for Research and Therapy of Homosexuality (NARTH), 212–14
National Association for the Advancement of Colored People (NAACP), 178
National Book Award, 93